Puritan Insights on the Psalms

Puritan Insights on the Psalms

A Year of Meditations to Grow Deeper

David J. McKinley

Foreword by Joel R. Beeke
and Fraser E. Jones

RESOURCE *Publications* · Eugene, Oregon

PURITAN INSIGHTS ON THE PSALMS:
A Year of Meditations to Grow Deeper

Copyright © 2025 David J. McKinley. All rights reserved. Except for brief quotations in critical publications or reviews, no part of this book may be reproduced in any manner without prior written permission from the publisher. Write: Permissions, Wipf and Stock Publishers, 199 W. 8th Ave., Suite 3, Eugene, OR 97401.

Resource Publications
An Imprint of Wipf and Stock Publishers
199 W. 8th Ave., Suite 3
Eugene, OR 97401

www.wipfandstock.com

PAPERBACK ISBN: 979-8-3852-1423-5
HARDCOVER ISBN: 979-8-3852-1424-2
EBOOK ISBN: 979-8-3852-1425-9

VERSION NUMBER 052825

Scripture quotations marked (ESV) are from the ESV® Bible (The Holy Bible, English Standard Version®), copyright © 2001 by Crossway, a publishing ministry of Good News Publishers. Used by permission. All rights reserved. May not copy or download more than 500 consecutive verses of the ESV Bible or more than one half of any book of the ESV Bible.

Scripture quotations marked (KJV) are taken from The Authorized (King James) Version. Rights in the Authorized Version in the United Kingdom are vested in the Crown. Reproduced by permission of the Crown's patentee, Cambridge University Press

Scripture quotations marked (NASB) are taken from the NASB® (New American Standard Bible®), Copyright © 1960, 1971, 1977, 1995, 2020 by The Lockman Foundation. Used by permission. All rights reserved. www.lockman.org"

Scripture marked (NKJV) are taken from the New King James Version®. Copyright © 1982 by Thomas Nelson. Used by permission. All rights reserved.

Scripture quotations marked (NIV) are taken from the Holy Bible, New International Version®, NIV®. Copyright © 1973, 1978, 1984, 2011 by Biblica, Inc.™ Used by permission of Zondervan. All rights reserved worldwide. www.zondervan.comThe "NIV" and "New International Version" are trademarks registered in the United States Patent and Trademark Office by Biblica, Inc.™

Scripture quotations marked (NLT) are taken from the Holy Bible, New Living Translation, copyright ©1996, 2004, 2015 by Tyndale House Foundation. Used by permission of Tyndale House Publishers, Carol Stream, Illinois 60188. All rights reserved.

To my

loving sister and brother-in-law

Brenda and Grant Del Begio

who have been a constant source

of encouragement and inspiration

throughout my spiritual pilgrimage

Foreword

"The Psalms are wonderful," remarked the Presbyterian theologian William Swan Plumer (1802–1880). This is evident, observed Plumer, because "they have been read, repeated, chanted, sung, studied, wept over, rejoiced in, expounded, loved and praised by God's people for thousands of years."* As the book of Psalms is indeed so wonderful—a masterpiece of divine inspiration and a realistic portrait of human experience in all its variety—what better way is there to spend the year than saturating your mind in the depths of this inspired hymnbook? And what better way is there to dive into the depths of the Psalter than to be led by the Puritans—those skilled physicians of the soul who knew well the terrain of vital, experiential piety because of their acquaintance with faithful biblical exegesis, intricate cases of conscience, and (oftentimes) difficult personal experience.

It is for this reason that brother David McKinley has collected a treasury of Puritan insights on the Psalms to serve as a spiritual banquet for hungry readers over the course of a year. And it is for this reason that I am grateful to see such a devotional in print—replete with the power of Puritan piety, the sensibleness of Puritan spirituality, and the precision of Puritan exegesis. You will find in the pages to follow insights from such spiritual giants as Joseph Alleine, Isaac Ambrose, John Bunyan, Jeremiah Burroughs, Stephen Charnock, John Collinges, Jonathan Edwards, John Flavel, Thomas Goodwin, Matthew Henry, John Owen, and Thomas Watson—each of whom are some of our favorite Puritans.

Before proceeding further, however, we must first define what we mean by the *Puritans*. The question of Puritan identity has drawn much debate in academic circles in recent years.** Was Puritanism primarily a political or a spiritual movement? Was it centered on a particular doctrine or concept, such as predestination, covenant, or conversion? Was it primarily a lay or a clerical movement? And was it focused more on ecclesiology and doxology or doctrine and practice? Likewise, the chronological boundaries of Puritan identity have also drawn debate. Did Puritanism begin during the English Reformation? And did it extend only to the expulsion of ministers from

---

*. Plumer, *Psalms*, 5.
**. For more on debates over Puritan identity, see Pederson, *Unity in Diversity*.

their pulpits in 1662 or to the Act of Toleration in 1689 or well into the eighteenth century?

To these questions we respond by declaring that in the strictest historical sense, the Puritans were a group of ministers and laymen within the Church of England who opposed the halfway reforms of the Elizabethan Settlement and promoted Reformed doctrine, liturgy, and church government in a national church that was increasingly adopting remnants of Roman Catholic worship and teaching. In other words, they sought to "purify" the national church of the remnants of Roman Catholic religion, even while they remained in the national church.

Many ministers who opposed such Roman Catholic influences in the Church of England were deposed from their pulpits upon the passing of the Act of Uniformity in 1662, and most of them had died by the dawn of the eighteenth century. With the passing of the Act of Uniformity, those who were once considered "Puritans" eventually came to be known as "Nonconformists," as they were no longer working to purify the Church of England from within but were expelled from it and worked for spiritual and ecclesiastical change from the outside of its ecclesiastical structures. The term "Nonconformist" came to be especially significant after the Glorious Revolution of 1688, when William III and Mary II granted religious toleration across England and thereby legalized nonconformity.

Thus, the Puritans were active between the start of Queen Elizabeth's reign in 1558 and the close of the seventeenth century. However, some ministers in the eighteenth century are also considered to be Puritans for their Reformed doctrine and experiential piety, even though they technically were not ministers working to purify the Church of England from within (the narrow definition of "Puritans") but were either Nonconformists or a related group (such as the New England Congregationalists) who carried on the doctrinal and spiritual tradition of the Puritans after they were forced out of the national church. Jonathan Edwards is one such example. Similarly, a group of divines who formed part of what some academics have called a "North Sea piety"[*] are often considered to be Puritans in a wider sense, although they are not Puritans in the strict historical sense. This group includes the Scottish Covenanters and the Dutch *Nadere Reformatie* (or Further Reformation) divines.

One reason why the Puritans have been so popular in the English-speaking world is that they were the most significant representatives of the Reformed faith in the English language. In other words, the Puritans are essentially the English "face" of the Reformed movement that was articulated

---

[*]. See op 't Hof, "Piety in the Wake of Trade," 263–65.

by such theologians as Ulrich Zwingli, John Calvin, and Heinrich Bullinger in theological hotbeds like Geneva and Zurich.

Another reason why the Puritans have been so popular—not only in the English-speaking world but increasingly around the globe—is that they clothed the Reformed theology of Zwingli, Calvin, and Bullinger in the garb of experiential piety, profound spirituality, and warm doxology in a way that surpassed their Reformed forebears. Above all, their emphasis on how Reformed doctrine—including covenant theology, the regulative principle of worship, and especially the doctrines of grace—should shape daily life for the individual, the family, and the church, has captured the imaginations of believers around the world ever since the resurgence of Puritan literature in the 1950s.

Furthermore, the Puritans were well-equipped to speak to matters of piety in the spheres of personal life, family life, and church life because they were experienced in various overlapping roles—as pastors, theologians, writers, husbands, fathers, and scholars. John Owen, for example, was simultaneously a pastor-theologian, a popular author, an academic heavyweight, and a family man (as well as the vice-chancellor of the University of Oxford!). Through each of these roles, he gleaned valuable insights that enriched his preaching, teaching, exegesis, catechesis, and practical theology. Such insights were the legacy that Owen (and other Puritans) bequeathed to future generations of Christians up to the present day.

The Puritan movement was wide, diverse, multifaceted, and eminently fruitful. Yet there are at least four facets of Puritan theology that are worth mentioning briefly.

First, the Puritan movement was *biblical*. The Puritans longed to subject every aspect of life to the lordship of Jesus Christ and the authority of His Word. They preached Scripture, taught Scripture, expounded Scripture, wrote about Scripture, defended the truths of Scripture, crystallized the doctrines of Scripture, meditated upon Scripture, prayed Scripture, and memorized Scripture. In sum, they loved Scripture. The Bible, "the library of the Holy Ghost," as the Puritans called it, was the lifeblood of Puritanism.

Second, the Puritan movement was *doctrinal*. For the Puritans, there should be no such thing as "dead orthodoxy." The entire corpus of sound doctrine is rich, beautiful, and lifegiving. From trinitarian theology, to Calvinistic soteriology, to orthodox Christology, to well-ordered ecclesiology, the Puritans loved to unpack and articulate the mind of the Holy Spirit as expressed throughout the canon of Scripture.

Third, the Puritan movement was *experiential*. For the Puritans, biblical doctrine should promote the experience of that doctrine. While believers cannot depend upon their experiences, nor should they fall prey to unbiblical subjectivism or mysticism, they should still test their experiences by the objective standard of God's Word. The faith of believers, said the Puritans, should not only touch the heart, but it should also penetrate the emotions and the will and thereby transform the entire person. Passionate about piety, the Puritans stressed such disciplines of spirituality as prayer, Scripture-reading, and meditation as keys of the Christian life which unlock a sweeter taste, stronger sense, and deeper experience of the grace which God has poured into the believer's soul by the Holy Spirit.

And fourth, the Puritan movement was *practical*. The result of biblical fidelity, doctrinal orthodoxy, and experiential piety is a metamorphosis of the believer's experience of daily life, whether on the level of the individual, the home, the church, the workplace, or the nation. The Puritans composed detailed manuals of Christian living, and particularly books on marriage and family life. With the transformation of practice, the entire person was being shaped and conformed to the image of Christ for joy and doxology in both this life and in the life to come.

From such descriptions of the Puritans, it should come as no surprise that the Puritans loved the Psalter. As the inspired hymnbook of God's people, the Psalms combine everything that the Puritans valued most—such as doctrine, experience, and practice—in 150 Spirit-inspired songs. There are at least five reasons why the Puritans so loved the Psalms.

First, the Psalter is *realistic*. John Calvin, who in a very real sense was a predecessor to the Puritans because of his articulation of the Reformed faith and his seismic influence upon the English Reformed movement, famously declared that the book of Psalms is "an anatomy of all the parts of the soul." For that reason, "there is not an emotion of which any one can be conscious that is not here represented as in a mirror," Calvin said. He went on: "The Holy Spirit has here drawn to the life all the griefs, sorrows, fears, doubts, hopes, cares, perplexities, in short, all the distracting emotions with which the minds of men are wont to be agitated."[*]

Second, the Psalter is *Christocentric*. In other words, it is about Jesus Christ. Unlike the modernist and postmodernist interpretations of the Psalms which are so in vogue these days, the Puritans saw Christ on every page of the Psalter. As Christ Himself declared, the Psalter is about Him (Luke 24:44).

Third, the Psalter is *pastoral*. On each page of the Psalter, the Puritan pastor had content from which to glean for the comfort, exhortation, warning, conviction, and praise of his parishioners. Puritan manuals of casuistry

---

[*]. John Calvin, "The Author's Preface," 1:xxxvii. Capitalization has been modernized in this quote.

(the precursor of modern-day pastoral counseling) were replete with references to the Psalms.

Fourth, the Psalter is *meditative*. The Puritans were masters of meditation. By feasting upon the Psalter, the believer can meditate much upon God, Christ, the gospel, and the daily vicissitudes of Christian experience. Such meditations sustain the believer's soul.

Fifth, the Psalter is *practical*. The psalmists do not shy away from the difficulties of the pious life. In fact, they portray cross-bearing as a hallmark of the life that is truly devoted to God.

Sixth and finally, the Psalter is *experiential*. It is the greatest manual of experiential piety ever produced, for it is a gift bequeathed to the church by the Holy Spirit Himself. As a manual of piety, the Psalter promotes true prayer in the soul of the believer.

Now as you turn to the smorgasbord of theological insight that lies before you, do so as the Puritans would have exhorted—prayerfully, meditatively, joyfully, experientially, practically, with worship, and with dependence upon the Holy Spirit. Stand in wonder at the privilege that you have to read, sing, and meditate upon the inspired hymnbook that has been so skillfully expounded and applied over the centuries. And wonder, as did the German theologian Johann Gerhard (1582–1637), that God has given you such a book to guide you on your pilgrim path to heavenly glory. It is with his words that we close:

> The Psalter is a theater, where Go" all'ws us to behold both himself and his works; a most pleasant green field, a vast garden, where we see all manner of flowers; a paradise, having the most delicious flowers and fruits; a great sea in which are hid costly pearls; a heavenly school, where we have God for our teacher; a [compendium] of all Scripture; a mirror of divine grace, reflecting the lovely face of our heavenly Father; and the anatomy of our souls.[*]

Dr. Joel R. Beeke
Chancellor and Professor of Systematic Theology and Homiletics
Puritan Reformed Theological Seminary
Grand Rapids, MI

Fraser E. Jones
Research Assistant to the Chancellor
Puritan Reformed Theological Seminary
Grand Rapids, MI

---

[*]. Plumer, *Psalms*, 7–8. Spelling has been modernized.

Preface

During the pleasant days of one summer in my hometown of Winnipeg, Manitoba, I enjoyed reading large portions of Matthew Henry's commentary on the Bible. Although I was only in my late teens, I was captivated by this Puritan's writing. His love for Jesus Christ stirred my heart. Years later, perhaps not surprisingly, I chose the Puritan, John Owen, for my doctoral dissertation on the topic of spiritual illumination. With an increased interest in the Puritans, I began reading many contemporary books on the Puritans' views on godliness and their outlook on the Christian life.

More recently, I devoted an entire year to reading through six old clothbound volumes of *The Treasury of* David which contains Charles Spurgeon's verse-by-verse commentary on the Psalms. Spurgeon highly valued the Puritans' writings, and consequently, his expositional notes are filled with doctrinal depth, experiential vigor, and applicable insights. In addition to his commentary, the *Treasury* contains the "Explanatory Notes and Quaint Sayings." Here I discovered a treasure-trove of excerpts from many authors including Puritan writers such as: Thomas Adams, Joseph Caryl, Matthew Henry, Thomas Goodwin, John Owen, and numerous others. What a goldmine of insights on the Psalms!

As I had previously done with Spurgeon's commentary on the Psalms, I began writing daily meditations, this time weaving in excerpts from these Puritans with my observations. The *Puritan Insights on the Psalms* incorporates over ninety Puritans' writings into a year of daily meditations and brief prayers. Each day includes a Scripture passage with at least one *highlighted* verse to focus either on the insights of a Puritan or on a limited number of non-Puritans (noted by an asterisk by their names). In my Appendix, I provide a list of all writers with the accompanying dates of their excerpts for reference in the meditations.

For the last several years (five and counting), my wife, Laura, and I have read daily from the Psalms, completing the entire Psalter in one year. Since these prayers and songs have been read by the church for many centuries, we continue to read the Psalms for our spiritual formation. I invite you to join us on this enriching journey!

I am thankful for the advice and encouragement received from Joel Beeke and Fraser Jones. For the reader who is unfamiliar with the Puritans and their writings, I encourage you to read *Meet the Puritans: A Guide to Modern Reprints*, co-authored by Dr. Joel Beeke who provides brief biographies of many of the Puritans mentioned in my book. To Janice F. Vessey for her professional copyediting, I am very thankful. A big "thank you" to the Wipf & Stock team; they have been a delight to work with throughout the entire publication process.

This publication completes my trilogy on the *Treasury of David*. My other books, *The Psalms for Everyday Living* and *Growing in Holiness*, highlight respectively, Spurgeon's exposition on the entire Psalter, and Spurgeon's emphasis on personal holiness. I pray that each reader will gain a greater love for the Psalms, an enlarged appreciation for the Puritans, and a deepened commitment to Jesus Christ. May this one-year journey be a spiritually transformative experience!

January 1 Psalm 1

1 Blessed is the man who walks not in the counsel of the wicked, nor stands in the way of sinners, nor sits in the seat of scoffers; 2 *but his delight is in the law of the* LORD, *and on his law he meditates day and night.* 3 He is like a tree planted by streams of water that yields its fruit in its season, and its leaf does not wither. In all that he does, he prospers. 4 The wicked are not so but are like chaff that the wind drives away. 5 Therefore the wicked will not stand in the judgment, nor sinners in the congregation of the righteous; 6 for the LORD knows the way of the righteous, but the way of the wicked will perish. (ESV)

Meditation on Scripture. When our minds are preoccupied with many things, we frequently find ourselves rushing through our daily Scripture reading. We may go away disappointed and dissatisfied that the Bible did not address our needs. Joseph Caryl understood this situation. He notes, "It may be, at once reading or looking, we see little or nothing . . . you may look lightly upon a Scripture and see nothing." To make Scripture reading more meaningful, he suggests that "if we in prayer and dependence upon God did sit down and study it, we should behold much more than appears to us . . . Meditate often upon it, and there you shall see a light, like the light of the sun." Meditation includes studying the Bible while asking God to reveal what he wants to say to us. This divine encounter with Scripture will inform our minds and affect our hearts. Like a light, God's truth illuminates those areas of our lives where sin exists, whether it be desires, thoughts, speech, or actions. We become aware of the need for growth in these areas that need to be brought into alignment with God's truth. As we meditate on Scripture, God guides us into the appropriate application for our spiritual growth and transformation. Then, we will be able to enjoy God's favor with a fruitful life on God's righteous path (vv. 1, 3, 6).

Prayer. Lord, I confess that I frequently read Scripture too quickly. Help me to slow down to create space in my heart and mind to ruminate on your word so that it may transform my life. Amen.

January 2   Psalm 2

1 Why are the nations restless and the peoples plotting in vain? 2 The kings of the earth take their stand and the rulers conspire together against the LORD and against His Anointed, saying, 3 "Let's tear their shackles apart and throw their ropes away from us!" 4 *He who sits in the heavens laughs, the Lord scoffs at them.* 5 Then He will speak to them in His anger and terrify them in His fury, saying, 6 "But as for Me, I have installed My King upon Zion, My holy mountain." 7 "I will announce the decree of the Lord: he said to me, 'You are My Son, today I have fathered you. 8 Ask it of Me, and I will certainly give the nations as Your inheritance, and the ends of the earth as Your possession. 9 You shall break them with a rod of iron, you shall shatter them like earthenware.'" 10 Now then, you kings, use insight; let yourselves be instructed, you judges of the earth. 11 Serve the Lord with reverence and rejoice with trembling. 12 Kiss the Son that He not be angry and you perish on the way, for His wrath may be kindled quickly. How blessed are all who take refuge in Him! (NASB)

God who scoffs. Mocking others is understandably cruel. Yet, God scoffs at those who oppose his rule. Thomas Adams comments, "Laugh? This seems a hard word at the first view: are the injuries of his saints, the cruelties of their enemies, the derision, the persecution of all that are round about us, no more but matter of laughter?" In light of the evil schemes plotted against the Lord's people (v. 3), God's laughter is appropriate. Adams explains, "He laughs, but it is in scorn; he scorns, but it is with vengeance." God will have the final say with those who oppose his rule on earth because he is the sovereign ruler who wants people to revere him by with their service and worship (v. 11). When we choose to humble ourselves before God, then it is possible to enjoy his blessing on our lives (v. 12).

Prayer. Lord, I despair when I see what is happening in the world with so much turmoil. Forgive me for not trusting your sovereign rule over the world's affairs. You are my sovereign King who is worthy of my worship. Amen.

January 3 — Psalm 3

1 O Lord, I have so many enemies; so many are against me. 2 So many are saying, "God will never rescue him!" 3 But you, O Lord, are a shield around me; you are my glory, the one who holds my head high. 4 I cried out to the Lord, and he answered me from his holy mountain. 5 *I lay down and slept, yet I woke up in safety, for the Lord was watching over me.* 6 I am not afraid of ten thousand enemies who surround me on every side. 7 Arise, O Lord! Rescue me, my God! Slap all my enemies in the face! Shatter the teeth of the wicked! 8 Victory comes from you, O Lord. May you bless your people. (NLT)

God's peace. When we are filled with anxieties and pressures, we commonly find it very difficult to experience any measure of peace. However, William Gurnall reminds us of King David who experienced peace (v. 5) "not when he lay on his bed of down in his stately palace at Jerusalem, but when he fled for his life from his unnatural son Absalom and possibly was forced to lie in the open field under the canopy of heaven. Truly it must be a soft pillow indeed that could make him forget his danger, who then had such a disloyal army at his back hunting of him." Such peace cannot be conjured up by us, but instead, "This peace of the gospel, and sense of the love of God in the soul, does so admirably contribute to the enabling of a person in all difficulties, and temptations, and troubles, that ordinarily, before he calls his saints to any hard service, or hot work, he gives them a draught of this cordial wine next their hearts, to cheer them up and embolden them in the conflict." Throughout the centuries, this supernatural peace has enabled God's people to rejoice in the most difficult times of their lives.

Prayer. Lord, my day is filled with problems, and I have wrongly sought peace in ways which have ignored you. Give me your abiding peace to quiet my soul so that I can live with confidence amid great challenges. I am thankful that I can rest in you, regardless of the circumstances swirling around me. Amen.

January 4 — Psalm 4

1 Answer me when I call to you, my righteous God. Give me relief from my distress; have mercy on me and hear my prayer. 2 How long will you people turn my glory into shame? How long will you love delusions and seek false gods? 3 Know that the Lord has set apart his faithful servant for himself; the Lord hears when I call to him. 4 *Tremble and do not sin; when you are on your beds, search your hearts and be silent.* 5 Offer the sacrifices of the righteous and trust in the Lord. 6 Many, Lord, are asking, "Who will bring us prosperity?" Let the light of your face shine on us. 7 Fill my heart with joy when their grain and new wine abound. 8 In peace I will lie down and sleep, for you alone, Lord, make me dwell in safety. (NIV)

Communion with God. During the day, our concerns can pile up and weigh us down, prompting us to look for relief from God (v. 1). Turning to him, the psalmist suggests, involves inward self-examination (v. 4). Joseph Caryl comments, "David shows us divine work when we go to rest. The bed is not all for sleep: 'Commune with your own heart upon your bed, and be still.' Be still or quiet, and then commune with your hearts; and if you will commune with your hearts, God will come and commune with your hearts, too, his Spirit will give you a loving visit and visions of his love." Upon awakening in the morning, we can enjoy talking and listening to the Lord. Caryl explains, "When we are most retired from the world, then we are most fit to have, and usually have, most communion with God." Communing with God in bed suggests that we can also enjoy his presence in life's ordinary routines when we can listen to his voice, assuring us of his presence and care (v. 7). Whether we are driving or walking, we may be confident that God hears us and will fill us with his presence (vv. 3, 6).

Prayer. Lord, with busy days I scarcely have time to listen and speak to you. Enable me to slow down so that I may discipline my mind and heart to create space to hear your voice and enjoy your joyful presence. Amen.

January 5 — Psalm 5:1–7

1 Listen to my words, Lord, consider my sighing. 2 Listen to the sound of my cry for help, my King and my God, for to You I pray. 3 In the morning, Lord, You will hear my voice; in the morning I will present my prayer to You and be on the watch. 4 For You are not a God who takes pleasure in wickedness; no evil can dwell with You. 5 *The boastful will not stand before Your eyes; You hate all who do injustice.* 6 You destroy those who speak lies; the Lord loathes the person of bloodshed and deceit. 7 But as for me, by Your abundant graciousness I will enter Your house, at Your holy temple I will bow in reverence for You. (NASB)

Hatred of sin. We may have varied responses to sin. Denying and excusing our sin with rationalizations is common. We may also blame others or become indifferent and callous to sin. This psalm serves as a reminder that God hates sin such as arrogance, wickedness, and deception (vv. 4–6). David Clarkson challenges us: "Avoid all that Christ hates . . . What is that which Christ hates? The psalmist tells us, making it one of Christ's attributes, to hate wickedness." How does this affect our relationships with those who do not know Jesus Christ? While we must form friendships with non-Christians, Clarkson cautions, "We must not love them, so as to be intimate with them [and] delight in the company of evil doers." This is a valid warning because we may begin to enjoy others' sinful behavior to the extent that we "openly profane" and become "scorners of godliness." Clarkson reminds us that we must hate sin because it affects our relationship with Jesus. "If you would have communion with Christ in sweet acts of love, you must have no fellowship with the unfruitful works of darkness, nor those that act them." If we want to develop an intimate relationship with Jesus Christ, we must be averse to sin dominating and controlling our lives.

Prayer. Lord, help me to love those who do not yet know you. Give me wisdom to do this without succumbing to the values and activities which would displease you. Guard my heart from falling prey to evil while loving those who do not know Jesus Christ as their Savior. Amen.

January 6 — Psalm 5:8–12

8 Lord, lead me in Your righteousness because of my enemies; make Your way straight before me. 9 For there is nothing trustworthy in their mouth; their inward part is destruction itself. Their throat is an open grave; they flatter with their tongue. 10 Make them pay, God; have them fall by their own schemes! Scatter them in the multitude of their wrongdoings, for they are rebellious against You. 11 But rejoice, all who take refuge in You, sing for joy forever! And may You shelter them that those who love Your name may rejoice in You. 12 *For You bless the righteous person,* Lord, *You surround him with favor as with a shield.* (NASB)

Dependence on God. Timothy Rogers, who suffered bouts of depression, reminds us to continually depend on the Lord. He writes, "When the strong man armed comes against us, when he darts his fiery darts, what can hurt us, if God compass us about with his lovingkindness as with a shield? He can disarm the tempter and restrain his malice and tread him under our feet. If God be not with us, if he do not give us sufficient grace, so subtle, so powerful, so politic an enemy, will be too hard for us." When we assume we can face life's challenges on our own, Rogers offers a somber warning, "How surely are we foiled, and get the worse, when we pretend to grapple with him in our own strength! How many falls, and how many bruises by those falls have we got, by relying too much on our own skill?" God is gracious in response when we turn to him. Rogers encourages us: "How often have we had the help of God when we have humbly asked it! And how sure are we to get the victory, if Christ pray for us that we do not fail! Where can we go for shelter but unto God our Maker?" Regardless of our difficulties, God's grace is sufficient, if we depend on him.

Prayer. Lord, too many times I have relied on my experience, knowledge and skills without first turning to you. Forgive me for my self-sufficiency and lack of dependency on you. I acknowledge that you offer all that I need for life—wisdom, comfort, and strength. Help me to increasingly rely on you throughout this day. Amen.

January 7 — Psalm 6

1 O Lord, don't rebuke me in your anger or discipline me in your rage. 2 Have compassion on me, Lord, for I am weak. Heal me, Lord, for my bones are in agony. 3 I am sick at heart. How long, O Lord, until you restore me? 4 Return, O Lord, and rescue me. Save me because of your unfailing love. 5 For the dead do not remember you. Who can praise you from the grave? 6 *I am worn out from sobbing. All night I flood my bed with weeping, drenching it with my tears. 7 My vision is blurred by grief; my eyes are worn out because of all my enemies.* 8 Go away, all you who do evil, for the Lord has heard my weeping. 9 The Lord has heard my plea; the Lord will answer my prayer. 10 May all my enemies be disgraced and terrified. May they suddenly turn back in shame. (NLT)

Dark days. The psalmist went through very dark times in his life. Sufferer Timothy Rogers describes depression's impact on individuals: "Soul-trouble is attended usually with great pain of body too, and so a man is wounded and distressed in every part . . . In this inward distress we find our strength decay and melt, even as wax before the fire; for sorrow darkens the spirits, obscures the judgment, blinds the memory, as to all pleasant things, and beclouds the lucid part of the mind, causing the lamp of life to burn weakly. In this troubled condition the person cannot be without a countenance that is pale, and wan, and dejected, like one that is seized with strong fear and consternation; all his motions are sluggish, and no sprightliness nor activity remains . . . Long weakness of body makes the soul more susceptible of trouble, and uneasy thoughts." In those darkest days, the psalmist offers us hope. We are not alone for we can cry out to the Lord knowing that he hears (vv. 8–9) and can restore us (v. 3).

Prayer. Lord, I have experienced very dark days and although I do not welcome such times, I am thankful that you have always been with me. In the darkness, I cling to you and hold on to the hope you give me. Amen.

January 8 — Psalm 7:1–5

1 O Lord my God, in you do I take refuge; save me from all my pursuers and deliver me, 2 lest like a lion they tear my soul apart, rending it in pieces, with none to deliver. 3 O Lord my God, if I have done this, if there is wrong in my hands, 4 *if I have repaid my friend with evil or plundered my enemy without cause,* 5 let the enemy pursue my soul and overtake it, and let him trample my life to the ground and lay my glory in the dust. *Selah* (ESV)

Refusing revenge. This psalm's context may be situated in I Sam 24 which describes David's encounter with king Saul who had been seeking to kill him. When Saul entered the cave in which David had been hiding, David could have killed the king but he refused to harm him (24:12–13). Thomas Manton comments on Saul's subsequent response to David, "Saul was melted, and said to David, 'You are more righteous than I' (24:17). Though [Saul] had such a hostile mind against [David], and chased and pursued him up and down, yet when David forbore revenge when it was in his power, it overcame him, and he [Saul] falls a-weeping." David's unwillingness to kill the king was not due to cowardice but as Manton states, it was God's "grace victorious" which gave David "a noble and brave spirit." Manton concludes that David's bravery and humility is "God's way to shame the party that did the wrong, and to overcome him [Saul] too; it is the best way to get the victory over him." When others mistreat us, we have two options. We can take matters into our own hands and expect a negative outcome (vv. 4–5). The better option is to trust in God who can address the wrongful actions of others (vv. 1–2). Rather than living with guilt for wrongdoing, we live freely with innocence (v. 3).

Prayer. Lord, it is so tempting to strike back at people who have offended and deeply hurt me. I know revenge is not the way you want me to respond, and I need your Spirit's enabling grace to love those who have hurt me. Amen.

January 9 — Psalm 7:6–11

6 Arise, O LORD, in anger! Stand up against the fury of my enemies! Wake up, my God, and bring justice! 7 Gather the nations before you. Rule over them from on high. 8 The LORD judges the nations. Declare me righteous, O LORD, for I am innocent, O Most High! 9 End the evil of those who are wicked, and defend the righteous. For you look deep within the mind and heart, O righteous God. 10 God is my shield, saving those whose hearts are true and right. 11 *God is an honest judge. He is angry with the wicked every day.* (NLT)

God's anger. Reading about God's wrath may create personal internal discomfort. Yet, God's righteous anger is an aspect of his character (v. 11). William Gurnall provides the reason for divine fury. He states, "At every door where sin sets its foot, there the wrath of God meets us. Every faculty of soul, and member of body, are used as a weapon of unrighteousness against God; so everyone hath its portion of wrath, even to the tip of the tongue. As man is sinful all over, so is he cursed all over. Inside and outside, soul and body, is written all with woes and curses, so close and full, that there is not room for another to interline, or add to what God hath written." Gurnall notes that our sin is an affront to the holiness of God who hates sin. Today's meditation on this psalm invites us to reflect on our lives by asking: Do I take sin seriously, so that I do not intentionally sin and grieve God? Accepting God's attitude toward sin is a step forward in our spiritual growth.

Prayer. Lord, the Bible reminds me that I cannot trifle with sin. Disobeying your will brings hurt and grief to my life and relationships. More importantly, violating your will grieves you. Recognizing both the pervasiveness of sin in my being and your profound love for me, I confess my absolute need for your power to resist sin in every area of my life. Amen.

January 10   Psalm 7:12–17

12 If one does not repent, He will sharpen His sword; He has bent His bow and taken aim. 13 He has also prepared deadly weapons for Himself; He makes His arrows fiery shafts. 14 Behold, an evil person is pregnant with injustice, and he conceives harm and gives birth to lies. 15 *He has dug a pit and hollowed it out and has fallen into the hole which he made.* 16 His harm will return on his own head, and his violence will descend on the top of his own head. 17 I will give thanks to the LORD according to his righteousness and will sing praise to the name of the LORD Most High. (NASB)

The consequences of sin. When a person is unwilling to repent of sin (v. 12), there are consequences. One will experience God's wrath (vv. 12–13). In addition, an unrepentant person, "pregnant" with evil, gives birth to trouble and disillusionment (v. 14). Finally, God judges his opponents with destruction by their own evil schemes (v. 15). While judgment may come in this life, it will certainly come after death. Thomas Adams applies today's Scripture reading to the parable of the rich man and Lazarus (Luke 16:19–31). Hell is an inescapable reality for those who are unwilling to repent and believe in the resurrection of Jesus Christ (vv. 30–31). Adams writes, "These wretched guests [of hell] were too busy with the waters of sin; behold, now they are in the depth of a pit, 'where no water is.'" The rich man who "wasted so many tons of wine, cannot now procure water, not a pot of water, not a handful of water, not a drop of water, to cool his tongue . . . A just recompense! He would not give a crumb; he shall not have a drop . . . As he denied the least comfort to Lazarus living, so Lazarus shall not bring him the least comfort dead. Thus, the pain for sin answers the pleasure of sin." The psalmist reminds us that we cannot trifle with sin. How much better it is to seek God's blessing on our lives!

Prayer. Lord, Scripture reminds me that I am ultimately accountable to you. Enable me to hate sin as you do, and to love you and others in gratitude for all you have done for me. Amen.

January 11   Psalm 8

1 Lord, our Lord, how majestic is your name in all the earth! You have set your glory in the heavens. 2 Through the praise of children and infants you have established a stronghold against your enemies, to silence the foe and the avenger. 3 *When I consider your heavens, the work of your fingers, the moon and the stars, which you have set in place,* 4 *what is mankind that you are mindful of them, human beings that you care for them?* 5 You have made them a little lower than the angels and crowned them with glory and honor. 6 You made them rulers over the works of your hands; you put everything under their feet: 7 all flocks and herds, and the animals of the wild, 8 the birds in the sky, and the fish in the sea, all that swim the paths of the seas. 9 Lord, our Lord, how majestic is your name in all the earth! (NIV)

The spiritual value of creation. Taking time to observe God's creation fills us with awe and contributes to our spiritual growth. Stephen Charnock instructs us to "draw spiritual inferences" from nature. When David reflects on God's creation, he "breaks out into self-abasement and humble admiration of God." Charnock encourages giving "praise to your Maker from everything you see . . . Dwell not upon any created object only as a virtuoso, to gratify your rational curiosity, but as a Christian, call religion to the feast, and make a spiritual improvement." Since observing nature is a means to spiritual growth, Charnock invites us to study many facets of God's creation. He states, "No creature can meet our eyes but affords us lessons worthy of our thoughts, besides the general notices of the power and wisdom of the Creator. Thus, may the sheep read us a lesson of patience, the dove of innocence, the ant and bee raise blushes in us for our sluggishness, and the stupid ox and dull ass correct and shame our ungrateful ignorance . . . He whose eyes are open cannot want [lack] an instructor, unless he wants [lacks] a heart." Yes, God's creation provides spiritual lessons which contribute to our spiritual growth.

Prayer. Lord, thank you for your creation which instructs me to know more about you and leads me to worship you. Direct my eyes to learn from your created order. Amen.

January 12 — Psalm 9:1–14

1 I will give thanks to the Lord with all my heart; I will tell of all Your wonders. 2 I will rejoice and be jubilant in You; I will sing praise to Your name, O Most High. 3 When my enemies turn back, they stumble and perish before You. 4 For You have maintained my just cause; You have sat on the throne judging righteously. 5 You have rebuked the nations, You have eliminated the wicked; You have wiped out their name forever and ever. 6 The enemy has come to an end in everlasting ruins, and You have uprooted the cities; the very memory of them has perished. 7 But the Lord sits as King forever; He has established His throne for judgment, 8 *and He will judge the world in righteousness; He will execute judgment for the peoples fairly.* 9 The Lord will also be a stronghold for the oppressed, a stronghold in times of trouble; 10 and those who know Your name will put their trust in You, for You, Lord, have not abandoned those who seek You. 11 Sing praises to the Lord, who dwells in Zion; declare His deeds among the peoples. 12 For He who requires blood remembers them; He does not forget the cry of the needy. 13 Be gracious to me, Lord; see my oppression from those who hate me, You who lift me up from the gates of death, 14 so that I may tell of all Your praises, that in the gates of the daughter of Zion I may rejoice in Your salvation. (NASB)

The reality of judgment. The psalmist states that God will equitably judge those who oppose him (v. 8). Though his judgment is warranted, Henry Smith reminds us that people dislike such an idea. If they could take a financial collection to cancel judgment day, he writes, "then God would be so rich that the world would go a-begging and be a waste wilderness." Although God's judgment is certain, we can avoid it through faith in Jesus Christ who died in our place (Rom 8:1).

Prayer. Lord, I am thankful that I no longer stand condemned through my relationship with Jesus Christ. Increase my sensitivity to sin so that I may live pleasingly before you. Use me to tell others of God's great love for them and how they can be spared from his judgment. Amen.

January 13 — Psalm 9:15–20

15 The nations have fallen into the pit they dug for others. Their own feet have been caught in the trap they set. 16 The Lord is known for his justice. The wicked are trapped by their own deeds. 17 The wicked will go down to the grave. This is the fate of all the nations who ignore God. 18 But the needy will not be ignored forever; the hopes of the poor will not always be crushed. 19 Arise, O Lord! Do not let mere mortals defy you! Judge the nations! 20 Make them tremble in fear, O Lord. Let the nations know they are merely human. (NLT)

Consider the afterlife. While individuals may deny God's judgment, the psalmist affirms its reality. Richard Baxter asks, "How many times did God by his messengers here call upon them, 'Sinners, consider where you are going. Do but make a stand awhile, and think where your way will end, what is the offered glory that you so carelessly reject: will not this be bitterness in the end?'" There will be a time when they will be trapped by their own actions and then face God's justice (vv. 16–17). For them, Baxter states that "God has arrested them, and judgment is passed upon them, and vengeance is poured out upon them to the full, then they cannot choose but consider it, whether they will or no." Since people are so busy with their lives, he notes, "Now they have no leisure to consider, nor any room in their memories for the things of another life." They are too preoccupied with daily life, but after they have passed away, "they shall have leisure enough, they shall be where they shall have nothing else to do but consider it: their memories shall have no other employment to hinder them; it shall even be engraven upon the tables of their hearts." It is unwise to ignore or deny God's judgment in the future. Now is the time to consider one's eternal destiny and turn to Jesus Christ who offers us eternal life (John 3:16–18).

Prayer. Lord, I have heard people wanting to postpone their consideration of a relationship with you until later in life. However, your Word reminds me that people's hearts are ensnared by sin with no desire for you. Use my life to encourage people to turn to you. Amen.

January 14   Psalm 10:1–11

1 Why do You stand far away, LORD? Why do You hide yourself in times of trouble? 2 In arrogance the wicked hotly pursue the needy; let them be caught in the plots which they have devised. 3 For the wicked boasts of his soul's desire, and the greedy person curses and shows disrespect to the LORD. 4 The wicked, in his haughtiness, does not seek Him. There is no God in all his schemes. 5 His ways succeed at all times; yet Your judgments are on high, out of his sight; as for all his enemies, he snorts at them. 6 He says to himself, "I will not be moved; throughout the generations I will not be in adversity." 7 His mouth is full of cursing, deceit, and oppression; under his tongue is harm and injustice. 8 He sits in the lurking places of the villages; he kills the innocent in the secret places; his eyes surreptitiously watch for the unfortunate. 9 *He lurks in secret like a lion in his lair; he lurks to catch the needy; he catches the needy when he pulls him into his net.* 10 *Then he crushes the needy one, who cowers; and unfortunate people fall by his mighty power.* 11 He says to himself, "God has forgotten; He has hidden His face; he will never see it." (NASB)

The destructive nature of sin. While sin may appear attractive, the psalmist portrays it in brutal terms. Thomas Brooks comments, "Oppression turns princes into roaring lions, and judges into ravening wolves. It [oppressing others] is an unnatural sin, against the light of nature. No creatures do oppress them of their own kind. Look upon the birds of prey, as upon eagles, vultures, hawks, and you shall never find them preying upon their own kind. Look upon the beasts of the forest, as upon the lion, the tiger, the wolf, the bear, and you shall ever find them favourable to their own kind; and yet men unnaturally prey upon one another, like the fish in the sea, the great swallowing up the small." Paul warns that we can either devour and destroy one another (Gal 5:15), or love our neighbors with Christ's love (v. 14).

Prayer. Lord, your word and my reflections on humanity's self-destruction reminds me of sin's tragic effects. I am thankful for your Spirit who liberates by changing human hearts to love. Amen.

January 15   Psalm 10:12-18

12 Arise, Lord! Lift up your hand, O God. Do not forget the helpless. 13 Why does the wicked man revile God? Why does he say to himself, "He won't call me to account?" 14 But you, God, see the trouble of the afflicted; you consider their grief and take it in hand. The victims commit themselves to you; you are the helper of the fatherless. 15 Break the arm of the wicked man; call the evildoer to account for his wickedness that would not otherwise be found out. 16 The Lord is King for ever and ever; the nations will perish from his land. 17 *You,* Lord, *hear the desire of the afflicted; you encourage them, and you listen to their cry,* 18 defending the fatherless and the oppressed, so that mere earthly mortals will never again strike terror. (NIV)

Heartfelt prayers. The psalmist provides some characteristics of our petitions to God. First, we come depending on him. The writer wisely looks to the Lord to encourage the afflicted and the orphans (vv. 17–18). Relying on God is a genuine mark of humility. Thomas Watson states, "A spiritual prayer is a humble prayer." Asking God to provide relief for the afflicted "requires humility." Second, our prayers should not be uttered in a perfunctory manner but with heartfelt desires (v. 17). These desires are not selfish but are prompted by the indwelling Holy Spirit, in alignment with God's will who is a "helper of the fatherless" (v. 14). Watson comments, "Prayer is the offering up of our desires to God in the name of Christ, for such things as are agreeable to his will. It is an offering of our desires. Desires are the soul and life of prayer . . . as the body without the soul is dead, so are prayers unless they are animated with our desires." Like the psalmist, we can be confident that God hears our desires (v. 17).

Prayer. Lord, I confess that too often I do not depend on you. As a result, many of my prayers are selfish demands asking you to answer them, according to my wishes. I want to humble myself by submitting to your purposes. May I grow closer to you so that my desires will align with your divine and good will. Amen.

January 16   Psalm 11

1 In the LORD I take refuge; how can you say to my soul, "Flee as a bird to your mountain? 2 For, behold, the wicked bend the bow, they have set their arrow on the string to shoot in darkness at the upright in heart. 3 If the foundations are destroyed, what can the righteous do?" 4 *The LORD is in his holy temple; the Lord's throne is in heaven; his eyes see, his eyelids test the sons of mankind.* 5 The LORD tests the righteous and the wicked, and his soul hates one who loves violence. 6 He will rain coals of fire upon the wicked, and brimstone and burning wind will be the portion of their cup. 7 For the LORD is righteous, he loves righteousness; the upright will see his face. (ESV)

God sees. When David's enemies threatened him (vv. 1–3), he did not despair because he knew God's nature (vv. 4–7). God's divine presence ensures that he observes both the righteous and wicked (vv. 4–5). For those who know him, they will enjoy God's presence and favor (v. 7). Those who oppose him will experience what they had intended for others (v. 6). Ezekiel Hopkins explains that, under the Lord's watchful eye, "God not only sees into all you do, but he sees it to that very end that he may examine and search into it. He does not only behold you with a common and indifferent look, but with a searching, watchful, and inquisitive eye: he pries into the reasons, the motives, [and] the ends of all your actions." Since God knows our hearts, he calls us to end our religious pretense. Hopkins reminds us that God "knows and discerns how much your very purest duties have in them of mixture, and base ends of formality, hypocrisy, distractedness, and deadness: he sees through all your specious pretenses . . . he is a God that can look through all those fig-leaves of outward profession, and discern the nakedness of your duties through them." This is a call to genuine faith in Jesus Christ and to wholehearted living for him.

Prayer. Lord, often I forget that you are watching everything I do. Enable me to live obediently for you, not out of fear, but in the knowledge of your love for me. Your loving presence also gives me hope in my difficulties. Amen.

January 17 — Psalm 12

1 Help, Lord, for the godly person has come to an end, for the faithful have disappeared from the sons of mankind. 2 They speak lies to one another; they speak with flattering lips and a double heart. 3 May the Lord cut off all flattering lips, the tongue that speaks great things; 4 who have said, "With our tongue we will prevail; our lips are our own; who is lord over us?" 5 "Because of the devastation of the poor, because of the groaning of the needy, now I will arise," says the Lord; "I will put him in the safety for which he longs." 6 *The words of the Lord are pure words; like silver refined in a furnace on the ground, filtered seven times.* 7 You, Lord, will keep them; You will protect him from this generation forever. 8 The wicked strut about on every side when vileness is exalted among the sons of mankind. (NASB)

Scripture's reliability. David contrasts God's word with those whose speech consists of lies and flattery. In response to verse 6, Thomas Manton mentions that two characteristics of the Bible include "the infallible certainty of the word; and, secondly, the exact purity." Regarding the former, he comments, "The infallible certainty of the word, [is] as gold endures in the fire when the dross is consumed. Vain conceits comfort us not in a time of trouble: but the word of God, the more it is tried, the more you will find the excellency of it—the promise is tried, as well as we are tried, in deep afflictions; but when it is so, it will be found to be most pure . . . As pure gold suffers no loss by the fire, so the promises suffer no loss when they are tried but stand to us in our greatest troubles." The purity of Scripture, Manton explains, is the "exact perfection of the word: there is no dross in silver and gold that hath been often refined; so there is no defect in the word of God." Scripture is trustworthy because it reflects God's nature.

Prayer. Lord, I am thankful for the truthfulness and reliability of Scripture which has sustained me throughout life's challenges. I am also grateful that I have been able to depend on your promises which have stood the test of time. Amen.

January 18 — Psalm 13

1 O Lord, how long will you forget me? Forever? How long will you look the other way? 2 How long must I struggle with anguish in my soul, with sorrow in my heart every day? How long will my enemy have the upper hand? 3 Turn and answer me, O Lord my God! Restore the sparkle to my eyes, or I will die. 4 Don't let my enemies gloat, saying, "We have defeated him!" Don't let them rejoice at my downfall. 5 But I trust in your unfailing love. I will rejoice because you have rescued me. 6 *I will sing to the Lord because he is good to me.* (NLT)

God and our trials. John Bunyan, author of the well-known *Pilgrim's Progress,* spent at least seventeen years in prison, undergoing times of severe hardships. He testifies, "I never knew what it was for God to stand by me at all turns, and at every offer of Satan to afflict me . . . as I have found him since I came in hither; for look how fears have presented themselves, so have supports and encouragements; yes, when I have started, even as it were at nothing else but my shadow, yet God, as being very tender to me, has not suffered me to be molested, but would with one Scripture or another, strengthen me against all; insomuch that I have often said, 'Were it lawful, I could pray for greater trouble, for the greater comfort's sake.'" In prison, no trial grew greater than the comfort God gave Bunyan. The apostle Paul testified how, in numerous ways (Phil 4:25; 2 Tim 4:13, 17), God had cared for him in prison (Acts 16:25)! We too can be confident that the Lord will be faithful by sustaining us with his comfort through Scripture, the Holy Spirit, godly friends, and divine providence.

Prayer. Lord. I admit life has had its challenging moments. In those times, I have been filled with despair, loneliness, and fear. However, you have been with me every step along the way by providing your strengthening presence. I am also thankful for the Scriptures which have sustained me throughout my life journey. You have been good to me. Amen.

January 19   Psalm 14

1 The fool says in his heart, "There is no God." They are corrupt, they do abominable deeds; there is none who does good. 2 The Lord looks down from heaven on the children of man, to see if there are any who understand, who seek after God. 3 They have all turned aside; together they have become corrupt; there is none who does good, not even one. 4 Have they no knowledge, all the evildoers who eat up my people as they eat bread and do not call upon the Lord? 5 There they are in great terror, for God is with the generation of the righteous. 6 *You would shame the plans of the poor, but the* Lord *is his refuge.* 7 Oh, that salvation for Israel would come out of Zion! When the Lord restores the fortunes of his people, let Jacob rejoice, let Israel be glad. (ESV)

Opposing God. David describes those who ignore God and oppress the poor whose refuge is the Lord (v. 6). John Owen provides some reasons for their opposition to God, "One, they know not God; and it is a foolish thing to trust one knows not whom. Two, they are enemies to God, and God is their enemy; and they account it a foolish thing to trust their enemy. Three, they know not the way of God's assistance and help. Four, they seek for such help, such assistance, such supplies, as God will not give; to be delivered, to serve their lusts; to be preserved, to execute their rage, filthiness, and folly." Owen warns people of all generations, "It is a foolish thing in any man to trust God to be preserved in sin. It is true, their folly is their wisdom, considering their state and condition. It is a folly to trust in God to live in sin and despise the counsel of the poor." To live wisely involves willingly submitting to the Lord of the universe.

Prayer. Lord, you have given me insight into the reasons others do not trust you. They do not know you and do not want to change their lives in accordance with your will. Help me understand that others' ridicule often reflects their opposition to you. I am thankful that I can come to you who is my personal refuge at any time. Amen.

January 20 — Psalm 15

1 LORD, who may dwell in your sacred tent? Who may live on your holy mountain? 2 *The one whose walk is blameless, who does what is righteous, who speaks the truth from their heart;* 3 whose tongue utters no slander, who does no wrong to a neighbor, and casts no slur on others; 4 who despises a vile person but honors those who fear the LORD; who keeps an oath even when it hurts, and does not change their mind; 5 who lends money to the poor without interest; who does not accept a bribe against the innocent. Whoever does these things will never be shaken. (NIV)

Integrity. This psalm contrasts the previous psalm's portrayal of an ungodly person with a description of a godly person. In response to his rhetorical question (v. 1), David declares that those who "walk blamelessly" (v. 2) can come before God's presence. While we may feel we are disqualified because we are not perfect, George Downame correctly believes that blamelessness is made possible only by God's grace transforming all areas of our lives. This blamelessness indicates, in his words, "the soundness of all grace and virtues, as also of all religion and worship of God." He is suggesting that blamelessness involves a spiritually changed inner life (the "heart") and outer life, such as our speech (v. 2). Integrity is the integration of these two areas. Without a heart change, "the best graces we seem to have are counterfeit, and, therefore, but glorious sins; the best worship we can perform is but hypocrisy, and therefore abominable in God's sight." Without the integration of an ongoing transformation of the inner life, an outwardly moral and religious life does not impress God. Our actions are simply "sins under the masks or vizards of virtue" before Him. When we live with integrity, we are not "shaken" (v. 5) because we are cognizant of God's presence in our lives.

Prayer. Lord, I want to have a godly life before you. However, I confess that I have tried to live a moral life apart from depending on your grace working in my life. I need your Spirit to change my heart so that my actions and words ultimately honor you. Enable me, by your grace, to live with integrity so that there is consistency between my inner and outer life. Amen.

January 21 — Psalm 16:1–4

1 Keep me safe, O God, for I have come to you for refuge. 2 I said to the Lord, *"You are my Master! Every good thing I have comes from you." 3 The godly people in the land are my true heroes! I take pleasure in them! 4 Troubles multiply for those who chase after other gods. I will not take part in their sacrifices of blood or even speak the names of their gods.* (NLT)

Trusting God. With continual social upheaval and global turbulence, people search for ways to cope with life's uncertainties. Based on his own observations in the sixteenth century, Richard Greenham comments, "Some we see trust in friends." Others, he says, place their trust in "their goods; some fence themselves with authority; others bathe and baste themselves in pleasure to put the evil day far from them; others make flesh their arm; and others make the wedge of gold their confidence." Five centuries later, people still unduly trust influential individuals, materialism, power, lavish lifestyles, excessive self-gratification, and financial portfolios to distance themselves from the swirling chaos around them. Greenham's experience told him that those who outwardly say that they seek God's help "mean in their hearts to find it in their friends, good authority and pleasure, howsoever for fear, they dare not say this outwardly." Rather than pursuing all these avenues which will ultimately disappoint us, we must observe "under what shelter we may harbour ourselves in the showers of adversity." It is the Lord (v. 1) who is able to protect us (Ps 91:1). We are secure in him! Of course, our security comes from trusting the promises that "if we come with like faith, we may obtain the like deliverance." Trusting the Lord during adversities can be very challenging, but this trust is God's way for our faith to grow as we see Him work in these circumstances.

Prayer. Lord, it is tempting to place my trust in many alluring ways rather than in you. You have reminded me that placing my confidence in possessions, position, and others will eventually be shaken. Reveal the reasons I place my hope in temporal things rather than you who is sovereign. Enable me, by your grace, to continue growing in my trust in you. Amen.

January 22   Psalm 16:5–11

5 Lord, you alone are my portion and my cup; you make my lot secure. 6 The boundary lines have fallen for me in pleasant places; surely I have a delightful inheritance. 7 I will praise the Lord, who counsels me; even at night my heart instructs me. 8 I keep my eyes always on the Lord. With him at my right hand, I will not be shaken. 9 Therefore my heart is glad and my tongue rejoices; my body also will rest secure, 10 because you will not abandon me to the realm of the dead, nor will you let your faithful one see decay. 11 You make known to me the path of life; you will fill me with joy in your presence, with eternal pleasures at your right hand. (NIV)

God's presence with us. In today's meditation, David continues to explain why he trusts the Lord. He focuses on God's presence dwelling among his people. God is the "delightful inheritance" of David (vv. 5–6). This secure inheritance flows out of a deep love relationship between God and his people. James Janeway, who faced his own share of suffering and persecution, comments on God's presence, "No greater mercy can be bestowed upon any people, family, or person than this, for God to dwell among them. If we value this mercy according to the excellence and worth of that which is bestowed, it is the greatest; if we value it according to the goodwill that gives it, it will appear likewise to be the greatest favour. The greatness of the good will of God in giving himself to be our acquaintance, is evident in the nature of the gift. A man may give his estate to them to whom his love is not very large, but he never gives himself but upon strong affection." Jesus spoke about his presence abiding among those who have a relationship with him (John 15:3, 9). God dwells within his people through the Holy Spirit who is a "deposit" of our future inheritance (Eph 1:13–14).

Prayer. Lord, I am grateful for your love and presence through the Holy Spirit who dwells within me. When overwhelming circumstances come my way, I am thankful that I can remain secure in your love and delight in you and all that you have given to me! Amen.

January 23   Psalm 17:1-9

1 Hear a just cause, LORD, give Your attention to my cry; listen to my prayer, which is not from deceitful lips. 2 Let my judgment come forth from Your presence; let Your eyes look with integrity. 3 You have put my heart to the test; You have visited me by night; You have sifted me and You find nothing; my intent is that my mouth will not offend. 4 As for the works of mankind, by the word of Your lips I have kept from the ways of the violent. 5 My steps have held to Your paths. My feet have not slipped. 6 I have called upon You, for You will answer me, God; incline Your ear to me, hear my speech. 7 Show Your wonderful faithfulness, Savior of those who take refuge at Your right hand from those who rise up against them. 8 *Keep me as the apple of the eye; hide me in the shadow of Your wings* 9 from the wicked who deal violently with me, my deadly enemies who surround me. (NASB)

God's protective care. When people oppose us, we can feel unloved. David tells us how he responded when he faced hostile opposition (v. 9). He asked the Lord to keep him as the "apple of the eye" (v. 8). Jeremiah Burroughs comments on David's petition, "I can look up to you, and know that I am dear unto you as the apple of your eye. All the saints of God are dear to God at all times, but the persecuted saints, they are the apple of God's eye; if at any time they are dear to God, then especially when they are most persecuted; now they are the apple of his eye, and the apple of an eye is weak, and little able to resist any hurt, but so much the more is the man tender of the apple of his eye." We can be assured of God's love for us in the most difficult times.

Prayer. Lord, I confess that I often take matters into my hands when I face attacks from those who dislike and even hate me. Help me to see myself from your perspective. Thank you for your persistent love and protective care for me during life's overwhelming circumstances. Amen.

January 24 Psalm 17:10–15

10 They have closed their unfeeling hearts, with their mouths they speak proudly. 11 They have now surrounded us in our steps; they set their eyes to cast us down to the ground. 12 He is like a lion that is eager to tear, and as a young lion lurking in secret places. 13 Arise, LORD, confront him, make him bow down; save my soul from the wicked with Your sword, 14 from people by Your hand, Lord, from people of the world, whose portion is in this life, and whose belly You fill with Your treasure; they are satisfied with children, and leave their abundance to their babies. 15 *As for me, I shall behold Your face in righteousness; I shall be satisfied with Your likeness when I awake.* (NASB)

True satisfaction. What satiates one's deepest longings? Some find satisfaction in the things "in this life" (v. 14). In contrast, David finds his greatest satisfaction in a personal and intimate communion with God (v. 15). John Howe expresses this relationship: "I look upon the face of a stranger and it moves me not; but upon a friend and his face presently transforms mine into a lively, cheerful aspect." Time spent in intimate fellowship with the heavenly Father becomes a transformative experience for us (2 Cor 3:18). Of course, our sinful nature hampers our communion with and transformation by God. However, when we pass into eternity, we will see the Lord "face to face" (1 Cor 13:12) and "we shall be like him (1 John 3:2). Howe comments, "The soul that loves God, opens itself to him, admits his influence and impressions, is easily molded and wrought to his will, yields to the transforming power of his appearing glory. There is no resistant principle remaining when the love of God is perfected in it; and so overcoming is the first sight of his glory upon the awaking soul, that it perfects it, and so his likeness, both at once." There is nothing more satisfying than this!

Prayer. Lord, too often I long for, and sometimes taste, those things which really do not bring any lasting satisfaction to my soul. Forgive me for pursuing the things of this world rather than communion with you. Satisfy my longing with intimate fellowship with you so that I can become increasingly more like Jesus. Amen.

January 25   Psalm 18:1–3

> 1 *I love you,* Lord; *you are my strength.* 2 *The* Lord *is my rock, my fortress, and my savior; my God is my rock, in whom I find protection. He is my shield, the power that saves me, and my place of safety.* 3 I called on the Lord, who is worthy of praise, and he saved me from my enemies. (NLT)

Our primary focus. Salvation in Jesus Christ provides us with many blessings. However, Joseph Caryl urges us to focus more on God than salvation's accrued blessings. He says, "It is God himself who is the salvation and the portion of his people. They would not care much for salvation if God were not their salvation. It more pleases the saints that they enjoy God, than that they enjoy salvation." Those who are not seriously committed to Christ may have greater interest in salvation's benefits rather than a focus on loving God. He notes that people "will express a great deal of desire after salvation, for they like salvation, heaven, and glory well; but they never express any longing desire after God and Jesus Christ. They love salvation, but they care not for a Saviour." Caryl sets us in the right direction. He explains, "Now that which faith pitches most upon is God himself; he shall be my salvation, let me have him, and that is salvation enough; he is my life, he is my comfort, he is my riches, he is my honour, and he is my all . . . It pleased holy David more that God was his strength, than that God gave him strength; that God was his deliverer, than that he was delivered; that God was his fortress, his buckler, his horn, his high tower, than that he gave him the effect of all these. It pleased David, and it pleases all the saints more that God is their salvation, whether temporal or eternal, than that he saves them: the saints look more at God than at all that is God's."

Prayer. Lord, I have often loved you because of the benefits which come from my relationship to you. These are wonderful blessings! However, I want to increase in my desire and love for you alone, apart from all the other privileges of salvation. You are worthy of my love. Amen.

January 26   Psalm 18:4–19

4 The ropes of death encompassed me, and the torrents of destruction terrified me. 5 The ropes of Sheol surrounded me; the snares of death confronted me. 6 *In my distress I called upon the* Lord *and cried to my God for help; He heard my voice from His temple, and my cry for help before Him came into His ears.* 7 *Then the earth shook and quaked; and the foundations of the mountains were trembling and were shaken, because He was angry.* 8 Smoke went up out of His nostrils, and fire from His mouth was devouring; coals burned from it. 9 He also bowed the heavens down low and came down with thick darkness under His feet. 10 He rode on a cherub and flew; and He sped on the wings of the wind. 11 He made darkness His hiding place, His canopy around Him, darkness of waters, thick clouds. 12 From the brightness before Him passed His thick clouds, hailstones and coals of fire. 13 The Lord also thundered in the heavens, and the Most High uttered His voice, hailstones and coals of fire. 14 He sent out His arrows, and scattered them, and lightning flashes in abundance, and routed them. 15 Then the channels of water appeared, and the foundations of the world were exposed by Your rebuke, Lord, at the blast of the breath of Your nostrils. 16 He sent from on high, He took me; He drew me out of many waters. 17 He saved me from my strong enemy, and from those who hated me, for they were too mighty for me. 18 They confronted me in the day of my disaster, but the Lord was my support. 19 He also brought me out into an open place; He rescued me, because He delighted in me. (NASB)

The power of prayer. God responds to our prayers! John Flavel comments, "The prayer of a single saint is sometimes followed with wonderful effects." When God answered Martin Luther's prayers, "his enemies felt the weight of his prayers; and the church of God reaped the benefits thereof. The Queen of Scots professed she was more afraid of the prayers of Mr. Knox, than of an army of ten thousand men."

Prayer. Lord, sometimes I doubt that you hear my prayers. Thank you for these reminders that you not only hear but respond in your wise ways. Amen.

January 27   Psalm 18:20-28

20 The LORD has rewarded me according to my righteousness; according to the cleanness of my hands He has repaid me. 21 For I have kept the ways of the LORD and have not acted wickedly against my God. 22 For all His judgments were before me, and I did not put away His statutes from me. 23 *I was also blameless with Him, and I kept myself from my wrongdoing.* 24 Therefore the LORD has repaid me according to my righteousness, according to the cleanness of my hands in His eyes. 25 With the faithful You show Yourself faithful; with the blameless You prove Yourself blameless; 26 with the pure You show Yourself pure, and with the crooked You show Yourself astute. 27 For You save an afflicted people, but You humiliate haughty eyes. 28 for You light my lamp; the LORD my God illumines my darkness. (NASB)

Resisting sin. David states that he kept himself from sin (v. 23). We may think we are spiritually thriving when we do not succumb to various sins. However, Thomas Goodwin wisely cautions that believers "may deceive themselves when they estimate their progress herein by having overcome such lusts as their natures are not so prone unto." Spiritual progress cannot be measured by what does not tempt a person. To aid our spiritual growth, Goodwin makes two suggestions. First, we need to carefully assess how resilient we are to those things that really do tempt us. He provides two illustrations. A physician must carefully assess each ailment a person has in order to cure the illness. Also, a conqueror does not measure military strength by "taking or burning of a few villages . . . but by taking the forts and strongest holds." Am I experiencing victory over the great temptations which come my way? Second, he asks us to consider by what force we "cut off of the main army?" We err if we assume we can defeat Satan's strongholds by mustering up our willpower. Instead, we need God's powerful resources to "cut off" and defeat the forces of evil (Eph 6:10-18).

Prayer. Lord, I can be fooled about my spiritual resiliency to sin and by my strategies to defeat sin. I need to face my real temptations in life by your word and Spirit to enable me to live with a pure heart. Amen.

January 28   Psalm 18:29-36

29 For by You I can run at a troop of warriors; and by my God I can leap over a wall. 30 As for God, His way is blameless; the word of the Lord is refined; He is a shield to all who take refuge in Him. 31 For who is God, but the Lord? And who is a rock, except our God, 32 the God who encircles me with strength, and makes my way blameless? 33 *He makes my feet like deer's feet and sets me up on my high places.* 34 He trains my hands for battle, so that my arms can bend a bow of bronze. 35 You have also given me the shield of Your salvation, and Your right hand upholds me; and Your gentleness makes me great. 36 You enlarge my steps under me, and my feet have not slipped. (NASB)

God's strength. Life's struggles undeniably wear us down both physically and emotionally, leaving us with less zest for life than we would wish. The psalmist encourages us with his testimony. God enabled him to run like a deer, energetically and speedily (v. 33). The significance of this experience is more fully seen in its context. Edward Marbury notes, "Consider David, as he then was, when he composed this Psalm, it was at the time when God had delivered him from the hand of all his enemies, and from the hand of Saul. For then God set his feet on high places, setting his kingdom, and establishing him in the place of Saul." 2 Samuel 22:31-46 provides a commentary on God empowering King David during these campaigns. In the heat of battle, the Lord enabled him to run speedily "like the feet of the deer" (v. 34) echoing today's Scripture passage (18:33). While David had both military prowess and mighty warriors, he ultimately depended on God's strength. Whatever we are facing at this moment, Marbury reminds us that "[God] does give swiftness and speed to his church." David's testimony reminds us to always depend on the Lord.

Prayer. Lord, I often feel weary facing life's many challenges. In addition to my physical and emotional fatigue, I fail to turn to you which results only in increasing my weariness. Forgive me for not turning to you! I want to experience your empowering grace so that new heights in life may be reached. Amen.

January 29 — Psalm 18:37-45

37 I pursued my enemies and overtook them, and I did not turn back until they were consumed. 38 I shattered them, so that they were not able to rise; they fell under my feet. 39 For You have encircled me with strength for battle; You have forced those who rose up against me to bow down under me. 40 You have also made my enemies turn their backs to me, and I destroyed those who hated me. 41 *They cried for help, but there was no one to save, they cried to the* Lord, *but He did not answer them.* 42 Then I beat them fine like the dust before the wind; I emptied them out like the mud of the streets. 43 You have rescued me from the contentions of the people; You have placed me as head of the nations; a people whom I have not known serve me. 44 As soon as they hear, they obey me; foreigners pretend to obey me. 45 Foreigners lose heart and come trembling out of their fortresses. (NASB)

Unanswered prayers. We are puzzled when God does not answer our prayers (v. 41). This verse's context is instructive for these situations. Those who cried to God actively opposed him by aggressively fighting against his anointed king, David. They were David's "enemies" and "foes" (2 Sam 22:41) and God did not answer their cries (22:42). John Trapp correctly applies the psalmist's statement (18:41) for our lives. He states, "As nature prompts men in an extremity to look up for help; but because it is but the prayer of the flesh for ease, and not of the Spirit for grace, and [not] a good use of calamities, and not but in extreme despair of help elsewhere, therefore God hears them not." Rather than praying for God to meet our selfish wishes and needs, he wants us to seek his will so that our prayers align with his purposes. God, in his great mercy, hears our cries and appropriately responds (Matt 15:21-28; Luke 18:13-14).

Prayer. Lord, forgive me when I come to you with my selfish requests. I want to cultivate a greater longing for you to be honored. Therefore, it is my desire to pray according to your will and then willingly submit to your divine purposes. Thank you that, for your name's sake, you listen to my prayer. Amen.

January 30 — Psalm 18:46–50

46 *The* LORD *lives, and blessed be my rock; and exalted be the God of my salvation,* 47 *the God who executes vengeance for me, and subdues peoples under me.* 48 *He rescues me from my enemies; You indeed lift me above those who rise up against me; You rescue me from a violent man.* 49 *Therefore I will give thanks to You among the nations,* LORD, *and I will sing praises to Your name.* 50 *He gives great salvation to His king, and shows faithfulness to His anointed, to David and His descendants forever.* (NASB)

God lives. After recounting his many struggles, David concludes this psalm with a doxology affirming that God lives (v. 46). Oliver Heywood states, "With all of God's promises and resources available to us, we can only blame ourselves if we remain discouraged." He illustrates with a story of a godly mother whose two young children passed away far too soon. For each child she could say, "God lives." His story continues, "At last her dear husband dies, and she sat oppressed and most overwhelmed with sorrow. A little child she had yet surviving, having observed what before she spoke to comfort herself, comes to her and said, 'Is God dead, mother? Is God dead?' This reached her heart, and by God's blessing recovered her former confidence in her God, who is a living God." He challenges us, "Thus do you chide yourselves? Ask your fainting spirits under pressing outward sorrows, is not God alive? And why then does not your soul revive? Why does your heart die within you when comforts die! Cannot a living God support your dying hopes? Thus, Christians, argue down your discouraged and disquieted spirits as David did." Heywood reminds us that we have entered a deeply personal covenant relationship with the Lord who is committed to love and care for us. Because he lives, we can be assured that he will provide us with everything we need for daily difficulties, whether great or small.

Prayer. Lord, I am thankful that you are alive. Yet, I often fail to consider how your life relates to my problems. Forgive me for living as if you are not living! Because you live, I want to turn to your many mercies which give me all I need to press on. I can always count on you. Amen.

January 31   Psalm 19:1–6

1 *The heavens declare the glory of God, and the sky above proclaims his handiwork.* 2 *Day to day pours out speech, and night to night reveals knowledge.* 3 *There is no speech, nor are there words, whose voice is not heard.* 4 *Their voice goes out through all the earth, and their words to the end of the world. In them he has set a tent for the sun,* 5 *which comes out like a bridegroom leaving his chamber, and, like a strong man, runs its course with joy.* 6 *Its rising is from the end of the heavens, and its circuit to the end of them, and there is nothing hidden from its heat.* (ESV)

Natural revelation. The Puritans believed that God makes himself known through special revelation (Scripture and Jesus Christ) and general revelation (creation). Today's meditation focuses on the latter. David rejoices that "the heavens declare the glory of God" (v. 1) and therefore God's creation speaks to us (v. 1). As Joseph Caryl states, "The heavens preach to us every day . . . Sun, moon, and stars are preachers; they are universal, they are natural apostles." Since these heavenly bodies enables us to learn about God, he advises that "we should observe what that glory is which they declare." Through the heavens, he further explains, "We may have good doctrine from them, especially this doctrine in the text, of the wisdom and power of God." We see God's wisdom by his design of the natural world to provide everyone warmth from the sun (vv. 4b–6). Caryl continues, "The gospel, like the sun, casts his beams over, and sheds his light into all the world." He shows how the apostle Paul repeats Psalm 19:4 in Romans 10:18, "Their voice has gone out to all the earth" as "a proof of gospel preaching to the whole world." If the universe's created bodies are "preachers" and "natural apostles," we should also tell others about God's greatness.

Prayer. Lord, I am awed by the immensity and beauty of your creation. I see your power to sustain life on this planet. Your design of the natural world reveals your wisdom. I am grateful that what I learn about you through your creation strengthens my trust in you. Amen.

February 1   Psalm 19:7–11

7 The law of the Lord *is perfect, reviving the soul; the testimony of the* Lord *is sure, making wise the simple;* 8 *the precepts of the* Lord *are right, rejoicing the heart; the commandment of the* Lord *is pure, enlightening the eyes;* 9 *the fear of the* Lord *is clean, enduring forever; the rules of the* Lord *are true, and righteous altogether.* 10 *More to be desired are they than gold, even much fine gold; sweeter also than honey and drippings of the honeycomb.* 11 *Moreover, by them is your servant warned; in keeping them there is great reward.* (ESV)

Special revelation. In addition to the created world, God reveals himself through Scripture. In the verses above, David uses five terms ("law", "testimony", "precepts", "commandments", and "rules") to capture the various aspects of God's written revelation. He also lists descriptions of God's word ("perfect", "sure", "right", "pure", "clean", "true", and "righteous"). God's revelation through Scripture impacts our lives; it rejoices the heart, enlightens the eyes (vs. 8), and revives the soul" (v. 7a). Thomas Manton notes that Scripture also makes the simple wise (v. 7b). He states, "It seems the law may also be a word of salvation to the creature" and therefore, the law refers to "the whole word, for the whole doctrine of the covenant of life and salvation . . . the law is of great use as joined with the gospel, to awaken and startle the sinner, to show him his duty, to convince him of sin and judgment; but it is the gospel properly that pulls in the heart." God's word does bring life to us, and with it we gain wisdom, joy and illumination for our benefit (vv. 7, 8, 11).

Prayer. Lord, thank you for your written revelation which leads me into a relationship with you and deepens my walk with you. I want your word to transform my heart and actions so that I may become more like Jesus. By your Holy Spirit, enable me to obey your word so that I may honor you and thereby experience the richness of your truth. Amen.

February 2 Psalm 19:12-14

12 *Who can discern his errors? Declare me innocent from hidden faults.* 13 Keep back your servant also from presumptuous sins; let them not have dominion over me! Then I shall be blameless, and innocent of great transgression. 14 Let the words of my mouth and the meditation of my heart be acceptable in your sight, O Lord, my rock and my redeemer. (ESV)

Secret sins. We may believe that our private sins are not too serious, but Obadiah Sedgewick challenges this thought. He states, "Secret sins are more dangerous to the person in some respects than open sins." To support his claim, he provides several reasons for their danger. One, we do not get the help we need. When a person's "sin breaks out, there is a minister at hand, a friend near, and others to reprove, to warn, to direct." But we deny "all public remedy" when we cover our secret sins "with some plausible varnish" which creates only others' good opinion of us. Two, when we privately enjoy our sins, "the mind is fed all the day long either with sinful contemplations or projectings, so that the very strength of the soul is wasted and corrupted." Our minds continue to feed on those particular sins. Three, when a person allows the heart "to act a secret sin, this begets a present, and quick, and strong flame in corruption to repeat and multiply and throng out the acts." He continues, "If the heart gives way for one sin, it will be ready for the next; if it will yield to bring forth once at the devil's pleasure, it will bring forth twice by its own motion." Four, Sedgwick states that when a person covers up private sins, this individual strives to be "an exact hypocrite" and the "more cunning" one is in excusing the sin, "the more perfect he is in his hypocrisy." Whether our sin is private or willful (v. 13), every sin is dangerous. Like David, we ought to ask God to forgive our hidden sins (v. 12).

Prayer. Lord, I readily admit that I have cherished and excused my private sins. I want my mind to embrace the same perspective of sin that you have so that I will freely confess and repent of my secret sins. I now see how this will enable me to grow spiritually. Amen.

February 3   Psalm 20

1 In times of trouble, may the Lord answer your cry. May the name of the God of Jacob keep you safe from all harm. 2 May he send you help from his sanctuary and strengthen you from Jerusalem. 3 May he remember all your gifts and look favorably on your burnt offerings. 4 May he grant your heart's desires and make all your plans succeed. 5 *May we shout for joy when we hear of your victory and raise a victory banner in the name of our God. May the* Lord *answer all your prayers.* 6 Now I know that the Lord rescues his anointed king. He will answer him from his holy heaven and rescue him by his great power. 7 Some nations boast of their chariots and horses, but we boast in the name of the Lord our God. 8 Those nations will fall down and collapse, but we will rise up and stand firm. 9 Give victory to our king, O Lord! Answer our cry for help. (NLT)

Spiritual battle. As David prepares for an upcoming battle, the people pray for God's blessing on him (vv. 1–5) because the Lord alone grants military victory (v. 7). Matthew Henry expresses the people's pledge, "We will wage war in his [God's] name, we will see that our cause be good, and make his glory our end in every expedition; we will ask counsel at his mouth, and take him along with us; we will follow his conduct, implore his aid, and depend upon it, and refer the issue to him." With victory anticipated, the people make a promise to David (v. 5). Henry paraphrases their commitment, "We will celebrate our victories in his name. When 'we lift up our banners' in triumph, and set up our trophies, it shall be 'in the name of our God,' he shall have all the glory of our success, and no instrument shall have any part of the honour that is due to him." In our spiritual battles, we must depend on God's resources to defeat Satan (Eph 6:10–18) and praise the Lord for the victory.

Prayer. Lord, too often when I have fought my spiritual battles, I have foolishly taken the credit without depending on you. I need you to experience spiritual victory over Satan's forces who are too great for me. Thank you for your empowering grace for every day! Amen.

February 4   Psalm 21:1-6

1 The king rejoices in your strength, LORD. How great is his joy in the victories you give! 2 You have granted him his heart's desire and have not withheld the request of his lips. 3 You came to greet him with rich blessings and placed a crown of pure gold on his head. 4 He asked you for life, and you gave it to him—length of days, for ever and ever. 5 *Through the victories you gave, his glory is great; you have bestowed on him splendor and majesty.* 6 Surely you have granted him unending blessings and made him glad with the joy of your presence. (NIV)

Spiritual victory. While the previous psalm focused on the king prior to a battle, this psalm dwells on God who gave David a great military victory (v. 5). While this conquest is glorious, it pales in comparison to God's glory. To describe his glory, Isaac Ambrose states, "It involves an eternal contradiction that the creature can see to the bottom of the Creator. Suppose all the sands on the sea-shore, all the flowers, herbs, leaves, twigs of trees in woods and forests, all the stars of heaven, were all rational creatures; and had they that wisdom and tongues of angels to speak of the loveliness, beauty, glory, and excellency of Christ, as gone to heaven, and sitting at the right hand of his Father, they would, in all their expressions, stay millions of miles on this side [of] Jesus Christ. Oh, the loveliness, beauty, and glory of his countenance!" On this side of eternity, we praise the "Father of our Lord Jesus Christ, who has blessed us in the heavenly realms with every spiritual blessing in Christ (Eph 1:3). One day, we will experience the fullness of salvation (glorification) and, with expectation, we can now say, "Thanks be to God! He gives us the victory through our Lord Jesus Christ." (1 Cor 16:57)

Prayer. Lord, I am filled with inexpressible joy as I ponder on your ineffable beauty. Your glory is too great for me, and yet, you have come to indwell me by your Holy Spirit. Thank you for all the spiritual blessings which are mine through Jesus Christ. Through your supernatural power, I know that it is possible to have victory over the Enemy. Amen.

February 5   Psalm 21:7–13

7 For the king trusts in the Lord; through the unfailing love of the Most High he will not be shaken. 8 Your hand will lay hold on all your enemies; your right hand will seize your foes. 9 *When you appear for battle, you will burn them up as in a blazing furnace. The Lord will swallow them up in his wrath, and his fire will consume them.* 10 You will destroy their descendants from the earth, their posterity from mankind. 11 Though they plot evil against you and devise wicked schemes, they cannot succeed. 12 You will make them turn their backs when you aim at them with drawn bow. 13 Be exalted in your strength, Lord; we will sing and praise your might. (NIV)

God's judgment. In contrast to the prior verses which focused on military victory, today's meditation concentrates on the enemy's defeat. The language is graphic, depicting God's earthly foes burning "in a blazing furnace" which consumes them (v. 9). Such vivid imagery is also found in Isaiah 31:9, which refers to the Lord's "fire . . . and furnace" and Malachi 4:1, which describes the day of the Lord as "burning like an oven." With the eternal fire of hell in mind, Matthew Henry states, "They shall not only be cast into a furnace of fire (Matt 13:42), but he [God] shall make them themselves as a fiery oven or furnace, they shall be their own tormentors, the reflections and terrors of their own consciences will be their hell. Those that might have had Christ to rule and save them, but rejected him, and fought against him, even the remembrance of that will be enough to make them to eternity a fiery oven to themselves." Henry rightly places the responsibility where it belongs—on the individual. While emphasizing God's love is important, his justice amplifies the fullness of his divine nature. This psalm and other scriptures call us to commit our lives to Jesus Christ in whom we can be secure (v. 7), both in this world and for eternity.

Prayer. Lord, I know hell is reserved for those who reject your love for them. Their refusal to accept your forgiveness and reconciliation results in eternal separation from you. May the Scripture's truths and your love for all people draw family and friends into a personal relationship with you. Amen.

February 6   Psalm 22:1–10

1 My God, my God, why have you abandoned me? Why are you so far away when I groan for help? 2 Every day I call to you, my God, but you do not answer. Every night I lift my voice, but I find no relief. 3 Yet you are holy, enthroned on the praises of Israel. 4 Our ancestors trusted in you, and you rescued them. 5 They cried out to you and were saved. They trusted in you and were never disgraced. 6 But I am a worm and not a man. I am scorned and despised by all! 7 Everyone who sees me mocks me. They sneer and shake their heads, saying, 8 "Is this the one who relies on the Lord? Then let the Lord save him! If the Lord loves him so much, let the Lord rescue him!" 9 Yet you brought me safely from my mother's womb and led me to trust you at my mother's breast. 10 I was thrust into your arms at my birth. You have been my God from the moment I was born. (NLT)

Christ forsaken. During his crucifixion on the cross, Jesus cries out to his Father in Matthew 27:46, "My God, why have you abandoned me?" These are the same words found in the first verse of Psalm 22. John Flavel explains two ways in which Jesus' cry strengthens our faith. First, "Christ's desertion is preventive of your final desertion. Because he was forsaken for a time you shall not be forsaken forever. For he was forsaken for you." Our relationship with God is secure because Jesus was "forsaken of God for a time" and therefore, "God will never finally withdraw from you." Second, Flavel states, "This sad desertion of Christ becomes a comfortable pattern to poor deserted souls in divers [various] respects . . . So, Christian, just so shall it be with you. Your God may turn away his face; he will not pluck away his arm." God, in his great love for us, is committed to us no matter what we may face in life (Rom 8:37–39). We can be confident that he will not desert us!

Prayer. Heavenly Father, I cannot fathom the depth of your relationship with your Son, Jesus, on the cross. I am so grateful that the abandonment he experienced has allowed me to know the reality and security found in a relationship with you. The cost of your redemptive love is truly amazing! Amen.

February 7   Psalm 22:11–21

11 Do not be far from me, for trouble is near and there is no one to help. 12 Many bulls surround me; strong bulls of Bashan encircle me. 13 Roaring lions that tear their prey open their mouths wide against me. 14 I am poured out like water, and all my bones are out of joint. My heart has turned to wax; it has melted within me. 15 My mouth is dried up like a potsherd, and my tongue sticks to the roof of my mouth; you lay me in the dust of death. 16 Dogs surround me, a pack of villains encircles me; they pierce my hands and my feet. 17 All my bones are on display; people stare and gloat over me. 18 They divide my clothes among them and cast lots for my garment. 19 But you, Lord, do not be far from me. You are my strength; come quickly to help me. 20 Deliver me from the sword, my precious life from the power of the dogs. 21 *Rescue me from the mouth of the lions; save me from the horns of the wild oxen.* (NIV)

The devil. David describes his enemies as lions (vv. 13, 21). Thomas Adams compares these lions to the devil. He notes, "Satan is called a lion, and that fitly; for he has all the properties of the lion: as bold as a lion, as strong as a lion, as furious as a lion, as terrible as the roaring of a lion. Yes, worse: the lion wants subtlety and suspicion; herein the devil is beyond the lion. The lion will spare the prostrate, the devil spares none. The lion is full and forbears, the devil is full and devours." He cautions, "He [Satan] seeks all; let not the simple say, 'He will take no notice of me'; nor the subtle, 'He cannot overreach me"; nor the noble say, 'He will not presume to meddle with me'; nor the rich, 'He dares not contest with me'; for he seeks to devour all. He is our common adversary, therefore let us cease all quarrels amongst ourselves, and fight with him." We can resist him by God's power.

Prayer. Lord, I can become lackadaisical about spiritual warfare. Keep me alert to the ways Satan wants to destroy me. Thank you for the divine resources you offer me to resist him. Amen.

February 8   Psalm 22:22-26

22 I will proclaim Your name to my brothers; in the midst of the assembly I will praise You. 23 You who fear the LORD, praise him; all you descendants of Jacob, glorify Him, and stand in awe of Him, all you descendants of Israel. 24 For He has not despised nor scorned the suffering of the afflicted; nor has He hidden His face from Him; but when He cried to Him for help, He heard. 25 *From you comes my praise in the great assembly; I shall pay my vows before those who fear Him.* 26 The afflicted will eat and be satisfied; those who seek Him will praise the LORD. May your heart live forever! (NASB)

Revering God. When David describes joining those who fear God (v. 25), he is telling the congregation to revere the Lord. For those who love him, fearing God is akin to holding him in great awe. William Gouge notes, "None but true saints do truly fear God." How do we fear or revere him? Revering God includes joyful, exuberant worship! When God answers his prayer, David joins the congregation in praising the Lord (v. 25a). David also makes a vow or a promise before the Lord (v. 25b). William Gouge encourages us to follow David's example: "This property of God's people, that they fear the Lord, shows that they will make the best use of such sacred, solemn duties performed in their presence. They will glorify God for this your zeal; they will join their spirits with your spirit in this open performance of duty; they will become followers of you, and learn of you to vow and pay unto the Lord, and that openly, publicly." It is possible that this vow or "duty" was to provide food for the "afflicted" so that they would be "satisfied" (v. 26). Revering God may result in caring for the needy among his people. Those who fear God cultivate both a vertical relationship with him and horizontal relationships with others.

Prayer. Lord, I adore you for you are most worthy of my worship and my commitment. Yet, it would be wrong to ignore the needs of those who love you. Help me to revere you by caring for those who are desperate and in need of your love. Amen.

February 9 — Psalm 22:27–31

27 All the ends of the earth will remember and turn to the LORD, and all the families of the nations will worship before You. 28 For the kingdom is the LORD's and He rules over the nations. 29 *All the prosperous of the earth will eat and worship, all those who go down to the dust will kneel before Him, even he who cannot keep his soul alive.* 30 A posterity will serve Him; it will be told of the Lord to the coming generation. 31 They will come and will declare His righteousness to a people who will be born, that He has performed it. (NASB)

Global homage. In these verses, homage to God spreads geographically, demographically and generationally to the Gentiles. The prosperous (v. 29a) will join in worship with the poor and suffering (v. 26) who "go down to the dust" (v. 29b). Explaining this verse, Joseph Caryl comments, "To be brought to the dust, is, at first, a circumlocution or description of death: 'Shall the dust praise you; shall it declare your truth?' (Ps 30:9) That is, shall I praise you when I am among the dead?" The reality of death is a wake-up call to those who have not committed their lives to Jesus Christ. Caryl mentions another meaning of "dust." He states, "Secondly, to be brought to the dust is a description of any low and poor condition . . . As if he had said, rich and poor, high and low, the king and the beggar, have alike need of salvation by Jesus Christ, and must submit unto him, that they may be saved" because no one can "keep his soul alive" (v. 29c). The proud must humble themselves by repenting and surrendering their lives to Jesus Christ who reigns over the nations (v. 28). If they do, they join God's kingdom of redeemed people and worship him (v. 27; Rev 5:9–13). The promise of salvation to future generations should stir us to pray for people around the globe to enter into a personal relationship with Jesus Christ.

Prayer. Lord, my mortality challenges me to consider my relationship with Jesus Christ. I am grateful for your salvation through Jesus Christ. Help me to daily submit to your reign in my life. Thank you for bringing people around the globe into a personal relationship with you. You alone are worthy of praise. Amen.

February 10   Psalm 23

1 The Lord *is my shepherd; I shall not want.* 2 He maketh me to lie down in green pastures: he leadeth me beside the still waters. 3 He restoreth my soul: he leadeth me in the paths of righteousness for his name's sake. 4 *Yea, though I walk through the valley of the shadow of death, I will fear no evil: for thou art with me; thy rod and thy staff they comfort me.* 5 Thou preparest a table before me in the presence of mine enemies: thou anointest my head with oil; my cup runneth over. 6 Surely goodness and mercy shall follow me all the days of my life: and I will dwell in the house of the Lord *forever. (KJV)*

Facing death. This much-loved psalm has comforted people with its reassuring words (v. 2). Yet, David also described the reality of his enemies and his possible death. William Gurnall comments, "Holy David, in this place, brings in, as it were, a death's head with his feast. In the same breath almost, he speaks of his dying (v. 4), and of the rich feast he at present sat at through the bounty of God (v. 5), to which he was not so tied by the teeth, but if God, that gave him this cheer, should call him from it, to look death in the face, he could do it, and fear no evil when in the valley of the shadow of it." Gurnall mentions Peter who was thrown in jail and would be tried by Caesar (Acts 12:4–6). Peter was able to fall asleep between two soldiers because he knew "the gospel of peace—he was ready to die, and that made him able to sleep. Why should that break his rest in this world, which if it had been effected, would have brought him to his eternal rest in the other?" Gurnall defines the source of Peter's peace: "A readiness of spirit to suffer gives the Christian the true enjoyment of life." Knowing Jesus, the good shepherd (v. 1) and the promise of his presence and eternal life (v. 6), enables us to face whatever comes our way.

Prayer. Lord, reflecting on my relationship with you, you have shown your faithfulness and goodness to me throughout the years. Regardless of the dark days and death I will experience, your presence and blessings will continue to be with me. How comforting this is! Amen.

February 11 — Psalm 24:1-6

1 The earth is the Lord's and the fullness thereof, the world and those who dwell therein, 2 for he has founded it upon the seas and established it upon the rivers. 3 Who shall ascend the hill of the Lord? And who shall stand in his holy place? 4 He who has clean hands and a pure heart, who does not lift up his soul to what is false and does not swear deceitfully. 5 He will receive blessing from the Lord and righteousness from the God of his salvation. 6 *Such is the generation of those who seek him, who seek the face of the God of Jacob. Selah* (ESV)

Seeking God. In response to his question regarding who can worship God (v. 3), David lists having clean hands and a pure heart, avoiding what is false, and pursuing God (vv. 4, 6). Concerning the latter, Richard Sibbes asserts, "Christians must be seekers. This is the generation of seekers. All mankind, if ever they will come to heaven, they must be a generation of seekers. Heaven is a generation of finders, of possessors, of enjoyers, seekers of God. But here we are a generation of seekers. We want somewhat that we must seek. When we are at best, we want the accomplishment of our happiness. It is a state of seeking here, because it is a state of want; we want something always." He specifically reminds us that we should be "seeking the face of God, or the presence of God . . . He [God]shows a presence in need and necessity, that is, a gracious presence to his children, a gracious face. As in want of direction, he shows his presence of light to direct them; in weakness he shows his strength; in trouble and perplexity he will show his gracious and comfortable presence to comfort them. In perplexity he shows his presence to set the heart at large, answerable to the necessity. So, in need God is present with his children, to direct them, to comfort them, to strengthen them, if they need that." Sibbes encourages us to enjoy seeking the Lord, expecting him to reveal himself to us.

Prayer. Lord, too often I fail to seek a personal relationship with you. Recognizing that you want to cultivate a relationship with me, by your Spirit I want to pursue you with a greater hunger for your presence. Amen.

February 12 — Psalm 24:7-10

7 Lift up your heads, O gates! And be lifted up, O ancient doors, that the King of glory may come in. 8 *Who is this King of glory? The* LORD, *strong and mighty, the* LORD, *mighty in battle!* 9 Lift up your heads, O gates! And lift them up, O ancient doors, that the King of glory may come in. 10 Who is this King of glory? The LORD of hosts, he is the King of glory! *Selah* (ESV)

The glorious King. After reflecting on God's creativity (vv. 1–2) and holiness (vv. 3–6), David dwells on God's glory (vv. 7–10) which is the totality of his attributes, including power. John Boys elaborates, "If the Lord of hosts, strong and mighty in battle, be the King of glory, then Christ (having conquered all his enemies, and made them his footstool, triumphing over death, and the devil which is the founder of death, and sin which is the sting of death, and the grave which is the prison of death, and hell itself which is the proper dominion of the devil and death) is doubtless in himself, 'the King of glory.'" Boys applies David's celebration of God's power to our lives. He comments, "And for as much as he died for our sins, and is risen again for our justification, and is ascended on high to give gifts unto men—in this life grace, in the next glory—what is he less than a 'King of glory' towards us, of whom and through whom alone we that fight his battles are delivered from the hands of all that hate us, and so made victors (1 Cor 15:57), yes, 'more than conquerors' (Rom 8:37)." When we are discouraged because we feel inept to defeat the sin within us, the psalmist reminds us of God's power. The King of glory who can defeat armies opposed to his people can certainly overcome sin through the Holy Spirit. Although the apostle Paul knew times of weakness, he also experienced the "all-surpassing power" which came from God (2 Cor 4:7).

Prayer. Father, I am thankful that your Son, Jesus, is the King of glory! He is my friend, but he is also the one who reigns over this world and its spiritual forces. What he has accomplished through his death and resurrection evokes joy in my heart and praise on my lips. Amen.

February 13   Psalm 25:1–7

1 In you, Lord my God, I put my trust. 2 I trust in you; do not let me be put to shame, nor let my enemies triumph over me. 3 No one who hopes in you will ever be put to shame, but shame will come on those who are treacherous without cause. 4 Show me your ways, Lord, teach me your paths. 5 *Guide me in your truth and teach me, for you are God my Savior, and my hope is in you all day long.* 6 Remember, Lord, your great mercy and love, for they are from of old. 7 Do not remember the sins of my youth and my rebellious ways; according to your love remember me, for you, Lord, are good. (NIV)

Hoping in God. David trusts and hopes in the Lord "all day long" (v. 5). Reflecting on this verse, Matthew Henry offers four suggestions for us. We must "live a life of desire towards God; to wait on him as the beggar waits on his benefactor, with earnest desire to receive supplies from him." Second, we must "live a life of delight in God, as the lover waits on his beloved." Desiring God suggests that "we must be wishing for more of God" and "we must never wish for more than God." Third, waiting on God requires us "to live of dependence on God, as the child waits on his father, whom he has confidence in, and on whom he casts all his care. To wait on God is to expect all good to come to us from him, as the worker of all good for us and in us, the giver of all good to us, and the protector of us from all evil." Fourth, to wait on God, requires us "to live a life of devotedness to God, as the servant waits on his master, ready to observe his will, and to do his work, and in everything to consult his honour and interest . . . Thus must we wait on God, as those that have no will of our own but what is wholly resolved into his, and must therefore study to accommodate ourselves to his."

Prayer. Lord, it is hard to wait for you to act in difficult times. As a result, I take matters into my hands and find myself in greater difficulty. Help me to remain focused on you! Cultivate in me a greater desire to depend on you and delight in you. Amen.

February 14   Psalm 25:8-15

8 Good and upright is the LORD; therefore he instructs sinners in his ways. 9 He guides the humble in what is right and teaches them his way. 10 All the ways of the LORD are loving and faithful toward those who keep the demands of his covenant. 11 *For the sake of your name, LORD, forgive my iniquity, though it is great.* 12 Who, then, are those who fear the LORD? He will instruct them in the ways they should choose. 13 They will spend their days in prosperity, and their descendants will inherit the land. 14 The LORD confides in those who fear him; he makes his covenant known to them. 15 My eyes are ever on the LORD, for only he will release my feet from the snare. (NIV)

For God's glory. As David asks God to forgive his sin (v. 11), so should we. What motivates us to seek God's forgiveness? The answer David gives is "the sake of [God's] name" (v. 11). Nathanael Hardy explains this phrase: "It is a very usual notion by 'name' to understand honour and glory . . . Thus, when God forgives sin, he does it for his name's sake, that is, for his own honour and glory. Indeed, God's own glory is the ultimate end of all his actions. As he is the first, so is he the last, the efficient, and the final cause; nor is there anything done by him which is not for him." Hardy applies this truth, "The end of our actions must be in his glory, because both our being and working are from him; but the end of his work is his own glory, because his being and acting are of and from himself. Among all divine works, there is none which more sets forth his glory than this of remission. Sin, by [our] committing it, brings God a great deal of dishonour, and yet, by forgiving it, God raises to himself a great deal of honour."

Prayer. Lord, I know that I often dishonor you by my wayward ways. For your name's sake, I am sorry and repent for my sins. I am so grateful for your willingness to forgive me for the ways that I have fallen short. Your mercy and love extended to me glorify your name. Amen.

February 15   Psalm 25:16–22

16 Turn to me and be gracious to me, for I am lonely and afflicted. 17 Relieve the troubles of my heart and free me from my anguish. *18 Look on my affliction and my distress and take away all my sins.* 19 See how numerous are my enemies and how fiercely they hate me! 20 Guard my life and rescue me; do not let me be put to shame, for I take refuge in you. 21 May integrity and uprightness protect me, because my hope, Lord, is in you. 22 Deliver Israel, O God, from all their troubles! (NIV)

Soul and physical sickness. David is troubled about his condition. He is relationally isolated, emotionally anguished, and physically and spiritually afflicted (vv. 16–18). Richard Sibbes offers wise counsel when we feel like the psalmist. He comments, "It is for the sickness of the soul that God visits with the sickness of the body. He aims at the cure of the soul in the touch of the body. And therefore in this case, when God visits with sickness, we should think our work is more in heaven with God than with men or physic [medicine]. Begin first with the soul." Sibbes reminds us that when David, on another occasion (Ps 32:3–5), faced physical illness and "dealt directly and plainly with God, and confessed his sins, then God forgave him them, and healed his body too". In light of David's prayer, he advises "the best method, when God visits us in this kind, is to think that we are to deal with God. Begin the cure there with the soul. When he visits the body, it is for the soul's sake." We err if we believe that all illnesses are due to sin that we have committed. We are wise to search our inner lives for shortcomings. When we discover our sins and, confess them, the Lord will forgive and heal us (Jas 5:15–16).

Prayer. Lord, when I am suffering physically, remind me to look inwardly in order that I might discover any known sin which needs to be confessed. I am thankful for your forgiveness so that I may experience your spiritual and physical healing in my life. Amen.

February 16   Psalm 26:1-8

1 Vindicate me, LORD, for I have led a blameless life; I have trusted in the LORD and have not faltered. 2 Test me, LORD, and try me, examine my heart and my mind; 3 for I have always been mindful of your unfailing love and have lived in reliance on your faithfulness. 4 I do not sit with the deceitful, nor do I associate with hypocrites. 5 *I abhor the assembly of evildoers and refuse to sit with the wicked.* 6 I wash my hands in innocence, and go about your altar, LORD, 7 proclaiming aloud your praise and telling of all your wonderful deeds. 8 LORD, I love the house where you live, the place where your glory dwells. (NIV)

Integrity with friendships. In these verses, David describes how living with integrity keeps him from destructive relationships. Twice he testifies that he does not sit with deceitful and hypocritical people (vv. 4–5). George Swinnock explains David's actions, "Consider that there can be no true friendship betwixt a godly and a wicked person; therefore, it concerns you to be the more wary in your choice . . . Friendship, according to the philosopher, is one soul in two bodies." For example, we learn that "the soul of Jonathan was knit with the soul of David" (1 Sam 18:1 KJV). They were united in spirit because they both loved and trusted God. In contrast to godly friendships, Swinnock asks, "But how can they [the godly and ungodly] ever be of one soul that are as different as air and earth, and as contrary as fire and water?" It is not possible without sacrificing one's integrity. Yet, we are expected to love everyone just as Jesus did while on earth. A person can love one's "neighbours for God's sake" but we cannot "truly love" the individual "who does not love his Maker." If we want to live with integrity, Swinnock advises, "God is the only foundation upon which we can build friendship."

Prayer. Lord, I want to live with integrity but, I admit that some of my friendships have steered me away from you. I need godly friends who will draw me closer to you and your purposes. Also, grant me wisdom on how to love those who do not know you, without being allured to whatever displeases you. Amen.

February 17 — Psalm 26:9–12

9 Do not take away my soul along with sinners, my life with those who are bloodthirsty, 10 in whose hands are wicked schemes, whose right hands are full of bribes. 11 I lead a blameless life; deliver me and be merciful to me. 12 *My feet stand on level ground*; in the great congregation I will praise the Lord. (NIV)

Commitment to integrity. David began this psalm affirming that he has led a "blameless" life (v. 1). He knows he is not perfect or faultless, but he also knows that he is living wholeheartedly for God. Now, he comes to the end of his psalm re-affirming his commitment to live with integrity before God (v. 11). He is assured that he is living this way because his "feet stand on level ground" (v. 12). William Gurnall contrasts two groups of people, "The upright man's foot, is said to stand in an even place; he walks not haltingly and uncomely, as those who go in unequal ways, which are hobbling, and up and down." The upright man makes sure his feet stand evenly or solidly on a firm foundation. Gurnall notes that this individual is "conscientious to the whole will of God" in contrast to the hypocrite who does not firmly put down both feet. Wise people recognize it is impossible to live with integrity by sheer willpower, and so the psalmist asks God for divine help and mercy (v. 11). In any culture which is diametrically opposed to God and his ways (vv. 9–10), living with integrity requires God's empowering grace.

Prayer. Lord, I want to be known as a person of integrity. However, I confess that I have often failed to depend on your resources. Thank you for the Bible which gives me the solid foundation to establish my life in this confusing culture. When society's many temptations begin to draw me away from you, deliver me by your truth, and when I do fail, be merciful to me. I unreservedly commit myself to live with integrity for you. Amen.

February 18 — Psalm 27:1-6

1 The LORD is my light and my salvation— whom shall I fear? The LORD is the stronghold of my life— of whom shall I be afraid? 2 When the wicked advance against me to devour me, it is my enemies and my foes who will stumble and fall. 3 Though an army besiege me, my heart will not fear; though war break out against me, even then I will be confident. 4 *One thing I ask from the LORD, this only do I seek: that I may dwell in the house of the LORD all the days of my life, to gaze on the beauty of the LORD and to seek him in his temple.* 5 For in the day of trouble he will keep me safe in his dwelling; he will hide me in the shelter of his sacred tent and set me high upon a rock. 6 Then my head will be exalted above the enemies who surround me; at his sacred tent I will sacrifice with shouts of joy; I will sing and make music to the LORD. (NIV)

Seeking God's presence. Almost daily, Christians witness and experience opposition. When David's enemies are trying to destroy him (vv. 2–3a), he shows us how to respond to these challenges. He places high priority on being in the temple and gazing on the "beauty of the LORD" (v. 4; 26:8). Richard Sibbes comments, "[This] was one end of his desire, to dwell in the house of God; not to feed his eyes with speculations and goodly sights (as indeed there were in the tabernacle goodly things to be seen). No; he had a more spiritual sight than that. He saw the inward spiritual beauty of those spiritual things." How do we behold God's beauty? Sibbes explains that our whole being should "delight" in God. Jesus, who is God, is "delightful and sweet" and is "the object of all [our] senses, inward and outward." Today, we can enjoy Jesus' presence through the Holy Spirit dwelling within us. He invites us to seek him so that we may bring our challenges to him.

Prayer. Lord, I want to come into your presence, not to escape from my challenges, but in order that I may live in the confidence that you are always with me. I am so thankful that I can delight in you! Amen.

February 19   Psalm 27:7-14

7 Hear my voice when I call, LORD; be merciful to me and answer me. 8 *My heart says of you, "Seek his face!" Your face, LORD, I will seek.* 9 Do not hide your face from me, do not turn your servant away in anger; you have been my helper. Do not reject me or forsake me, God my Savior. 10 Though my father and mother forsake me, the LORD will receive me. 11 Teach me your way, LORD; lead me in a straight path because of my oppressors. 12 Do not turn me over to the desire of my foes, for false witnesses rise up against me, spouting malicious accusations. 13 I remain confident of this: I will see the goodness of the LORD in the land of the living. 14 Wait for the LORD; be strong and take heart and wait for the LORD. (NIV)

Communing in God's presence. For good reason, David seeks to be in God's presence (v. 4). With a request for God to answer his prayer (v. 7), the psalmist does not want God to hide from him (v. 9) but to reveal himself (v. 8). Richard Sibbes describes God's availability, "God is willing to be known. He is willing to open and discover himself; God delights not to hide himself . . . The more we know of him, the more we shall admire him . . . Therefore he hides not himself, nay, he desires to be known; and all those that have his Spirit desire to make him known." We sometimes feel that God is hiding from us, but Sibbes challenges this assumption, "He loves not strangeness to his poor creatures. It is not a point of his policy . . . No; the fault is altogether in us. We walk not worthy of such a presence; we want [lack] humility and preparation. If there be any darkness in the creature that he finds God does not so shine on him as in former times, undoubtedly the cause is in himself; for God said, 'Seek my face.'" This is intimacy with him!

Prayer. Lord, I am overwhelmed that you would want to reveal yourself to me. How can I, a finite and sinful person, seek and know you? I am thankful for your indwelling Holy Spirit so that I may commune with you. Create within me a greater hunger to know and enjoy you. Amen.

February 20   Psalm 28:1–5

1 To you, LORD, I call; you are my Rock, do not turn a deaf ear to me. For if you remain silent, I will be like those who go down to the pit. 2 Hear my cry for mercy as I call to you for help, as I lift up my hands toward your Most Holy Place. 3 *Do not drag me away with the wicked, with those who do evil, who speak cordially with their neighbors but harbor malice in their hearts.* 4 Repay them for their deeds and for their evil work; repay them for what their hands have done and bring back on them what they deserve. 5 Because they have no regard for the deeds of the LORD and what his hands have done, he will tear them down and never build them up again. (NIV)

Deception. At the outset of this psalm, David cries to the Lord (vv. 1–2). Facing the possibility of death, he does not want to be disgraced by being associated with deceptive people (v. 3). He is not like them! Thomas Watson explains David's attitude, "The godly man abhors dissimulation [deception] towards men; his heart goes along with his tongue, he cannot flatter and hate, commend and censure." In contrast to a godly person is the fool: "Whoever conceals hatred with lying lips and spreads slander is a fool" (Prov 10:18 NIV). Deception reveals a lack of love for another. This false portrayal of love, Watson states, "is worse than hatred; counterfeiting of friendship is no better than a lie." As an example, Watson mentions Joab who called Amasa a "brother" and then kissed him before stabbing him to death (2 Sam 20:9–10). To illustrate deception, Watson mentions a river in Spain "where the fish seem to be of a golden colour, but take them out of the water, and they are like other fish. All is not gold that glitters; there are some pretend much kindness" but it is not genuine love. We want Paul's instruction to be true in our lives, "Let love be genuine. Abhor what is evil; hold fast to what is good" (Rom 12:9).

Prayer. Lord, my conversations with others have periodically failed to be honest because of a lack of genuine love. Forgive me and purify my heart so that Jesus' love will motivate me to speak truthfully. Amen.

February 21   Psalm 28:6–9

6 Praise be to the Lord, for he has heard my cry for mercy. 7 The Lord is my strength and my shield; my heart trusts in him, and he helps me. My heart leaps for joy, and with my song I praise him. 8 *The Lord is the strength of his people*, a fortress of salvation for his anointed one. 9 Save your people and bless your inheritance; be their shepherd and carry them forever. (NIV)

God's strength. David no longer feels the despair that he expressed earlier. Now he praises God for answering his prayer by providing strength to him and his people (vv. 7–8). Matthew Henry states that God "is the strength of all Israel, because he is the saving strength of his anointed" who is David, Israel's king. God strengthens David, Henry notes, by divinely fighting Israel's battles which, in turn, strengthen the nation. Henry reminds us that, as King David cares for his people, "the saints rejoice in their friends' comforts as well as their own; for as we have not the less benefit by the light of the sun, so neither by the light of God's countenance, for others sharing therein; for we are sure there is enough for all, and enough for each. This is our communion with all saints, that God is their strength and ours; Christ their Lord and ours." As God strengthens David, so God strengthens the apostle Paul (2 Cor 12:9–10) to bolster others' walk with Christ (12:19). When we are discouraged and feel weak, we can turn to the Lord who fortifies us through Scripture, the presence of the Holy Spirit, and godly people who encourage us in our walk with the Lord (Rom 12:10–13). We are strengthened through fellowship with God and with his people.

Prayer. Lord, I confess that all too often life's demands weary me. I humbly come to you asking you to buttress my faith in order that I may serve you and those around me. But I know many others are also exhausted by daily pressures. I want to be sensitive to their needs so that I may encourage them through Scripture, loving words, or practical assistance. Thank you for your supernatural strength! Amen.

February 22   Psalm 29

1 Ascribe to the Lord, you heavenly beings, ascribe to the Lord glory and strength. 2 *Ascribe to the Lord the glory due his name; worship the Lord in the splendor of his holiness.* 3 The voice of the Lord is over the waters; the God of glory thunders, the Lord thunders over the mighty waters. 4 The voice of the Lord is powerful; the voice of the Lord is majestic. 5 The voice of the Lord breaks the cedars; the Lord breaks in pieces the cedars of Lebanon. 6 He makes Lebanon leap like a calf, Sirion like a young wild ox. 7 The voice of the Lord strikes with flashes of lightning. 8 The voice of the Lord shakes the desert; the Lord shakes the Desert of Kadesh. 9 The voice of the Lord twists the oaks and strips the forests bare. And in his temple all cry, "Glory!" 10 The Lord sits enthroned over the flood; the Lord is enthroned as King forever. 11 The Lord gives strength to his people; the Lord blesses his people with peace. (NIV)

Worshipping the Lord. The four calls to worship God (vv. 1–2) are addressed to "heavenly beings." Joseph Caryl asks, "Why is the Lord to be worshipped? Why must he have such high honours from those that are high?" Caryl states that David answers the question "meteorologically as well as theologically." God is the Lord over the thunderous storms (vv. 3–10a). He is also King over his people (vv. 10b–11). Caryl expounds on God's reign, "Although the Lord Jesus Christ will not set up an outward, pompous, political kingdom . . . yet by the ministry of the gospel he will erect a spiritual kingdom, and gather to himself a church that shall abide forever, out of all the nations of the earth; for the gospel shall be carried and preached, to not only the people of Israel, the Jews, but to the Gentiles, all the world over." In the midst of the storms, God blesses us with his peace (v. 11).

Prayer. Lord, you are worthy of worship as the creator and king. I praise and adore you for who you are. By surrendering and obeying you, I want you to be the Lord over my life. Amen.

February 23   Psalm 30:1–5

1 I will extol you, O Lord, for you have drawn me up and have not let my foes rejoice over me. 2 O Lord my God, I cried to you for help, and you have healed me. 3 O Lord, you have brought up my soul from Sheol; you restored me to life from among those who go down to the pit. 4 Sing praises to the Lord, O you his saints, and give thanks to his holy name. 5 For his anger is but for a moment, and his favor is for a lifetime. *Weeping may tarry for the night, but joy comes with the morning.* (ESV)

Weeping and joy. When we go through periods of adversity, we frequently feel that those times will never end. Thomas Brooks, a Puritan pastor in London, knew such experiences. His church building burned down, he was forced to resign his pastorate due to a law, and his beloved wife died. After these trials, he continued preaching and remarried. For those who go through extended trials, Brooks, with his pastoral heart and experience, encourages us by reminding us that "joy comes with the morning" (v. 5). He comments, "Their mourning shall last but till morning. God will turn their winter's night into a summer's day, their sighing into singing, their grief into gladness, their mourning into music, their bitter into sweet, their wilderness into a paradise. The life of a Christian is filled up with interchanges of sickness and health, weakness and strength, want and wealth, disgrace and honour, crosses, and comforts, miseries and mercies, joys and sorrows, mirth and mourning." Brooks explains that God uses these diverse experiences for our spiritual well-being. He notes, "It is best and most for the health of the soul that the south wind of mercy, and the north wind of adversity, do both blow upon it; and though every wind that blows shall blow good to the saints, yet certainly their sins die most, and their graces thrive best, when they are under the drying, nipping north wind of calamity, as well as under the warm, cherishing south wind of mercy and prosperity."

Prayer. Lord, I often chafe when I experience extended times of adversity. Teach me to accept your providential rhythms in my life. Help me to patiently wait for you, knowing that in your good time you will bring joy to me. Amen.

February 24   Psalm 30:6–12

6 *As for me, I said in my prosperity, "I shall never be moved."* 7 By your favor, O Lord, you made my mountain stand strong; you hid your face; I was dismayed. 8 To you, O Lord, I cry, and to the Lord I plead for mercy: 9 "What profit is there in my death, if I go down to the pit? Will the dust praise you? Will it tell of your faithfulness? 10 Hear, O Lord, and be merciful to me! O Lord, be my helper!" 11 You have turned for me my mourning into dancing; you have loosed my sackcloth and clothed me with gladness, 12 that my glory may sing your praise and not be silent. O Lord my God, I will give thanks to you forever! (ESV)

Prosperity's snare. While resources are a blessing, they may also insidiously affect our spiritual well-being. Richard Gilpin warns us, "We are apt to get proud, careless, and confident, after or upon such employments and favours." When David says, "I shall not be moved," Gilpin comments, "David enjoying the favour of God in a more than ordinary measure, though he was more acquainted with vicissitudes and changes than most of men, grows secure in his apprehension that he should 'never be moved.'" Fortunately, "David acknowledged his mistake, and leaves it upon record as an experience necessary for others to take warning by, that when he became warm under the beams of God's countenance, then he was apt to fall into security." Then David mentions he was dismayed when God hid his face (v. 7). Gilpin identifies a pattern here, "Enjoyments beget confidence; confidence brings forth carelessness; carelessness makes God withdraw and gives opportunity to Satan to work unseen." Jesus warns us that we are prone to trust our assets for our security rather than God (Matt 19:23–24). In the same vein, Paul instructs followers of Christ not to "put their hope in wealth, which is so uncertain, but to put their hope in God, who richly provides us with everything for our enjoyment" (1 Tim 6:17). When we place our security in the Lord, then we can be "rich in good deeds," generously sharing with others (v. 18).

Prayer. Lord, I confess that I am tempted to view my resources as my greatest security. Forgive me for my self-sufficiency, and turn my heart to trust in you who are, my greatest security. Amen.

February 25 — Psalm 31:1–8

1 O LORD, I have come to you for protection; don't let me be disgraced. Save me, for you do what is right. 2 Turn your ear to listen to me; rescue me quickly. Be my rock of protection, a fortress where I will be safe. 3 You are my rock and my fortress. For the honor of your name, lead me out of this danger. 4 Pull me from the trap my enemies set for me, for I find protection in you alone. 5 I entrust my spirit into your hand. Rescue me, LORD, for you are a faithful God. 6 I hate those who worship worthless idols. I trust in the LORD. 7 *I will be glad and rejoice in your unfailing love, for you have seen my troubles, and you care about the anguish of my soul.* 8 You have not handed me over to my enemies but have set me in a safe place. (NLT)

Joy in adversity. David believes that he will experience joy amid his trials (v. 7). Although he faces his enemies' threats (vv. 4, 8), he possesses a joyful outlook. He focuses, not on his circumstances, but on God who is his "refuge" and a "fortress" (vv. 1–4). The Lord is not only strong, but he is faithful (v. 5). David Dickson elaborates on the psalmist's gladness in God's faithfulness. He comments, "In the midst of trouble, faith will furnish matter of joy, and promise to itself gladness, especially from the memory of past experiences of God's mercy." It is important for us to look back to the many times God has showed us his faithfulness. Yet, Dickson issues a caveat. He cautions that our gladness "should not be in the benefit so much as in the fountain of the benefit." That is, our rejoicing should not be based on the received blessings but on the Giver of the blessings. When future trials come our way, it is an opportunity to focus on the Lord himself and nothing more.

Prayer. Lord, I often focus on the many benefits of knowing you, rather than simply delighting in you. I want to turn from this selfishness to thoroughly enjoying you. The many expressions of your love are encouragement to focus on you who is the source of true joy, even in the most difficult days. Amen.

February 26   Psalm 31:9-18

9 Have mercy on me, Lord, for I am in distress. Tears blur my eyes. My body and soul are withering away. 10 I am dying from grief; my years are shortened by sadness. Sin has drained my strength; I am wasting away from within. 11 I am scorned by all my enemies and despised by my neighbors—even my friends are afraid to come near me. When they see me on the street, they run the other way. 12 I am ignored as if I were dead, as if I were a broken pot. 13 I have heard the many rumors about me, and I am surrounded by terror. My enemies conspire against me, plotting to take my life. 14 But I am trusting you, O Lord, saying, "You are my God!" 15 *My future is in your hands. Rescue me from those who hunt me down relentlessly.* 16 Let your favor shine on your servant. In your unfailing love, rescue me. 17 Don't let me be disgraced, O Lord, for I call out to you for help. Let the wicked be disgraced; let them lie silent in the grave. 18 Silence their lying lips—those proud and arrogant lips that accuse the godly. (NLT)

In God's hands. David recognizes that his life is in God's hands (v. 15). Awareness of this truth means that we cannot presume upon God by living foolishly. Edward Reynolds warns, "We may not neglect our body, nor shipwreck our health, nor anything to hasten death" to gain personal benefits such as financial success. He reminds us that "our times are in God's hands, and therefore to his holy providence we must leave them." Believing everything is in God's hands, we may also become lazy. Reynolds challenges us, "We have a great deal of work to do." The apostle Paul agrees. When some Thessalonian believers stopped working, assuming that Jesus would soon return to earth, they received Paul's rebuke for their idleness (2 Thess 3:11–12). God's providence teaches us to trust and obey him in all areas of life.

Prayer. Lord, it is easy to say that my life is in your hands. How foolish of me to take matters into my own hands when I think of who you are! I submit to your providential care so that I can live confidently and responsibly before you and those around me. Amen.

February 27 Psalm 31:19–24

19 How abundant are the good things that you have stored up for those who fear you, that you bestow in the sight of all, on those who take refuge in you. 20 In the shelter of your presence you hide them from all human intrigues; you keep them safe in your dwelling from accusing tongues. 21 Praise be to the Lord, for he showed me the wonders of his love when I was in a city under siege. 22 *In my alarm I said, "I am cut off from your sight!" Yet you heard my cry for mercy when I called to you for help.* 23 Love the Lord, all his faithful people! The Lord preserves those who are true to him, but the proud he pays back in full. 24 Be strong and take heart, all you who hope in the Lord. (NIV)

Rash words. By painful experience, we know the deep regret we feel for the words we have spoken. The hearer is often shocked by our unthoughtful words. We wish we could take them back, but we cannot. David rashly declares that he is cut off from God's sight (v. 22) and his words dumbfound us. Even though David feels isolated from his friends (vv. 9–13), he knows that God cares for him and his people (vv. 19–20). However, when the city is attacked (v. 21), David panics and utters words which dishonor God. Feelings can cloud our thoughts and corrupt our speech. Richard Alleine comments on hasty words, "Sometimes a sudden passion arises, and out it goes in angry and froward [uncouth] words, setting all in an uproar and combustion: by and by our hearts recur upon us, and then we wish, 'O that I had bit my tongue, and not given it such an unbridled liberty.'" As a corrective, we must assess difficult situations based on what we know to be true (vv. 19–20) and then wait on God to act in his good time (v. 24).

Prayer. Lord, I have often panicked and spoken words which dishonor you and others. Forgive me when my feelings override what I know to be true. Teach me to trust in your character and promises so that I may learn to wait for you to act. Amen.

February 28 — Psalm 32:1–5

1 Blessed is the one whose transgression is forgiven, whose sin is covered. 2 Blessed is the man against whom the LORD counts no iniquity, and in whose spirit there is no deceit. 3 For when I kept silent, my bones wasted away through my groaning all day long. 4 For day and night your hand was heavy upon me; my strength was dried up as by the heat of summer. *Selah* 5 *I acknowledged my sin to you, and I did not cover my iniquity; I said, "I will confess my transgressions to the* LORD*," and you forgave the iniquity of my sin. Selah* (ESV)

Confession of sin. Sometimes we ask: Since Jesus paid for the guilt of our sin on the cross, why should we confess our sins to God? As Christopher Love expresses it, "What are the reasons why persons justified and pardoned are yet bound to make confession of sin unto God in private?" In response to this question, Love provides us with five excellent reasons we should confess our sins to the Lord. He states, "First, they are to confess sin unto God because holy confession gives a great deal of ease and holy quiet unto the mind of a sinner: concealed and indulged guilt contracts horror and dread on the conscience. Secondly, because God loves to hear the complaints and the confessions of his own people." Love continues, "A third reason is, because confession of sin does help to quicken the heart to strong and earnest supplication to God (see Ps 32:6)." In other words, confession sharpens our prayers. He continues, "A fourth reason is, because confession of sin will work a holy contrition and a godly sorrow in the heart . . . A fifth reason is, because secret confession of sin does give a great deal of glory to God . . . It gives glory to God's mercy. I confess sin, yet mercy may save me. It gives glory to God's omniscience. In confessing sin, I do acknowledge that God knows my sin."

Prayer. Lord, I confess that I often fail to admit my many sins before you. Cultivate in my heart a greater desire to acknowledge my sins to you, not only for my well-being, but to honor you by your continued forgiveness and mercy shown to me. Amen.

February 29   Psalm 32:6–11

6 Therefore let everyone who is godly offer prayer to you at a time when you may be found; surely in the rush of great waters, they shall not reach him. 7 You are a hiding place for me; you preserve me from trouble; you surround me with shouts of deliverance. *Selah* 8 *I will instruct you and teach you in the way you should go; I will counsel you with my eye upon you.* 9 Be not like a horse or a mule, without understanding, which must be curbed with bit and bridle, or it will not stay near you. 10 Many are the sorrows of the wicked, but steadfast love surrounds the one who trusts in the Lord. 11 Be glad in the Lord, and rejoice, O righteous, and shout for joy, all you upright in heart! (ESV)

God's way. Even as God's children, due to the destructive influence of our own unbridled passions (v. 9). we may be tempted to live unwisely. However, Thomas Taylor encourages us to learn the Lord's pathway. His way is the best because it is based on his thorough knowledge of us (v. 8b). Taylor offers four reasons why we need to pay attention to the divine road. He states, "If we compare this way with all other ways, it will whet our care to enter into and continue in it; for, first, this is the King's highway, in which we have promise of protection (Ps 91:11). Secondly, God's ways are the cleanest of all (2 Sam 22:31). Thirdly, God's ways are the rightest ways; and, being rightest, they be also the shortest ways (Hos 14:9). Fourthly, God's ways are most lightsome and cheerful (Prov 3:17). Therefore, God's ways being the safest, cleanest, rightest, shortest, and lightsomest ways, we must be careful to walk in them." Today's meditation on God's ways reflects Psalm 1 which spells out two distinct to live: the "way of sinners" (v. 1) and "the way of the righteous" (v. 6). There is no middle ground; we must decide. The best choice is God's way if we want a fruitful life (v. 3).

Prayer. Lord, I have been tempted to choose my own way to live. However, I have discovered that my own pathway proves to be messy, painful, and costly. Help me to unreservedly follow your ways which are the best for living well. Amen.

March 1 — Psalm 33:1–7

1 Sing for joy in the LORD, you righteous ones; praise is becoming to the upright. 2 Give thanks to the LORD with the lyre; sing praises to Him with a harp of ten strings. 3 Sing to Him a new song; play skillfully with a shout of joy. 4 For the word of the LORD is right, and all His work is done in faithfulness. 5 He loves righteousness and justice; the earth is full of the goodness of the LORD. 6 *By the word of the* LORD *the heavens were made, and by the breath of His mouth all their lights.* 7 He gathers the waters of the sea together as a heap; He puts the depths in storehouses. (NASB)

God's powerful promises. In verses 6–7, when the psalmist describes how God creates, he shows that God does what he speaks. David Clarkson expresses this fact in this way, "It is all one with God to do as to say, to perform as to promise; it is as easy, he is as willing, as able, to do the one as the other. There is no such distance betwixt God's saying and doing, as amongst men. His saying is doing." He states why God's words can create, "There is omnipotence in his word; both of command and promise . . . One word of his can do more in an instant than the united powers of heaven and earth can do in eternity." Clarkson applies God's creative and powerful words for our lives. While we may experience people's broken promises, we can trust in God's promises to us. He encourages us to think about God's power to perform his promises: "This consideration removes at once the chief discouragements that hinder the lively actings of faith; for what is it that weakens our confidence of the promises' performance, but because we look upon the accomplishment as uncertain or difficult, or future and afar off! Now from hence faith may conclude the performance is certain, easy, and present." God's promises in Scripture are trustworthy because he is omnipotent in all that he speaks.

Prayer. Lord, thank you for your numerous promises throughout Scripture. However, I find myself doubting your promises, especially in the difficult times when I need them! Since you created the world by your powerful words may my trust grow in your promises for daily living. Amen.

March 2 — Psalm 33:8-11

8 Let the whole world fear the LORD and let everyone stand in awe of him. 9 For when he spoke, the world began! It appeared at his command. 10 The LORD frustrates the plans of the nations and thwarts all their schemes. 11 *But the LORD's plans stand firm forever; his intentions can never be shaken.* (NLT)

God's providence. Yesterday's meditation considered God's creation and its application to his promises. In today's Scripture reading, the psalmist relates how God created the world and works out his plans in human history. He directs the course of world events to fulfill his purposes. God stymies the nations' plans (v. 10) and no nation can undermine God's eternal purposes (v. 11). However, when we see and hear about tragic events among the nations, we quietly wonder, and may even question, if God has lost control of the world. Richard Sibbes addresses this issue. He illustrates, "The wheels in a watch or a clock move contrary one to another, some one way, some another, yet all serve the intent of the workman, to show the time, or to make the clock strike." Then he makes his point, "So in the world, the providence of God may seem to run cross to his promises; one man takes this way, another runs that way; good men go one way, wicked men another, yet all in conclusion accomplish the will, and centre in the purpose of God the great Creator of all things." Although we sometimes wonder how nations' evil and destructive ways can serve God's purposes Sibbes reminds us that nothing will derail God's providential rule over the nations. This very fact should cause us to revere God and "stand in awe of him" (v. 8).

Prayer. Lord, your ways are so mysterious, causing me to question what you are doing in this troubled and chaotic world. Thank you for the truth that your sovereignty extends over this globe. This encourages me in my small world with its hectic activities among family and friends. Thank you, Father, that I can place my confidence in your providence wherever I go and whatever I do throughout the day. Amen.

March 3 — Psalm 33:12-22

12 Blessed is the nation whose God is the Lord, the people He has chosen for His own inheritance. 13 The Lord looks from heaven; He sees all the sons of mankind; 14 from His dwelling place He looks out on all the inhabitants of the earth, 15 He who fashions the hearts of them all, He who understands all their works. 16 The king is not saved by a mighty army; a warrior is not rescued by great strength. 17 *A horse is a false hope for victory; nor does it rescue anyone by its great strength.* 18 Behold, the eye of the Lord is on those who fear Him, on those who wait for His faithfulness, 19 to rescue their soul from death and to keep them alive in famine. 20 Our soul waits for the Lord; He is our help and our shield. 21 For our heart rejoices in Him, because we trust in His holy name. 22 Let Your favor, Lord, be upon us, just as we have waited for You. (NASB)

False hopes. Society entices us to trust visible sources of power. The psalmist warns his people not to place their ultimate hope in powerful resources (v. 17). Commenting on this verse, Joseph Caryl states it is wrong to place confidence in a horse because it is "a horse of the greatest strength imaginable." He is addressing the danger of placing our trust in any power which can supplant our confidence in God. He explains, "But do not trust the strength of horses. If you trust the strength which God has given to horses, you make them your god. How often does God forbid trusting in the strength of horses, as knowing that we are apt to trust in anything that is strong, though but a beast." Apart from God, no other power can save and deliver us from the forces of wickedness. We can move away from the idols of power and trust in God Almighty. He knows what is occurring in our world (vv. 13–15) and has the power to protect us (vv. 18–21).

Prayer. Lord, the gods of power have seduced me, and I have pursued them. Forgive me for my lack of trust in your power. Deepen my confidence in your strength for daily living. Amen.

March 4 — Psalm 34:1–10

1 I will bless the Lord at all times; His praise shall continually be in my mouth. 2 My soul will make its boast in the Lord; the humble will hear it and rejoice. 3 Exalt the Lord with me, and let's exalt His name together. 4 *I sought the Lord and He answered me and rescued me from all my fears.* 5 They looked to Him and were radiant, and their faces will never be ashamed. 6 This wretched man cried out, and the Lord heard him, and saved him out of all his troubles. 7 The angel of the Lord encamps around those who fear Him and rescues them. 8 Taste and see that the Lord is good; how blessed is the man who takes refuge in Him! 9 Fear the Lord, you His saints; for to those who fear Him there is no lack of anything. 10 The young lions do without and suffer hunger; but they who seek the Lord will not lack any good thing. (NASB)

Deliverance from fear. It is common to hear people asking God to deliver them from an awful situation in the home or workplace. Here, David writes about an event (1 Sam 21:10–15) which threatened his life and made him very fearful (v. 4), before God spared him. Richard Baker comments on the issue of fear. He notes, "To have delivered me from all my troubles had been a great favour, but a far greater to deliver me from all my fears . . . now I enjoy not only tranquillity, but security, a privilege only of the godly." Baker explains, "The wicked may be free from trouble, but can they be free from fear? No; God knows, though they be not in trouble like other men, yet they live in more fear than other men. Guiltiness of mind, or mind of the world, never suffers them to be secure." Baker concludes, "Seeing the Lord has done this for me, has delivered me from all my fears, have I not cause, just cause, to magnify him, and exalt his name?"

Prayer. Lord, I confess that I succumb to fear in my life because of my own experiences in an unsafe world. While no one is immune from danger, help me to battle my fears and grow confident in your secure loving arms. Through you, I know that I can experience your much needed peace. Amen.

March 5   Psalm 34:11-14

11 Come, my children, listen to me; I will teach you the fear of the Lord. 12 Whoever of you loves life and desires to see many good days, 13 keep your tongue from evil and your lips from telling lies. 14 *Turn from evil and do good; seek peace and pursue it.* (NIV)

Going to heaven. For various reasons, most people assume that they will eventually go to heaven. Thomas Watson confronts this assumption. He states, "Negative goodness is not sufficient to entitle us to heaven. There are some in the world whose religion runs all upon negatives; they are not drunkards, they are not swearers, and for this they do bless themselves." While they are to "turn from evil" they should also "do good" (v. 14). Then Watson asks us to think about what it means to be good. He asks, "But what good is there in you? It is not enough for the servant of the vineyard that he does no hurt there, he does not break the trees or destroy the hedges; if he does not work in the vineyard he loses his pay. It is not enough for us to say at the last day, we have done no hurt, we have lived in no gross sin; but what good have we done in the vineyard?" Watson agreed with the biblical doctrine on human depravity. While individuals may do good works, their nature falls short of God's standard (Rom 3:23). Since we cannot earn our way to heaven, our only assurance rests on God's grace which saves us (Eph 2:8-9). Having experienced salvation, we respond with good works (Eph 2:10). David's good actions flow out of humbling himself before God whom he reveres (v. 11) and indicate that he is a "man after God's own heart" (1 Sam 13:14). For us today, Watson asks a pivotal question, "Where is the grace we have gotten? If we cannot show this, we shall lose our pay and miss of salvation." If we do accept God's grace and his salvation provided by Jesus Christ, we will enjoy life in this life (v. 12) and forever.

Prayer. Lord, thank you for the assurance of salvation by your saving grace. Thank you also for your empowering grace which enables me to do good to others. Thank you that I can live fully now and in heaven. Amen.

March 6   Psalm 34:15–22

15 The eyes of the Lord watch over those who do right; his ears are open to their cries for help. 16 But the Lord turns his face against those who do evil; he will erase their memory from the earth. 17 The Lord hears his people when they call to him for help. He rescues them from all their troubles. 18 *The Lord is close to the brokenhearted; he rescues those whose spirits are crushed.* 19 The righteous person faces many troubles, but the Lord comes to the rescue each time. 20 For the Lord protects the bones of the righteous; not one of them is broken! 21 Calamity will surely destroy the wicked, and those who hate the righteous will be punished. 22 But the Lord will redeem those who serve him. No one who takes refuge in him will be condemned. (NLT)

Broken heartedness. Painful experiences usually leave us broken-hearted. David assures us that during these times, God is close to us (v. 18) and is attentive to our cries (vv. 15, 17). James Janeway comments, "As for these broken ones, he will be sure not to leave them long, nor go far from them, but will be ready at hand to set their bones, to bind up their wounds to keep them from festering." To those who feel forgotten by God, Janeway offers assurance, "It is possible that they may look upon themselves as forgotten by God, they may not know their Physician when he is by them, and they may take their Friend for an enemy . . . God will let them know that he loves to act like himself, that is, like a God of love, mercy, and goodness; and that they are the persons that he has set his heart upon; he will have them in his bosom, never leave them nor forsake them; and though these contrite ones many times look upon themselves as lost, yet God will save them, and they shall sing a song of thankfulness amongst his delivered ones." Knowing God loves us in adversities is the best perspective for life (vv. 19–20, 22).

Prayer. Lord, I am thankful you are always with me, even in my pain. Even when my heart is broken, I am thankful for your loving care. I am so grateful for your mercy and promise never to abandon me. With you by my side, I have renewed hope that I can go on living. Amen.

March 7 — Psalm 35:1–10

1 Contend, LORD, with those who contend with me; fight against those who fight against me. 2 Take hold of buckler and shield and rise up as my help. 3 Draw also the spear and the battle-axe to meet those who pursue me; say to my soul, "I am your salvation." 4 Let those be ashamed and dishonored who seek my life; let those be turned back and humiliated who devise evil against me. 5 Let them be like chaff before the wind, with the angel of the LORD driving them on. 6 Let their way be dark and slippery, with the angel of the LORD pursuing them. 7 For they hid their net for me without cause; without cause they dug a pit for my soul. 8 *Let destruction come upon him when he is unaware, and let the net which he hid catch him; let him fall into that very destruction.* 9 So my soul shall rejoice in the LORD; it shall rejoice in His salvation. 10 All my bones will say, "Lord, who is like you, who rescues the afflicted from one who is too strong for him, and the afflicted and the poor from one who robs him?" (NASB)

Self-destructive evil. David shocks us with his prayer to see his enemies destroyed (v. 8). However, rather than taking matters into his own hands, he wants God to allow the enemies to fall into their own destructive trap. David knew wickedness backfires on nations and individuals who inflict evil on others (Ps 7:16; 9:15–18). Thomas Brooks points to Ahithophel to illustrate this moral principle. This man was David's trusted counselor (2 Sam 15:12) but in time, Ahithophel joined a conspiracy to kill David (17:1–4). When others rejected his advice, Ahithophel hanged himself (17:23), and David's life was spared. Brooks states the principle: "The wicked shall be undone by their own doings; all the arrows that they shoot at the righteous shall fall upon their own pates [heads]." God upholds his justice and at the same time, he longs for people to turn to him.

Prayer. Lord, as I consider all the evil in the world, thank you for the reminder that you carry out justice against evil offenders either in this world or in the world to come. In the meantime, I pray that they will come to know your love for them. Amen.

March 8   Psalm 35:11–18

11 Malicious witnesses rise up; they ask me things that I do not know. 12 They repay me evil for good, to the bereavement of my soul. 13 But as for me, when they were sick, my clothing was sackcloth; I humbled my soul with fasting, but my prayer kept returning to me. 14 I went about as though it were my friend or brother; I bowed down in mourning, like one who mourns for a mother. 15 *But at my stumbling they rejoiced and gathered themselves together; the afflicted people whom I did not know gathered together against me, they slandered me without ceasing.* 16 Like godless jesters at a feast, they gnashed at me with their teeth. 17 Lord, how long will You look on? Rescue my soul from their ravages, my only life from the lions. 18 I will give You thanks in the great congregation; I will praise You among a mighty people. (NASB)

Misfortunes of others. It hurts when we attempt to love difficult people, and they reject us. David describes how his love for people (vv. 12–14) meets with false accusations and derision (vv. 11, 15–16). They are "malicious" (v. 11) and "evil" (v. 12). Thomas Brooks admonishes us not to follow their example because God's people must reflect a different attitude. He states, "Do not glory in your neighbour's ruins. The firefly leaps and dances in the fire, and so do many wicked men rejoice in the sufferings of others. Such as rejoice in the sufferings of others are sick of the devil's disease; but from that disease the Lord deliver all your souls." Since we do not want sin to control us, Brooks paraphrases Proverbs 24:17 in admonishing us: "There cannot be a greater evidence of a wicked heart, than for a man to be merry because others are in misery . . . do not make other's mourning your music, do not make other's tears your wine; as you would not be made drunk at last with the wine of astonishment." This is the godly and wise way to live.

Prayer. Lord, enjoying others' failures and setbacks is a sin which offends them and you. Since you desire that I show mercy, shape and fill my heart with your love so that I may express genuine love to them. Amen.

March 9   Psalm 35:19-28

19 Do not let those who are wrongfully my enemies rejoice over me; nor let those who hate me for no reason wink maliciously. 20 For they do not speak peace, but they devise deceitful words against those who are quiet in the land. 21 *They opened their mouth wide against me; they said, "Aha, aha! Our eyes have seen it!"* 22 You have seen it, LORD, do not keep silent; Lord, do not be far from me. 23 Stir yourself, and awake to my right and to my cause, my God and my Lord. 24 Judge me, LORD my God, according to Your righteousness, and do not let them rejoice over me. 25 Do not let them say in their heart, "Aha, our desire!" Do not let them say, "We have swallowed him up!" 26 May those be ashamed and altogether humiliated who rejoice at my distress; may those who exalt themselves over me be clothed with shame and dishonor. 27 May those shout for joy and rejoice, who take delight in my vindication; and may they say continually, "The LORD be exalted, who delights in the prosperity of His servant." 28 And my tongue shall proclaim Your righteousness and Your praise all day long. (NASB)

False accusations. As part of the wrongful actions of David's enemies (vv. 19-20), they falsely accuse him (v. 21). Ezekiel Hopkins notes, "What is more common than for the vilest sinners to plead [give evidence] for their excuse [justification}" for their actions against God's people. Spite causes people to view others in the worst conceivable way. For example, Hopkins observes, "The unclean sensualist quotes David, and calls him in to be the patron of his debauchery." In other words, people's false accusations say more about them than the one accused. If they continue to boldly sin, they will not be "monuments of mercy" but instead, "God will set them up as pillars of salt" (Gen 19:26) because of their love for wickedness. However, if they should repent of their sin, Hopkins states "how great sins he [God] can pardon."

Prayer. Lord, you have reminded me of sin's powerful influence on human nature. Apart from your Spirit controlling me, I can destroy people's reputations. By your empowering grace, deliver me from hateful and deceitful speech which wrongly accuses others. Use my life to love others by seeking their well-being. Amen.

March 10 — Psalm 36:1-4

1 Transgression speaks to the wicked deep in his heart; there is no fear of God before his eyes. 2 *For he flatters himself in his own eyes that his iniquity cannot be found out and hated.* 3 The words of his mouth are trouble and deceit; he has ceased to act wisely and do good. 4 He plots trouble while on his bed; he sets himself in a way that is not good; he does not reject evil. (ESV)

Flattery. David reminds us that those who do not think highly of God think too highly of themselves (vv. 1–2). Jonathan Edwards warns us about following those who brag about themselves for several reasons. First, he states, "Some flatter themselves with a secret hope, that there is no such thing as another world." Second, others, "flatter themselves that death is a great way off, and that they shall hereafter have much opportunity to seek salvation." The third reason illustrates a misunderstanding of salvation. Edwards explains, "Some flatter themselves that they lead moral and orderly lives, and therefore think that they shall not be damned . . . There are some who flatter themselves that they do, and have done, a great deal for their salvation, and therefore hope they shall obtain it." In other words, he says, "Some hope by their strivings to obtain salvation of themselves. They have a secret imagination that they shall, by degrees, work in themselves sorrow and repentance of sin, and love towards God and Jesus Christ. Their striving is not so much an earnest seeking to God, as a striving to do themselves that which is the work of God." Fourth, Edwards comments, "Some sinners flatter themselves that they are already converted. They sit down and rest in a false hope, persuading themselves that all their sins are pardoned; that God loves them; that they shall go to heaven when they die; and that they need trouble themselves no more." We are wisest when we listen to God, and not ourselves, about eternal matters.

Prayer. Lord, thinking too highly of myself affects every area of my life. Recognizing my true condition before you, I want to turn away from bragging about myself to accept your view of me. Help me to make you the center of my life knowing that your unconditional love for me is what matters the most in life. Amen.

March 11 — Psalm 36:5-12

5 Your mercy, Lord, extends to the heavens, Your faithfulness reaches to the skies. 6 Your righteousness is like the mountains of God; Your judgments are like the great deep. Lord, You protect mankind and animals. 7 How precious is Your mercy, God! And the sons of mankind take refuge in the shadow of Your wings. 8 They drink their fill of the abundance of Your house; and You allow them to drink from the river of Your delights. 9 For the fountain of life is with You; in Your light we see light. 10 Prolong Your mercy to those who know You, and Your righteousness to the upright of heart. 11 May the foot of pride not come upon me and may the hand of the wicked not drive me away. 12 Those who do injustice have fallen there; they have been thrust down and cannot rise. (NASB)

Turning to God. After describing people's animosity toward David and God (vv.1-4), now the psalmist praises God's greatness. William Sedgwick* wants us to do the same. Commenting on verse 5, he notes, "God is gathering up all goodness, mercy, and peace from man to himself; and though there is cruelty, mischief, and wickedness in the world, in the earth, yet there is mercy, truth, and faithfulness in the clouds; and it's good that wisdom, goodness, truth, and righteousness leave the world, and cleave to God, that so we may follow it; and that what goodness, mercy, truth, and faithfulness we formerly enjoyed in man, we may enjoy it in God." Sedgwick also reminds us to be mindful of God's righteousness, judgments and protection which offer great hope in a hostile world (v. 6). While evil in society continues thrive, Sedgwick believes that now is the time "of sweetest admiration and love in God" whom we can enjoy and therefore be genuinely "happy."

Prayer. Lord, I confess that society's disdain for you and your people discourages me. Unfortunately, I pay more attention to social evils, rather than focusing on your nature. Guide my heart and mind to dwell more on your attributes which, in a troubled world, give me hope and joy. True happiness is based on a right relationship with you. Amen.

March 12   Psalm 37:1–6

1 Do not fret because of those who are evil or be envious of those who do wrong; 2 for like the grass they will soon wither, like green plants they will soon die away. 3 Trust in the Lord and do good; dwell in the land and enjoy safe pasture. 4 *Take delight in the* Lord, *and he will give you the desires of your heart.* 5 Commit your way to the Lord; trust in him and he will do this: 6 He will make your righteous reward shine like the dawn, your vindication like the noonday sun. (NIV)

Enjoying God. David encourages us to "delight" in God (v. 4). Knowing that this admonition is fundamental to our relationship with the Lord, John Howe explains the nature of delighting in God in his "Treatise of Delight in God." This delight, he says, is not one specific action but includes all our "holy and religious" conversations with him. To delight "in the Lord", "with the Lord", "by the Lord", "beside the Lord", "before the Lord", and "in the presence of the Lord"—all these phrases broaden our understanding "as a man may be said to delight himself with a friend that puts himself under his roof, and besides personal converse with himself, freely enjoys the pleasure of all the entertainments, accommodations, and provisions which he is freely willing to communicate with him." In the same way, we delight in God when we enjoy fellowship with him. Our conversation with God is "seasoned . . . with delight." David's invitation to "delight in the Lord" is captured by Howe's paraphrase, "Come and sit down with God, retire yourself to him, and solace yourself in the delights which are to be found in his presence and converse, in walking with him, and transacting your course as before him, and in his sight." Delighting in the Lord captures the essence of our relationship with him. When we fully enjoy God, then there is little room for us to fret or be anxious about the challenges we face in life (v. 1).

Prayer. Lord, I admit that I have searched for delight in too many things other than you. However, none of them has given me true delight. Turn my heart away from those fading delights in order that I may genuinely enjoy my relationship with you throughout the day! Amen.

March 13 — Psalm 37:7–11

7 Rest in the Lord *and wait patiently for him: fret not thyself because of him who prospereth in his way, because of the man who bringeth wicked devices to pass.* 8 Cease from anger and forsake wrath: fret not thyself in any wise to do evil. 9 For evildoers shall be cut off: but those that wait upon the Lord, they shall inherit the earth. 10 For yet a little while, and the wicked shall not be: yea, thou shalt diligently consider his place, and it shall not be. 11 But the meek shall inherit the earth; and shall delight themselves in the abundance of peace. (KJV)

Spiritual rest. We worry about so many things in life. So, it is not surprising that David tells us three times not to fret (vv. 1, 7, 8). However, since his exhortation is given amid very threatening circumstances (v. 7b), it surprises us. Is David mouthing a religious platitude? No, the psalmist is assuring us that we do not need to get all worked up about others' success, despite their wrongdoings. He is instructing us to "rest in the Lord" (v. 7), the corrective to our frequent fretfulness. James Hervey* notes that there are two Hebrew words which "express the privilege and the duty of resting on Christ." One word "signifies the refreshment and repose of a weary pilgrim, when he arrives at the end of his journey, and is settled for life in a secure, commodious, plentiful habitation." While we might be able to escape from troubles which encircle us, the psalmist suggests that we can rest amid the surrounding evil. The other Hebrew word "implies such a state of acquiescence, as silences the clamours of conscience, and composes the perturbation of the spirit." As other translations suggest, we can "still" our hearts and minds. Being "still" demands an intentional focus on the Lord. Then we do not have to react in hurtful ways (v. 11).

Prayer. Lord, too often I get all worked up about what is going on around me. Fretting is a way of life for me. I ask you to calm my heart by focusing on your presence and promises. I want to be still in you and find true rest, regardless of the surrounding chaos. Amen.

March 14   Psalm 37:12–17

12 The wicked plot against the godly; they snarl at them in defiance. 13 But the Lord just laughs, for he sees their day of judgment coming. 14 The wicked draw their swords and string their bows to kill the poor and the oppressed, to slaughter those who do right. 15 But their swords will stab their own hearts, and their bows will be broken. 16 *It is better to be godly and have little than to be evil and rich.* 17 For the strength of the wicked will be shattered, but the Lord takes care of the godly. (NLT)

True contentment. David knows that the human heart is inclined to envy those who are financially successful, albeit by corrupt means. While they may achieve the so-called "good life," he unequivocally assures us that it is far better to be "godly and have little" (v. 16). While we may conclude that "little" is insufficient, George Swinnock assures us that "little" is more. Known for his great skill in using illustrations, he makes his case with a few examples. He comments that the "lump of sugar in your cup would make the liquor sweet, be it never so small." He also explains that although small, the ring "with a very costly diamond in it is far more worth than many great ones without it." A third illustration points to our homes. To live in a humble home "perfumed" by love has "infinitely more worth" than to live in an expensive home, ignorant of God's goodness. David was not alone in his claim about the nature of a better life. In Proverbs 28:6, David's son, Solomon, wrote, "Better is a poor man who walks in his integrity than a rich man who is crooked in his ways." And the apostle Paul reminds us that, even if we only have life's necessities, "godliness with contentment is great gain" (1 Tim 6:6). Compared to the illusory and fading contentment of our possessions, contentment with God is supremely and eternally satisfying.

Prayer. Lord, I confess that I am often jealous of others' wealth and resentful of my limited resources. Teach me to be content with what you have given me. Jesus, I recall how you took a few fish and multiplied them to bless others. Take what I have and use it for your kingdom purposes. Amen.

March 15 — Psalm 37:18-26

18 The LORD knows the days of the blameless, and their inheritance will be forever. 19 They will not be ashamed in the time of evil, and in the days of famine they will have plenty. 20 But the wicked will perish; and the enemies of the LORD will be like the glory of the pastures, they vanish—like smoke they vanish away. 21 The wicked borrows and does not pay back, but the righteous is gracious and gives. 22 For those blessed by Him will inherit the land, but those cursed by Him will be eliminated. 23 *The steps of a man are established by the* LORD, *and He delights in his way.* 24 *When he falls, he will not be hurled down, because the* LORD *is the One who holds his hand.* 25 I have been young and now I am old, yet I have not seen the righteous forsaken or his descendants begging for bread. 26 All day long he is gracious and lends, and his descendants are a blessing. (NASB)

A secure path. David emphatically states that God directs our steps (v. 23). We need this assurance because we will still experience difficulties over time (v. 24a). However, since the Lord daily holds our hand, we will not be "hurled down" and destroyed (v. 24b). Drawing from marine imagery, James Janeway encourages us with his comments, "When this Pilot undertakes to steer [our] course, [our] vessel shall never split upon the rock, run upon the sands, or spring a leak, so as to sink in the seas. To be sure he will see [us] safe in [our] harbour." To drive home this truth, Janeway quotes a philosopher who said, "If a man will choose God for his Friend, he shall travel securely through a wilderness that has many beasts of prey in it; he shall pass safely through this world; for he only is safe that has God for his guide." When troubles come our way, they ought not to disillusion us. The psalmist is unequivocal—we will experience tough times. However, since the Lord directs our paths and holds our hands, we are secure in his love.

Prayer. Lord, I am grateful that you walk with me through life, even during life's challenges. Knowing that you hold my hand, no calamity can deliver a knock-down punch. You will pick me up and keep me going. Amen.

March 16 — Psalm 37:27–33

27 Turn away from evil and do good; so shall you dwell forever. 28 For the LORD loves justice; he will not forsake his saints. They are preserved forever, but the children of the wicked shall be cut off. 29 The righteous shall inherit the land and dwell upon it forever. 30 The mouth of the righteous utters wisdom, and his tongue speaks justice. 31 *The law of his God is in his heart; his steps do not slip.* 32 The wicked watches for the righteous and seeks to put him to death. 33 The LORD will not abandon him to his power or let him be condemned when he is brought to trial. (ESV)

Spiritual stability. David informs us that the one who follows God will not "slip" in life (v. 31b). Although this promise contradicts the psalmist's earlier comment that one can expect to fall from time to time (v. 24), the context of today's passage resolves the issue. David mentions that God's law in a person's heart (v. 31a). A love for God's truth impacts the very core ("heart") of one's being and how an individual walks through life. In contrast to an elderly person who may walk feebly, God's law internalized in our hearts, enables us to walk with spiritual strength. Richard Steele highlights the importance of allowing Scripture to permeate our being. He states, "The flock of sheep that's indisposed and unwilling to drive, start out of the way into every lane's end, one this way and another that; and just so is it with an unwilling heart; one thought starts this way, and another that, and it's a piece of skill to drive them through. But a willing heart, a heart prepared and ready to every good work, it flies quite up an end and delights itself in the Lord." With hearts firmly rooted in Scripture, we can "turn away from evil and do good" (v. 27) knowing God is with us every step of the way and will keep us secure with him (vv. 28, 33).

Prayer. Lord, I have paid too much attention to head knowledge regarding the Bible. I want biblical truth to percolate in my heart and then permeate every area of my life. May I be spiritually stable amid the evil which seeks to knock me off my feet to destroy me. Thank you for walking alongside me! Amen.

March 17 — Psalm 37:34-40

34 Wait for the Lord and keep His way, and He will exalt you to inherit the land; when the wicked are eliminated, you will see it. 35 I have seen a wicked, violent person spreading himself like a luxuriant tree in its native soil. 36 Then he passed away, and behold, he was no more; I searched for him, but he could not be found. 37 Observe the blameless person and look at the upright; for the person of peace will have a future. 38 But wrongdoers will altogether be destroyed; the future of the wicked will be eliminated. 39 But the salvation of the righteous is from the Lord; He is their strength in time of trouble. 40 The Lord helps them and rescues them; He rescues them from the wicked and saves them, because they take refuge in Him. (NASB)

Following God's way. Facing difficult circumstances can cause us to become impatient, waiting on God (v. 34). Then we may be tempted to take matters into our own hands. Thomas Watson cautions us, "While we are waiting let us take heed of wavering. Go not a step out of God's way, though a lion be in the way." When we are inclined to figure out the best way to respond to challenges, we risk disobeying God. Watson challenges us, "Keep God's highway, the good old way (Jer 6:16), the way which is paved with holiness." He also points us to Isaiah 35:8 (NIV), "And a highway will be there; it will be called the Way of Holiness." Psalm 1 describes two ways, "the way of the righteous" (v. 6a) or" the way of sinners" (vv. 1, 6b). Considering these two roads, Watson warns us, "Avoid crooked paths, take heed of turning to the left hand, lest you be set on the left hand. Sin does cross our hopes, it barricades up our way; a man may as well expect to find heaven in hell, as in a sinful way." Our best route is to follow Jesus who is "the way" (John 14:6).

Prayer. Lord, I confess that it is difficult to wait for you to work out your purposes in my life. I get impatient and my actions only make matters worse! I need your grace to remain faithful to Jesus and your way of living in this world. This is the best way to live! Amen.

March 18 — Psalm 38:1–9

1 Lord, do not rebuke me in Your wrath, and do not punish me in Your burning anger. 2 *For Your arrows have sunk deep into me, and Your hand has pressed down on me.* 3 There is no healthy part in my flesh because of Your indignation; there is no health in my bones because of my sin. 4 For my guilty deeds have gone over my head; like a heavy burden they weigh too much for me. 5 My wounds grow foul and fester because of my foolishness. 6 I am bent over and greatly bowed down; I go in mourning all day long. 7 For my sides are filled with burning, and there is no healthy part in my flesh. 8 I feel faint and badly crushed; I groan because of the agitation of my heart. 9 Lord, all my desire is before You; and my sighing is not hidden from You. (NASB)

The nature of afflictions. No stranger to adversities, David begins this psalm by launching into an intimate description of his suffering, guilt (vv. 1, 4), and physical torment (vv. 3, 5–8). He uses the "arrows" (v. 2) as a metaphor for his afflictions. Joseph Caryl suggests four ways by which arrows are analogous to suffering. He observes first, "Afflictions often come very speedily, with a glance as an arrow, quick as a thought. Second, afflictions come suddenly, unexpectedly; an arrow is upon a man afore he is aware, so are afflictions. Though Job said, the thing he feared came upon him, he looked for this arrow before it came; yet usually afflictions are unlooked for guests, they thrust in upon us when we dream not of them." Caryl describes the third characteristic: "They come with little noise; an arrow is felt before, or, as soon as it is heard; an arrow flies silently and secretly, stealing upon and wounding a man, unobserved and unseen. Lastly, all afflictions are sharp, and in their own nature killing and deadly. That any have good from them, is from the grace of God, not from their nature." Since God loves us, he assures us that he will use the afflictions for our good and his purposes.

Prayer. Father, I have gone through deep waters and have felt like I was drowning. I am thankful that you care for me and sustain me through my trials. Amen.

March 19 — Psalm 38:10–15

10 My heart pounds, my strength fails me; even the light has gone from my eyes. 11 My friends and companions avoid me because of my wounds; my neighbors stay far away. 12 Those who want to kill me set their traps, those who would harm me talk of my ruin; all day long they scheme and lie. 13 *I am like the deaf, who cannot hear, like the mute, who cannot speak;* 14 I have become like one who does not hear, whose mouth can offer no reply. 15 Lord, I wait for you; you will answer, Lord my God. (NIV)

Wise silence. When others speak critically of us, we may react with an angry tone and harsh words. When his opponents scheme to take David's life and speak of his demise (v. 12), he demonstrates a unique way of responding to his critics. Richard Baker paraphrases David's response (v. 13), "For why should I hear when I meant not to speak? And why should I speak when I knew beforehand I should not be heard?" Baker explains David's thinking, "I knew by contesting I should but provoke them, and make them more guilty ... [who] were guilty too much before. I therefore thought it better myself to be silent than to set them a roaring and make them grow outrageous." Baker suggests that the psalmist is an example for us. He states, "No doubt [there was] a great wisdom in David, to know that to be deaf and dumb was in this case his best course, but yet a far greater virtue that knowing it, he was able to do it. Oh, how happy should we be, if we could always do that which we know is best to be done, and if our wills were as ready to act, as our reason is able to enact; we should then decline many rocks we now run upon, we should then avoid many errors we now run into." Jesus who remained silent before his antagonists serves as an example for those who follow him (1 Pet 2:18–23).

Prayer. Lord, it is very tempting to lash out at those who attack me. However, such actions will only aggravate them and make matters worse. With your Spirit's help, I want to act wisely by remaining silent in conflicts to allow you to work out your purposes. Amen.

March 20　　　　　　　　Psalm 38:16–22

16 For I said, "Do not let them gloat or exalt themselves over me when my feet slip." 17 For I am about to fall, and my pain is ever with me. 18 *I confess my iniquity; I am troubled by my sin.* 19 Many have become my enemies without cause; those who hate me without reason are numerous. 20 Those who repay my good with evil lodge accusations against me, though I seek only to do what is good. 21 Lord, do not forsake me; do not be far from me, my God. 22 Come quickly to help me, my Lord and my Savior. (NIV)

Genuine confession. In the context of chronic suffering (v. 17b), David confesses his sin before the Lord (v. 18a). Confession involves the difficult admittance of wrongdoing. Nathanael Hardy suggests two issues related to confession. First, doing "good" to those who have no reason to hate us (vv. 19–20), may lead us to think that we are doing well spiritually. Then we often ignore the sins which no one sees. Hardy encourages self-examination for the "private sin," and when we recognize it, "we must not leave out that sin" in our confession to God. Second, confession includes not only the admittance of sinful deeds, but also the posture of remorse for our sins (v. 18b). As Hardy states, "David does not only say, 'I will declare' but 'I will be sorry for my sin.'" He explains that the psalmist may rightly express remorse with tears (Ps 119:136); however, tears themselves do not reveal the true condition of the heart. One may shed tears due to negative consequences while holding on to a defiant spirit. Hardy concludes, "It is only the heart broken with godly sorrow that sends forth a true confession." With this kind of "godly grief," the apostle Paul rejoices because we will genuinely confess and repent of our wrongdoing (2 Cor 7:9–10).

Prayer. Lord, I admit that when I am doing well, I gloss over sinful attitudes and emotions which lurk in the recesses of my heart. Expose those areas so that I may genuinely grieve over my sins and then confess them to you. Thank you for your forgiveness through Jesus Christ. Amen.

March 21   Psalm 39:1–6

1 I said, "I will keep watch over my ways so that I do not sin with my tongue; I will keep watch over my mouth as with a muzzle while the wicked are in my presence." 2 I was mute and silent, I refused to say even something good, and my pain was stirred up. 3 *My heart was hot within me, while I was musing the fire burned; then I spoke with my tongue:* 4 "Lord, let me know my end, and what is the extent of my days; let me know how transient I am. 5 Behold, You have made my days like hand widths, and my lifetime as nothing in Your sight; certainly all mankind standing is a mere breath. *Selah* 6 Certainly every person walks around as a fleeting shadow; they certainly make an uproar for nothing; he amasses riches and does not know who will gather them. (NASB)

Meditation and prayer. While we might assume that meditation on Scripture and prayer are two distinct activities, they are really two sides of a one coin. David spent time "musing" on Scripture and then he expressed those thoughts to God (v. 3). Reflecting on these two related disciplines, Thomas Watson comments, "Now meditation is a help to prayer . . . Meditation is like oil to the lamp; the lamp of prayer will soon go out unless meditation cherish and support it. Meditation and prayer are like two turtles, if you separate one the other dies." Watson continues with another illustration, "When the gun is full of powder it is fittest to discharge. So, when the mind is full of good thoughts, a Christian is fittest by prayer for discharge; now he sends up whole volleys of sighs and groans to heaven." Watson says, "Meditation has a double benefit in it, it pours in and pours out; first it pours good thoughts into the mind, and then it pours out those thoughts again into prayer; meditation first furnishes with matter to pray and then it furnishes with a heart to pray."

Prayer. Lord, I admit that I often separate meditation on Scripture from my prayer life. I fail to turn my musing on biblical truth into an intimate conversation with you. Help me to really talk to you about those insights I have discovered in the Bible and in my life. Amen.

March 22 — Psalm 39:7–13

7 And now, Lord, what wait I for? My hope is in thee. 8 Deliver me from all my transgressions: make me not the reproach of the foolish. 9 I was dumb, I opened not my mouth; because thou didst it. 10 Remove thy stroke away from me: I am consumed by the blow of thine hand. 11 When thou with rebukes dost correct man for iniquity, thou makest his beauty to consume away like a moth: surely every man is vanity. *Selah.* 12 Hear my prayer, O LORD, and give ear unto my cry; hold not thy peace at my tears: *for I am a stranger with thee, and a sojourner, as all my fathers were.* 13 O spare me, that I may recover strength, before I go hence, and be no more. (KJV)

Strangers and sojourners. David describes himself as a stranger and sojourner (v. 12). Thomas Manton clarifies ways that we also are "strangers" in this world. He says, "A stranger is one that is absent from his country, and from his father's house: so are we, heaven is our country, God is there, and Christ is there. Two, a stranger in a foreign country is not known, nor valued according to his birth and breeding: so the saints walk up and down in the world like princes in disguise." He also explains, "A stranger is thankful for the least favour; so, we must be thankfully contented with the things God has bestowed upon us: anything in a strange country is much." As a final comparison, Manton notes that "a stranger's heart is in his country; so is a saint's." Manton also reflects on our status as "sojourners." He writes, "A sojourner is one that intends not to settle, but only passes through a place, and is in motion travelling homeward. So, the children of God in relation to a country of their own in another place, namely, heaven; they are denizens [aliens] there, but strangers in the world; and they are sojourners and pilgrims in regard of their motion and journey towards their country." We too are "aliens and strangers" in this world (1 Pet 2:11).

Prayer. Lord, I confess I can love this world too much without giving thought about heaven. Increase my longing to be in your presence, and until then, help me to live well here on earth. Amen.

March 23 — Psalm 40:1–5

1 I waited patiently for the Lord; he inclined to me and heard my cry. 2 He drew me up from the pit of destruction, out of the miry bog, and set my feet upon a rock, making my steps secure. 3 He put a new song in my mouth, a song of praise to our God. Many will see and fear and put their trust in the Lord. 4 Blessed is the man who makes the Lord his trust, who does not turn to the proud, to those who go astray after a lie! 5 *You have multiplied, O Lord my God, your wondrous deeds and your thoughts toward us; none can compare with you!* I will proclaim and tell of them, yet they are more than can be told. (ESV)

God's thoughts on us. While experiencing life's trials, we may feel that God has forgotten us. David gives us hope! While going through a dark time in his life (v. 2) he patiently waits for the Lord's deliverance (v. 1a). After hearing his cries, God rescues him from his adversity (vv. 1b–2). With praise on his lips (v. 3), David reflects on this past trial (vv. 4–5). He tells us that we can trust in the Lord to do miraculous deeds, and to think about us (v. 5). Thomas Goodwin marvels that God constantly thinks about us, "My brethren, if God have been thinking thoughts of mercy from everlasting to those that are his, what a stock and treasury do these thoughts arise to, besides those that are in his nature and disposition! This is in his actual purposes and intentions, which he has thought, and does think over, again and again, every moment." With all of God's "treasury" of thoughts towards us, we are far from forgotten. Goodwin continues, "God has studied mercies, mercies for his children, even from everlasting . . . Not that any mercies are new, but he actually thinks over mercies again and again, and so he brings out of his treasury, mercies both new and old, and old are always new."

Prayer. Lord, although I often forget about you, I am profoundly thankful that you never forget about me. This gives me confidence for future challenges which will come my way. Amen.

March 24   Psalm 40:6–10

6 In sacrifice and offering you have not delighted, but you have given me an open ear. Burnt offering and sin offering you have not required. 7 Then I said, "Behold, I have come; in the scroll of the book it is written of me: 8 *I delight to do your will, O my God; your law is within my heart.*" 9 I have told the glad news of deliverance in the great congregation; behold, I have not restrained my lips, as you know, O Lord. 10 I have not hidden your deliverance within my heart; I have spoken of your faithfulness and your salvation; I have not concealed your steadfast love and your faithfulness from the great congregation. (ESV)

Delight in obedience. The psalmist delights to do God's will (v. 8a) and more than our worship, God delights in our obedience with an "open ear" to him (v. 6). In addition to our gratitude to God for his daily mercies (vv. 2–5), we gladly obey him because his will and his word are in our hearts (8b). The writer of Hebrews quotes Psalm 40:6–8 to show how these words reflect Jesus' willing obedience to his heavenly Father (Heb 10:5–7). John Flavel provides four reasons why Jesus delighted to do his Father's will. The first one is that by his own sacrificial death, Jesus revealed that God "had still a regard, a special respect" to a sacrifice (Lev 1:3). The second reason is to reveal the "unity of Christ's will with the Father's." Jesus' joy was rooted in the display of unity among the Godhead. The third reason for Jesus' humble willingness to die for us was showing us "mercy of the first magnitude; he came in love to our souls and underwent all his sufferings with such willingness for our sakes." He had joy knowing that his death obtained our salvation (Heb 12:2). Finally, by his suffering and death Jesus gave us a "pattern" so that, by "seeing and setting this great example of obedience before us, we might never grudge nor grumble at any duty of suffering that God should call us to." We joyfully offer our lives as a living sacrifice to the Lord (Rom 12:1).

Prayer. I confess that I sometimes serve you out of obligation. Lord, forgive me for those times when I obey you reluctantly. Stir within me a deeper love for your will and a delight to obey you. Amen.

March 25 — Psalm 40:11–17

11 As for you, O Lord, you will not restrain your mercy from me; your steadfast love and your faithfulness will ever preserve me! *12 For evils have encompassed me beyond number; my iniquities have overtaken me, and I cannot see; they are more than the hairs of my head; my heart fails me.* 13 Be pleased, O Lord, to deliver me! O Lord, make haste to help me! 14 Let those be put to shame and disappointed altogether who seek to snatch away my life; let those be turned back and brought to dishonor who delight in my hurt! 15 Let those be appalled because of their shame who say to me, "Aha, Aha!" 16 But may all who seek you rejoice and be glad in you; may those who love your salvation say continually, "Great is the Lord!" 17 As for me, I am poor and needy, but the Lord takes thought for me. You are my help and my deliverer; do not delay, O my God! (ESV)

Confronting our sins. David's troubles are his personal sins which are more than the hairs on his head (v. 12). The Puritans, such as David Clarkson, also took sin seriously. He admits, "We lose ourselves [become disappointed] when we speak of the sins of our lives. It may astonish any considering man to take notice how many sins he is guilty of any one day." Clarkson elaborates on this theme. Whenever we "do anything forbidden" or "neglect that which is enjoined," we commit the sin of "omission or commission." He points us to James who instructs us that if we break one of the Ten Commandments, we are guilty of breaking all of them (Jas 2:10). Thus, "the apostle [James] makes every sin tenfold . . . He [the sinner] breaks every command by sinning directly against one and so sins ten times at once." Even with our "best religious duty," such as prayer, we may find "a swarm of sins as cannot be numbered" such as "irreverence, lukewarmness, unbelief, spiritual pride, self-seeking, hypocrisy, distractions . . . and many more." David confesses his sin because he knows God's mercy (v. 11).

Prayer. Lord, I come before you honestly confessing my numerous sins. I am thankful for your mercy by which I am forgiven through Jesus Christ who paid the penalty for all my sin. Amen.

March 26   Psalm 41:1–4

1 Blessed is one who considers the helpless; the LORD will save him on a day of trouble. 2 The LORD will protect him and keep him alive, and he will be called blessed upon the earth; and do not turn him over to the desire of his enemies. 3 *The LORD will sustain him upon his sickbed; in his illness, You restore him to health.* 4 *As for me, I said,* "LORD, *be gracious to me; heal my soul, for I have sinned against You.*" (NASB)

Personal healing. The king pronounces a blessing on those who care for the weak and affirms that God will help the caregivers when they are weak (vv. 2–3). David, a helper to others, now applies this principle to his own situation by asking God to help him in his own weakness. He acknowledges his sin and pleads for God's mercy by asking for his soul to be healed (v. 4). Thomas Goodwin elaborates on David's confession: "Destroy my lusts, which are the diseases of my soul, Lord; and heal my soul, and renew life and communion with you, which is the health and strength of my soul. Do not take this sickness and death only away; but this sin away, that has dishonoured you, has separated between me and you: Heal my soul, for I have sinned against you." Many times, we pray for physical healing without considering the possible need for spiritual healing. We naturally pay more attention to physical illness compared to the aching soul. While a physical illness may not be due to a committed sin, sometimes, as in David's case, sin can be the cause (Jas 5:14–16). When sickness afflicts us, Goodwin suggests that this is the opportune time to explore our inner life because the soul's well-being is foundational for intimacy with Jesus Christ. Just as consistent physical examinations are important, so too must we practice the regular rhythm of probing our inner lives. While the healing of the body is wonderful, the healing of soul is of far greater benefit.

Prayer. Lord, I have prayed for my physical healing. However, I have not used these times to search my heart to reveal any sin. I invite you to probe my life, so that I may confess any sin because I want to experience physical and spiritual healing for your glory. Amen.

March 27 — Psalm 41:5–13

5 My enemies speak evil against me, "When will he die, and his name perish?" 6 And when he comes to see me, he speaks empty words; his heart gathers wickedness to itself; when he goes outside, he tells it. 7 All who hate me whisper together against me; they plot my harm against me, saying, 8 "A wicked thing is poured out upon him, so that when he lies down, he will not get up again." 9 Even my close friend in whom I trusted, who ate my bread, has lifted up his heel against me. 10 But You, Lord, be gracious to me and raise me up, that I may repay them. 11 By this I know that You are pleased with me, because my enemy does not shout in triumph over me. 12 As for me, You uphold me in my integrity, and You place me in Your presence forever. 13 *Blessed be the* Lord, *the God of Israel, from everlasting to everlasting. Amen and Amen.* (NASB)

Glory to God. David describes to God in detail the difficulties he is experiencing (vv. 5–9) and pleads for God's help (v. 10). When God answers, David rejoices "my enemy does not shout in triumph over me" (v. 11). With his prayers heard and his sin confessed (v. 4), David is now lives with integrity, enjoying God's sustaining presence (v. 12). With a renewed and intimate fellowship with God, David closes the psalm with doxology of praise (v. 13) giving glory (Greek *doxa*) to the Lord. Matthew Henry explains why and how we should sing a doxology to God: "We are here taught, One, to give glory to God, as 'the Lord God of Israel,' [KJV] a God in covenant with his people; that has done great and kind things for them and has more and better in reserve. Two, to give him glory as an eternal God that has both his being and his blessedness 'from everlasting and to everlasting.' Three, to do this with great affection and fervour of spirit, intimated in a double seal set to it, 'Amen, and Amen.' We say Amen to it, and let all others say Amen too."

Prayer. Lord, your graciousness to me fills my heart with joy and my mouth praises you for your unfathomable goodness. You deserve all the glory! Amen and Amen.

March 28   Psalm 42:1–5

1 As the deer pants for streams of water, so my soul pants for you, my God. 2 My soul thirsts for God, for the living God. When can I go and meet with God? 3 My tears have been my food day and night, while people say to me all day long, "Where is your God?" 4 These things I remember as I pour out my soul: how I used to go to the house of God under the protection of the Mighty One with shouts of joy and praise among the festive throng. 5 Why, my soul, are you downcast? Why so disturbed within me? *Put your hope in God,* for I will yet praise him, my Savior and my God. (NIV)

Hope in God. The psalmist is very discouraged (vv. 3, 5a). Spiritually dry, he asks God when he can meet with him (vv. 1–2). While others ask David where his God is (v. 3), David reflects on his times of fellowship with God. In his distress, he exhorts himself to place his hope in God again (v. 5b). William Gurnall provides us with two excellent reasons why hope has a "powerful influence" during our afflictions. First, he says, hope "stills and silences" the believer who is undergoing adversities. By way of contrast, he notes, "A hopeless soul is clamorous: one while it charges God, another while it reviles his instruments" which are the ways trials come to a believer. With no hope, this person cannot "long rest." Gurnall makes his point, "Hope has a rare art in stilling a froward [restless] spirit, when nothing else can; as the mother can make the crying child quiet by laying it to the breast, when the rod makes it cry worse." Second, in addition to stillness, the psalmist praises God (v. 5c), Gurnall states, "This hope fills the afflicted soul with such inward joy and consolation, that it can laugh while tears are in the eye, sigh and sing all in a breath; it is called "the rejoicing of hope" (Heb 3:6). And hope never affords more joy than in affliction."

Prayer. Father, as your child, you know when I feel downcast and discouraged. I turn to you for you are my hope! Still my troubled heart with your peace so that I may hear you. Then fill my heart with joy so that I may praise you. You are my true hope! Amen.

March 29 — Psalm 42:6–11

6 My soul is downcast within me; therefore I will remember you from the land of the Jordan, the heights of Hermon—from Mount Mizar. 7 Deep calls to deep in the roar of your waterfalls; all your waves and breakers have swept over me. 8 By day the Lord directs his love, at night his song is with me—a prayer to the God of my life. 9 I say to God my Rock, "Why have you forgotten me? Why must I go about mourning, oppressed by the enemy?" 10 My bones suffer mortal agony as my foes taunt me, saying to me all day long, *"Where is your God?"* 11 Why, my soul, are you downcast? Why so disturbed within me? Put your hope in God, for I will yet praise him, my Savior and my God. (NIV)

God is not hidden. Like the psalmist's adversaries, we may question where God is in our trials (v. 10). In response to such a question, Richard Sibbes reflects, "David might rather have said to them, 'Where are your eyes? Where is your sight? for God is not only in heaven, but in me.' Though David was shut out from the sanctuary, yet his soul was a sanctuary for God. Sibbes explains, "God has two sanctuaries, he has two heavens—the heaven of heavens and a broken spirit. God dwelt in David as in his temple. God was with David and in him; and he was never more with him, nor never more in him than in his greatest afflictions." Although we may see God at work in us in tough times, we may also feel God is hiding because of our painful circumstances. For example, Mary "could not see Christ distinctly, but thought him to be the gardener" (John 20:15). Sibbes instructs us, "There is a kind of concealment awhile in heavenly wisdom, yet notwithstanding, God is with his children always, and they know it by faith though not by feeling always . . . he is a God hiding himself oft times; and he shows himself in contrary conditions most of all, most comfortably. His work is by contraries."

Prayer. Lord, in challenging times, I have felt you are hiding from me. Grant me discernment to see your presence and faith to know you are working out your purposes. Amen.

March 30   Psalm 43

1 Vindicate me, my God, and plead my cause against an unfaithful nation. Rescue me from those who are deceitful and wicked. 2 You are God my stronghold. Why have you rejected me? Why must I go about mourning, oppressed by the enemy? 3 Send me your light and your faithful care, let them lead me; let them bring me to your holy mountain, to the place where you dwell. 4 Then I will go to the altar of God to God, my joy and my delight. I will praise you with the lyre, O God, my God. 5 *Why, my soul, are you downcast? Why so disturbed within me? Put your hope in God,* for I will yet praise him, my Savior and my God. (NIV)

Recurring despondency. In verse 5, David returns to the issue of personal discouragement which he describes in Psalm 42. He already knows the remedy for that which ails his soul—fixing his eyes on the Lord. With pastoral insight, Richard Sibbes notes, "You see how David's passions here are interlaced with comforts, and his comforts with passions, till at last he gets the victory of his own heart. Beloved, neither sin nor grief for sin, are stilled and quieted at the first." It is common to chide ourselves for repeated despondency. While some believers may give up trying to find inner peace, Sibbes believes that this is "not so with a true Christian soul, with the best soul living." He goes on to explain, "It was not so with David when he was in distemper [inwardly troubled]; he checks himself, the distemper was not yet stilled; he checks himself again, then the distemper breaks out again; he checks himself again, and all little enough to bring his soul to a holy, blessed, quiet, temper, to that blessed tranquility and rest that the soul should be in before it can enjoy its own happiness, and enjoy sweet communion with God." Sibbes encourages us to persist in seeking God although "it may be [that] there will be breaking out of the grief and malady again." Despite reoccurrences, we "go to God again" because this is "the right temper [disposition] of a Christian."

Prayer. Father, I confess that so many things really discourage me. I am very thankful for your patience as I learn to place my hope in you. As I do, I will praise you, my Savior. Amen.

March 31   Psalm 44:1-8

1 We have heard it with our ears, O God; our ancestors have told us what you did in their days, in days long ago. 2 With your hand you drove out the nations and planted our ancestors; you crushed the peoples and made our ancestors flourish. 3 It was not by their sword that they won the land, nor did their arm bring them victory; it was your right hand, your arm, and the light of your face, for you loved them. 4 *You are my King and my God, who decrees victories for Jacob.* 5 Through you we push back our enemies; through your name we trample our foes. 6 I put no trust in my bow, my sword does not bring me victory; 7 but you give us victory over our enemies, you put our adversaries to shame. 8 In God we make our boast all day long and we will praise your name forever. (NIV)

Our victorious King. The psalmist credits Israel's past victories to God (vv. 1-3) who, as King, makes it possible for his people to be victorious once again (vv. 4-8). David Clarkson elaborates on God's kingship, "His bare word is sufficient, all sufficient, for it, whatever it be, how great, how difficult, how impossible soever it seems. Such a power there is even in the word of the great King. There needs no more to deliver you, to deliver his people anywhere, how deep soever plunged, but only the command of him that sits on the throne." Clarkson notes that God also brings life to individuals, "If the gospel, the interests of Christ, in these parts of the world, and the dear concerns of our souls, and the souls of posterity, were all as dry bones, in a more forlorn and hopeless condition than they are, he could make all live with a word. He, that is our King, that sits upon the throne, can command life into that which seems as far from living as a dry bone. While he keeps the throne, it is a senseless heart that fails through distrust of his power, even when all visible power and help fail." We can have full confidence in God our King!

Prayer. Lord, when my life is chaotic, I need this reminder that you are my king who sits on the throne in control of all that takes place. Amen.

April 1   Psalm 44:9–16

9 Yet You have rejected us and brought us to dishonor, and do not go out with our armies. 10 You cause us to turn back from the enemy; and those who hate us have taken spoils for themselves. 11 You turn us over to be eaten like sheep, and have scattered us among the nations. 12 You sell your people cheaply, and have not profited by their sale. 13 You make us an object of reproach to our neighbors, of scoffing and ridicule to those around us. 14 You make us a proverb among the nations, a laughingstock among the peoples. 15 *All day long my dishonor is before me and I am covered with my humiliation,* 16 because of the voice of one who taunts and reviles, because of the presence of the enemy and the avenger. (NASB)

Our absent King. Although God had given Israel past military victories over their enemies, the nation now is experiencing devastating defeats (vv. 9–15). In addition to the loss of property and possessions (v. 10), people of surrounding nations mock (vv. 13–14, 16) and put the Israelites to shame (vv. 9, 15). Rather than blaming powerful enemies for Israel's demise, the psalmist complains to God, Israel's king, who has withdrawn and rejected his people (v. 9). Today, Jesus' followers witness churches decreasing in numbers and compromising biblical truth. As a result of scandals, churches face ridicule and embarrassment. In the seventeenth century, David Dickson observed similar reactions: "When the visible church is visited with sad calamities, the true members thereof are partakers of the trouble, and sorrow, and shame of that condition." While we may rightfully long to see God's power displayed, we must remember that prior to his death, Jesus enters Jerusalem as a king, riding a colt (Matt 21:4). Soon after, the authorities crucify Jesus as the "King of the Jews" (Matt 27:29). Yet, Christ's conquering death proves his eternal, kingly power. One day, he will appear as the "King of kings" (Rev 19:16). In the meantime, he still reigns by accomplishing his divine purposes in the universal church.

Prayer. Lord, I am thankful that you are the eternal King who reigns on the throne and will make all things right one day. I pray that those who oppose you will submit to you and allow you to reign in their lives. Amen.

April 2   Psalm 44:17–26

17 All this has come upon us, but we have not forgotten You, and we have not dealt falsely with Your covenant. 18 Our heart has not turned back, and our steps have not deviated from Your way, 19 yet You have crushed us in a place of jackals and covered us with deep darkness. 20 If we had forgotten the name of our God or extended our hands to a strange god, 21 would God not find this out? For He knows the secrets of the heart. 22 But for Your sake we are killed all day long; we are regarded as sheep to be slaughtered. 23 Wake yourself up, why do You sleep, Lord? Awake, do not reject us forever. 24 Why do you hide Your face and forget our affliction and oppression? 25 For our souls have sunk down into the dust; our bodies cling to the earth. 26 Rise up, be our help, and redeem us because of Your mercy. (NASB)

Faithfulness. The writer believes that God is not acting on behalf of his people (vv. 23–26). His inaction is puzzling because his people have been faithful to the Lord (vv. 17–20). Joseph Caryl reflects on believers' unwavering commitment to God throughout the centuries. He observes, "The church having reported her great troubles, speaks it as an argument of much sincerity towards God, and strength of grace received from him." Caryl paraphrases the psalmist's words, "These afflictions have been strong temptations upon us to cause us to decline from your ways, but through grace we have kept our ground and remained constant in thy covenant." Caryl notes that "most of the saints" he observes, have "improved" or grown spiritually stronger under trials by God's grace, although others have suffered spiritually. Although God's ways are mysterious, we are encouraged to remain faithful to him through our troubles (v. 17), knowing God is irrevocably committed to us in the present and future (1 Pet 1:1–9). Even when we falter and wonder where God is, he will be faithful to us (2 Tim 2:13).

Prayer. Lord, sometimes I question your unpredictable ways and wonder if you are with me. Thank you for the reminders that you are faithful to me. This motivates me to be faithful to you. Amen.

April 3 — Psalm 45:1–9

1 My heart is stirred by a noble theme as I recite my verses for the king; my tongue is the pen of a skillful writer. 2 You are the most excellent of men and *your lips have been anointed with grace*, since God has blessed you forever. 3 Gird your sword on your side, you mighty one; clothe yourself with splendor and majesty. 4 In your majesty ride forth victoriously in the cause of truth, humility and justice; let your right hand achieve awesome deeds. 5 Let your sharp arrows pierce the hearts of the king's enemies; let the nations fall beneath your feet. 6 Your throne, O God, will last for ever and ever; a scepter of justice will be the scepter of your kingdom. 7 You love righteousness and hate wickedness; therefore God, your God, has set you above your companions by anointing you with the oil of joy. 8 All your robes are fragrant with myrrh and aloes and cassia; from palaces adorned with ivory the music of the strings makes you glad. 9 Daughters of kings are among your honored women; at your right hand is the royal bride in gold of Ophir. (NIV)

Gracious words. The description of a wedding song for the king (vv. 1–8) and his bride (v. 9) receives its fulfillment in Jesus Christ who is the greatest king. Among all the people, he is the "most excellent" because of his grace-filled speech (v. 2). John Boys details how this grace is exemplified in Jesus' life. In contrast to the "harsh and hard words" of the Law, grace fills the content or the "matter" of his teaching (Matt 11:28; Luke 4:18, 22; John 1:17). Jesus "deliver[s] acceptable doctrine." Grace also characterizes the "manner" of Jesus' speaking to people. He notes that people follow Jesus because he speaks "so sweetly" and "so graciously." Finally, he observes that gracious speech involves "sometimes correcting" when love is the motivation. The apostle Paul reminds his readers, "Let your conversations be always full of grace" (Col 4:6). Since harsh words stir up anger (Prov 15:1), it is no wonder that pleasant and winsome speech is a mark of excellence (v. 2).

Prayer. Lord, help me not to be harsh but gracious in my relationships so that I may reflect Jesus by my words and attitudes. Amen.

April 4 — Psalm 45:10–17

10 Hear, O daughter, and consider, and incline your ear: forget your people and your father's house, 11 and the king will desire your beauty. Since he is your lord, bow to him. 12 The people of Tyre will seek your favor with gifts, the richest of the people. 13 All glorious is the princess in her chamber, with robes interwoven with gold. 14 In many-colored robes she is led to the king, with her virgin companions following behind her. 15 *With joy and gladness they are led along as they enter the palace of the king.* 16 In place of your fathers shall be your sons; you will make them princes in all the earth. 17 I will cause your name to be remembered in all generations; therefore nations will praise you forever and ever. (ESV)

The greatest wedding. After describing the king, the next verses focus on the bride who leaves behind her people and goes to the groom (vv. 11, 15). Jesus is also our groom, and we are his bride (2 Cor 11:2). When we are in heaven, we will enjoy the wedding and the feast with our groom, Jesus the Lamb (Rev 19:7–9; Matt 22:1–14). John Flavel comments on this marriage, "No marriage was ever consummated with that triumphal solemnity as the marriage of Christ and believers shall be in heaven." Those in heaven, he notes, will rejoice at this wonderful event. First, "God the Father will rejoice to behold the blessed accomplishment and consummation of that glorious design and project of his love." Jesus Christ, the groom, will rejoice. The Holy Spirit will also rejoice "to see those souls, whom he once found as rough stones, now to shine as the bright polished stones of the spiritual temple." The angels will rejoice because they will see their announcement of salvation fulfilled (Luke 2:13). Finally, "the saints themselves shall rejoice unspeakably, when they shall enter into the king's palace, and be forever with the Lord (1 Thess 4:17)." Because we are Christ's bride, Jesus must be our primary love and we must pray that we not lose our love for him (Rev 2:4).

Prayer. Lord, I am grateful that you want me to enjoy a life of intimacy with you. Since this is my longing, guard my heart so that I may remain faithful to you. Amen.

April 5   Psalm 46:1–3

1 *God is our refuge and strength, a very ready help in trouble.*
2 *Therefore we will not fear, though the earth shakes and the mountains slip into the heart of the sea;* 3 *though its waters roar and foam, though the mountains quake at its swelling pride. Selah* (NASB)

Our strong fortress. Even in the turbulent times described, these verses exude confidence. The writer looks to God who has power over nature's mighty earthquakes and storms. If the immoveable mountains can shake, where can we place our confidence? We discover our true and certain security in God himself (v. 1). It is not surprising that these and the following verses have encouraged countless individuals throughout the centuries. S. W. Christophers* comments on the times Martin Luther faced troubles, "Luther and his companions, with all their bold readiness for danger and death in the cause of truth, had times when their feelings were akin to those of a divine singer, who said, 'Why are you cast down, O my soul?' But in such hours, the unflinching Reformer would cheerily say to his friend Melanchthon, 'Come, Philip, let us sing the forty-sixth Psalm.'" The assurance of this psalm stirred Martin Luther* to pen the words which we know as "A Mighty Fortress." In his words, Luther comments, "We sing this Psalm to the praise of God, because God is with us, and powerfully and miraculously preserves and defends his church and his word, against all fanatical spirits, against the gates of hell, against the implacable hatred of the devil, and against all the assaults of the world, the flesh and sin." The Psalter frequently uses the imagery of God as a fortress (18:2; 31:3; 59:9; 62:3; 71:3; 94:22; 144:2). God is our fortress, and we can find refuge in him (2:12; 7:1; 11:1; 16:1; 18:2; 31:1; 62:7; 71:3; 91:2; 94:22). Psalm 46:1 reminds us that our security is in God; we can confidently trust him, regardless of what we are going through.

Prayer. Lord, I confess that when I experience alarming situations, I get nervous and my heart trembles. Forgive me for considering only my limited resources rather than looking to you for what I really need. Build my confidence in your inexhaustible strength. I come to you, my refuge and strength, who to give me confidence to face life. Amen.

April 6   Psalm 46:4–7

4 *There is a river whose streams make the city of God happy,* the holy dwelling places of the Most High. 5 God is in the midst of her, she will not be moved; God will help her when morning dawns. 6 The nations made an uproar, the kingdoms tottered; He raised his voice, the earth quaked. 7 The LORD of armies is with us; the God of Jacob is our stronghold. *Selah* (NASB)

God's indwelling presence. Not only does nature shake and roar (vv. 2–3) but nations are also in an "uproar" (v. 6). Amid this turbulence, the "city of God" remains immoveable (vv. 4–5). This phrase focuses not on the city of Jerusalem or Zion itself, but on the place where God dwells (v. 4b). In addition, the river's symbolism (v. 4) contributes to the imagery of God living among his people (Rev 22:1–2). In response to his own question, "What is the river that makes glad the city of God?" Ralph Erskine replies, "I answer, God himself is the river, as in the following verse, 'God is in the midst of her.'" On this theme, he elaborates by providing a Trinitarian perspective. First, he states that "God the Father is the river" because he calls himself 'the fountain of living waters' (Jer 2:13)." He continues, "Second, God the Son is the river, the fountain of salvation: 'In that day there shall be a fountain opened to the house of David, and the inhabitants of Jerusalem for sin and for uncleanness' (Zech 13:1)." Erskine concludes, "God the Spirit is the river" referring to John 7:38–39, where Jesus says, "whoever believes in me . . . 'Out of his heart will flow rivers of living water.'" The apostle John interprets this living water to be the Holy Spirit who was given after Jesus' resurrection, at Pentecost. Erskine also describes "streams" or tributaries (v. 4) connected to the Godhead. These streams are "the perfections of God, the fullness of Christ, the operations of the Spirit" which flow in the "channel" of God's "covenant of promise." By these "streams", the Lord makes his presence known to us!

Prayer. Lord, I am very thankful that you have made it possible for me to know and enjoy your indwelling presence whatever each day brings. Help me to live joyfully in your living and refreshing presence. Amen.

April 7   Psalm 46:8–11

8 Come and see what the LORD *has done, the desolations he has brought on the earth.* 9 He makes wars cease to the ends of the earth. He breaks the bow and shatters the spear; he burns the shields with fire. 10 *He says, "Be still, and know that I am God;* I will be exalted among the nations, I will be exalted in the earth." 11 The LORD *Almighty is with us; the God of Jacob is our fortress.* (NIV)

Be still. The psalmist invites us to see God revealing his power over the nations (vv. 8–9). When chaos around the globe troubles us, we need spiritual eyes to discern God's purposes. To do so, God asks us to "be still" and wait for him to be exalted among the nations (v. 10). Jonathan Edwards describes how we can be still before God. We must be quiet by limiting our "words" rather than "speaking against" and "complaining" about God's ways, or, by "justifying ourselves and speaking great swelling words of vanity." Edwards suggests two further ways, "We must be still as to actions and outward behaviour, so as not to oppose God in his dispensations; and as to the inward frame of our hearts, cultivating a calm and quiet submission of soul to the sovereign pleasure of God, whatever it may be." The basis for being still before God rests with God's nature. Edwards comments, "His being God is a sufficient reason why we should be still before him, in no wise murmuring, or objecting, or opposing, but calmly and humbly submitting to him." Finally, to truly be still before the Lord, Edwards instructs us to "know him to be God. Our submission is to be such as becomes rational creatures. God does not require us to submit contrary to reason, but to submit as seeing the reason and ground of submission." We can rest in God's sovereignty because "God is God." To those who create chaos in the world, God commands them to be still and see that he is the Lord over all the nations.

Prayer. Lord, teach me more about yourself so that I may learn to be still. Amid the uncertainties of life, I need your grace to silence my words, my actions, and my anxious heart. Help me to gladly submit and rest in who you are today. Amen.

April 8 — Psalm 47

1 Clap your hands, all peoples! Shout to God with loud songs of joy! 2 For the Lord, the Most High, is to be feared, a great king over all the earth. 3 He subdued peoples under us, and nations under our feet. 4 *He chose our heritage for us,* the pride of Jacob whom he loves. *Selah* 5 God has gone up with a shout, the Lord with the sound of a trumpet. 6 Sing praises to God, sing praises! Sing praises to our King, sing praises! 7 For God is the King of all the earth; sing praises with a psalm! 8 God reigns over the nations; God sits on his holy throne. 9 The princes of the peoples gather as the people of the God of Abraham. For the shields of the earth belong to God; he is highly exalted! (ESV)

Our inheritance. Throughout this psalm, including this section, the writer declares that God is above all other powers as the "King" (vv. 6–7) and the "Most High" (v. 2). By subduing the nations and providing his people with land for their inheritance (v. 4), God shows his absolute reign. Through faith in Jesus Christ, we will also receive an inheritance (Eph 1:14; Col 3:24; 1 Pet 1:4). John Boys notes that God chooses our inheritance (v. 4). His wise choosing "means that he knows what is better for us than ourselves." Our inheritance includes "the hope of a better life, to wit, a kingdom that cannot be shaken, an everlasting habitation, and inheritance which is immortal and undefiled, and fades not away, reserved for us in heaven." This vastly superior inheritance is available to all who are the "people of the God of Abraham" (v. 9a). This expansive group of heirs includes Gentiles who are the spiritual children of Abraham (Rom 4:11–12). Throughout all generations, the Lord rightly deserves all praise and adoration (vv. 1, 6). One day we will enter heaven and enjoy the fullness of a glorious inheritance.

Prayer. Lord, with so many ongoing global conflicts, I often fail to remember that you are the almighty king who reigns on the throne. I want to loosen my grip on earthly matters and embrace being an heir to my present and future inheritance. Amen.

April 9 — Psalm 48:1-8

1 *Great is the Lord, and greatly to be praised in the city of our God, His holy mountain.* 2 Beautiful in elevation, the joy of the whole earth, is Mount Zion in the far north, the city of the great King. 3 In its palaces, God has made Himself known as a stronghold. 4 For, behold, the kings arrived, they passed by together. 5 They saw it, then they were amazed; they were terrified, they fled in a hurry. 6 Panic seized them there, anguish, as that of a woman in childbirth. 7 With the east wind You smash the ships of Tarshish. 8 Just as we have heard, so have we seen in the city of the Lord of armies, in the city of our God; God will establish her forever. *Selah* (NASB)

The focus of worship. The psalmist mentions Mount Zion (vv. 1-2) but his interest is on God, the "great King," who dwells there (v. 2). Robert Bellarmine* comments, "The prophet, being about to praise a certain edifice, commences by praising the architect, and says that in the holy city the wonderful skill and wisdom of God, who built it, is truly displayed." Therefore, God deserves to be praised because "whether we look at his essence, his power, his wisdom, his justice, or his mercy, all are infinite, everlasting, and incomprehensible; and thus, so much is God 'greatly to be praised' that all the angels, all men, even all his own works would not suffice thereto." After emphasizing God's nature, Bellarmine relates Jerusalem's Mount Zion to the church. "There is no one thing can give us a greater idea of his greatness, or for which were should praise and thank him more," he states, "than the establishment of his church; and therefore, the prophet adds, 'in the city of our God, in the mountain of his holiness' (KJV); that is to say, the greatness of God, and for which he deserves so much praise, is conspicuous in the foundation and construction of his church." We are his temple because the Holy Spirit dwells within each believer and among his redeemed people (1 Cor 3:16).

Prayer. Lord, I praise you for choosing to dwell by your Spirit among your people. Enable me by your grace to live a holy life pleasing to you. May your church reflect your Spirit to the world. Amen.

April 10 — Psalm 48:9-14

9 We have thought over your goodness, God, in the midst of your temple. 10 As is Your name, God, so is Your praise to the ends of the earth; Your right hand is full of righteousness. 11 Mount Zion shall be glad, the daughters of Judah shall rejoice because of Your judgments. 12 Walk around Zion and encircle her; count her towers; 13 consider her ramparts; go through her palaces, so that You may tell of her to the next generation. 14 *For such is God, our God forever and ever;* He will lead us until death. (NASB)

Our eternal God. While the beauty of religious buildings may enrapture us, the psalmist wants us to delight in God himself. The psalmist tells us three times that he is "our God" (vv. 1, 8, 14). George Swinnock notes that God is a "satisfying portion filling every crevice of [our] soul with the light of joy and comfort." He is our "sanctifying portion" enabling us to grow spiritually. God is also our "universal portion" for every area of life not just "health, or wealth, or friends, or honours, or liberty, or life, or house, or wife, or child, or pardon, or peace, or grace, or glory, or earth, or heaven, but all these, and infinitely more." He gives us all the resources we need for life! As Swinnock eloquently describes, "Our portion is so full that [we] desire no more; [we] enjoy variety and plenty of delights above what [we] are able to ask or think, and want nothing but to have it fixed [unchangeable]." Finally, the Lord is our "eternal portion" because he is "for ever and ever" (v. 14). In order for us to realize the incomprehensibility of eternity, Swinnock makes a contrast, "All the arithmetical figures of days, and months, and years, and ages, are nothing to this infinite cipher 'ever' which, though it stand for nothing in the vulgar account, yet contains all our millions; yea, our millions and millions of millions are less than drops in this ocean 'ever.'"

Prayer. Lord, I am thankful that you are our eternal God for those who have come into a personal relationship with you. Thank you for your unlimited resources for my daily life. Amen.

April 11 — Psalm 49:1-4

1 Listen to this, all you people! Pay attention, everyone in the world! 2 *High and low, rich and poor—listen!* 3 For my words are wise, and my thoughts are filled with insight. 4 I listen carefully to many proverbs and solve riddles with inspiration from a harp. (NLT)

A call to wisdom. With our busy lives, we are often too preoccupied to stop, listen and ponder how to live wisely. While a sizable percentage of the Psalter is devoted to praising God, this psalm offers wise instruction (v. 3) To set the stage, today's verses serve as a prelude, calling all people to hear, consider and respond to the psalmist's words. Joseph Caryl comments on the nature of the first two verses which "summon and divide" humankind. In verse 1, God summons all the people to hear what he has to say. Then the writer divides humanity into two groups based on social and economic standing (v. 2). Society is composed of the high and rich, and low and poor. Caryl points out the phrase "high and rich" employs two Hebrew words *ish* (all humanity) and *adam* (each person) and "if we should translate the text directly, according to the letter, the words must run, 'sons of men and sons of men.'" Everyone must seriously "listen" (vv. 1, 2, 4) to the psalmist's godly wisdom regarding the brevity of life (in verses 5–13 which follow). Those who have low status and are poor need to be warned not to envy those who have high status and are wealthy. The rich also need to listen. While the wealthy often pay little attention to the brevity of life, everyone needs to heed the reality of human mortality. Living wisely entails the lowly living with contentment, knowing God will provide all that they need. For those who are proud of their social standing, wisdom calls them to live humbly, sharing what they have with others.

Prayer. Lord, I confess that it is easy to allow pride to flood my heart when I consider my status in life compared to others. At other times, I am upset by those who flaunt what they have received by ill-gotten means. Teach me to live wisely, content with what you have provided. Amen.

April 12   Psalm 49:5–13

5 Why should I fear in days of adversity, when the injustice of those who betray me surrounds me, 6 those who trust in their wealth and boast in the abundance of their riches? 7 No one can by any means redeem another or give God a ransom for him—8 for the redemption of his soul is priceless, and he should cease imagining forever—9 that he might live on eternally, that he might not undergo decay. 10 For he sees that even wise people die; the foolish and the stupid alike perish and leave their wealth to others. 11 *Their inner thought is that their houses are forever and their dwelling places to all generations; they have named their lands after their own names.* 12 But man in his splendor will not endure; he is like the animals that perish. 13 This is the way of those who are foolish, and of those after them who approve their words. *Selah* (NASB)

Death and wealth. The psalmist warns those who place their ultimate trust in their wealth (vv. 5–6) that wealth has limitations (vv. 7–8), and death is inevitable (vv. 9–10a). He challenges the belief that personal possessions will last forever (vv. 10b–11). Richard Sibbes elaborates, "God makes fools of them [the wealthy], for how few have you that go beyond the third generation? How few houses have you that the child or the grandchild can say, 'This was my grandfather's and my great grandfather's?' How few houses have you that those that are now in them can say, 'My ancestor dwelt here, and these were his lands?' Go over a whole country, few can say so. Men when they build, together with building in the earth they build castles in the air; they have conceits." Then their dreams crumble. Sibbes notes, "God crosses them. Either they have no posterity, or by a thousand things that fall out in the world, it falls out otherwise. The time is short, and the fashion of this world passes away; that is, the buildings pass away, the owning passes away, all things here pass away." He urges us not to allow earthly possessions to control us, and to be sure that we have the "best possession" which is heaven.

Prayer. Lord, in this materialistic society, I find myself preoccupied with obtaining more and more in order to find security. Teach me not to place my full confidence in my possessions but in you who is eternal. Amen.

April 13   Psalm 49:14–20

14 Like sheep they sink down to Sheol; death will be their shepherd; and the upright will rule over them in the morning, and their form shall be for Sheol to consume so that they have no lofty home. 15 But God will redeem my soul from the power of Sheol, for He will receive me. *Selah* 16 Do not be afraid when a person becomes rich, when the splendor of his house is increased; 17 for when he dies, he will take nothing with him; his wealth will not descend after him. 18 *Though while he lives he congratulates himself—and though people praise you when you do well for yourself—*19 he will go to the generation of his fathers; they will never see the light. 20 Mankind in its splendor, yet without understanding, is like the animals that perish. (NASB)

Death and adulation. We must view personal wealth in light of death's inevitability (vv. 11–12). Ezekiel Hopkins cautions, "How foolish is it to account yourself a better man than another, only because your dunghill is a little bigger than his!" It is silly to determine our value based on our possessions because as he states, "These things are not at all to be reckoned into the value and worth of a man." If one has wealth, the psalmist challenges us not to congratulate ourselves and be impressed by others' adulation (v. 18). Hopkins warns, "It is wealth, indeed, that makes all the noise and bustle in the world, and challenges all the respect and honour to itself; and the ignorant vulgar, whose eyes are dazzled with pomp and bravery, pay it with a stupid and astonished reverence. Yet know, that it is but your silks and velvet, your lands, or your retinue and servants, they venerate, not you: and if you think otherwise, you are as justly ridiculous as that ass in the apologue, that grew very gravely proud, and took state, when the people fell prostrate before him, adoring, not him, but to the idol he carried." If we like others' adulation, the psalmist reminds us that we cannot take our wealth with us when we die (vv. 17, 19–20). We are to trust God and seek his favor.

Prayer. Lord, forgive me for enjoying people's praise more than your commendation. Help me to live with an eternal perspective. Amen.

April 14   Psalm 50:1–6

1 The Mighty One, God the LORD, speaks and summons the earth from the rising of the sun to its setting. 2 Out of Zion, the perfection of beauty, God shines forth. 3 Our God comes; he does not keep silence; before him is a devouring fire, around him a mighty tempest. 4 He calls to the heavens above and to the earth, that he may judge his people: 5 *"Gather to me my faithful ones, who made a covenant with me by sacrifice!"* 6 The heavens declare his righteousness, for God himself is judge! *Selah* (ESV)

God speaks to his people. Among God's roles, he is a judge (vv. 4, 6). Using the imagery of fire, the psalmist draws our minds to Mount Sinai where God appeared before his people (v. 3; Exod 19:18). Now, in this psalm, God calls his people to gather before him to hear what he will declare to them (v. 5). Whatever his pronouncement may be, he addresses them as the covenant people to whom he is irrevocably committed. Commenting on the nature of this covenant relationship between God and his people, William Gurnall states, "Formerly soldiers used to take an oath not to flinch from their colours, but faithfully to cleave to their leaders; thus, they called *sacramentum militaire*, a military oath; such an oath lies upon every Christian. It is so essential to the being of a saint, that they are described by this [covenant]." Through Jesus' death on the cross, he made it possible for us to enter a new covenant with the Godhead (1 Cor 11:5; 2 Cor 3:6). Gurnall challenges us, "We are not Christians till we have subscribed [signed] this covenant, and that without any reservation. When we take upon us the profession of Christ's name, we enlist ourselves in his muster roll, and by it do promise that we will live and die with him in opposition to all his enemies . . . He will not entertain [maintain] us till we resign up [surrender] ourselves freely to his disposal, that there may be no disputing with his commands afterwards, but, as one under his authority, go and come at his word." As God's covenant people, we express our commitment by lovingly obeying Him.

Prayer. Lord, thank you for your commitment to me. As an expression of my gratitude and relationship to you, enable me by your Spirit to love and obey you. Amen.

April 15   Psalm 50:7-15

7 Hear, O my people, and I will speak; O Israel, I will testify against you. I am God, your God. 8 Not for your sacrifices do I rebuke you; your burnt offerings are continually before me. 9 I will not accept a bull from your house or goats from your folds. 10 For every beast of the forest is mine, the cattle on a thousand hills. 11 I know all the birds of the hills, and all that moves in the field is mine. 12 If I were hungry, I would not tell you, for the world and its fullness are mine. 13 Do I eat the flesh of bulls or drink the blood of goats? 14 Offer to God a sacrifice of thanksgiving, and perform your vows to the Most High, 15 *and call upon me in the day of trouble; I will deliver you, and you shall glorify me.* (ESV)

Relationship, not religiosity. Religious activities can consume our lives while we forget that God places a higher priority on a genuine relationship with him. Through the psalmist, the Lord tells his people that he does not need their religious sacrifices because he owns everything (vv. 9–13). Instead, he wants their gratitude ("thanksgiving") and their trust ("call upon me") during challenging times (vv. 14–15). Thomas Adams addresses the importance of us calling on God. He notes, "The Lord has promised his children supply of all good things, yet they must use the means of impetration [petition]; by prayer." For example, God "feeds the young ravens, but first they call upon him [Ps 147:9]." He suggests two reasons why it is important to call on God. First, "God withholds from them that ask not, lest he should give to them that desire not." Second, he observes, "Those things we pray for, we must work for." Adams refers to David who, though he depended on God to deliver him and his people from Goliath, nevertheless was "valiant" using his skills, working for victory (1 Sam 17:37). Gratitude and genuine dependence are marks of a genuine relationship with the Lord.

Prayer. Lord, I must admit that I can become so preoccupied with my religious duties that I neglect my personal relationship with you. Forgive me for not giving proper attention to cultivating gratitude and dependence on you. Amen.

April 16   Psalm 50:16-23

16 But to the wicked God says: "What right have you to recite my statutes or take my covenant on your lips? 17 For you hate discipline, and you cast my words behind you. 18 If you see a thief, you are pleased with him, and you keep company with adulterers. 19 You give your mouth free rein for evil, and your tongue frames deceit. 20 You sit and speak against your brother; you slander your own mother's son. 21 These things you have done, and I have been silent; you thought that I was one like yourself. But now I rebuke you and lay the charge before you. 22 Mark this, then, you who forget God, lest I tear you apart, and there be none to deliver! 23 *The one who offers thanksgiving as his sacrifice glorifies me;* to one who orders his way rightly I will show the salvation of God!" (ESV)

Our words. No one, including God, likes hypocrites. In this psalm, the people are hypocritical because they worship God with sacrifices (v. 8) but they deceive and slander others (vv. 19-20). God hates such hypocrisy and rebukes "those who forget God" (v. 22) and their sinful speech. This is certainly not a unique situation because centuries later, James identifies the same issue among Jesus' followers. They praise God but curse others (Jas 3:9-10). A new attitude of giving thanks to the Lord (v. 23a) must replace their hate for others. Thomas Watson underlines the importance of sincere thanksgiving. He states, "Thanksgiving is a God exalting work. Though nothing can add the least cubit to God's essential glory, yet praise exalts him in the eyes of others. Praise is a setting forth of God's honour, a lifting up of his name, a displaying the trophy of his goodness, a proclaiming his excellency, a spreading his renown, a breaking open the box of ointment, whereby the sweet savour and perfume of God's name is sent abroad into the world." Because God provides salvation for us (v. 23b), we are "to continually offer to God a sacrifice of praise—the fruit of lips that confess his name" (Heb 13:15).

Prayer. Lord, by your grace, empower me to praise you and to speak well of others. I want my speech to be consistent with my faith so that I may honor you and others. Amen.

April 17   Psalm 51:1–5

1 Have mercy on me, O God, according to your unfailing love; according to your great compassion blot out my transgressions. 2 Wash away all my iniquity and cleanse me from my sin. 3 *For I know my transgressions, and my sin is always before me.* 4 Against you, you only, have I sinned and done what is evil in your sight; so you are right in your verdict and justified when you judge. 5 Surely I was sinful at birth, sinful from the time my mother conceived me. (NIV)

Self-examination. We are not inclined to admit that we sin and therefore, we downplay or deny any wrongful deeds and speech. However, the mark of godliness is not necessarily the number of our sins, but the recognition of those sins which we do commit. The more we grow in intimacy with Christ, the more acutely sensitive we are to those actions and attitudes which offend God (1 Tim 1:15). David, a man after God's heart (1 Sam 13:14), addresses his sins by acknowledging and confessing them before the Lord (v. 3). Nathanael Hardy offers us his insight into recognizing sin. He states, "There cannot be *agnitio* [acknowledgement] if there be not *cognitio peccati* [knowledge of sin], and acknowledging, unless there precede a knowledge of sin. David puts them together. If our sins be not before us, how can we set them before God?" Hardy offers practical advice, "And therefore, to the right exercise of this duty, there is required a previous examination of our hearts, inspection into our lives, that we may be enabled to see our sins. He that has not yet asked himself that question, 'What have I done?' can never make the confession, thus and thus have I done; and in this respect I would, though not require, yet advise it as a pious and prudent practice, and that which I doubt not but many Christians have found benefit by, to keep a constant daily catalogue, as of mercies received, so of sins committed." We do well to search our lives for sins we have committed and to confess them to the Lord who forgives.

Prayer. Holy Spirit, I ask you to reveal my sins to me so that I may willingly acknowledge and confess them to you. Thank you for forgiving me so that I can grow in my relationship with you. Amen.

April 18　　　　　　　　Psalm 51:6–9

6 Yet you desired faithfulness even in the womb; you taught me wisdom in that secret place. 7 Cleanse me with hyssop, and I will be clean; wash me, and *I will be whiter than snow.* 8 Let me hear joy and gladness; let the bones you have crushed rejoice. 9 Hide your face from my sins and blot out all my iniquity. (NIV)

Spiritual cleansing. After his confessing his sin, David asks God for a spiritual cleansing and then he will be "clean" and "whiter than snow" (v. 7). Richard Baker asks, "But how is this possible? All the dyers on earth cannot dye a red into a white; and how, then, is it possible that my sins which are as red as scarlet should ever be made as white as snow?" It is certainly "no work of human art," and therefore, he says, "It must be only his [God's] doing" whose grace "can bring not only the redness of scarlet sins, but even the blackness of deadly sins, into its native purity and whiteness again." Baker raises another question, "What need is there of so great a whiteness, as to be 'whiter than snow?'" He reasons that a white wall is not white on the exterior and dirty within the paint, but it is "white within and without, throughout and all over." Yet, a layer of whiteness is insufficient, Baker continues, for Gehazi who sinned and "went from Elisha a leper as white as snow" (2 Kgs 5:27) shows us that we must be "whiter than snow" (v. 7). Baker explains what this whiteness signifies to us, "Such a whiteness it is that God's washing works upon us, makes within us; for no snow is so white in the eyes of men as a soul cleansed from sin is in the sight of God. And yet, a whiter whiteness than this too; for being purged from sin we shall put on the whiter robe; and this is a whiteness as much whiter than snow as angelical whiteness is more than elemental." God's Spirit transforms us, within and without, so that we can gradually become more like Jesus.

Prayer. Lord, I recognize those areas in my life that need changing. I ask you to purify my thoughts, attitudes, speech, and behavior. I am thankful that your Holy Spirit works to align my nature with your will for me. Amen.

April 19 — Psalm 51:10–12

10 Create in me a clean heart, O God. Renew a loyal spirit within me. 11 Do not banish me from your presence, and don't take your Holy Spirit from me. 12 *Restore to me the joy of your salvation and make me willing to obey you.* (NLT)

A joyful relationship. After his painful experience and strained relationship with God, David needs to take steps to experience restoration with the Lord. Working through the process of confession of sin and repentance, he experiences God's forgiveness and now he longs to enjoy the fruit of forgiveness. With a renewed desire to be in God's presence (v. 11), he asks the Lord to restore joy in his life once again (v. 12a). When we find ourselves making the same request to God, Richard Baker raises questions we should ask ourselves in order to know our motivation. Constructive self-examination questions should include: "Why am I so earnest for restoring? What good will restoring do [for] me?" Having answered these questions, we must further ask ourselves, "How shall I more keep [the joy of my salvation] being restored?" In other words, we must consider how we sustain joyful restoration with the Lord. One might assume seeking joy is the answer. However, Baker raises a concern, "And if I so enjoy [restoration], as still to fear to lose it, what joy can there be in such enjoying?" Feeling exhilarating joy is not enough to maintain a restored relationship with the Lord. For answer to his final question, Baker turns our attention to David's words, "make me willing to obey you" (v. 12b). David is not only asking for God to restore joy to his life, but he also asking God to work in his life so that, in Baker's words, "by [God's] restoring [he] may enjoy [restoration] entirely . . . [he] may enjoy it securely." Sustained joyful restoration cannot rest on an emotional experience, but on God's continual sanctifying work within us.

Prayer. Father, I admit that oftentimes I lack joy in my relationship with you. I know that I have created my own distance from you because of my selfish disobedience. I want to be joyfully restored to you, not only for today but for the long term. Holy Spirit, work in my life so that I may willingly obey you with joy. Amen.

April 20   Psalm 51:13-19

13 Then I will teach wrongdoers Your ways, and sinners will be converted to You. 14 Save me from the guilt of bloodshed, God, the God of my salvation; then my tongue will joyfully sing of Your righteousness. 15 Lord, open my lips, so that my mouth may declare Your praise. 16 For You do not delight in sacrifice, otherwise I would give it; You do not take pleasure in burnt offering. 17 *The sacrifices of God are a broken spirit; a broken and a contrite heart, God, You will not despise.* 18 By Your favor do good to Zion; build the walls of Jerusalem. 19 Then You will delight in righteous sacrifices, in burnt offering and whole burnt offering; then bulls will be offered on Your altar. (NASB)

Contrite hearts. Although God demanded the sacrifice of animals without defects (Lev 22:19-20), he does not expect us to be perfect. God is delighted when we offer ourselves to him as broken and contrite individuals (v. 17). Yet Richard Baker observes that, because we prefer doing religious activities rather than giving God our hearts, contrition is difficult. However, he reasons that God receives contrite hearts because "he cares for [them]; and if [they] be broken, and offered up by penitence and contrition [they are] the only sacrifice that now he delights in." Considering the Jewish sacrificial requirements, Baker asks, "But can we think God to be so indifferent that he will accept of a broken heart? Is a thing that is broken good for anything? Can we drink in a broken glass? Or can we lean upon a broken staff?" We may ask: Is a broken heart worthless to God? Baker answers, "But though other things may be the worse for breaking, yet a heart is never at the best till it be broken; for till it be broken we cannot see what is in it; till it be broken, it cannot send forth its sweetest odour; and therefore, though God loves a whole heart in affection, yet he loves a broken heart in sacrifice." Since the Lord desires our wholehearted affection for him, he allows our hearts to be broken in order that we may love him more fully.

Prayer. Father, accept my broken heart so that I may love you with my whole heart. Amen.

April 21 — Psalm 52:1–5

1 Why do you boast of evil, O mighty man? The steadfast love of God endures all the day. 2 Your tongue plots destruction, like a sharp razor, you worker of deceit. 3 You love evil more than good, and lying more than speaking what is right. Selah 4 You love all words that devour, O deceitful tongue. 5 *But God will break you down forever;* he will snatch and tear you from your tent; he will uproot you from the land of the living. *Selah* (ESV)

Adversity. The psalm's title, "When Doeg, the Edomite, came and told Saul, 'David has come to the house of Ahimelech,'" provides the historical background. Fleeing from king Saul, David asks Ahimelech for provisions and a sword (1 Sam 21:5–6, 8–9). Doeg, overhearing the conversation, informs Saul about David's request for a sword to presumably kill Saul (22:9–10). In a rage, Saul orders Doeg to kill Ahimelech and his family of priests—a total of eighty-five people (22:18). This event is a painful and bitter experience for David because he feels responsible for this mass murder tragedy (22:22). Now, in Psalm 52:1–4, David rebukes Doeg for his betrayal of Ahimelech with deceitful and destructive words expressed to Saul. David knows that the Almighty God will deal with Doeg, the "mighty man" (vv. 1, 5). John Trapp expands verse 5 with his paraphrase, "As you have destroyed the Lord's priests, and their whole city, razing and harassing it; so God will demolish and destroy you utterly, as a house pulled down to the ground, so that one stone is not left upon another (Lev 14:45); so shall God pull down Doeg from that high preferment, which he by sycophancy [mean tale-bearing] has got at court." When individuals malign us, the psalmist's words serve as a reminder to trust in God who opposes evil. We can trust God's power to confront the worst evil perpetrated in the world. Our responsibility is not to seek revenge but to wait patiently for God to act and remain confident by trusting in God's continual "steadfast love" (v. 1b).

Prayer. Lord, forgive me when I want to retaliate against those who have deeply hurt me. Grant me the patience to wait on you to act, and the confidence to trust in your abiding love for me. Amen.

April 22   Psalm 52:6–9

6 The righteous shall see and fear, and shall laugh at him, saying, 7 *"See the man who would not make God his refuge, but trusted in the abundance of his riches and sought refuge in his own destruction!"* 8 *But I am like a green olive tree in the house of God. I trust in the steadfast love of God forever and ever.* 9 I will thank you forever, because you have done it. I will wait for your name, for it is good, in the presence of the godly. (ESV)

Thriving in adversity. The psalmist paints a stark contrast between two groups (vv. 7–8). William Gurnall describes the first group (v. 7) who profess faith in God but experience "little growth in love to God, humility, heavenly mindedness, mortification." Telling them that it is "worth the digging to see what lies at the root of [their] profession," Gurnall determines a "legal influence" has led these people to maintain a moralistic standard which places high hopes on actions. Their approach to the Christian life has resulted in "so much dead earth, which must be thrown out." Instead of attempting to live by legal principles, Gurnall instructs them to live by "gospel principles" which will allow them to experience God's grace. The second group (v. 8), represented by David, "gives an account how he came to stand and flourish when some that were rich and mighty, on a sudden withered and came to nothing." David trusted in the abundance of God's "steadfast love" rather than the "abundance" of personal wealth. In contrast to the ungodly, David thrived like an olive tree in adversity. Gurnall applies today's Scripture passage for us, "While others trust in the riches of their own righteousness and services, and make not Christ their strength, you do renounce all, and trust in the mercy of God in Christ, and you shall be like a green olive when they fade and wither."

Prayer. Father, living by legalistic standards with its external focus has misled me to disregard my inner life. I want to live in your continual love which allows me to change inwardly and outwardly so that I may be fruitful for your purposes. Help me, with your power and love, to live vibrantly for you and others. Amen.

April 23 — Psalm 53

1 The fool says in his heart, "There is no God." They are corrupt, doing abominable iniquity; there is none who does good. 2 God looks down from heaven on the children of man to see if there are any who understand, who seek after God. 3 They have all fallen away; together they have become corrupt; there is none who does good, not even one. 4 *Have those who work evil no knowledge, who eat up my people as they eat bread, and do not call upon God?* 5 There they are, in great terror, where there is no terror! For God scatters the bones of him who encamps against you; you put them to shame, for God has rejected them. 6 Oh, that salvation for Israel would come out of Zion! When God restores the fortunes of his people, let Jacob rejoice, let Israel be glad. (ESV)

Our conscience. David asks whether those who commit evil have any knowledge of what they are doing (v. 4). In response, Thomas Goodwin, in agreement with biblical (Rom 2:15) and other Puritans' teaching, argues that these violent perpetrators have a conscience. He states, "Conscience is a means to curb and restrain, control and rebuke corrupt nature, and the swelling forms of it. It is not there as a native inhabitant, but as a garrison planted in a rebellious town by the great Governor [God] of the world, to keep the rebellion of the inhabitants within compass, who else would break forth into present confusion." Goodwin is suggesting that if it were not for one's conscience, evil would be more rampant in society. In response to David's question about whether these people possess knowledge (v. 4), Goodwin suggests that they do know and therefore they live with great "terror" or fear (v. 5). He comments, "God placed this[conscience] there to overcome them with fear; and by that to restrain them from many outrages against God's people, whom in their desires, and sometimes practice, they eat up as bread. Therefore, this knowledge is put in as a bridle to corrupt nature." Without people's consciences and their fear of God there would be no restraints on cruelty.

Prayer. Lord, thank you for weaving the conscience into the fabric of each person. I want to be more aware of my conscience so that I may be more sensitive to temptations to sin, resisting them and obeying you. Amen.

April 24   Psalm 54

1 Save me, God, by Your name, and vindicate me by Your power. 2 Hear my prayer, God; listen to the words of my mouth. 3 For strangers have risen against me and violent men have sought my life; they have not set God before them. *Selah* 4 *Behold, God is my helper*; the Lord is the sustainer of my soul. 5 He will pay back the evil to my enemies; destroy them in Your faithfulness. 6 Willingly I will sacrifice to You; I will praise Your name, LORD, for it is good. 7 For He has saved me from all trouble, and my eye has looked with satisfaction upon my enemies. (NASB)

God our helper. When our circumstances overwhelm us, it is common to panic and create plans to alleviate our fears. In this psalm, once again, David faces ruthless enemies who seek to kill him (v. 3a). In response to this antagonism, he turns to God knowing that he will listen and vindicate him (vv. 1–2). He prays with confidence because he knows that "God is my helper" (v. 4). David Dickson suggests three specific ways that the Lord helps the psalmist. First, he says, "Fervent prayer has readily a swift answer, and sometimes wonderfully swift, even before a man [has] ended speech, as here David finds in experience." Second, he states, "The sight of faith is very clear and piercing through all clouds when God holds forth the light of his Spirit unto it, it can demonstrate God present in an instant; ready to help in greatest straits." Finally, Dickson notes, "There is more joy in God's felt presence than grief in felt trouble. [God is] more comfortable to David than his friends' unkindness, and strangers' malice [is] grievous." When we go through deep waters, the Lord is our helper as well. Sometimes God immediately answers our prayers to meet our crisis, perhaps when we may need to ask God for wisdom to know how to respond to a conflict. The Lord makes his presence known to us amid the trial we are in. Finally, God grants us a profound comfort which allows us to sing and worship God during trials (Acts 5:41; 16:5).

Prayer. Almighty Lord, forgive me for not trusting in you and thank you for the supernatural ways you meet me in my times of need. You are my helper! Amen.

April 25 — Psalm 55:1–8

1 Listen to my prayer, God; and do not hide Yourself from my pleading. 2 Give Your attention to me and answer me; I am restless in my complaint and severely distracted, 3 because of the voice of the enemy, because of the pressure of the wicked; for they bring down trouble upon me and in anger they hold a grudge against me. 4 My heart is in anguish within me, and the terrors of death have fallen upon me. 5 *Fear and trembling come upon me, and horror has overwhelmed me.* 6 I said, "Oh, that I had wings like a dove! I would fly away and be at rest. 7 Behold, I would flee far away, I would spend my nights in the wilderness. Selah 8 I would hurry to my place of refuge from the stormy wind and heavy gale." (NASB)

Facing fears. Few of us are immune from fear's stranglehold. The psalmist experiences fear (v. 5) because his angry and vindictive enemies cause him trouble and plan his death. Is it any wonder David, the man of God, trembles with fear? Though fear is a natural response to circumstances, we may wonder about fear's presence with those who follow the Lord. Although Scripture commands us 365 times to "Fear not," we feel fearful and guilty. How do we manage this emotion of fear? We can consider escaping from our frightful circumstances as David did (vv. 6–8), or we can accept our fear as a means of spiritual growth. David Dickson offers wise counsel, "In this pitiful condition of mind, learn, that it is not a thing inconsistent with godliness to be much moved with fear in time of danger; natural affections are not taken away in conversion, but sanctified and moderated." We should not expect that our fears will vanish when we become Jesus' followers. As we grow spiritually in the process of sanctification, we learn that we can go to God knowing that he will hear us (vv. 1–2) and give us confident hope amid our fears.

Prayer. Lord, I am a fearful person. Although I wish my fears would disappear, I want to draw closer to you because of my fears. Amen.

April 26   Psalm 55:9–19

9 Confuse them, Lord, divide their tongues, for I have seen violence and strife in the city. 10 Day and night they go around her upon her walls, and evil and harm are in her midst. 11 Destruction is in her midst; oppression and deceit do not depart from her streets. 12 For it is not an enemy who taunts me, then I could endure it; nor is it one who hates me who has exalted himself against me, then I could hide myself from him. 13 But it is you, a man my equal, my companion and my confidant; 14 we who had sweet fellowship together, walked in the house of God among the commotion. 15 May death come deceitfully upon them; may they go down alive to Sheol, for evil is in their dwelling, in their midst. 16 As for me, I shall call upon God, and the LORD will save me. 17 Evening and morning and at noon, I will complain and moan, and He will hear my voice. 18 *He will redeem my soul in peace from the battle which is against me, for they are many who are aggressive toward me.* 19 God will hear and humiliate them—even the one who sits enthroned from ancient times—*Selah*—with whom there is no change, and who do not fear God. (NASB)

Deliverance. With the threat of death about him, David calls on God to save him (vv. 16–17). As a veteran of many afflictions, he asks God to rescue him. When David prays for help, God answers and gives him assurance of God's power to deliver him from his enemies. Many years later, the apostle Paul also asks God for deliverance from a desperate situation and God delivers him (2 Cor 1:11). David Dickson assures us, "In the midst of war the Lord can keep a man as safe as in the time of peace, and in extreme perils preserve him from danger. He that depends upon God in the time of trouble, albeit he had a host against him, yet has he more with him when God is with him, than can be against him." Then we experience "peace" or *shalom* in our lives (v. 18).

Prayer. Lord, thank you for being with me in the most challenging times because I know that I can rely on your resources. Amen.

April 27   Psalm 55:20-23

20 My companion attacks his friends; he violates his covenant. 21 *His talk is smooth as butter, yet war is in his heart; his words are more soothing than oil, yet they are drawn swords.* 22 Cast your cares on the LORD and he will sustain you; he will never let the righteous be shaken. 23 But you, God, will bring down the wicked into the pit of decay; the bloodthirsty and deceitful will not live out half their days. But as for me, I trust in you. (NIV)

Betrayal. The writer describes a friend who has betrayed him by attacking and breaking the covenant previously made between these two close companions (v. 20). The former friend's attack is not vicious but "smooth as butter" or oil (v. 21). John Bunyan describes a similar personal experience, "Well, when I came to the justice again, there was Mr. Foster, of Bedford, who coming out of another room, and seeing me by the light of the candle, for it was dark night when I came thither, he said unto me, 'Who is there? John Bunyan?' with much seeming affection, as if he would have leaped in my neck and kissed me, (a right Judas), which made me somewhat wonder that such a man as he, with whom I had so little acquaintance, and, besides, that had ever been a close opposer of the ways of God, should carry himself so full of love to me, but afterwards when I saw what he did, it caused me to remember, 'Their tongues were softer than oil, yet were they drawn swords.'" How should we respond when betrayals have deeply hurt us? The psalmist encourages us to cast our cares on the Lord because he will sustain us when someone has betrayed us (v. 22). We can take any of our concerns to the Lord because he cares for us (1 Pet 5:7).

Prayer. Heavenly Father, you know that close friends have betrayed and have deeply hurt me. Memories are so painful! However, your faithful love for me overwhelms me. I come to you with my pain, in full confidence knowing that you are always my closest friend. Help me to be a faithful friend to others because I do not want to inflict such pain on them. Amen.

April 28 — Psalm 56:1-6

1 Be merciful to me, my God, for my enemies are in hot pursuit; all day long they press their attack. 2 My adversaries pursue me all day long; in their pride many are attacking me. 3 *When I am afraid, I put my trust in you.* 4 In God, whose word I praise—in God I trust and am not afraid. What can mere mortals do to me? 5 All day long they twist my words; all their schemes are for my ruin. 6 They conspire, they lurk, they watch my steps, hoping to take my life. (NIV)

From fear to trust. The psalm's title informs us that David flees Saul to the Philistine city of Gath (1 Sam 21:10-15). When Gath's leader speaks, David becomes very afraid (v. 12). He has escaped from Saul who tried to kill him and now he ends up in another dangerous situation (56:5-6). It is no wonder David experiences fear (vs. 3a; 55:5). When we run into fearful situations, God longs for us to learn to trust him (v. 3b). John Bunyan comments on the importance of faith, "There is nothing like faith to help at a pinch; faith dissolves doubts as the sun drives away the mists. And that you may not be put out, know that your time for believing is always. There are times when some graces may be out of use, but there is no time wherein faith can be said to be so. Wherefore faith must be always in exercise. Faith is the eye, is the mouth, is the hand, and one of these is of use all the day long. Faith is to see, to receive, to work, or to eat; and a Christian should be seeing or receiving, or working, or feeding all day long. Let it rain, let it blow, let it thunder, let it lighten, a Christian must still believe." Bunyan reminds us that we need to trust in the Lord throughout the day in every sphere of life. When we place our confidence in God during the difficult circumstances, we can come to the point when we do not fear (v. 4).

Prayer. Lord, there are various areas of life which cause me to fear. Teach me to trust in you throughout the day so that fear does not have to control me. Amen.

April 29   Psalm 56:7–13

7 For their crime will they escape? In wrath cast down the peoples, O God! 8 You have kept count of my tossings; put my tears in your bottle. Are they not in your book? 9 Then my enemies will turn back in the day when I call. This I know, that God is for me. 10 *In God, whose word I praise, in the* Lord, *whose word I praise,* 11 in God I trust; I shall not be afraid. What can man do to me? 12 I must perform my vows to you, O God; I will render thank offerings to you. 13 For you have delivered my soul from death, yes, my feet from falling, that I may walk before God in the light of life. (ESV)

Divine names. Throughout the Psalter, the writers employ numerous names to God in order to describe his character. Some of the commonly used Hebrew names include: *Adonai* (Lord), *Elyon* (Most High), *Shaddai* (Most High), and *Sabaoth* (Almighty). Two of the most frequently used names include: *Elohim* (365 times), and *Yahweh* or Jehovah (almost 700 times). Both names are intentionally mentioned in verse 10. "God" is *Elohim*, and "Lord" is *Yahweh*. Stephen Charnock observes, "The first word, *Elohim*, is a name belonging to God as a judge, the second word, *Jehovah*, is a name of mercy." Knowing all that David experiences at the hands of his enemies, it is not surprising that he cries out to God to judge them. He also wants *Jehovah* or *Yahweh* (Lord) to extend lovingkindness to himself. He knows that God keeps a record of his misery by catching his tears in a bottle (v. 8). The longed-for divine compassion, rooted in the name *Yahweh*, defines God's faithful covenant relationship between him and his people. Twice in Psalm 56, David praises God's word and declares his trust in God (vv. 4, 10). Charnock concludes, "I will praise God whether he deal with me in a way of justice or in a way of mercy, when he has thunder in his voice, as well as when he has honey under his tongue. Oh, how should we praise God, and pleasure ourselves by such a frame!"

Prayer. Lord, I am thankful that your character is so multi-dimensional that I can count on you to respond to the numerous ways I need you in my life. Amen.

April 30   Psalm 57:1-6

1 *Have mercy on me, O God, have mercy! I look to you for protection. I will hide beneath the shadow of your wings until the danger passes by.* 2 *I cry out to God Most High, to God who will fulfill his purpose for me.* 3 *He will send help from heaven to rescue me, disgracing those who hound me. My God will send forth his unfailing love and faithfulness.* 4 *I am surrounded by fierce lions who greedily devour human prey—whose teeth pierce like spears and arrows, and whose tongues cut like swords.* 5 *Be exalted, O God, above the highest heavens! May your glory shine over all the earth.* 6 *My enemies have set a trap for me. I am weary from distress. They have dug a deep pit in my path, but they themselves have fallen into it.* (NLT)

God's mercy. We fully appreciate God's vast mercy when we are in despair. After fleeing from Saul, David is now in a cave (according to the psalm's title) but still surrounded by his enemies (v. 4). Describing David's dangerous situation in verse 1, John Flavel comments, "This excellent Psalm was composed by David when there was enough to discompose the best man in the world. The repetition [for mercy] notes both the extremity of the danger, and the ardency of the supplicant. Mercy! Mercy! Nothing but mercy, and that exerting itself in any extraordinary way, can now save him from ruin. The arguments he pleads for obtaining mercy in this distress are very considerable." First, Flavel states that David "pleads his reliance upon God as an argument to move mercy." Looking to God for protection, he demonstrates "his trust and dependence upon God, though it be not argumentative in respect of the dignity of the act; yet it is so in respect both of the nature of the object, a compassionate God who will not expose any that take shelter under his wings, and in respect of the promise, whereby protection is assured to them that fly to him for sanctuary." Second, David "pleads former experiences of his help in past distresses, as an argument encouraging hope under the present strait." Our trust in the Lord grows as we see his past faithfulness to us.

Prayer. Lord, thank you for the times you have shown me your mercy which have encouraged me. I am incredibly grateful for your protection and care for me. Amen.

May 1 — Psalm 57:7–11

7 My heart is confident in you, O God; my heart is confident. No wonder I can sing your praises! 8 Wake up, my heart! Wake up, O lyre and harp! I will wake the dawn with my song. 9 I will thank you, Lord, among all the people. I will sing your praises among the nations.10 For your unfailing love is as high as the heavens. Your faithfulness reaches to the clouds. 11Be exalted, O God, above the highest heavens. May your glory shine over all the earth. (NLT)

Confidence in the Lord. With a dependence on God's mercy, David moves from petition (vv. 1–2) to twice declaring his confidence in the Lord (v. 7). His confidence is steadfast and calm, knowing God will rescue him (vv. 3, 6b). Richard Gilpin reflects on the importance of rock-solid confidence if we expect to serve the Lord. He comments, "Fitness for duty lies in the orderly temper of body and mind, making a man willing to undertake, and able to finish his work with comfortable satisfaction. If either the body or mind be distempered [unsettled], a man is unfit for such an undertaking; both must be in a suitable frame, like a well-tuned instrument, else there will be no melody: hence when David prepares himself for praises and worship, he tells us 'his heart [is] ready and fixed' (v. 7 KJV). His tongue [is] ready also (Ps 45:1), as [is] his hand with psaltery and harp; all these [are] awakened into a suitable posture." How can we know if we or others are prepared to serve the Lord in the face of adversities? Gilpin provides three characteristics. The first is an "alacrity to undertake a duty." There is an enthusiastic willingness to serve. The second characteristic is a certain "activity in the prosecution." The activity of turning to God, as the psalmist does, reveals trust in Him. The final characteristic is "satisfaction afterward." Like David, we praise God for how he helps us, and we exalt and glorify him. Our greatest satisfaction is to know that God's glory is known around the world (vv. 5, 11).

Prayer. Lord, forgive me for my self-assurance. Instead, I want to reflect on what you have already done in my life, and I want to grow in my confidence of who you are. Amen.

May 2 — Psalm 58:1–5

1 Do ye indeed speak righteousness, O congregation? Do ye judge uprightly, O ye sons of men? 2 *Yea, in heart ye work wickedness; ye weigh the violence of your hands in the earth.* 3 The wicked are estranged from the womb: they go astray as soon as they be born, speaking lies. 4 Their poison is like the poison of a serpent: they are like the deaf adder that stoppeth her ear; 5 Which will not hearken to the voice of charmers, charming never so wisely. (KJV)

The workings of evil. This psalm confronts those who treat others unjustly. Joseph Caryl reiterates David's claim that evil schemes originate in the heart (v. 2). He asserts, "The heart is a shop within, an underground shop; there they [do] closely contrive, forge, and hammer out their wicked purposes, and fit them into actions." The wicked are like merchants who "weigh" their actions. That is, "they do not oppress grossly, but with a kind of exactness and skill, they sit down and consider what and how much violence they may use in such a case, or how much such a person may endure, or such a season may bear. They are wiser than to do all at once, or all to one, lest they spoil all. They weigh what they do, though what they do be so bad that it will hold no weight when God comes to weigh it." Caryl goes on to detail when this evil begins. He notes that these evil people do not develop their "skill" later in life. Rather, they serve as apprentices in evil and they bind themselves "to the trade very early" in their lives. David tells us that their evil begins as soon as they are babbling as infants; they are born "estranged" and "go astray" from birth (v. 3). Caryl states that their actions occur "both by nature and by early practice; they lose no time, they go to it young, even 'as soon as they are born,' as soon as they are fit for any use, or to do anything, they are using and setting themselves to do wickedly." The psalmist's teaching on humanity's sinful depravity is buttressed by the apostle Paul (Rom 3:9–20, 23).

Prayer. Father, I readily admit that I am sinful, and I desperately need your Spirit to deliver me from the power of sin. I want my life to honor you! Amen.

May 3   Psalm 58:6–11

6 Break off their fangs, O God! Smash the jaws of these lions, O Lord! 7 May they disappear like water into thirsty ground. Make their weapons useless in their hands. 8 May they be like snails that dissolve into slime, like a stillborn child who will never see the sun. 9 God will sweep them away, both young and old, faster than a pot heats over burning thorns. 10 *The godly will rejoice when they see injustice avenged. They will wash their feet in the blood of the wicked.* 11 Then at last everyone will say, "There truly is a reward for those who live for God; surely there is a God who judges justly here on earth." (NLT)

Responding to evil. After describing evil men, David asks God to destroy them. What may startle us is David's saying that "the godly will rejoice when they see injustice avenged" (v. 10). While it initially seems that the righteous are gloating over their enemies, Joseph Caryl clarifies the reason for their response, "Not that [they] shall be glad of the vengeance purely as it is a hurt, or a suffering to the creature, but the righteous shall be glad when they sees the vengeance of God, as it is a fulfilling of the threatening of God against the sin of man, and so evidence of [their] own holiness." The people do not focus on themselves but instead, they praise a holy God who opposes all forms of evil. William Greenhill, offers a similar rationale, citing two reasons for people's rejoicing. He notes, "When angels execute God's judgments upon sinners, the saints see much in it; they see matter of fear and praise; of fear, in that God's power, wrath, and hatred are manifested in them against sin and sinners; of praise, in that themselves are delivered and justice performed. When the wicked are taken away by a divine stroke, by the hand of justice, and God has the glory of his justice, the righteous rejoice at it." While we may not use the language of this psalm, it teaches us to pray against evil by asking God to defeat wickedness for the sake of his glory.

Prayer. Lord, knowing that evil dulls my spiritual sensitivity, arouse within me a hatred of sin so that I plead with you to vanquish evil for the sake of your powerful name. Amen.

May 4 — Psalm 59:1-5

1 Deliver me from my enemies, O my God; defend me from those who rise up against me. 2 Deliver me from the workers of iniquity and save me from bloodthirsty men. 3 For look, they lie in wait for my life; The mighty gather against me not for my transgression nor for my sin, O LORD. 4 They run and prepare themselves through no fault of mine. Awake to help me and behold! 5 You therefore, O LORD God of hosts, the God of Israel, awake to punish all the nations; Do not be merciful to any wicked transgressors. Selah (NKJV)

Unfair treatment. Most people have experienced others' unfair mistreatment. In this psalm, David's enemies are abusing him. From the psalm's preface title, we learn that Saul's men pursue David to his house and threaten to kill him in the morning (1 Sam 19:11). David pleads to God that he is innocent of any wrongdoing to them. For times when people mistreat us, Matthew Henry offers pastoral counsel. First, he says, "The innocency of the godly will not secure them from the malignity of the wicked. Those that are harmless like doves, yet for Christ's sake are hated of all men, as if they were noxious like serpents, and obnoxious accordingly." Because Jesus himself prepared his disciples for hostility (John 15:18–21), Henry reminds us that we can also expect to suffer as followers of Jesus. He continues with an additional pastoral insight, "Though our innocency will not secure us from troubles, yet it will greatly support and comfort us under our troubles. The testimony of our conscience for us, that we have behaved ourselves well toward those that have behaved themselves ill towards us, will be very much our rejoicing in the day of evil. If we are conscious to ourselves of our innocency, we may with humble confidence appeal to God and beg of him to plead our injured cause which he will do in due time." Rather than becoming resentful and angry at God, we can find comfort with a conscience free of any wrongdoing which gives us the freedom to ask God to intervene on our behalf.

Prayer. Father, it is hard when others malign me because I am following you. Forgive me when I feel like verbally lashing out. I need your wisdom to respond in ways which will honor you. Amen.

May 5   Psalm 59:6–13

6 Each evening they come back, howling like dogs and prowling about the city. 7 There they are, bellowing with their mouths with swords in their lips—for "Who," they think, "will hear us?" 8 But you, O LORD, laugh at them; *you hold all the nations in derision.* 9 *O my Strength, I will watch for you, for you, O God, are my fortress.* 10 My God in his steadfast love will meet me; God will let me look in triumph on my enemies. 11 Kill them not, lest my people forget; make them totter by your power and bring them down, O LORD, our shield! 12 For the sin of their mouths, the words of their lips, let them be trapped in their pride. For the cursing and lies that they utter, 13 consume them in wrath; consume them till they are no more that they may know that God rules over Jacob to the ends of the earth. *Selah* (ESV)

A sovereign God. When bleak issues such as poor health, relational hatred, or economic hardships confront us, we need good theology to help us. David has good reason to fear Saul and his allies who hate him, yet he focuses on God's sovereignty over the nations (v. 8b) to help him trust God. In the words of John Calvin*, while these nations "[may]equal the whole world in numbers, they [will] prove a mere mockery with all their influence and resources . . . One thing is obvious, that David ridicules the vain boasting of his enemies, who [think] no undertaking too great to be accomplished by their numbers." David sees God as far superior to the nations. He affirms that God is his strength and fortress (vv. 9, 17). Calvin comments, "However intemperately Saul [may] boast of his strength, he [David] [will] rest satisfied in the assurance that there is a secret divine providence restraining his actions. We must learn to view all men as subordinated in this manner, and to conceive of their strength and their enterprises as depending upon the sovereign will of God."

Prayer. Lord, forgive me when I become fearful because of the actions of others. I need to pay more attention to your control and power over all situations. Then I can experience more of your peace in a turbulent world. Amen.

May 6   Psalm 59:14-17

14 *Each evening they come back, howling like dogs and prowling about the city.* 15 *They wander about for food and growl if they do not get their fill.* 16 *But I will sing of your strength; I will sing aloud of your steadfast love in the morning. For you have been to me a fortress and a refuge in the day of my distress.* 17 *O my Strength, I will sing praises to you, for you, O God, are my fortress, the God who shows me steadfast love.* (ESV)

Empty lives. In these verses, David describes his hateful enemies as dogs (vv. 6, 16). During the night these scavengers roam, devouring what they can and then vomiting destruction (vv. 7, 14). And when they cannot find anything to eat, they "growl" (v. 15). This growling and "howling" (v. 14) comes from individuals, Matthew Henry observes, whose "hearts are hardened when they are in trouble." For them, their god is "their belly, [and] if that be not filled and its appetites gratified, [they] fall out both with God and themselves. It is not poverty, but discontent that makes a man unhappy." Nothing in life truly satisfies them for they are inwardly discontented people. Qoheleth, the wise teacher of Ecclesiastes, instructs us about the emptiness experienced by so many in society. He states that people can devour pleasures, social advancement, wealth, and so much more and still inwardly starve. Why? While all these areas may appear to satisfy the human appetite, they are all vanity or emptiness. To those who are hungry in their souls, he tells them to "stand in awe of God" (Eccl 5:7b). People remain dissatisfied with what they taste because, in Augustine's words, their "hearts are restless until they find their rest in God." Then we can begin to experience true contentment which makes a significant difference. Matthew Henry notes, "A contented man, if he has not what he would have, yet does not grudge, does not quarrel with providence, nor fret within himself." God fills our hungry souls with his presence, through the Holy Spirit, and then we are truly satisfied.

Prayer. Father, I have tasted so much in life, but I am still inwardly hungry. Come into my whole being so that I may be filled with all that you offer me, and I will be satisfied. Amen.

May 7 — Psalm 60:1-4

1 God, you have rejected us. You have broken us; You have been angry; restore us! 2 You have made the land quake, You have split it open; heal its cracks, for it sways. 3 You have made Your people experience hardship; You have given us wine to drink that makes us stagger. 4 *You have given a banner to those who fear You, that it may be displayed because of the truth. Selah* (NASB)

Despair. When circumstances overwhelm us, we may feel that God has let us down. These experiences are not unique to us as we observe in the opening of this psalm. Many Bible versions include a psalm's title which provides us with the historical setting. In this case, the title refers to David and his men, far from home, who face an alliance of military forces which hope to defeat him and his nation (2 Sam 8:5a, 13). In great distress, David complains that the Lord has rejected and broken his people with hardships. However, the title also indicates that this psalm is a *miktam*, written for our instruction. What do we learn from this section? Verse four teaches that God offers a glimmer of hope in the direst circumstances. Mathew Poole suggests that we can understand the "banner" in three ways. First, the banner refers to "people, who were lately divided and under several banners" and now God has brought them together, "united under one banner." The banner represents the "union" of God's people. Second, the banner refers to "battle." God's people had a banner in opposition to the enemies' banner. In effect, this banner expresses the thought, "You have given us an army and power to oppose our enemies." Third, the banner suggests "triumph." As Poole explains, "We have not lost our banner but gained theirs, and brought it away in triumph" (Ps 20:5). Each of these interpretations offers hope to God's people who wait on him.

Prayer. Lord, when hardships come my way, I feel that you are rejecting me. In those times, I confess that I resent your apparent lack of love and concern for me. Thank you for your truth reminding me of your love and power which gives me the hope of victory in my battles. I know that there is victory through you! Amen.

May 8   Psalm 60:5-12

5 Now rescue your beloved people. Answer and save us by your power. 6 *God has promised this by his holiness:* "I will divide up Shechem with joy. I will measure out the valley of Succoth. 7 Gilead is mine, and Manasseh, too. Ephraim, my helmet, will produce my warriors, and Judah, my scepter, will produce my kings. 8 But Moab, my washbasin, will become my servant, and I will wipe my feet on Edom and shout in triumph over Philistia." 9 Who will bring me into the fortified city? Who will bring me victory over Edom? 10 Have you rejected us, O God? Will you no longer march with our armies? 11 Oh, please help us against our enemies, for all human help is useless. 12 With God's help we will do mighty things, for he will trample down our foes. (NLT)

A plea for help. When our circumstances are out of control, David's words in this section offer wise insights. First, we are God's beloved and cherished children (v. 5a), even when we feel that he has rejected us (v. 1). Second, God has the power to answer our prayers (v. 5b). Nothing is beyond his ability to intervene. Third, God acts out of his holiness (v. 6a). Joseph Caryl explains that God's holiness means that "there is nothing but holiness in his word," nothing but holiness in his promise. Caryl points out that David, having received God's promise (v. 6), "stands assured" that "Shechem and Succoth, Gilead and Manasseh, Ephraim and Judah [will] willingly submit to him and yield obedience; so, also, that Moab, Edom, and Philistia, who [are] his professed enemies, [shall] be subdued to him. He expects to conquer and triumph over them, to put them to the basest offices, as his vassals, because God has decreed and spoken it in his holiness." In our adversities, we do well to remember that God is sovereign, and he will accomplish his purposes, even with those who hurt us.

Prayer. Father, I am thankful that I am your beloved child, and I can rest in your tender but powerful arms. Strengthen my trust in your holy character while I wait on you to act on my behalf. Amen.

May 9 — Psalm 61

1 Hear my cry, O God, listen to my prayer; 2 *from the end of the earth I call to you when my heart is faint.* Lead me to the rock that is higher than I, 3 for you have been my refuge, a strong tower against the enemy. 4 Let me dwell in your tent forever! Let me take refuge under the shelter of your wings! *Selah* 5 For you, O God, have heard my vows; you have given me the heritage of those who fear your name. 6 Prolong the life of the king; may his years endure to all generations! 7 May he be enthroned forever before God; appoint steadfast love and faithfulness to watch over him! 8 So will I ever sing praises to your name, as I perform my vows day after day. (ESV)

All alone. We can feel alone and uncomfortable in distant, unfamiliar places. In pursuit of enemies or on military campaigns, David often finds himself far from home (2 Sam 8:3). In this psalm, David cries to God "from the end of the earth" (v. 2a). Regarding the meaning of this phrase, John Owen proposes that David is speaking "ecclesiastically with reference to the temple of God" located in Jerusalem, the "heart of the land where God manifested and gave tokens of his gracious presence and favour." Owen paraphrases David's thoughts, "I am at the end of the earth; far from any tokens, pledges, or manifestations of the love and favour of God, as well as from outward help and assistance." Removed from the visible symbols of God's presence, he cries out to God. Owen suggests that David's call to God is like a person who cries to one at a distance and is "afraid he will go farther" away. Nevertheless, David expresses a "great work of faith to cry out to God." His faith is rooted in God who is his "rock" and "strong tower" (vv. 2–3). Even when we feel distant from God, we can still find our security in him.

Prayer. Lord, for many reasons, I have felt distant from you, but I am thankful that you have not abandoned me and therefore, you hear my cries. My security rests in you. Amen.

May 10 — Psalm 62:1-4

1 Truly my soul finds rest in God; my salvation comes from him.
2 Truly he is my rock and my salvation; he is my fortress, I will never be shaken. 3 How long will you assault me? Would all of you throw me down—this leaning wall, this tottering fence? 4 Surely they intend to topple me from my lofty place; they take delight in lies. With their mouths they bless, but in their hearts they curse. (NIV)

Waiting on God. When adversity hits us, we may react by taking matters into our own hands. It's not uncommon to escape, lash out at others, or seek solutions which end up being counterproductive. Familiar with adversity, David instructs us to find "rest in God" during hardships (v. 1). William Gurnall indicates that this phrase, in Hebrew, means that we are to be "silent" before God. He expands this thought, "Indeed, waiting on God for deliverance, in an afflicted state, consists much in a holy silence. It is a great mercy, in an affliction, to have our bodily senses, so as not to lie raving, but still and quiet, much more to have the heart silent and patient." Developing holy silence in the heart before God should be our priority. The heart's quietness is crucial because, as Gurnall reminds us, "We find the heart is as soon heated into a distemper [unsettled state] as the head." Using the analogy of firing a cannon and then cooling it down, Gurnall explains that hope "cools the spirit and makes it meeker" and prevents the heart from breaking out into unsettled "thoughts or words against God." Being silent before God is so important that David reminds us to do the same. Ultimately, being silent before God requires us to rest in God's character. In the midst of chaos, he is our rock and fortress, providing us with the necessary stability in turbulent times (v. 2).

Prayer. Lord, you know how my mind spins and churns in demanding situations. Forgive me for constantly trying to figure out my responses before coming to you. I want to replace my unsettled heart with holy silence. Help me to truly wait on you by depending on your rock-solid character. Amen.

May 11 — Psalm 62:5–8

5 Yes, my soul, find rest in God; my hope comes from him. 6 Truly he is my rock and my salvation; he is my fortress, I will not be shaken. 7 My salvation and my honor depend on God; he is my mighty rock, my refuge. 8 *Trust in him at all times, you people; pour out your hearts to him, for God is our refuge.* (NIV)

Crying out to God. Waiting on God does not preclude communicating with him. While we must cultivate the discipline of waiting on him, we should also feel free to burst out in prayer before the Lord. Samuel Lee connects the various thoughts mentioned in verse 8, "According to our love, so is our faith and trust in God; and according to our trust, such is our freedom at the throne of grace. Trust in him and pour out your hearts before him; pour them out, like water, in joyful tears." We express our trust in the Lord by speaking to him from the depths of our being. It may be that our adversities have embittered our hearts toward the Lord to the extent that we do not pour out our thoughts to him. In that case, God must soften our hearts. As Lee notes, "When the stone in the heart is melted by mercy, the eyes will issue like a fountain of tears. Good men have melting spirits. It is a branch of the covenant and a fruit of the effusion of the Spirit of grace." Being well acquainted with chemistry, Lee provides us with an illustration. He observes, "It is asserted by the learned in chemistry that no menstruums [solvents] are so powerful as sulphureous and oily liquors to melt down the hardest minerals; to be sure there is nothing like the oil of mercy, so potent a solvent for an iron heart." In verse 8, David shifts from his personal testimony to challenge us ("you people") to trust in the Lord "at all times." As we experience God's mercy and faithfulness, we too can encourage others to always trust him!

Prayer. Lord, I say that I trust you, I inwardly complain and question you. Soften my heart and teach me not only to wait on you but to trust you by coming to you with my fervent and heart-felt prayers. Amen.

May 12 — Psalm 62:9-12

9 Common people are as worthless as a puff of wind, and the powerful are not what they appear to be. If you weigh them on the scales, together they are lighter than a breath of air. 10 *Don't make your living by extortion or put your hope in stealing. And if your wealth increases, don't make it the center of your life.* 11 God has spoken plainly, and I have heard it many times: Power, O God, belongs to you; 12 unfailing love, O Lord, is yours. Surely you repay all people according to what they have done. (NLT)

The snare of material possessions. We have a natural proclivity to place our trust in people or our material assets. However, David warns us that people are not what they appear to be (v. 9) and that the pursuit of riches can deceive and entice us. All that we own can control us and become the center of our lives (v. 10). Joseph Caryl addresses the seductive nature of our accumulated possessions. He notes, "We naturally love riches, and therefore as naturally spend many thoughts, both how to get and how to keep them. If a man have riches, or an increase in riches, it is not unlawful for him to think of them (yet we should be as sparing of our thoughts that way as may be, our thoughts and the bent of our souls should always be upon God), but that which the psalmist forbids is the settling of our hearts; as if he had said, 'Let not your thoughts stay or dwell here. Riches are themselves transient things, therefore they should have but our transient thoughts.'" Caryl stresses that if we set our hearts on our possessions (which may unexpectedly diminish), our hearts will be unsettled. Warnings by Solomon (Prov 11:4, 18) and Paul (1 Tim 6:17) reinforce David's admonition. Rather than allowing unreliable riches to ensnare us, we are to bind ourselves to the Lord (v. 11). In addition to his power, he promises us his love which will never fail (v. 12).

Prayer. Lord, I confess that the allure of the benefits of my possessions draws my heart away from you. But I need to fix my heart on you who offers me true security and joy in life. Help me to generously share my material goods with those in need. Amen.

May 13   Psalm 63:1-4

1 *O God, you are my God; I earnestly search for you. My soul thirsts for you; my whole body longs for you in this parched and weary land where there is no water.* 2 I have seen you in your sanctuary and gazed upon your power and glory. 3 *Your unfailing love is better than life itself;* how I praise you! 4 I will praise you as long as I live, lifting up my hands to you in prayer. (NLT)

Longing for God. This psalm's title indicates that David is in the desert, possibly pursued by his rebellious son Absalom (2 Sam 16:21). In that desert place, his greatest desire is for the Lord himself (vv. 1-2). Thomas Brooks beautifully captures the psalmist's yearning, "He does not say my soul thirsts for water, but my soul thirsts for 'you,' nor he does say my soul thirsts for the blood of my enemies, but my soul thirsts for 'you'; nor he does not say my soul thirsts for deliverance out of this dry and thirsty land, where no water is; nor he does not say my soul thirsts for a crown, a kingdom, but my soul thirsts for you,' my flesh longs for 'you.' These words are a notable metaphor . . . to note his earnest, ardent, and strong affections towards God." David expresses his longing for the Lord's unfathomable love. He unequivocally states that God's unfailing love "is better than life itself" (v. 3). Brooks paraphrases David's sentiment, "Divine favour is better than life; it is better than life with all its revenues, with all its appurtenances, as honours, riches, pleasures, applause . . . yes, it is better than many lives put together." Brooks concludes, "Many men have been weary of their lives, as is evident in Scripture and history; but no man was ever yet found that was weary of the love and favour of God." There is nothing in life that compares to the satisfaction of knowing and experiencing the Lord who is better than life (v. 3).

Prayer. Lord, I have longed for life's pleasures which I thought would satiate my deepest desires. But they have only left me empty, leaving me disappointed and craving something much better. You are the one who truly satisfies my longings! I desire you and your extravagant love for me. Amen.

May 14 — Psalm 63:5-8

5 You satisfy me more than the richest feast. I will praise you with songs of joy. 6 I lie awake thinking of you, meditating on you through the night. 7 Because you are my helper, I sing for joy in the shadow of your wings. 8 I cling to you; your strong right hand holds me securely. (NLT)

Communing with God. After describing his longing as a thirst for God, David now compares God to a feast. In spite of the most delectable foods, only the Lord fully satisfies him (v. 5). George Swinnock comments on David's spiritual gratification, "His solitary meditations [bring] him more solace and comfort than the whole creation [can] afford him." Swinnock compares communion with the Lord to other areas of life, "Communion with God in secret is a heaven upon earth. What food can compare with the hidden manna? Some persons have excellent banquets in their closets. That bread which the saints eat in secret, how pleasant is it! Ah! What stranger can imagine the joy, the melody, which even the secret tears of the saints cause! Believers find rich mines of silver and gold in solitary places; they fetch up precious jewels out of secret holes, out of the bottom of the ocean, where are no inhabitants." Swinnock reminds us of the importance of spending time alone with God. We must create space in our hearts, setting aside less crucial details cluttering our thoughts. Solitude allows us the opportunity to be still and listen to the voice of God speaking to us about those matters which we need to attend to in our lives. After he speaks into our lives through Scripture and the nudges in our hearts, we can talk to him about what he has said to us. This rich communion with the lover of our souls is far better than any feast before us. In response, we joyfully thank the Lord for the privilege of being in his presence (v. 5b).

Prayer. Father, I have spent time in prayer, but I have often failed to enjoy being in your presence. I want to enjoy spending time listening to you, whether it is during the day or night. Since this intimate communion will satisfy me more than anything else, I want to pursue my love relationship with you. Amen.

May 15 — Psalm 63:9–11

9 But those who seek to destroy my life shall go down into the depths of the earth; 10 they shall be given over to the power of the sword; they shall be a portion for jackals. 11 *But the king shall rejoice in God; all who swear by him shall exult, for the mouths of liars will be stopped.* (ESV)

Praising God. David concludes his psalm with a note of praise. Those who pursued him, including his son Absalom, now face the real possibility of death (vv. 9–10). However, even though his enemies forced him to flee his palace, he is still the rightful king anointed by God. When the Lord eventually executes justice upon them for their wickedness, David will praise him (v. 11). He has to depend on the protective care of God whose power is greater than the enemies' (v. 2). As a result of divine justice on his adversaries and the re-affirmation of David's kingship, his subjects "who swear by him" also praise God (v. 11b). Regarding the people's oath, Matthew Henry explains that, in the oath, the people give their allegiance to "the blessed name of God, and not by any idol (Deut 6:13–15)." He continues, "It means all good people that make a sincere and open profession of God's name . . . shall glory in God; they shall glory in David's advancement." They acknowledge that the Lord is protecting David so that he can continue reigning as their king. While we typically praise God when conflicts cease, this psalm reminds us to praise him during the conflicts, while we wait for him to work out his sovereign purposes. We can praise the Lord who has called us to himself and then continues to watch over us with his mercy and love (Jude 20–21). Like David, we may question God's calling on our lives, but he will certainly fulfill his purposes for and through us.

Prayer. Lord, when unsettling events intrude and interrupt what you have called me to, I begin to question your divine purposes. Teach me to be patient and allow you to reveal your plans. At the same time, I need to learn to praise you during adversities rather than waiting until everything is resolved. Amen.

May 16 — Psalm 64:1-6

1 Hear my voice, O God, in my complaint; preserve my life from dread of the enemy. 2 Hide me from the secret plots of the wicked, from the throng of evildoers, 3 *who whet their tongues like swords, who aim bitter words like arrows,* 4 *shooting from ambush at the blameless, shooting at him suddenly and without fear.* 5 They hold fast to their evil purpose; they talk of laying snares secretly, thinking, "Who can see them?" 6 They search out injustice, saying, "We have accomplished a diligent search." For the inward mind and heart of a man are deep. (ESV)

Destructive words. While incendiary devices cause physical destruction, the human tongue causes far-reaching damage to relationships and reputations. David describes how words hurt and destroy others. His enemies' weapons are their tongues which act like swords and arrows (vv. 3–4). Jeremiah Burroughs explains why the tongue is so deadly. As the sword "wounds, so the tongues of reproaching men cut deeply into the credits and reputations of their brethren, but a sword does mischief only near hand, not a far off." Malicious words are also like "an arrow that can hit at a distance: and so revilers do not ill offices to those only in the parish or town where they live, but to others far remote." When David uses the metaphor of a sharp razor to describe destructive speech (Ps 51:2), Burroughs notes, "To a razor, such a one as will take off every little hair: so a reviling tongue will not only take advantage of every gross sin committed by others, but those peccadilloes, the least infirmities which others better qualified cannot so much as discern." As Burroughs applies these three analogies (swords, arrows, razors) to our lives, he concludes, "How much, then, does it concern every man to walk circumspectly; to give no just cause of reproach, not to make himself a scorn to the fools of the world; but, if they will reproach (as certainly they will), let it be for forwardness in God's ways, and not for sin, that so the reproach may fall upon their own heads, and their scandalous language into their own throats."

Prayer. Lord, I have hurt individuals with my words and others' comments have deeply hurt me. I need grace-filled speech which will honor them and you. Amen.

May 17   Psalm 64:7–10

7 But God shoots his arrow at them; they are wounded suddenly. 8 *They are brought to ruin, with their own tongues turned against them;* all who see them will wag their heads. 9 Then all mankind fears; they tell what God has brought about and ponder what he has done. 10 Let the righteous one rejoice in the Lord and take refuge in him! Let all the upright in heart exult! (ESV)

Self-inflicted words. When people's words have deeply wounded us, we may find ourselves retaliating with a tongue-lashing. However, this is not the way Christ wants us to respond. In this psalm, David describes how God responds justly to verbal abusers. There are grave consequences for those who speak maliciously. Regarding these consequences, Joseph Caryl comments, "Their own words shall be brought as a testimony against them and condemn them. 'The tongue is a little member' (Jas 3:5), and therefore a light member; yet it falls heavy, as heavy as lead. A man were better have his house fall upon him, than that, in this sense, his tongue should fall upon him. Some have been pressed to death because they would not speak, but stood mute before the judge; but more have been pressed to death by their sinful freedom, or rather licentiousness in speaking; this has brought them to judgment, and cast them in judgment . . . A strange thing, that the fall of a man's tongue should oppress his body and whole estate; yet so it is, the weight of a man's tongue falling upon him crushes him to powder." God desires that the trials that he inflicts upon the slanderers (vv. 7–8) will cause them and others to fear him (v. 9) and ponder what he has done to them. He is showing mercy because their somber reflections may draw them to acknowledge and willingly submit to him. Since these matters are in God's hands, we can trust him and express praise (v. 10).

Prayer. Lord, I confess that it is tempting to respond to verbal abuse with the same mean-spirited words. I need to remember that you will deal with slanderers, and you have redemptive purposes which are far beyond my understanding. Amen.

May 18 — Psalm 65:1–4

1 There will be silence before You, and praise in Zion, God, and the vow will be fulfilled for You. 2 *You who hear prayer, to You all mankind comes.* 3 Wrongdoings prevail against me; as for our offenses, You forgive them. 4 Blessed is the one You choose and allow to approach You; he will dwell in Your courtyards. We will be satisfied with the goodness of Your house, Your holy temple. (NASB)

God hears and forgives. In this three-part psalm, David meditates on God's forgiveness (vv. 1–4), creation (vv. 5–8), and provisions (vv. 9–13). This first section declares that God hears and answers prayer (v. 2). David Clarkson reflects, "This is one of his titles of honour, he is a God that hears prayer; and it is as truly ascribed to him as mercy or justice. He hears all prayer and therefore 'all mankind comes'" to him (v. 2). Clarkson continues, "He never rejects any that deserves the name of prayer, how weak, how unworthy [whoever] the petitioner be . . . And will he (may faith say) reject mine only?" To affirm God's response to our prayers, Clarkson provides encouraging Scriptures, here in current English: "the same Lord is Lord of all and richly blesses all who call on him" (Rom 10:12 NIV); "You are kind and forgiving, O Lord, abounding in love to all who call on you" (Ps 86:5 NIV); and, "he rewards those who earnestly seek him" (Heb 11:6 NIV). These descriptions of God "must be believed as certainly as we believe that God is. As sure as God is the true God, so sure is it that none who sought him diligently departed from him without a reward. He rewards all seekers . . . if all, why not me?" If a person doubts this, he argues, "You may as well doubt that he is God, as doubt that he will not reward, not hear prayer." Clarkson reminds us of the promise in James 1:5, "If any of you lacks wisdom, he should ask God, who gives generously to all without finding fault, and it will be given to him." God will respond to our prayers!

Prayer. Father, I confess that I do not always believe you hear me. Thank you for your promises that you will hear and respond to my prayers. Amen.

May 19   Psalm 65:5-8

5 By awesome deeds You answer us in righteousness, God of our salvation, You who are the trust of all the ends of the earth and the farthest sea; 6 who establishes the mountains by His strength, who is encircled with might; 7 who stills the roaring of the seas, the roaring of their waves, and the turmoil of the nations. 8 They who dwell at the ends of the earth stand in awe of Your signs; *You make the sunrise and the sunset shout for joy.* (NASB)

God creates. God's power is revealed through his creation (vv. 6–7). We also see his wisdom in the beauty and design of the sunrise and sunset (v. 8). On the wonder of the beginning and the end of each day, Matthew Henry exclaims, "How contrary soever light and darkness are to each other, and how inviolable soever the partition between them (Gen 1:4)." As distinct as day is from night, he observes, "Both are equally welcome to the world in their season; it is hard to say which is more welcome to us, the light of the morning which befriends the business of the day, or the shadows of the evening which befriend the repose of the night. Does the watchman wait for the morning? So does the hireling earnestly desire the shadow." Society recognizes the value of both day and night and welcomes the benefits of each. The rhythms of the Levites' sacrifices follow the morning and evening pattern "which good people greatly rejoiced in, and in which God was constantly honoured." God received honor because "every morning and every evening songs of praise were sung by the Levites; it was that which the duty of every day required." Henry applies their daily rhythm for our lives, "We are to look upon our daily worship alone, and with our families, to be both the most needful of our daily business, and the most delightful of our daily comforts; and if therein we keep up our communion with God, the outgoings both of the morning and of the evening are thereby made truly to rejoice." When we use the mornings and evenings to draw close to God, he, through his creation, rejoices!

Prayer. Father, I am thankful that I can use your creation's wise designs to live for your purposes, communing with you and honoring you from morning to the evening. Amen.

May 20 — Psalm 65:9–13

9 You visit the earth and cause it to overflow; You greatly enrich it; the stream of God is full of water; You prepare their grain, for so You prepare the earth. 10 You water its furrows abundantly, You settle its ridges, You soften it with showers, You bless its growth. 11 *You have crowned the year with your goodness, and your paths drip with fatness.* 12 The pastures of the wilderness drip, and the hills encircle themselves with rejoicing. 13 The meadows are clothed with flocks and the valleys are covered with grain; they shout for joy, yes, they sing. (NASB)

God provides. David praises God who amply provides for his creation. Abundant water, grain, and flocks reveal his providential care for this world and his commitment to the covenant made with his people. If they obey the covenant, he promises to bless their land with rain, crops, and cattle (Deut 28:11–12). David testifies that God has been faithful to his promise because he "crowned the year with his goodness" (v. 11). Matthew Henry explains that the word "crowned" can also be translated as "compassed" (KJV), or "surrounded" (NIV). He continues "God has surrounded this year with his goodness, 'compassed and enclosed it' on every side" like a crown, Paraphrasing David in verse 11, Henry concludes, "He [God] has given us instances of his goodness in everything that concerns us; so that turn which way we will, we meet with the tokens of his favour; every part of the year has been enriched with the blessings of heaven, and no gap has been left open for any desolating judgment to enter by." Everywhere God's people turn, they will see sufficient evidence of God's provisions for nature, the flocks, and humankind. Jesus also reminds us of God's continual care for his creation, including the vegetation and the birds (Matt 6:26–30). God assures us in Psalm 65 and Jesus assures us in Matthew 6: 25–32 that he will take care of us, mitigating our worry about life's necessities. Freed from pre-occupied worrying, we can devote ourselves to pursuing God's reign in our lives and the world.

Prayer. Father, I praise you for all your provisions. In every direction I move, I see your generous blessings reminding me of your goodness. How can I doubt your care for me? Amen.

May 21 — Psalm 66:1–4

1 Shout for joy to God, all the earth! 2 Sing the glory of his name; make his praise glorious. 3 Say to God, "How awesome are your deeds! *So great is your power that your enemies cringe before you.* 4 All the earth bows down to you; they sing praise to you, they sing the praises of your name." (NIV)

Global honor. The psalmist calls on "all the earth" (vv. 2, 4) to praise God for his powerful deeds which reflect his glory (v. 2). While many will be filled with awe, not everyone will praise God. Although his enemies will participate by bowing before God (v. 4), they will "cringe" before his power (v. 3). Jeremiah Burroughs comments on their response, "In times of affliction every hypocrite—all tag and rag—will be ready to come in to God in an outward profession." He argues that the Hebrew word for "cringe" conveys the act of lying. That is, their "submission to God at this time is not out of truth." Charles Spurgeon* agrees that God's enemies will bow before him but with a "forced and false submission. Power brings a man to his knee but love alone wins his heart. Pharaoh said he would let Israel go, but he lied unto God; he submitted in word but not in deed. Tens of thousands, both in earth and hell, are rendering this constrained homage to the Almighty; they only submit because they cannot do otherwise; it is not their loyalty, but his power, which keeps them subjects of his boundless dominion." The apostle Paul taught that one day all people will bow before Christ (Phil 2:10–11). The apostle did not embrace universal salvation but reinforced the psalm's claim. There will be those who willingly bow before the Lord while others will begrudgingly do so. The latter will fail to recognize and accept Jesus' glory revealed in his earthly ministry (John 1:14). When we do embrace Jesus and his revelation of God's glory, praise fills our hearts!

Prayer. Lord, I joyfully bow before you in adoration of your glory and greatness. With the throngs of people around the globe, I join them with my praise! I pray that those who resist you will come to know your extravagant love for them so that they will also bow down before you in worship. Amen.

May 22 Psalm 66:5-12

5 Come and see the works of God, who is awesome in his deeds toward the sons of mankind. 6 He turned the sea into dry land; they passed through the river on foot; let's rejoice there, in Him! 7 He rules by his might forever; His eyes keep watch on the nations; the rebellious shall not exalt themselves! Selah 8 Bless our God, you peoples, and sound His praise abroad, 9 who keeps us in life, and does not allow our feet to slip. 10 For You have put us to the test, God; You have refined us as silver is refined. 11 You brought us into the net; you laid an oppressive burden upon us. 12 You made men ride over our heads; *we went through fire and through water*. Yet You brought us out into a place of abundance. (NASB)

Our trials. An idealistic view of the Christian life assumes that God will spare believers from hardships. Although verses 5-9 of today's Scripture passage describe God protecting his people from harm, the psalmist's subsequent verses describe their hardships. We will go through trials (vv. 10-11)! Thomas Goodwin comments on "a great variety of such perils; and not only of several, but of contrary sorts ('we went through fire and through water'), either of which singly and alone denotes an extremity of evils." He adds, "But when through both successively, one after the other, this denotes an accumulation of miseries, or trials." Yet this is not the end of the story! Goodwin points out that Isaiah 43:2 promises that God is with us and will preserve us in our deepest "water" and "fire" trials. Goodwin explains that God's promise is "acknowledged by the psalmist to have been performed: God was with the three children when they walked through the fire, in the very letter of Isaiah's speech; and with the children of Israel when they went through the water of the Red Sea." God's promises assure us that he supplies us his strength and hope during life's trials.

Prayer. Lord, I am thankful that you are with me through my personal challenges. Thank you for your grace to persevere and I cling to your love for me. Amen.

May 23   Psalm 66:13–15

13 I will come into your house with burnt offerings; I will perform my vows to you, 14 that which my lips uttered and my mouth promised when I was in trouble. 15 I will offer to you burnt offerings of fattened animals, with the smoke of the sacrifice of rams; I will make an offering of bulls and goats. *Selah* (ESV)

Dedication to God. The psalmist has told us that God, in his mercy, has been faithful to preserve them through their trials. Out of gratitude for God's mercy, the writer desires to present to the Lord extravagant offerings with fattened rams, bulls and goats (v. 15). By his sacrifice and vows, the psalmist rededicates himself to God. Thomas Adams reflects on personal dedication to the Lord. He comments, "For ourselves, be we sure that the best sacrifice we can give to God is obedience; not a dead beast, but a living soul. The Lord takes not delight in the blood of brutish creatures. It is the mind, the life, the soul, the obedience, that he requires" and he quotes 1 Samuel 15:22, "To obey is better than sacrifice." Thus, Adams issues the challenge, "Let this be our burnt offering, our holocaust, a sanctified body and mind given up to the Lord (Rom 12:1–2). We cannot be content offering only a part of our lives. To totally dedicate ourselves to the Lord, Adams tells us that we must offer our heart (Prov 23:26), hands (Isa 1:16), feet (Prov 4:27), lips (Mic 7:5), tongue (Ps 34:13), ears (Matt 11:15), eyes (Prov 4:25), body, and spirit (1 Cor 6:20). As to when we know that we have dedicated these areas to the Lord, he concludes, "When the eyes abhor lustful objects, the ear [abhors] slanders, the foot [abhors] erring paths, the hands [abhor] wrong and violence, the tongue [abhors] flattery and blasphemy, the heart [abhors] pride and hypocrisy; this is your holocaust, your whole burnt offering." Using the same analogy of sacrifices, Paul exhorts us to offer our lives as "living sacrifices" to the Lord (Rom 12:1). We do so out of gratitude for all he has done for us.

Prayer. Lord, I am filled with thankfulness for your generous grace. I dedicate my life to you each day so that I may gladly obey and serve you. Use me because I want my life to count for you by influencing others for you! Amen.

May 24 — Psalm 66:16–20

16 Come and hear, all you who fear God, *and I will tell what he has done for my soul.* 17 I cried to him with my mouth, and high praise was on my tongue. 18 If I had cherished iniquity in my heart, the Lord would not have listened. 19 But truly God has listened; he has attended to the voice of my prayer. 20 Blessed be God, because he has not rejected my prayer or removed his steadfast love from me! (ESV)

Our testimony. When we dedicate ourselves to the Lord (vv. 13–15), we eagerly tell others what he has done for us (v. 16). Timothy Rogers meditates on the value of recounting God's goodness to others: "After we are delivered from the dreadful apprehensions of the wrath of God, it is our duty to be publicly thankful. It is for the glory of our Healer to speak of the miserable wounds that once pained us; and of that kind hand that saved us when we were brought very low. It is for the glory of our Pilot to tell of the rocks and of the sands; the many dangers and threatening calamities that he, by his wise conduct, made us to escape: and to see us safe on the shore may cause others that are yet afflicted, and tossed with tempests, to look to him for help; for he is able and ready to save them as well as us. We must, like soldiers, when a tedious war is over, relate our combats, our fears, our dangers, with delight; and make known our experiences to doubting, troubled Christians, and to those that have not yet been under such long and severe trials as we have been." Yet too often, we prefer remaining silent. Rogers offers us much needed wise counsel here. Rather than keeping our painful experiences to ourselves, we must share how God's grace is given to us in our dark days. In his letters, the apostle Paul shares his many hardships with his readers. By doing so, he testifies of God's enduring grace (2 Cor 4:7–11).

Prayer. Lord, I confess that by keeping my personal pain from others, I fail to show how you have given me your grace through my difficulties. Help me to be a witness of the ways your presence and strength sustained me! Amen.

May 25   Psalm 67

1 God be gracious to us and bless us and cause His face to shine upon us—*Selah* 2 that Your way may be known on the earth, Your salvation among all nations. 3 May the peoples praise You, God; may all the peoples praise You. 4 May the nations be glad and sing for joy; for You will judge the peoples with fairness and guide the nations on the earth. *Selah* 5 May the peoples praise You, God; may all the peoples praise You. 6 The earth has yielded its produce; *God, our God, blesses us.* 7 God blesses us, so that all the ends of the earth may fear Him. (NASB)

Our personal God. Throughout this song, the psalmist encourages us to praise God (vv. 3–5) for his numerous blessings (vv. 1, 6b–7) such as his daily provisions (v. 6a). Here the psalmist addresses those who belong to and enjoy the covenant relationship with God (Deut 28:1–14). "The peoples" can rightly claim that he is "our God" (v. 6a) who shines the supreme blessing of his face upon them (v. 1). Reflecting on "the earth has yielded its produce; God, our God, blesses us" (v. 6), John Howe exclaims, "How inexpressible [is] the inward pleasure wherewith we may suppose those words to have been uttered. How delightful an appropriation [a total of assets devoted to a special purpose]! As if it were intended to be said, the blessing itself were less significant, it could not have that savour with it, if it were not from our own God." He applies the psalmist's statement to our lives, "Not only, therefore, allow but urge your spirits thus to look towards God, that you may both delight in him as being in himself the most excellent one, and also as being yours; for know [that] you are not permitted only, but obliged to eye [behold], accept, and rejoice in him as such." Through faith in Jesus Christ, we can enjoy the blessings of the "new covenant" (Luke 22:20). The greatest blessing is to know God as our "*Abba*, Father" (Rom 8:15, Gal 4:6) with whom we can enjoy an intimate relationship.

Prayer. Father, my heart overflows with praise for all your blessings, especially for the joy of personally knowing you and your commitment to me. Nothing else compares to a covenant relationship with you. Amen.

May 26   Psalm 68:1–6

1 *May God arise*, may His enemies be scattered, and may those who hate Him flee from His presence. 2 As smoke is driven away, so drive them away; as wax melts before a fire, so the wicked will perish before God. 3 But the righteous will be joyful; they will rejoice before God; yes, they will rejoice with gladness. 4 Sing to God, sing praises to His name; exalt Him who rides through the deserts, whose name is the Lord, and be jubilant before Him. 5 A father of the fatherless and a judge for the widows, is God in His holy dwelling. 6 God makes a home for the lonely; He leads out the prisoners into prosperity, only the rebellious live in parched lands. (NASB)

A mighty warrior. When life's storms overwhelm us, we may feel that God is asleep and disinterested in our well-being (Matt 8:23–25). Amid the enemies' threats, the psalmist calls on God to "arise" and act (v. 1). This summons to arise to conquer the enemy is a theme throughout the Psalter (7:6; 9:19; 10:12; 17:13; 74:22; 102:13). John Boys reflects on God's rising to act in world events. He notes, "The mercifulness of God is seen in his patience toward the wicked, implied in the word 'arise,' for he seems, as it were, to 'sleep' (Ps 44:23), and not to mark what is done amiss. The Lord is patient, and would have none to perish, but would have all men to come to repentance. He was longer in destroying one city (Jericho; Josh 6:4) than in building the whole world; slow to wrath, and ready to forgive, desiring not the death of a sinner, but rather he should amend. He does not arise to particular punishments, much less to the general judgement, but after long suffering and great goodness." While we may be impatient for God to act, Boys reminds us that God's delays are intentional because of his nature. He is full of mercy, desiring that people would turn to and follow him. God is not asleep! He is working out his divine purposes, even with those who oppose him.

Prayer. Lord, I get impatient that you do not appear to bring justice to those who defy you. Help me to become more patient and trust you while you are achieving your purposes amid turbulent world affairs. Amen.

May 27 — Psalm 68:7–19

7 God, when You went forth before Your people, when You marched through the desert, *Selah* 8 the earth quaked; the heavens also dropped rain at the presence of God; Sinai itself quaked at the presence of God, the God of Israel. 9 You made plentiful rain fall, God; You confirmed Your inheritance when it was parched. 10 Your creatures settled in it; in Your kindness You provided for the poor, God. 11 The Lord gives the command; the women who proclaim good news are a great army: 12 "Kings of armies flee, they flee, and she who remains at home will divide the spoils!" 13 When you lie down among the sheepfolds, you are like the wings of a dove covered with silver, and its pinions with glistening gold. 14 When the Almighty scattered the kings there, it was snowing in Zalmon. 15 The mountain of Bashan is a mountain of God; the mountain of Bashan is a mountain of many peaks. 16 *Why do you look with envy, you mountains of many peaks, at the mountain God has desired as His dwelling?* Indeed, the Lord will dwell there forever. 17 The chariots of God are myriads, thousands upon thousands; the Lord is among them as at Sinai, in holiness. 18 You have ascended on high, You have led captive Your captives; You have received gifts among people, even among the rebellious as well, that the Lord God may dwell there. 19 Blessed be the Lord, who daily bears our burden, the God who is our salvation. *Selah* (NASB)

The unimpressive. The psalmist describes the ark, symbolizing God's presence among his people, proceeding through the land (vv. 7–10). After the defeat of the opposing kings (vv. 11–14), the ark arrives at its destination, not at the "mountain of Bashan" with its peaks (v. 15) but at a significantly smaller hill, Mount Zion (v. 16). God's choice of this location should not surprise us. John Trapp notes: "This low, little, barren hill of Zion; and God's election makes the difference, as it did of Aaron's rod from the rest, and does still of the church from the rest of the world." God often chooses the unimpressive things of this world to reveal his grace.

Prayer. Lord, I often feel so inadequate to serve you but am thankful that you can use my limited abilities for your purposes. Amen.

May 28   Psalm 68:20-23

20 God is to us a God of salvation; and to God the Lord belong ways of escape from death. 21 God certainly will shatter the heads of his enemies, the hairy head of one who goes about in his guilt. 22 The Lord said, "I will bring them back from Bashan. I will bring them back from the depths of the sea, 23 so that your foot may shatter them in blood, and the tongue of your dogs may have its portion from your enemies." (NASB)

God saves. When we face danger, we have a proclivity to figure out how to get out of the mess. Sometimes, we simply do not know what to do. Joseph Caryl notes, "When a man is in the valley of the shadow of death, where shall he issue out? Where shall he have a passage? Nowhere, says man, he shall not escape." However, David reminds us that God saves his people (v. 20). The psalmist's use of "salvation" (v. 20) does not refer to spiritual salvation. Instead, as Caryl states, this salvation is related to God's "outward deliverance" of his people from their enemies to the land promised to them. To achieve this, the Lord provides "ways of escape" (v. 20b). Caryl observes, "God has all ways that lead out from death in his own keeping, he keeps the key of the door that lets us out from death." A notable "key" in Israel's history is the miraculous crossing of the Red Sea to escape from the Egyptians. Throughout the centuries, God provides other means to escape such as: military might, effective military strategies, political alliances, and betrayals. Rather than panicking when our troubles hem us in, we need to remember that, "God keeps all the passages; when men think they have shut us up in the jaws of death, he can open them, and deliver us . . . God is a faithful keeper, and a friendly keeper, who will open the door for the escape of his people, when they cry unto him." His deliverances should encourage us. He is the sovereign and omnipotent God who delivers!

Prayer. Lord, forgive me for always trying to solve my predicaments without including you. Teach me to wait for you to see the ways you will act on my behalf. Amen.

May 29   Psalm 68:24–31

24 They have seen Your procession, God, the procession of my God, my King, into the sanctuary. 25 The singers went on, the musicians after them, in the midst of the young women beating tambourines. 26 Bless God in the congregations, even the Lord, you who are of the fountain of Israel. 27 Benjamin, the youngest, is there, ruling them, the leaders of Judah in their company, the leaders of Zebulun, the leaders of Naphtali. 28 *Your God has commanded your strength; show Yourself strong,* God, You who acted in our behalf. 29 Because of Your temple at Jerusalem kings will bring gifts to You. 30 Rebuke the animals in the reeds, the herd of bulls with the calves of the peoples, trampling the pieces of silver; He has scattered the peoples who delight in war. 31 Messengers will come from Egypt; Cush will quickly stretch out her hands to God. (NASB)

God is our strength. The ark's movement to its destination (vv. 7–19) requires both God's deliverance (vv. 20–23) and people's involvement (vv. 24–27). At times, we may presume on God to act without our participation. However, because God gives strength to his people (v. 28), the ark's arrival in Jerusalem and the following celebration are possible. In Samuel Martin's words, "David can provide a sacred place for the ark of his God," and "thirty thousand chosen men can attend on this occasion, and a multitude besides. Then, why should they tarry at home . . . and why should they be silent?" Through the Lord's strength, they fulfill their responsibilities. In regard to verse 28, "Your God has commanded your strength," Martin stresses the importance of the psalmist's words for each of us. God's strength is "our best—all that is within you; all that you can do, and be, and become; and all that you have." In writing "I can do everything through Christ who gives me the strength" (Phil 4:13), the apostle Paul echoes Martin's exhortation.

Prayer. Lord, too many times I want you to act without my involvement or I want to act without depending on you. I confess I doubt that your power can really help me in my struggles. Help me to partner with you and your strength so that you receive praise through my life. Amen.

May 30 — Psalm 68:32-35

32 Sing to God, you kingdoms of the earth; Oh, sing praises to the Lord, *Selah* 33 To Him who rides on the heaven of heavens, which were of old! *Indeed, He sends out His voice, a mighty voice.* 34 Ascribe strength to God; His excellence *is* over Israel, And His strength *is* in the clouds. 35 O God, You are more awesome than Your holy places. The God of Israel is He who gives strength and power to His people. Blessed be God! (NKJV)

God's voice. The celebration surrounding the ark's arrival in Jerusalem reaches its grand finale in these verses. The strength to transport the ark (v. 28) came from the "God of Israel" (v. 34), who is strong, powerful, and mighty (v. 35), who speaks with a thunderous voice (v. 33) John Gill* observes that Scripture is the "strong and powerful voice" when it is "accompanied with the power and Spirit of God. It is a soul shaking and awakening voice; it is a heart melting and a heart breaking one; it is a quickening and an enlightening voice; it quickens dead sinners, gives life unto them, and the entrance of it gives light to dark minds; it is a soul charming and alluring one; it draws to Christ, engages the affections to him, and fills with unspeakable delight and pleasure." Scripture is God's voice speaking to us through both his revealed written word and the Holy Spirit who softens our hearts, illumines our minds to God's truth and leads us to a personal relationship with Jesus Christ. God's communication through Scripture is for all people including the world's powerful rulers (v. 32). God invites all people to submit to His voice and then praise Him who is both transcendent over the earth and indwells us through the Holy Spirit. We become the sanctuary or temple of God's Spirit (1 Cor. 6:19).

Prayer. Father, too often I do not take the Bible seriously and my spiritual ears are inattentive to your voice. At such times, I need you to speak with a mighty voice to wake me up from my complacency and call me to pay attention to what you are saying through Scripture. May your Holy Spirit reveal sin and convict me, instruct me and transform my life so that I may become increasingly more like the living Jesus Christ. Amen.

May 31   Psalm 69:1–4

1 Save me, O God, for the floodwaters are up to my neck. 2 *Deeper and deeper I sink into the mire;* I can't find a foothold. I am in deep water, and the floods overwhelm me. 3 I am exhausted from crying for help; my throat is parched. My eyes are swollen with weeping, waiting for my God to help me. 4 Those who hate me without cause outnumber the hairs on my head. Many enemies try to destroy me with lies, demanding that I give back what I didn't steal. (NLT)

Despair. David, the author of this psalm, faces troubles (v. 1) brought upon by enemies who want to destroy him with their slander (v. 4). All seems hopeless leaving him exhausted (vv. 2, 3a). To make matters worse, God appears slow to respond to his dire situation (v. 3b). David's plight resonates with so many, even though the specific circumstances vary. John Bunyan describes his despair brought about by his sinful condition, with no personal relationship with Jesus Christ. He testifies, "I saw indeed there was cause of rejoicing for those that held to Jesus; but as for me, I had cut myself off by my transgressions, and left myself neither foothold, nor handhold, amongst all the stays and props in the precious word of life. And truly I did now feel myself to sink into a gulf, as an house whose foundation is destroyed; I did liken myself, in this condition, unto the case of a child that was fallen into a mill pit, who, though it could make some shift to scrabble and sprawl in the water, yet, because it could find neither hold for hand nor foot, therefore, at last, it must die in that condition." Whatever deep waters we are facing, God desires that we recognize the need for him to save us (v. 1). Bunyan's eventual conversion to Christ serves as a reminder for us to have a relationship with Jesus. Or our need may require his strength, wisdom, and love to deal with those who treat us unfairly. Out of his mercy and love for us, he will respond to our heart cries.

Prayer. Lord, I need you in my life! Would you hear my cries and respond with your love? I have not always paid attention to you, but I now make a renewed commitment to you. Amen.

June 1   Psalm 69:5-12

5 God, You know my foolishness, and my guilt is not hidden from You. 6 May those who wait for You not be ashamed because of me, Lord God of armies; may those who seek You not be dishonored because of me, God of Israel, 7 because for Your sake I have endured disgrace; dishonor has covered my face. 8 I have become estranged from my brothers, and a stranger to my mother's sons. 9 *For zeal for Your house has consumed me, and the taunts of those who taunt You have fallen on me.* 10 When I wept in my soul with fasting, it became my disgrace. 11 When I made sackcloth my clothing, I became a proverb to them. 12 Those who sit in the gate talk about me, and songs of mockery by those habitually drunk are about me. (NASB)

Godly passion. David's passion ("zeal") for God provokes the hatred he experiences (vv. 4, 9). However, God uses these trials for his purposes. Thomas Brooks asserts, "Grace never rises to so great a height as it does in times of persecution. Suffering times are a Christian's harvest times." He continues, "All the reproaches, frowns, threatenings, oppositions, and persecutions that a Christian meets with in a way of holiness, do but raise his zeal and courage to a greater height." To illustrate, he mentions that a fire on a frosty winter day feels intensely hot, and thus "in the winter of affliction and persecution, that divine fire, the zeal of a Christian, burns so much the hotter, and flames forth so much the more vehemently and strongly." Brooks offers four reasons why we grow in godliness during afflictions. We have "a good captain [Jesus] to lead and encourage" us; a "righteous cause" which prompts us to be bold; a "gracious God" who helps us; and a "glorious heaven to receive and reward" us. Speaking to the individual believer, he states that, "these things cannot but mightily raise him and inflame him under the greatest opposition and persecution. These things will keep him from fearing, fawning, fainting, sinking, or flying in a stormy day." By God's goodness, we will be like an "adamant" or impenetrable stone, "invincible and unchangeable" during trials.

Prayer. Lord, I want my passion for you to be vibrant. By your strengthening grace, help me embrace the difficulties to become more like Jesus. Amen.

June 2   Psalm 69:13–18

13 But as for me, my prayer is to you, O LORD. *At an acceptable time, O God, in the abundance of your steadfast love answer me in your saving faithfulness.* 14 Deliver me from sinking in the mire; let me be delivered from my enemies and from the deep waters. 15 Let not the flood sweep over me, or the deep swallow me up, or the pit close its mouth over me. 16 Answer me, O LORD, for your steadfast love is good; according to your abundant mercy, turn to me. 17 Hide not your face from your servant, for I am in distress; make haste to answer me. 18 Draw near to my soul, redeem me; ransom me because of my enemies! (ESV)

God's time. In response to his enemies' hatred of him, David asks God to answer his prayer (v. 13) with "haste" (v. 17), although he knows that God's timetable is "acceptable" (v. 13). Mark Frank* describes how long we may wait to receive answers to our requests, "We may knock, and knock again, and yet stand without a while; sometimes, so long, till our knees are ready to sink under us, our eyes ready to drop out, as well as drop with expectation, and our hearts ready to break in pieces, while none hears, or none regards." At times, David feels exhausted and overwhelmed with waiting (vv. 2–3). We may join him in wondering when it is will be God's "acceptable time." Frank encourages us that "either God's being in a good or pleasing disposition towards us, or our being in a good and pleasing disposition towards him" guarantees that . . . we are sure to be accepted." God's pleasing "disposition" or attitude toward David (and us!) comes from his "steadfast love" and "faithfulness" (v. 13). His commitment to us will not allow him to give up on us, even though we may feel that he has. Also, David has a "pleasing disposition" toward God because he confesses his dependency on God to rescue him. While he complains about his circumstances, he prays rather than grumbling and ignoring God. In a dependent posture, we wait on God to answer our prayers.

Prayer. Lord, you know how impatient I can be with you! Teach me to be patient as I depend on you and wait for you to answer my prayers according to your perfect timetable. Amen.

June 3   Psalm 69:19-21

19 You know of my shame, scorn, and disgrace. You see all that my enemies are doing. 20 Their insults have broken my heart, and I am in despair. If only one person would show some pity; if only one would turn and comfort me. 21 But instead, they give me poison for food; they offer me sour wine for my thirst. (NLT)

Emotional pain. While David's enemies seek to kill him, they also inflict "shame, scorn and disgrace" (v. 19) upon him. Although he is experiencing emotional pain and has no person to give him comfort, God recognizes David's sufferings. Jeremiah Burroughs comments, "It is a great deal of comfort that God does take notice of our reproaches; this [is] the comfort of the psalmist. If a man suffer reproach, and disgrace, and trouble for his friends, while he is abroad from them; O, says he, did my friends know what I suffer, and suffer for them, it would comfort me." We find comfort when others understand our pain but, like David, sometimes no one empathizes with us (v. 20). Fortunately, God fully understands our hurts, not only because he is omniscient, but because Jesus personally experienced shame, scorn, and disgrace. Earlier verses of this psalm allude to Jesus' suffering as David describes his pain. Without cause or any reason, David and Jesus experience hatred (v. 4; John 15:23–25). Their "zeal" for God's temple angers the religious authorities (v. 9; John 2:17). Finally, David and Jesus on the cross, are offered "sour wine" (v. 21; John 19:29). As Burroughs notes, "Christ is acquainted with all the sufferings of every member; and, therefore, do not say, I am a poor creature; who takes notice of my sufferings? Heaven takes notice of your sufferings; Christ takes notice of them better than yourselves." There is no room for us to have self-pity because Jesus' emotional pain was far worse than ours. When Paul challenges his audience to refrain from pleasing themselves, he refers to this psalm and points to Jesus who willingly faced insults and experienced shame from those who hated him (Rom 15:1–3).

Prayer. Lord, I often think that no one else understands my pain. I find comfort knowing that Jesus, who experienced far more emotional pain than I, perfectly understands my emotional wounds. You provide me with the safe place I need! Amen.

June 4   Psalm 69:22–27

> 22 Let their own table before them become a snare; and when they are at peace, let it become a trap. 23 Let their eyes be darkened, so that they cannot see, and make their loins tremble continually. 24 Pour out your indignation upon them, and let your burning anger overtake them. 25 May their camp be a desolation; let no one dwell in their tents. 26 For they persecute him whom you have struck down, and they recount the pain of those you have wounded. 27 *Add to them punishment upon punishment*; may they have no acquittal from you. (ESV)

Justice. After asking God to rescue him, David requests justice for those who have persecuted him. Specifically, he wants justice in their areas of enjoyment. For example, he prays that their food will become a "snare," their eyes will become blind (v. 23), and their camaraderie will become desolation (v. 25). While God executes justice by supernatural means, Samuel Annesly explains that divine justice is also exercised by unexpected means, "Sin, carried far enough, becomes its own punishment. Let but a voracious glutton be bound to sit at a well-furnished table but two hours after he had filled his stomach, he would account it an intolerable penance. Let but the drunkard be forced to drink on with those that can drink him down, how is he a burden to himself, and a scorn to his fellow drunkards! Let but a lazy sluggard be confined three days to his bed, and how weary will he be of his bed of down!" People face unpleasant consequences when their sins harm them. For our part, we do not seek revenge on others, but we ask God to forgive them as, in Acts 7:60, Stephen asks God to forgive those who are stoning him. God will bring justice to those who persecute his people. Until that day of judgment, we demonstrate God's love to our enemies.

Prayer. Father, I have witnessed how evil doers suffer at their own hands. They bring upon themselves a type of divine justice with relational and physical consequences. Help me not to gloat over their misfortune. Instead, I pray that they will turn to you. In the meantime, enable me to love those who hate you. Amen.

June 5 — Psalm 69:28–36

28 Let them be blotted out of the book of the living; let them not be enrolled among the righteous. 29 But I am afflicted and in pain; let your salvation, O God, set me on high! 30 I will praise the name of God with a song; I will magnify him with thanksgiving. 31 This will please the Lord *more than an ox or a bull with horns and hoofs. 32 When the humble see it they will be glad; you who seek God, let your hearts revive. 33 For the* Lord *hears the needy and does not despise his own people who are prisoners. 34 Let heaven and earth praise him, the seas and everything that moves in them. 35 For God will save Zion and build up the cities of Judah, and people shall dwell there and possess it; 36 the offspring of his servants shall inherit it, and those who love his name shall dwell in it.* (ESV)

God's lists. David asks God to bring justice on the wicked by blotting them from the book of life and not counting them among the righteous (v. 28). In reflecting on this verse, Thomas Adams asks: if one's name is written in the book of life, does this offer an "infallible assurance of salvation," or can one's name be blotted out? He replies, "The truth is, that none written in heaven can ever be lost." To suggest that one's name could be entered into the book of life and then blotted out, "casts a double aspersion on God himself." God would have to be ignorant about the future and deceived by choosing some to be saved but who eventually reject him. If this would occur, God's decree of election would have to change because he would have to exclude those he had formerly chosen. Adams reminds us that Paul teaches that "the Lord knows those who are his" (2 Tim 2:19). Those whom God has chosen "can never come into hell." In the context of his day, David asks God not to allow the wicked to live any longer and certainly not classify these people as righteous (v. 28).

Prayer. Jesus, I am thankful that I can have the assurance of eternal life, not through my good works but through a personal relationship with you. Amen.

June 6 — Psalm 70

1 Make haste, O God, to deliver me! O Lord, make haste to help me! 2 Let them be put to shame and confusion who seek my life! Let them be turned back and brought to dishonour who delight in my hurt! 3 Let them turn back because of their shame who say, "Aha, Aha!" 4 May all who seek you rejoice and be glad in you! *May those who love your salvation say evermore, "God is great!"* 5 But I am poor and needy; hasten to me, O God! You are my help and my deliverer; O Lord, do not delay! (ESV)

Love's priority. In desperation, David pleads for God to deliver him (vv. 1, 4, 5). In this context, "salvation" (v. 4) refers to physical deliverance from one's enemies. The application for us is clear. Out of our spiritual impoverishment and need for deliverance from sin's consequences, we call out to God to save us. Through faith in Christ, we experience spiritual salvation which includes the deliverance from sin's guilt and dominance in our lives. For this reason, we should "love" the salvation that we experience in Christ. James Frame* elaborates on believers' love. He comments, "They love it for its own sake; they love it for the sake of him who procured it by his obedience until death; they love it for the sake of that Holy Spirit who moved them to seek it and accept it; and they love it for the sake of their own souls, which they cannot but love, and which, without it, would be the most miserable outcasts in the universe. No wonder that in the light of its intrinsic importance, and of its intrinsic relations, they should be 'such as love God's salvation.'" However, we have numerous competitors for our love. Frame points out, "All men are lovers as well as seekers; for all men love. Some love money more than God's salvation; others love pleasure, even the pleasures of sin, more than God's salvation; and others love bustle and business more than God's salvation." He challenges us who are "friends of Jesus," to "elevate above [all other loves], as the worthier object of [our] regard and embrace, the salvation of God." His salvation reveals his greatness (v. 4).

Prayer. Father, I love you for your wonderful salvation which enables me to know and love you for all eternity. Amen.

June 7 — Psalm 71:1-8

1 In you, Lord, I have taken refuge; let me never be put to shame. In your righteousness, rescue me and deliver me; turn your ear to me and save me. 3 Be my rock of refuge, to which I can always go; give the command to save me, for you are my rock and my fortress. 4 Deliver me, my God, from the hand of the wicked, from the grasp of those who are evil and cruel. 5 *For you have been my hope, Sovereign* Lord, *my confidence since my youth.* 6 From birth I have relied on you; you brought me forth from my mother's womb. I will ever praise you. 7 I have become a sign to many; you are my strong refuge. 8 My mouth is filled with your praise, declaring your splendor all day long. (NIV)

Memories of the past. Reflecting from childhood days on God's faithfulness is beneficial. Throughout the years, the psalmist affirms that God has been his hope (v. 5). Since this truth has anchored him amid past trials, he asks God not to abandon him in his advanced years (vv. 9, 17-18). Oliver Heywood applies the psalmist's example to our lives, "The remembering and acknowledging of God in youth will be great satisfaction in old age. O what joy will reflection upon youthful piety yield!" He provides examples of those who looked back to God's presence from their childhood days. Polycarp, who, when asked to deny Christ and give his allegiance to the emperor, replied, "I have served Christ these eighty-six years, and he has not once injured me, and shall I now deny him?" When Jacob blessed Joseph, he declared that God had been his [Jacob's] shepherd for his entire life (Gen 48:15). Heywood paraphrased Jacob: "God has fed me all my life long unto this day; he has been kind to me all my days, and I trust he will look to me even in the end; and shall I now turn my back on him?" Job, who faced great trials, looked back on his younger days and recollected God's faithfulness to him over the years (Job 29:2-4).

Prayer. Lord, I am filled with gratitude for your faithfulness throughout the years. Even though there have been many difficulties, you have constantly loved me. I will hold on to your love until the end of my life. Amen.

June 8 — Psalm 71:9-18

9 Do not cast me away at the time of my old age; do not abandon me when my strength fails. 10 For my enemies have spoken against me; and those who watch for my life have consulted together, 11 saying, "God has abandoned him; pursue and seize him, for there is no one to save him." 12 God, do not be far from me; my God, hurry to my aid! 13 May those who are enemies of my soul be put to shame and consumed; may they be covered with disgrace and dishonor, who seek to injure me. 14 But as for me, I will wait continually and will praise You yet more and more. 15 My mouth shall tell of Your righteousness and of Your salvation all day long; for I do not know the art of writing. 16 I will come with the mighty deeds of the Lord God; I will make mention of Your righteousness, Yours alone. 17 *God, You have taught me from my youth*, and I still declare Your wondrous deeds. 18 And even when I am old and gray, God, do not abandon me, until I declare Your strength to this generation, Your power to all who are to come. (NASB)

Teaching from the past. The elderly psalmist tells us that God has not only been faithful since childhood but has also taught him from his youth (v. 17a). Thomas Watson asks how the psalmist, according to Psalm 119:99-100, can understand more than his teachers and elders. With God's law (vv. 97-100), the psalmist has "a Father to teach him; God [is] his instructor." The Law is the divine textbook for his learning. Although "many a child of God complains of ignorance and dullness," Watson reminds us that "our Father will be our tutor" which suggests is very encouraging for us. He notes that God gives the Holy Spirit to lead us into all truth (John 6:13). The Spirit does this by illuminating our minds and hearts so that we can understand the fundamental truths of Scripture. God also "inclines the will" so that we are enabled to do his will (Ezek 36:27).

Prayer. Father, deepen my understanding of your word and reveal areas in my life which need to align with your will so that by your Spirit I will obey you more. Amen.

June 9 — Psalm 71:19-24

19 For Your righteousness, God, reaches to the heavens, You who have done great things; God, who is like You? 20 You who have shown me many troubles and distresses will revive me again, and will bring me up again from the depths of the earth. 21 May You increase my greatness and turn to comfort me. 22 *I will also praise You with a harp*, and Your truth, my God; I will sing praises to You with the lyre, Holy One of Israel. 23 My lips will shout for joy when I sing praises to You; and my soul, which You have redeemed. 24 My tongue also will tell of Your righteousness all day long; for they are put to shame, for they are humiliated who seek my harm. (NASB)

The essence of worship. In their church services, the Puritans sought to honor God by their purity of worship. They excluded rituals which distracted from glorifying God and would only gratify or please the worshippers. They believed that freedom from a preoccupation with the externalities of worship encouraged praising God from one's heart. Writing from such a background, John Cotton proposes that "singing with instruments [was] not typical" in the Old Testament, but music from instruments was "only an external solemnity of worship, fitted to the solace of the outward senses of children under age, such as the Israelites were in the Old Testament (Gal 4:1–3)." With this perspective, Cotton not surprisingly asserts that "now, in the grown age of the heirs of the New Testament, such external pompous solemnities are ceased, and no external worship reserved." Since "simplicity" is the goal, worship services should not use musical instruments. While many today likely do not accept Cotton's perspective, he reminds us that we can become preoccupied or distracted with the external means of worship. The Puritans' emphasis on worshipping God from our hearts rather than focusing on any externalities is extremely important. The apostle Paul writes that the first evidence of the Spirit's filling our lives involves singing and making "music in [our hearts] to the Lord" (Eph 5:19). This is the mark of genuine worship.

Prayer. Lord, too often I view worship as a performance by others and am impressed by their abilities. I need to become an active participant by examining and preparing my heart so that I may genuinely praise and honor you. Amen.

June 10 — Psalm 72:1-7

1 Give the king Your judgments, God, and Your righteousness to the king's son. 2 May he judge Your people with righteousness and Your afflicted with justice. 3 *May the mountains bring peace to the people*, and the hills, in righteousness. 4 May he vindicate the afflicted of the people, save the children of the needy, and crush the oppressor. 5 May they fear You while the sun shines, And as long as the moon shines, throughout all generations. 6 May he come down like rain upon the mown grass, like showers that water the earth. 7 May the righteous flourish in his days, as well as an abundance of peace, until the moon is no more. (NASB)

The righteous king. This psalm's title, "Of Solomon," suggests that he wrote this psalm as a prayer for his own reign. Although not a prophetic psalm, this prayer finding its fullest expression in Jesus' rule over the world, has inspired hymns for congregational singing. In addition to the request for the king to exercise "righteousness" (vv. 1, 2, 3b, 7), the prayer includes the longing for peace to come to the people (v. 3a). When justice ("righteousness") rules over them, then they can experience *shalom* or wholesome relationships with each other. Joseph Caryl elaborates on the changes produced by *shalom*, "You may be sure to have peace when your mountains shall bring forth peace; when those mountains, which heretofore were mountains of prey and hills of the robbers, shall be a quiet habitation; when peace shall not be walled up in cities, or fenced in by bulwarks, but the open fields and highways, the mountains and the hills shall yield it abundantly; under every hedge, and under every green tree, there shall you find it; when the cottagers and the mountaineers shall have their fill of it; when they shall eat and be satisfied, lie down and none shall make them afraid, then the blessing is universal: and this is the work of righteousness." The originating point for experiencing God's peace begins by personally knowing the Prince of Peace who is Jesus Christ (Isa 9:6). When we have peace with God, we can extend peace to others.

Prayer. Lord, I desire to be filled with your *shalom* so that I may have wholesome, flourishing relationships. Give me a heart to seek the well-being of others and reflect Jesus' true peace with them. Amen.

June 11   Psalm 72:8-14

8 May he also rule from sea to sea, and from the Euphrates River to the ends of the earth. 9 May the nomads of the desert bow before him, and his enemies lick the dust. 10 May the kings of Tarshish and of the islands bring gifts; may the kings of Sheba and Seba offer tributes. 11 And may all kings bow down before him, all nations serve him. 12 *For he will save the needy when he cries for help*, the afflicted also, and him who has no helper. 13 He will have compassion on the poor and needy, and he will save the lives of the needy.14 He will rescue their life from oppression and violence, and their blood will be precious in his sight; (NASB)

The compassionate king. The prayer continues by focusing on the surrounding nations paying homage to the king (vv. 8–11). In addition to his political might, the king exercises power to show compassion to those who cry out for help because they are oppressed and poor (vv. 12–14). Solomon tells us three times that they are "needy" people! Unfortunately, as king, he fails to show compassion to his people but lashes them with whips and makes their yoke of work heavy (1 Kings 12:1–15). What a difference to David's eventual royal successor, Jesus, who will reign with compassion. In contrast to the imperfect king, Solomon, Jesus declares that those who are "weary and burdened" can come to him and find that "his yoke is easy and his burden is light" (Matt 11:28–30). David Dickson comments on Jesus who hears the cries of the needy, "There needs no mediator between him [Jesus] and his subjects . . . The man that has nothing within him or without him to commend him to Christ, to assist, help, relieve, or comfort him in heaven or earth, is not despised by Christ, but delivered from that which he fears." We can turn to Jesus who, full of compassion, will not turn us away but lovingly care for our needs.

Prayer. Lord, I am needy in so many ways, and I turn to you in desperation for your help. Thank you for extending your loving care which sustains me. Amen.

June 12 — Psalm 72:15-20

15 So may he live, and may the gold of Sheba be given to him; and they are to pray for him continually; they are to bless him all day long. 16 May there be abundance of grain on the earth on top of the mountains; its fruit will wave like the cedars of Lebanon; and may those from the city flourish like the vegetation of the earth. 17 May his name endure forever; may his name produce descendants as long as the sun shines; and may people wish blessings on themselves by him; may all nations call him blessed. 18 Blessed be the LORD God, the God of Israel, who alone works wonders. 19 And blessed be His glorious name forever; and may the whole earth be filled with His glory. *Amen and Amen.* 20 The prayers of David the son of Jesse are ended. (NASB)

Amen! The prayer for the king culminates with a blessing for him and his land (vv. 15–17), followed by blessing God with praise (vv.18–19). This doxology concludes both this psalm and Book Two (Ps 42–72). Similar doxologies are an appropriate finale for each of the five books or sections of the Psalter (Ps 41:13; 89:52; 106:48; 150). Two hearty "Amens" conclude this psalm, emphasizing a congregation's heartfelt agreement with the prayer. In relation to "Amen," Richard Sibbes elaborates, "Amen is a short word, but marvellously pregnant, full of sense, full of spirit. It is a word that seals all the truths of God [and] that seals every particular promise of God." Thus, it is not surprising that this psalm and section conclude with a double "Amen." Regarding the significance of saying "Amen," Sibbes adds, "It [Amen] is never likely to arise in the soul, unless there be first an almighty power from heaven, to seize on the powers of the soul, to subdue them, and make it say, 'Amen.' There is such an inward rising of the heart, and an innate rebellion against the blessed truth of God, that unless God, by his strong arm, bring the heart down, it never will nor can say, 'Amen.'"

Prayer. Lord of glory, you are worthy of all praise and honor. With all my heart I worship you with my voice! Amen and amen!

June 13   Psalm 73:1–3

1 *Truly God is good to Israel, to those who are pure in heart.* 2 But as for me, my feet had almost stumbled, my steps had nearly slipped. 3 For I was envious of the arrogant when I saw the prosperity of the wicked. (ESV)

God's goodness. Asaph opens his psalm with God's promise to extend his goodness to the "pure in heart" (v. 1). Thomas Watson comments, "Purity of heart is the characteristic note of God's people." He goes on to say, "As chastity distinguishes a virtuous woman from a harlot, so the true saint is distinguished from the hypocrite by his heart purity." He notes that a "true saint" possesses a pure heart, in contrast to a hypocrite who only outwardly professes faith in God. A pure heart reflects a genuine commitment to the Lord. About God's goodness, Watson observes that while "we all desire that God should be good to us . . . it is the sick man's prayer: 'The Lord be good to me.'" Affliction makes us long for God's goodness. When we go through a season of adversity (vv. 2–3), we may echo Watson's query, "But how is God good to [us]?" There are two ways that God shows his goodness to the pure in heart. First, those who have a pure heart make a positive impact on their work and relationships for to the pure "all things are pure" (Titus 1:15). To them, God shows his goodness by providing them with friends who will pray, encourage, and walk alongside of them through their trials. To contrast, he notes that the wicked experience negative consequences in their own lives (Deut 28:16–19). Second, God extends his goodness to the "clean-hearted" because he "works for the good of those who love him" (Rom 8:28). Not all good things from God appear to be good to us. In Watson's words, "Mercies and afflictions shall turn to [our] good; the most poisonous drugs shall be medicinal; the most cross providence shall carry on the design of [our] salvation. Who, then, would not be clean in heart?" In the most unlikely ways, God expresses his goodness!

Prayer. Lord, I confess that when adversities come into my life, I question your goodness. Reawaken me to the innumerable ways you show you goodness to me so that I will trust your goodness in tough times. Amen.

June 14 — Psalm 73:4-9

4 For they have no pangs until death; their bodies are fat and sleek. 5 They are not in trouble as others are; they are not stricken like the rest of mankind. 6 Therefore pride is their necklace; violence covers them as a garment. 7 Their eyes swell out through fatness; their hearts overflow with follies. 8 *They scoff and speak with malice; loftily they threaten oppression.* 9 They set their mouths against the heavens, and their tongue struts through the earth. (ESV)

Society's goodness. Having affirmed the goodness of God and the value of a pure heart, Asaph now describes the wicked (v. 3). They seem to have the good life. Prosperity allows them to enjoy the best foods and good health (vv. 2, 4). They believe that they can protect themselves from danger and are immune from life's troubles (v. 5). With their affluence, they have an arrogant attitude regarding what they have attained (v. 6). While they proudly strut around, they speak maliciously (vv. 8a, 9), and brutalize others (vv. 6b, 8b) who seem less important than themselves. John Calvin* graphically describes how sin progresses in these proud and mean people: "Indeed, we see that wicked men, after having for some time got everything to prosper according to their desires, cast off all shame, and are at no pains to conceal themselves, when about to commit iniquity, but loudly proclaim their own turpitude. 'What!' they will say 'is it not in my power to deprive you of all that you possess, and even to cut your throat?' Robbers, it is true, can do the same thing; but then they hide themselves for fear. These giants, or rather inhuman monsters, of whom David speaks, on the contrary not only imagine that they are exempted from subjection to any law, but, unmindful of their own weakness, foam furiously, as if there were no distinction between good and evil, between right and wrong." Knowing God's goodness, it is no wonder that Asaph questions how these mean-spirited people prosper in life. This question and its answer will be the focus of the remainder of the psalm.

Prayer. Lord, I confess my arrogance, believing that I do not need to depend on you. I need you to change my proud heart so that I can grow in humility and become truly thankful for all that you have given me. Amen.

June 15 — Psalm 73:10-14

10 Therefore his people turn back to them and find no fault in them. 11 And they say, "How can God know? Is there knowledge in the Most High?" 12 Behold, these are the wicked; always at ease, they increase in riches. 13 All in vain have I kept my heart clean and washed my hands in innocence. 14 *For all the day long have been stricken and rebuked every morning.* (ESV)

Daily afflictions. Those who do well in life but unjustly treat others (v. 12) disturb us. We are further troubled when we become victims of their abuse (v. 14). When this happens, we may be tempted to feel that our love and obedience to God is in "vain" (v. 13), making this treatment seemingly unfair and pointless. Does not God see our commitment to him and yet he allows others to prey upon us? To avoid such a limited perspective, Joseph Caryl explains that we should accept trials as a part of our everyday life. He notes, "If a man be watchful over his own ways, and the dealings of God with him, there is seldom a day but he may find some rod of affliction upon him; but, as through want of care and watchfulness, we lose the sight of many mercies, so we do of many afflictions. Though God does not every day bring a man to his bed, and break his bones, yet we seldom, if at all, pass a day without some rebuke and chastening. I have been chastened every morning, said the psalmist . . . As sure, or as soon, as I rise I have a whipping, and my breakfast is bread of sorrow and the water of adversity . . . Our lives are full of afflictions; and it is as great as part of a Christian's skill to know afflictions as to know mercies; to know when God smites, as to know when he girds us; and it is our sin to overlook afflictions as well as to overlook mercies." Caryl's wise counsel reminds us not to be surprised and embittered by those who use their elevated status to get what they want in life.

Prayer. Lord, for those who have taken advantage of me, I want to retaliate. Grant me the grace to accept and respond to these trials so that you may be honored through my life. Amen.

June 16 — Psalm 73:15–20

15 If I had said, "I will speak thus," I would have betrayed the generation of your children. 16 But when I thought how to understand this, it seemed to me a wearisome task, 17 until I went into the sanctuary of God; then I discerned their end. 18 *Truly you set them in slippery places; you make them fall to ruin.* 19 How they are destroyed in a moment, swept away utterly by terrors! 20 Like a dream when one awakes, O Lord, when you rouse yourself, you despise them as phantoms. (ESV)

God's judgment. When others afflict us, they impose a heavy burden upon us. When this happened to Asaph, he knows that he cannot complain about his woes to others. If he does, they may doubt God and suffer spiritually (v. 15). As Asaph struggles to understand the prosperity of the wicked (v. 16), he turns to God for insight (v. 17). When he spends time alone with the Lord, God gives him the much-needed discernment that God will execute judgment on them (v. 18). Asaph gains a new perspective, understanding that God is directly involved in punishing the wicked. George Swinnock describes their downfall, "They are but exalted, as the shellfish by the eagle, according to the naturalist, to be thrown down on some rock and devoured. Their most glorious prosperity is but like a rainbow, which shows itself for a little time in all its gaudy colours, and then vanishes." Their demise comes unexpectedly and conclusively. He continues, "The Turks, considering the unhappy end of their viziers, use this proverb, 'He that is in the greatest office is but a statue of glass.' Wicked men walk on glass or ice" and suddenly "their feet slip—they fall and break their necks." When we wonder why wicked people often succeed, Asaph reminds us that Almighty God deals with arrogant oppressors when the time is right.

Prayer. Lord, I confess that I often adopt a short-term view of acts of injustice which leaves me angry at successful evildoers. You have reminded me of your just judgment in world affairs. Thank you for making everything right in your time! Amen.

June 17   Psalm 73:21–24

21 Then I realized that my heart was bitter, and I was all torn up inside. 22 I was so foolish and ignorant—I must have seemed like a senseless animal to you. 23 Yet I still belong to you; you hold my right hand. 24 *You guide me with your counsel, leading me to a glorious destiny.* (NLT)

Overcoming bitterness. When a perplexing situation troubles us, we may not at first be aware of the causes of our inner turmoil. Asaph has admitted that he has been envious (v. 3), but now, because he has spent time alone with God), he not only trusts God's just dealings with the oppressors, but he acknowledges that he had a bitter spirit (v. 21) and that he has been ignorant (v. 22a). So, he concludes that from God's perspective, he has behaved like a "senseless animal" (v. 22b). Although he feels ashamed and useless before the Lord, God assures him of their relationship, of God's presence with him, holding his hand. With this assurance, Asaph gains confidence that God will guide his life. Thomas Manton comments, "After conversion, God still works with us: he does not only give grace, but actual help in the work of obedience . . . His actual help is necessary to direct, quicken, strengthen, protect and defend us. In our way to heaven, we need not only a rule and path, but a guide. The rule is the law of God; but the guide is the Spirit of God." Scripture provides the pathway to live but we need the Holy Spirit who enables us to follow his guidance. Because God has adopted us and loves us (Eph 1:3–5), he has given us everything we need to obey him.

Prayer. Father, forgive me for the destructive bitterness I have held in my heart toward you and others. Surrendering my bitter spirit to you, I ask you to cleanse my heart so that I may fully embrace your love for me. Amen.

June 18 — Psalm 73:25–28

25 Whom have I in heaven but you? I desire you more than anything on earth. 26 My health may fail, and my spirit may grow weak, but God remains the strength of my heart; he is mine forever. 27 Those who desert him will perish, for you destroy those who abandon you. 28 *But as for me, how good it is to be near God!* I have made the Sovereign Lord my shelter, and I will tell everyone about the wonderful things you do. (NLT)

Drawing near to God. Nothing matters as much as a personal relationship with God (vv. 25–26) and a desire to be near to him (v. 28a). Richard Sibbes mentions six degrees of increasing closeness to God. The first degree is when we realize that Jesus is the Son of God, when our "understanding is enlightened" and is near to accepting Jesus Christ as Savior. In the second degree, we are conscious of God's nearness because he is "present to our minds" in contrast to those whose minds do not have room for God (Ps 10:4). The third degree of nearness to the Lord occurs when we choose to "cleave to him." When we draw near to the Lord in the fourth degree "our whole affections are carried to God, loving him as the chief good. Love is the firstborn affection" which creates the desire for communion with God and our soul "pants" for him (Ps 42:1). The fifth degree occurs "when the soul is touched with the Spirit of God working faith, stirring up dependence, confidence, and trust on God." With the joy of "sweet communion" with the Lord, we grow inwardly "zealous and resolute, and hot in love" for him. Outwardly, we speak reverently "of him and to him," pray with strong "affection," as well as "hear him speak to us; consulting with his oracles; fetching comforts against distresses, directions against maladies." Sibbes observes that in the final degree of nearness "we draw near to him when we praise him" as the saints and angels do in God's presence in heaven. Through union with Jesus (John 15:4–5) an intimate relationship with God is possible.

Prayer. Lord, I commit myself to drawing near to you by cultivating my relationship with you. I am thankful for the privilege of being close to you so that I may enjoy this intimate friendship. Amen.

June 19   Psalm 74:1–11

1 God, why have You rejected us forever? *Why does Your anger smoke against the sheep of your pasture?* 2 Remember Your congregation which You purchased of old, which You have redeemed to be the tribe of Your inheritance; and this Mount Zion, where You have dwelt. 3 Step toward the irreparable ruins; the enemy has damaged everything in the sanctuary. 4 Your adversaries have roared in the midst of Your meeting place; they have set up their own signs as signs. 5 It seems like one bringing up his axe into a forest of trees. 6 And now they break down all its carved work with axes and hammers. 7 They have burned Your sanctuary to the ground; they have defiled the dwelling place of Your name. 8 They said in their heart, "Let's completely subdue them." They have burned all the meeting places of God in the land. 9 We do not see our signs; there is no longer any prophet, nor is there anyone among us who knows how long. 10 How long, God, will the enemy taunt You? Shall the enemy treat Your name disrespectfully forever? 11 Why do You withdraw Your hand, even Your right hand? Extend it from Your chest and destroy them! (NASB)

God's anger. Going through afflictions prompts us to ask God about our pain (v. 1). Our heartache is pronounced because God's interminable ("forever") anger seems directed at us, his people ("the sheep"). Although Christ's death has appeased God's wrath toward sin, yet, out of love, God disciplines us so that we may become more like him (Eph 4:30; Heb 12: 1–11). Joseph Alleine offers counsel regarding God's discipline. He encourages us to "take notice of, and be much affected with" God's displeasure, not due to the trial's pain, but because our sin affects him. Although we are not to "murmur" against God, Alleine reminds us to come to him and "humbly expostulate" or "enquire into the cause" of our pain. Talking to God about these matters is important because otherwise we "are apt to have misgiving thoughts of God" and wrongly assume that "God did cast off his people." We are assured that nothing shall separate us from our relationship with the Lord who unconditionally loves us (Rom 8:37–39).

Prayer. Lord, even though I question your ways with me, I am thankful you love me and will never cast me away from you! Amen.

June 20 — Psalm 74:12–17

12 Yet God is my King from long ago, who performs acts of salvation in the midst of the earth. 13 You divided the sea by Your strength; You broke the heads of the sea monsters in the waters. 14 You crushed the heads of Leviathan; You gave him as food for the creatures of the wilderness. 15 You broke open springs and torrents; You dried up ever-flowing streams. 16 Yours is the day, Yours also is the night; You have prepared the light and the sun. 17 You have established all the boundaries of the earth; You have created summer and winter. (NASB)

God is king. Our lives often parallel the people of Israel described in this psalm. Although we belong to God (v. 1), experiencing painful times leads us to believe that God has rejected us. He seems silent, uncaring about our plight (vv. 10–11), and leaving us to wonder if he will ever respond to us. Then he surprises us by mercifully showing up once again! He is not only our shepherd (v. 1) but also our king who delivers his people (v. 12)! He saves us by his power which he exercises over all his creation (vv. 13–17). Wolfgang Musculus* reflects on God's role as king, "Let us learn from this verse how to think of our God. First, that he is our King, and therefore we ought to be encouraged to pray for his help against the ungodly, and to place ourselves in entire submission to his will and government." Musculus reminds us that God is king over all the forces of the ungodly and thus, we need not despair in our afflictions. He adds, "Secondly, that he is not a new God, but the Ancient of Days ["from long ago"], and that whatever salvation has been wrought not only in the midst of his own people, but in the midst of the whole earth, even among those by whom he is not acknowledged, has been wrought by him. Let this meaning strike at the root of all trust in other gods, or in any creature." We must remain faithful to the Lord who is king over all!

Prayer. Lord, thank you for the reminder that you are my king who powerfully acts on my behalf during my darkest days. Amen.

June 21 — Psalm 74:18–23

18 Remember this, Lord that the enemy has taunted You, and a foolish people has treated Your name disrespectfully. 19 Do not give the soul of Your turtledove to the wild animal; do not forget the life of Your afflicted forever. 20 *Consider the covenant*; for the dark places of the land are full of the places of violence. 21 May the oppressed person not return dishonored; may the afflicted and the needy praise Your name. 22 Arise, God, and plead Your own cause; remember how the foolish person taunts You all day long. 23 Do not forget the voice of Your adversaries, the uproar of those who rise against You, which ascends continually. (NASB)

God's covenant with us. When God has seemingly rejected us (v. 1), we must remember that he has made a commitment or covenant never to abandon us. If God would forget, Asaph asks him to remember his covenant with his people (Gen 12:1–5). Yet we, like they, feel God does forget his commitment to us. Francis Taylor proposes a few reasons for our feeling forgotten. First, since our misery blinds us to reality, we "suspect" everyone who might come near to us, including God. Second, "self-love makes us suspect any rather than ourselves, yes, even God himself." As an example, he mentions Adam and Eve who each blame each other. Likewise, "when trouble is upon us, [we] suspect God's breaking covenant, rather than our own." Third, Taylor suggests that "in time of need we most commonly suspect such as are best able to help us." To illustrate, the sick man will not suspect his "ignorant neighbours, but his skilful physician." Likewise, "We know God is best able to help us; our corruption, therefore, makes us to suspect him most, if our troubles continue." Along a similar line, Taylor continues, "We most suspect those who, as we think, have most reason to help us in our miseries, and do it not." For example, if an employee has a complaint, the individual does not go to the other employees but turns to the employer "who is tied by covenant to provide" for the employee. While we may feel that God has abandoned us, we have his promise never to leave us.

Prayer. Lord, I am thankful for your love and unconditional commitment to me. By your grace, I want to remain faithful to you. Amen.

June 22 — Psalm 75:1-5

1 We praise you, God, we praise you, for your Name is near; people tell of your wonderful deeds. 2 You say, "I choose the appointed time; it is I who judge with equity. 3 When the earth and all its people quake, it is I who hold its pillars firm. 4 *To the arrogant I say, 'Boast no more,'* and to the wicked, 'Do not lift up your horns. 5 Do not lift your horns against heaven; do not speak so defiantly.'" (NIV)

The foolishness of arrogance. Asaph, who wrote the previous psalm, knew the evil committed against God's people. He concluded by asking God to deal with those who were "foolish" enough to mock him (74:22). In this current psalm, Asaph describes God as the just Judge who will confront the arrogant (vv. 2, 4). Their pride may cause them to disregard God, but he is in control of the time he will act and in control of the earth he will sustain (vv. 2, 3). Yet, they believe that they can assert their power ("horns") against God (vv. 4–5). Thomas Watson comments, "The ungodly are spiritual fools." While they may not be intellectually foolish, he suggests, "better be a fool void of reason, than a fool void of grace: this is the devil's fool." He highlights God's invitation to the ungodly, "Open wide your mouth and I will fill it" (Ps 81:11). However, not all respond. Watson asks, "Is not he a fool who refuses a rich portion? God offers Christ and salvation, but the sinner refuses this portion." Using metaphors to drive home this biblical truth, he asks, "Is not he a fool who tends his mortal part, and neglects his angelical part? As if one should paint the wall of his house and let the timber rot." We must not be so foolish to focus only on our bodies and ignore our spirits, our "angelical" parts. In contrast to arrogance, we praise God as judge over the world, knowing that God always acts righteously.

Prayer. Lord, I am thankful that you deal with evil in this world. In recognition of who you are, I humbly submit myself to you and your purposes for my life. Amen.

June 23 — Psalm 75:6–10

6 For no one on earth—from east or west, or even from the wilderness—should raise a defiant fist. 7 *It is God alone who judges;* he decides who will rise and who will fall. 8 For the LORD holds a cup in his hand that is full of foaming wine mixed with spices. He pours out the wine in judgment, and all the wicked must drink it, draining it to the dregs. 9 But as for me, I will always proclaim what God has done; I will sing praises to the God of Jacob. 10 For God says, "I will break the strength of the wicked, but I will increase the power of the godly." (NLT)

God's judgment. With the power they have (v. 5), the arrogant believe that they can do whatever they want, including defying God (v. 6). In response, the Lord declares that he alone is the judge (v. 7). Alexander Carson* elaborates on this thought, "The rise and fall of nations and empires are in this Psalm ascribed to God. He exalts one and puts down another at his pleasure. In this he generally uses instrumentality, but that instrumentality is always rendered effectual by his own agency. When nations or individuals are prosperous, and glorious, and powerful, they usually ascribe all to themselves or to fortune. But it is God who has raised them to eminence. When they boast he can humble them. In these verses God is considered as the governor of the world, punishing the wicked, and pouring out judgment on his enemies. The calamities of war, pestilence, and famine, are all ministers of providence to execute wrath." As a result of divine judgment, the wicked will get what they deserve (v. 8). In response to what God will do, Asaph resolves to wholeheartedly worship him. God acts consistently by humbling the proud and exalting those who are unreservedly committed to him (v. 10; Luke 1:51–53).

Prayer. Lord, I confess that the powerful seem to get their way at the expense of those who are vulnerable. This injustice upsets me! I am thankful that you have the power to address these wrongs, for the sake of what is right and fair. Help me to trust and wait on you when I feel beaten down by others. Amen.

June 24 — Psalm 76:1-6

1 God is known in Judah; His name is great in Israel. 2 *His tabernacle is in Salem; His dwelling place also is in Zion.* 3 There He broke the flaming arrows, the shield, the sword, and the weapons of war. Selah 4 You are resplendent, more majestic than the mountains of prey. 5 The stout-hearted were plundered, they sank into sleep; *and none of the warriors could use his hands.* 6 At Your rebuke, God of Jacob, both rider and horse were cast into a dead sleep. (NASB)

Our great deliverer. Asaph opens his psalm by focusing on God whose presence (v. 2) and power (v. 3) deliver his people from their enemies (vv. 4–6). Israel's foes may have been the Assyrians who sought to obliterate the city of Salem (2 Kgs 18:17–25). However, the Assyrian men could not use their hands (v. 5) and they fell into "sleep" (vv. 5-6). John Owen elaborates on their inability to fight, "The strength and power of a man is in his hands; if they be gone, all his hope is gone. If a man's sword be taken from him, he will do what he can with his hands; but if his hands be gone, he may go to sleep for any disturbance he will work. For men not to find their hands, is not to have that power for the execution of their designs which formerly they had." The Assyrians' defeat (Isa 37:36) comes about because God fights for his people with whom he dwells on Mount Zion (v. 2). Owen comments on God's presence, "The care of Salem, or Zion, lies at the bottom of all God's powerful acting and workings among the sons of men. Every mighty work of God throughout the world may be prefaced with these two verses [vv. 1–2]. The whole course of affairs in the world is steered by Providence in reference to the good of Salem." Today God, who indwells us through the Holy Spirit, supplies us with all the necessary resources to defeat Satan and everything he throws at us (Eph 6:10–18).

Prayer. Lord, too often I fail to rely on you, thinking that I can win spiritual battles in my strength. How shortsighted, because Satan is far greater than I! I am thankful that I can depend on all your resources to defeat this adversary. Amen.

June 25   Psalm 76:7–12

7 You, You indeed are to be feared, and who may stand in Your presence, once You are angry? 8 You caused judgment to be heard from heaven; the earth feared and was still 9 when God arose to judgment, to save all the humble of the earth. *Selah* 10 *For the wrath of mankind shall praise You*; You will encircle Yourself with a remnant of wrath. 11 Make vows to the LORD Your God and fulfill them; all who are around Him are to bring gifts to Him who is to be feared. 12 He will cut off the spirit of princes; He is feared by the kings of the earth. (NASB)

God's sovereignty. The nations' hostility toward God is surprisingly an expression of praise to God (v. 10). Ebenezer Erskine comments, "God turns the wrath of man to the praise of his adorable sovereignty." Erskine elaborates on four ways that God's antagonists praise him. First, God is praised by separating us, his children, from those of the world. God's "discovering work" reveals those who oppose and love him. He "separates between the precious and the vile, betwixt the chaff and the wheat . . . Like the chaff and the wheat in the barn floor, the Lord, like the husbandman, opens the door of his barn, and puts the wind of man's wrath through it, that the world may know which is which." Second, God is praised by sanctifying us through our trials. "God's purging work is advanced among his own children by the wrath of men . . . The Lord heats the furnace of man's wrath, and casts his people into it, that when he has tried them, he may bring them forth as gold." Others' animosity toward God and us purifies us and brings God praise. Third, God is praised as trials unite the body of Christ. "God's uniting work is hereby advanced. In a time of peace and external tranquility the sheep of Christ scatter and divide among themselves" but adversity brings God's people together in unity. Finally, "God's enlarging work, or his work of spreading the gospel, is sometimes advanced by the wrath of man (Acts 8:1–5)." God uses hostility to advance the gospel and his praise.

Prayer. Father, because you are sovereign, I am thankful that you are accomplishing your purposes through those who oppose you. Amen.

June 26   Psalm 77:1–3

1 I cry out to God; yes, I shout. Oh, that God would listen to me! 2 When I was in deep trouble, I searched for the Lord. All night long I prayed, with hands lifted toward heaven, but my soul was not comforted. 3 *I think of God, and I moan, overwhelmed with longing for his help.* (NLT)

A troubled soul. While turning to God often comforts us in difficulties, Asaph found no relief (vv. 2b–3). Commenting on verse 3, John Owen notes, "All had not been well between God and him; and whereas formerly, in his remembrance of God, his thoughts were chiefly exercised about [God's] love and kindness, now they were wholly possessed with his own sin and unkindness. This caused his trouble." Now the troubled individual inwardly asks, "Foolish creature, have you thus requited [repaid] the Lord? Is this the return that you have made unto him for all his love, his kindness, his consolations, mercies? Is this your kindness for him, your love to him? Is this your kindness to your friend? Is this your boasting of him, that you had found so much goodness and excellence in him and his love, that though all men should forsake him, you never would do so?" Owen continues, "Are all your promises, all your engagements which you made unto God, in times of distress upon prevailing obligations, and mighty impressions of his good Spirit upon your soul, now come to this, that you should so foolishly forget, neglect, despise, [and] cast him off?" When we realize that we have neglected and forgotten God, Owen asks, "Are you not even ashamed to desire him to return?" He does not believe that God rejects us but not surprisingly, God seems distant from us. When we confess our sins and return to meditating on him, the Lord is merciful and welcomes us back into a close relationship!

Prayer. Father, when my life is in turmoil, help me to recall all you have done for me so that I will turn to you with a fuller measure of love and commitment. Amen.

June 27   Psalm 77:4–9

4 You hold my eyelids open; *I am so troubled that I cannot speak.* 5 I consider the days of old, the years long ago. 6 I said, "Let me remember my song in the night; let me meditate in my heart." Then my spirit made a diligent search: 7 "Will the Lord spurn forever, and never again be favorable? 8 Has his steadfast love forever ceased? Are his promises at an end for all time? 9 Has God forgotten to be gracious? Has he in anger shut up his compassion?" *Selah* (ESV)

Troubled prayer. Confused by God's inaction, Asaph experiences sleepless nights (v. 4). He tries to remember his past relationship with the Lord, his "song in the night" (vv. 5–6) and meditate. Thinking about more pleasant days in the past only accentuates the contrast between the past and the present (vv. 4, 7–9). Timothy Rogers, in his *A Discourse on Trouble of Mind, and the Disease of Melancholy,* offers insight into those times when we are in agony before God questioning his actions. He comments, "Sometimes our grief is so violent that it finds no vent, it strangles us, and we are overcome. It is with us in our desertions as with a man that gets a slight hurt; at first, he walks up and down, but not looking betimes to prevent a growing mischief, the neglected wound begins to fester, or to gangrene, and brings him to greater pain and loss. So it is with us many times in our spiritual sadness; when we are first troubled, we pray and pour out our souls before the Lord; but afterwards the waters of our grief drown our cries and we are so overwhelmed, that if we might have all the world we cannot pray, or at least we can find no enlargement, no life, no pleasure in our prayers; and God himself seems to take no delight in them, and that makes us more sad." In time, we begin to discern those troubling, unexpressed questions which God fully knows. Even when we do not know how to pray, the Holy Spirit intercedes for us (Rom 8:26–27).

Prayer. Father, I am grateful that you understand my emotional anguish. Thank you for your unconditional love which allows me to come before you with my tough questions. Help me to pray. Amen.

June 28   Psalm 77:10–15

10 And I said, "This is my fate; the Most High has turned his hand against me." 11 *But then I recall all you have done, O Lord; I remember your wonderful deeds of long ago.* 12 They are constantly in my thoughts. I cannot stop thinking about your mighty works. 13 O God, your ways are holy. Is there any god as mighty as you? 14 You are the God of great wonders! You demonstrate your awesome power among the nations. 15 By your strong arm, you redeemed your people, the descendants of Jacob and Joseph. (NLT)

Turning points. Asaph makes a turnaround in his outlook on life by recalling God's "mighty" actions (vv. 11–14) which brought about Israel's deliverance from their enemies. William Gurnall comments on the importance of remembering God's active involvement in history, "Faith is a considering grace . . . Faith has a good memory and can tell the Christian many stories of ancient mercies." He challenges us, "Therefore, Christian, when you are in the depths of affliction, and Satan tempts you to asperse [falsely charge] God, as if he were forgetful of you, stop his mouth with this, 'No, Satan, God has not forgotten to do for me, but I have forgot what he has done for me, or else I could not question his fatherly care at present over me.'" Gurnall exhorts us, "Go, Christian, play [busy yourself] over your own lessons, praise God for past mercies, and it will not be long before you have a new song put into your mouth for a present mercy." When Jeremiah remembered God's faithfulness, his hope strengthened (Lam 3:31). Likewise, "David was famous for his hope, and not less eminent for his care to observe and preserve the experiences he had of God's goodness. He was able to recount the dealings of God with him; they were so often the subject of his meditation and matter of his discourse, that he had made them familiar to him." Gurnall concludes, "Thus, Christian, when your hope is at a loss, and you question your salvation in another world, then look backward and see what God has already done for you."

Prayer. Lord, I often forget the ways you have clearly revealed yourself to me. I want to develop the discipline of remembering the unmistakable ways you have stepped into the course of my daily events. Amen.

June 29   Psalm 77:16-20

16 When the Red Sea saw you, O God, its waters looked and trembled! The sea quaked to its very depths. 17 The clouds poured down rain; the thunder rumbled in the sky. Your arrows of lightning flashed. 18 Your thunder roared from the whirlwind; the lightning lit up the world! The earth trembled and shook. 19 *Your road led through the sea, your pathway through the mighty waters—a pathway no one knew was there!* 20 You led your people along that road like a flock of sheep, with Moses and Aaron as their shepherds. (NLT)

Renewed hope. When Asaph looks back at his nation's history, he recalls God's specific and active involvement by enabling his people to escape from their Egyptian captors via the Red Sea (vv. 16-20). David Dickson states that the Lord chose this body of water "where no man can wade, except God be before him, but where any man may walk if God take him by the hand and lead him through." Joseph Caryl states that God's footsteps "are not always known" (v. 19). A path across the Red Sea requires God's miraculous intervention and deliverance by a means completely unknown by anyone. By remembering how the Lord acted so decisively, Asaph's faith is strengthened and his doubts relieved. God's lovingkindness and his promises will not cease forever (v. 8). He will be gracious and will show his compassion to his people (v. 9). Furthermore, the Lord will not turn his hand against his people forever (v. 10). Although he may appear absent for a limited time in our lives, his actions, word, and character give assurance that he has not abandoned us. He is actively involved in our daily lives! God shepherds us, his sheep, long a pathway which includes trials (23:4) and risks. While we may be tempted to resist God's pathway, we recall that Jesus is our "Chief Shepherd" (1 Pet 5:4) who faithfully guides us until we see him in eternity. Therefore, we can give our heartfelt thanks to him (79:13).

Prayer. Jesus, you are my Shepherd who guides me. What a path I have been on through these years! Sometimes the pathway has been exceedingly difficult. However, you have provided your power so that I could continue journeying on your pathway. Thank you for your faithfulness! Amen.

June 30 — Psalm 78:1-8

1 Listen, my people, to my instruction; incline your ears to the words of my mouth. 2 I will open my mouth in a parable; I will tell riddles of old, 3 which we have heard and known, and our fathers have told us. 4 *We will not conceal them from their children, but we will tell the generation to come the praises of the* LORD, *and His power and His wondrous works that He has done.* 5 For He established a testimony in Jacob, and appointed a law in Israel, which He commanded our fathers that they were to teach them to their children, 6 so that the generation to come would know, the children yet to be born, that they would arise and tell them to their children, 7 *so that they would put their confidence in God and not forget the works of God, but comply with His commandments* 8 and not be like their fathers, a stubborn and rebellious generation, a generation that did not prepare its heart and whose spirit was not faithful to God. (NASB)

Remember the past. In this psalm, Asaph rehearses the lengthy history of his people and their relationship with God. The older generation must pass on their past experiences to their children (v. 4). They must not forget what they have heard for two reasons. First, since God's words are of "great weight" and his deeds are "worthy," George Swinnock states that we must keep them in perpetuity for God's praise. Second, recollecting lessons of the past benefits the younger generation (v. 7). For them, Swinnock notes, "Acquaintance with God's favour will encourage their faith; knowledge of his power will help them to believe his promise." He explains, "The more they be acquainted with the goodness, wisdom, power, and faithfulness of God which appear in his works, the more they will fear, love, and trust him." He adds, "By teaching your children God's actions, you will fix them the faster, and they will make the greater impression, upon your own spirit. A frequent mention of things is the best art of memory: what the mouth preaches often the mind will ponder much." Recounting the past stories of God's work benefits both the teller and hearer of the stories.

Prayer. Lord, help me to remember stories of your great works and then tell others of your involvement in my life. I want them to trust and follow you! Amen.

July 1 — Psalm 78:9–16

9 *The sons of Ephraim were archers equipped with bows, yet they turned back on the day of battle.* 10 They did not keep the covenant of God and refused to walk in His Law; 11 they forgot His deeds and His miracles that He had shown them. 12 He performed wonders before their fathers in the land of Egypt, in the field of Zoan. 13 He divided the sea and caused them to pass through, and He made the waters stand up like a heap. 14 Then He led them with the cloud by day and all the night with a light of fire. 15 He split the rocks in the wilderness and gave them plenty to drink like the ocean depths. 16 He brought forth streams from the rock and made waters run down like rivers. (NASB)

The disobedient heart. We may be impressed by outward displays of power such as social status, political position, or military might. So, we are surprised and shocked when the powerful fall apart, leaving us to wonder what happened. The tribe of Ephraim had military strength but unexpectedly, they "turned back" in the heat of the battle (v. 9). Their retreat was not due to cowardice but deliberate disobedience (v. 10) and spiritual amnesia (v. 11). William Gurnall asks the obvious question, "Why? What is the matter? So well-armed, and yet so cowardly?" In response to his own question, he points us back to verse 8 which indicates that their hearts were "stubborn" and "rebellious." He elaborates, "Let the armour be what it will, yes, if soldiers were in a castle, whose foundations were rock, and walls brass; yet if their hearts be not right to their prince, an easy storm will drive them from the walls, and a little scare open their gate, which has not this bolt of sincerity on it to hold it fast." Gurnall applies this lack of wholehearted commitment for God to us, "Look carefully to the ground of your active obedience, that it be sound and sincere. The same right principles whereby the sincere soul acts for Christ, will carry him to suffer for Christ, when a call from God comes with such an errand."

Prayer. Lord, even though I may appear strong in others' eyes, I know my weaknesses and ask for your strength so that my commitment to you is wholehearted. May your overwhelming love melt my disobedient heart so that I will gladly yield to your will for my life. Amen.

July 2 — Psalm 78:17–25

17 Yet they still continued to sin against Him, to rebel against the Most High in the desert. 18 And in their heart they put God to the test by asking for food that suited their taste. 19 Then they spoke against God; they said, "Can God prepare a table in the wilderness? 20 *Behold, He struck the rock so that waters gushed out, and streams were overflowing; can He also provide bread? Will He prepare meat for his people?*" 21 Therefore the LORD heard and was full of wrath; and a fire was kindled against Jacob, and anger also mounted against Israel, 22 because they did not believe in God and did not trust in His salvation. 23 Yet He commanded the clouds above and opened the doors of heaven; 24 He rained down manna upon them to eat and gave them food from heaven. 25 Man ate the bread of angels; He sent them food in abundance. (NASB)

The unsatisfied heart. Although the Lord provides water for his people while they wander in the wilderness, they still complain (v. 20). In William Gurnall's words, "This [complaining] was all that ungrateful Israel returned to God, for his miraculous broaching of the rock to quench their thirst . . . This, indeed, was their trade[habit]all the time they were in the wilderness." He notes that true character remains untested as it experiences God's feast of goodness, but character flaws come to light when the feast is removed from the "table" (v. 19). In the Israelites' case, "As soon as they feel their hunger return, like froward [rebellious] children, they are crying, as if God meant to starve them . . . they forgot his works and waited not for his counsel" (v. 11). "O how sad is this," he continues, because their faith was so weak, incapable of sustaining them when God did not respond as quickly as they had hoped. The application is clear for each one of us, "He is the most thankful man that treasures up the mercies of God in his memory and can feed his faith with what God has done for him, so as to walk in the strength thereof in present straits."

Prayer. Father, I complain too much about what you do not give me. I need your grace to wait for you and to be satisfied with your provisions for my daily needs. Amen.

July 3   Psalm 78:26–31

26 He caused an east wind to blow in the heavens; and by His power He brought in the south wind. 27 He also rained meat on them like the dust, feathered fowl like the sand of the seas; 28 And He let them fall in the midst of their camp all around their dwellings. 29 So they ate and were well filled, for He gave them their own desire. 30 *They were not deprived of their craving;* but while their food was still in their mouths, 31 the wrath of God came against them and slew the stoutest of them, and struck down the choice men of Israel. (NKJV)

The greedy heart. Unsatisfied with God's daily and abundant provision of manna (vv. 23–25), the people now craved meat (Num 11:4) which God gave them by providing quail (vv. 18–20). Yet, in spite of God's response to their plea, the people remain greedy. Asaph tells us that the Israelites were not "deprived of their craving" even though they had an abundance of meat (v. 30). John Calvin* comments on their craving, "This implies, that they were still burning with their lust. If it is objected that this does not agree with the preceding sentence, where it is said, that 'they did eat, and were thoroughly filled' [v. 29 KJV], I would answer, that if, as is well known, the minds of men are not kept within the bounds of reason and temperance, they become insatiable; and, therefore, a great abundance will not extinguish the fire of a depraved appetite." The condition of their hearts meant that they had rejected the Lord (Num 11:20). According to Asaph, the people's greedy hearts angered God (v. 31). We too are vulnerable to greed. Our materialistic society tempts us to desire far more than we possess to satisfy our longings. We must be on guard against greed when we ask from God. If we demand to receive, we may end up being sorely disappointed. Through what he provides, he may teach us that nothing, but God himself, will truly satisfy us.

Prayer. Forgive me Lord for my frequent demands, often asking for things which feed my sinful appetite but do not truly satisfy my soul. I resolve to feast on you and all that you wisely offer me. Amen.

July 4 — Psalm 78:32–37

32 In spite of all this they still sinned and did not believe in His wonderful works. 33 So He brought their days to an end in futility, and their years to an end in sudden terror. 34 When He killed them, then they sought Him, and they returned and searched diligently for God; 35 and they remembered that God was their rock, and the Most High God their Redeemer. 36 *But they flattered Him with their mouth and lied to Him with their tongue.* 37 For their heart was not steadfast toward Him, nor were they faithful with His covenant. (NASB)

The insincere heart. After facing God's discipline, his people seemingly repented and sought him (v. 34). However, their return was shallow, marked by flattering and lying to God (v. 36). Joseph Caryl observes that, "Man is flattered when that is ascribed to him which he has not, or when he is applauded for what he has, beyond the worth of it. God cannot be flattered thus: he is as much beyond flatterings as he is beyond sufferings." Caryl explains the Israelites' motives, "The Jews, then, are said to flatter God, not because they applauded him by fair speeches more than was his due, but because by fair speeches they hoped to prevent what themselves did deserve; or they flattered God with their own promises, not with his praises. They sinned against him, and he slew them; and when the sword found them they sought God, they creeped to him and fawned upon him, they came as with ropes about their necks, confessing they were worthy to die, yet humbly begging for life: and if God would but humbly sheathe his sword and spare them." Their repentance failed to impress God because their flattery stems from insincere hearts (v. 37). Our hearts clearly govern our words. When we speak highly of God's love, hoping thereby that he will forgive our misbehavior and our continued excuses, we are foolishly flattering him. He sees through our insincere praise. Caryl reminds us that God "cannot be flattered by over-praising him; so his person cannot be unduly honoured by over-respecting him."

Prayer. Lord, I do not often consider the ways I flatter you. Guard my heart from insincerely praising you with the hope of garnering your favor with my selfishness. I want to genuinely repent with my whole heart. Amen.

July 5   Psalm 78:38-41

38 But He, being compassionate, forgave their wrongdoing and did not destroy them; and often He restrained His anger and did not stir up all His wrath. 39 So He remembered that they were only flesh, a wind that passes and does not return. 40 How often they rebelled against Him in the wilderness and grieved Him in the desert! 41 Again and again they tempted God and pained the Holy One of Israel. (NASB)

God's overwhelming compassion. Asaph has detailed the Israelites' wretched spiritual condition before God (vv. 8–37). As shocking as their rebellion against the Lord is, who has done so much for them, God's compassion toward them astounds us more (v. 38). John Preston describes that "When [God's] hand was up, and he giving the blow, he called it back again, as one that could not find it in his heart to do it; and when he did it, 'he did not stir up all his wrath'; he let fall some drops of it, but would not shed the whole shower of it." God would not pour out his wrath on these rebellious people because "he remembered that they were only flesh." Preston explains that "[God's] primary scope is to show mercy; and that he afflicts is but upon occasions; and therefore, he is provoked and provoked much before he does it." Preston illustrates from nature, "As it is natural for the bee to give honey, but it stings; but it stings but by occasion when it is provoked; and this we see to be true in God by experience, who suffers men, and suffers them long; they continue in their sins, and yet he continues in his mercies, and withholds his judgments." God shows compassion with the purpose to prompt people to repent (Rom 2:4).

Prayer. Father, I do not want to take for granted your compassion or misuse it for my own selfish ways. I need to remember how much my sin grieves your heart. I want your mercy to move me to turn from my sins and wholeheartedly follow you. Thank you for your unfathomable compassion shown to me! Amen.

July 6   Psalm 78:42-53

42 They did not remember His power, the day when He redeemed them from the enemy, 43 when He performed His signs in Egypt and His marvels in the field of Zoan, 44 and turned their rivers to blood, and their streams, so that they could not drink. 45 He sent swarms of flies among them that devoured them, and frogs that destroyed them. 46 He also gave their crops to the grasshopper and the product of their labor to the locust. 47 He destroyed their vines with hailstones and their sycamore trees with frost. 48 He also turned their cattle over to the hailstones, and their herds to bolts of lightning. 49 He sent his burning anger upon them, fury and indignation and trouble, a band of destroying angels. 50 He leveled a path for his anger; He did not spare their souls from death, but turned their lives over to the plague, 51 and struck all the firstborn in Egypt, the first and best of their vigor in the tents of Ham. 52 But He led His own people out like sheep, and guided them in the wilderness like a flock; 53 He led them safely, so that they did not fear; but the sea engulfed their enemies. (NASB)

Forgotten compassion. Arthur Pridham* reflects on the consequences of spiritual amnesia, "To an Israelite a remembrance of the deliverance from Egypt is the test of active faith. In like manner, to the tried believer now it is the CROSS that furnishes the outlet of deliverance from the misty darkness with which Satan sometimes is permitted to envelope our conscience, when the Lord had not been kept watchfully before our face. Because Israel forgot that first deliverance, they went on frowardly [rebelliously] in the way of evil. Because a Christian sometimes stops short of the Cross in his spiritual conflicts, he fails to defeat the enemy and remains unfruitful and unhappy, until by some special intervention of the great Restorer, he is again brought, in spirit, to that place where God first met him, and welcomed him in Jesus in the fullness of forgiveness and of peace . . . It is at the cross alone that we regain a thorough right mindedness about ourselves as well as about God."

Prayer. Lord, forgive me when I intentionally choose not to remember all you have done for me and go on my own way. Cure me of my amnesia by drawing my mind to the many ways you have shown your love for me. Amen.

July 7 — Psalm 78:54–58

54 And he brought them to his holy land, to the mountain which his right hand had won. 55 He drove out nations before them; he apportioned them for a possession and settled the tribes of Israel in their tents. 56 Yet they tested and rebelled against the Most High God and did not keep his testimonies, 57 but turned away and acted treacherously like their fathers; *they twisted like a deceitful bow.* 58 For they provoked him to anger with their high places; they moved him to jealousy with their idols. (ESV)

The deceitful heart. Despite God's compassion for his people (vv. 54–55), they rebelled and disobeyed him (vv. 56–57). Their actions are analogous to a "deceitful bow" (v. 57). Christopher Ness describes what a deceitful bow does. Even though the archer's eye aims the arrow at the target, "the arrow, through the warping of the bow, flies a quite contrary way . . . sometimes one way and sometimes another way; yes, and sometimes it rebounds into his own sides; or if it be a rotten bow (though otherwise fair to look upon), when an arrow is drawn to the head it breaks in the hand and deceives the archer. The same thing happens when the string of the bow is naughty and breaks when the arrow is drawn." Ness applies a spiritual lesson from the deceptive bow, "Behold, such a fallacious, warping, and rotten bow is man's deceitful heart; his purposes and promises are the arrows that he puts upon the string, the mark he aims at is repentance, to the which (in affliction especially) he looks with an accurate and intent eye, as though he would repent indeed; but, alas! his heart deceives him . . . Thus a deceiving, as well as a deceived, heart, turns him aside." Ness challenges us, "Look to the secret warping of your own heart, and seeing you are God's bow, you must be bent by him, and stand bent for him." Since our hearts are so deceptive (Jer 17:9), we must be receptive when God's truth reveals our cherished falsehoods so that we will surrender them to him.

Prayer. Lord, because my heart is so deceitful, I need your Word to expose and convict me of wrong beliefs and attitudes so that your truth will bring my life into alignment with your perfect will. Amen.

July 8   Psalm 78:59–64

59 *When God heard them, He was filled with wrath and He utterly rejected Israel;* 60 *so that He abandoned the dwelling place at Shiloh, the tent which He had pitched among people,* 61 *and He gave up His strength to captivity and His glory into the hand of the enemy.* 62 *He also turned His people over to the sword, and was filled with wrath at His inheritance.* 63 *Fire devoured His young men, and His virgins had no wedding songs.* 64 *His priests fell by the sword, and His widows could not weep.* (NASB)

God's anger. The people's rebellion against God provoked his anger (v. 59). Charles Spurgeon* elaborates on God's wrath, "The mere report of it filled him with indignation; he could not bear it, he was incensed to the uttermost, and most justly so. And greatly abhorred Israel. He cast his idolatrous people from his favour, and left them to themselves, and their own devices." Spurgeon provides the reason for God's anger, "How could [God] have fellowship with idols? What concord has Christ with Belial? Sin is in itself so offensive that it makes the sinner offensive too. Idols of any sort are highly abhorrent to God, and we must see to it that we keep ourselves from them through divine grace, for rest assured idolatry is not consistent with true grace in the heart." He reminds us of the Philistine idol Dagon who fell to the ground before the Ark of the Lord (1 Sam. 5:1–5) and warns us against idols by drawing an analogy between Dagon and our idols: "If Dagon sit aloft in any soul, the ark of God is not there. Where the Lord dwells no image of jealousy will be tolerated." However, Spurgeon concludes, "Note that God did not utterly cast away his people Israel even when he greatly abhorred them, for he returned in mercy to them, so the subsequent verses tell us: so now the seed of Abraham, though for a while under a heavy cloud, will be gathered yet again, for the covenant of salt shall not be broken." God does not reject his children, but he wants us to surrender our existing idolatries.

Prayer. Lord, I admit that I do not take seriously your anger toward sin. I want to cast down anything that grieves your heart. Amen.

July 9 — Psalm 78:65-72

65 Then the Lord awoke as if from sleep, like a warrior overcome by wine. 66 He drove His adversaries backward; He put on them an everlasting disgrace. 67 *He also rejected the tent of Joseph, and did not choose the tribe of Ephraim,* 68 *but chose the tribe of Judah, Mount Zion, which He loved.* 69 And He built His sanctuary like the heights, like the earth which He has established forever. 70 He also chose His servant David and took Him from the sheepfolds; 71 from the care of the ewes with nursing lambs He brought him to shepherd Jacob His people, and Israel His inheritance. 72 So he shepherded them according to the integrity of his heart and guided them with his skillful hands. (NASB)

God's mysterious sovereignty. God confronts his people's enemies (vv. 65-66) and deals with Israel's two kingdoms by rejecting the northern region, Ephraim, and by choosing and loving the southern region, Judah (vv. 67-68). Although God's choice may seem unfair, Thomas Goodwin explains that "if God would love, it was fit he should be free. It is a strange thing that you will not allow God that which kings and princes have the prerogative of, and you will allow it them. They will have favourites whom they will love and will not love others; and yet men will not allow God that liberty, but he must either love all mankind, or he must be cruel and unjust. The specialness of his love, increases it, endears it to us. You shall find almost all along the Bible, that when God would express his love, he does it with a specialty to his own elect, which he illustrates by the contrary done to others." Following Solomon's years as the king, the northern kingdom collapses and God chooses the southern kingdom, Judah. God chooses Judah, Goodwin asserts "for no other reason than that he had loved them, and out of love had chosen them. For otherwise Judah was, as well as Ephraim, alike involved in the same guilt of sin." (vv. 56-60). Those who are God's elect, his chosen ones, are to live for his purposes (Eph 1:3-14).

Prayer. Lord, although I do not fully understand your ways, help me to live worthily of your calling on my life. Your love reassures me that you know what is best for my life and your purposes. Amen.

July 10 — Psalm 79:1-7

1 O God, pagan nations have conquered your land, your special possession. They have defiled your holy temple and made Jerusalem a heap of ruins. 2 They have left the bodies of your servants as food for the birds of heaven. The flesh of your godly ones has become food for the wild animals. 3 Blood has flowed like water all around Jerusalem; no one is left to bury the dead. 4 *We are mocked by our neighbors, an object of scorn and derision to those around us.* 5 O Lord, how long will you be angry with us? Forever? How long will your jealousy burn like fire? 6 Pour out your wrath on the nations that refuse to acknowledge you—on kingdoms that do not call upon your name. 7 For they have devoured your people Israel, making the land a desolate wilderness. (NLT)

Brokenness. When circumstances tear apart our lives, the pain is excruciating. Asaph writes this psalm, capturing the pathos of Jerusalem and its people, destroyed by the Babylonians. These conquerors defiled the "holy" temple where God's presence dwells (v. 1). When God's "servants" died, they are devoured by wild animals since there is no one left to bury them. Meanwhile, the enemies scorn and mock them (v. 4). About their national disgrace, Matthew Henry comments, "If God's professing people degenerate from what themselves and their fathers were, they must expect to be told of it; and it is well if a just reproach will help to bring us to a true repentance." In this case, their past sins and lack of repentance precipitate God's humiliating them. His actions stem from his anger and jealousy at their rebellion and idolatry. Even if they know why they are being punished, the survivors agonize under the unknown length of their suffering (v. 5). God does eventually bring them back to the land promised to them (v. 1). When we wonder whether there is hope for us in our darkest days, God's faithfulness to his people encourages us that he will accomplish his good purposes in our lives.

Prayer. Lord, it is not pleasant experiencing brokenness, but I am thankful to you for restoring and teaching me what I need in order that I may love you more. Amen.

July 11 — Psalm 79:8–13

8 Do not hold us guilty for the sins of our ancestors! Let your compassion quickly meet our needs, for we are on the brink of despair. 9 Help us, O God of our salvation! *Help us for the glory of your name.* Save us and forgive our sins for the honor of your name. 10 Why should pagan nations be allowed to scoff, asking," Where is their God?" Show us your vengeance against the nations, for they have spilled the blood of your servants. 11 Listen to the moaning of the prisoners. Demonstrate your great power by saving those condemned to die. 12 O Lord, pay back your neighbors seven times for the scorn they have hurled at you. 13 Then we your people, the sheep of your pasture, will thank you forever and ever, praising your greatness from generation to generation. (NLT)

For God's glory. When the psalmist calls for God's help, he appeals to the glory of God's name as the reason for giving help (v. 9). Writing as if God were speaking, William Greenhill quotes, "What I do (says God), I do for mine holy name's sake; there is nothing to move me but mine own name; that is holy, great, and glorious, and I will for my name's sake do much for my church and people." Greenhill enumerates biblical events which display God's glory. Early in Israel's history, their "temple, sacrifices, priests, prophets, ordinances" glorify God. During those years, their enemies nearly destroy the nation, but God spares them for his glory. God "preserved" his people in Babylon who then "brought out" and "replanted" in their homeland. "It is not for the enemies' sake that God does preserve or deliver his people; nor for their sakes, their prayers, tears, faith, obedience, holiness, that he does great things for them, bestows great mercies upon them; but it is for his own name's sake." For "his great name's sake," Greenhill concludes, God converts people, forgives sins, and leads people in righteousness. Both God's salvation and his continued work in our lives are for his glory (Eph 1:14; 3:21).

Prayer. Lord, I want to glorify you! But I must submit to your purposes and accept those demanding times. Help me to live to honor you, for your name's sake. Amen.

July 12 — Psalm 80:1–7

1 Hear us, Shepherd of Israel, you who lead Joseph like a flock. You who sit enthroned between the cherubim, shine forth 2 before Ephraim, Benjamin and Manasseh. Awaken your might; come and save us. 3 *Restore us, O God; make your face shine on us, that we may be saved.* 4 How long, Lord God Almighty, will your anger smolder against the prayers of your people? 5 You have fed them with the bread of tears; you have made them drink tears by the bowlful. 6 You have made us an object of derision to our neighbors, and our enemies mock us. 7 *Restore us, God Almighty; make your face shine on us, that we may be saved.* (NIV)

A cry for restoration. Some of our losses, such as aging, are inevitable; others are caused by our disobedience. Asaph describes the loss experienced by the northern kingdom's tribes (v. 2) who rebel against God. Defeated by the Assyrians, they grieve while their enemies mock them (vv. 5–6). In their plight, they turn to God, their Shepherd, asking him to deliver them from their enemies (vv. 1, 4, 7). David Dickson answers the question, "Will God save them?" in this way, "Salvation may be certainly expected in God's order; and if we labour to be sure of our turning to God, and living in the sense of communion with him, we need not make question of salvation." In verse 3, Asaph asks God to restore them and make his face shine on them. Girolamo Savonarola*, writing a prayer, elaborates on God's face shining on his people, "To yourself convert us, from the earthly to the heavenly; convert our rebellious wills to you, and when we are converted, show your countenance that we may know you; show your power that we may fear you; show your wisdom that we may reverence you; show your goodness that we may love your; show them once, show them a second time, show them always, that through tribulation we may pass with a happy face, and be saved. When you do save, we shall be saved." By God's grace, we can move from tears to a restored relationship, with God's face shining on us (vv. 3, 7).

Prayer. Lord, I have wandered from you and faced the consequences. I am broken and am in need of your healing. I humbly ask that you restore my life so that I and others may see how compassionate you are. Amen.

July 13   Psalm 80:8–11

8 *You transplanted a vine from Egypt; you drove out the nations and planted it.* 9 You cleared the ground for it, and it took root and filled the land. 10 The mountains were covered with its shade, the mighty cedars with its branches. 11 Its branches reached as far as the Sea, its shoots as far as the River. (NIV)

Divine restoration. When God's people cried out to him to deliver them from Egyptian oppression, God mercifully responded to their plea. Asaph recounts how God delivered his people from Egypt and planted them in a new land where they would prosper. Charles Spurgeon* comments on this significant event, "Small in appearance, very dependent, exceeding weak, and apt to trail on the ground, yet the vine of Israel was chosen of the Lord, because he knew that by incessant care, and abounding skill, he could make of it a goodly fruit bearing plant." Like a good gardener who properly "cleared the ground" so that the plants would thrive, the Israelites prospered (vv. 10–11). Spurgeon compares their experience to followers of Jesus and his church, "The Lord has planted us, we are growing downward, 'rooting roots,' and by his grace we are also advancing in manifest enlargement. The same is true of the church in a yet closer degree, for at this moment through the goodwill of the dresser of the vineyard her branches spread far and wide." He continues, "When the church pleases the Lord, her influence becomes immense, far beyond the proportion which her numbers or her power would lead us to expect." Jesus compared the kingdom of God to the exceedingly small mustard seed which grows into a tree with large branches (Mark 4:30–32). As God took a broken nation and restored it, he can graciously take our shattered lives and rebuild us. He wants us to cry out to him for his supernatural healing. When we do this, we will be amazed at the ways God will use our lives.

Prayer. Lord, what you have done for countless people gives me renewed hope for what you can also do in my life. I confess my brokenness; there is no one else who can heal and restore me like you. I invite you to do your work in me so that others may see your empowering grace for your glory. Amen.

July 14 — Psalm 80:12–19

12 Why have you broken down its walls so that all who pass by pick its grapes? 13 Boars from the forest ravage it, and insects from the fields feed on it. 14 Return to us, God Almighty! Look down from heaven and see! Watch over this vine, 15 the root your right hand has planted, the son you have raised up for yourself. 16 Your vine is cut down, it is burned with fire; at your rebuke your people perish. 17 *Let your hand rest on the man at your right hand, the son of man you have raised up for yourself.* 18 Then we will not turn away from you; revive us, and we will call on your name. 19 Restore us, Lord God Almighty; make your face shine on us, that we may be saved. (NIV)

The foundation for restoration. Although God restores us, we are still vulnerable to attacks which seek to subvert our spiritual life. God transplants the vine of Israel (v. 12) to a new land, but in time, adversities beat the nation down (v. 16). Again, they ask God to restore them (vv. 14–15, 19) so that their strong "son of man" will accomplish his sovereign purposes (v. 17). Verse 19 also points to Jesus, the Son of man. David Dickson describes Jesus' role to sustain and restore us, "Neither the church, nor any member thereof needs any more security for their stability and perpetuation, but Christ." He reminds us of our intimate relationship with Jesus who is the vine, and we are the branches (John 15:1–6). Jesus also serves as our advocate "at the right hand of the Father as God." As the Son of man, Jesus is a "partaker of flesh and blood with us, of the same stock that we are of, in all things like to us, except sin." He knows what we experience and shows us how to live for God by his Spirit. Dickson concludes, "The perpetuity of the church, and the perseverance of the saints, is founded upon the sufficiency of Christ; and the unfeigned believer may assure himself, as of the continuance of the church, so of his own perseverance and constant communion with God through him."

Prayer. Lord, I need you daily to help me live for your purposes. I am thankful for all you provide through a relationship with you. Amen.

July 15   Psalm 81:1-5

1 Sing for joy to God our strength; shout joyfully to the God of Jacob. 2 Raise a song, strike the tambourine, the sweet sounding lyre with the harp. 3 *Blow the trumpet at the new moon, at the full moon, on our feast day.* 4 For it is a statute for Israel, an ordinance of the God of Jacob. 5 He established it as a testimony in Joseph when he went throughout the land of Egypt. I heard a language I did not know. (NASB)

A call to worship. Asaph opens his psalm by calling his people to joyfully worship God (v. 1). They praise him by singing, shouting, and playing the tambourine, lyre, harp and trumpet (vv. 2-3). The blowing of trumpets, John Gill* explains, "was in commemoration of Isaac's deliverance, a ram being sacrificed for him, and therefore they sounded with trumpets made of ram's horns." This *shophar* announced the commencement of the first of three celebrations, starting on the first day of the seventh month ("the new moon"). After the Feast of Trumpets or the New Moon festival, the Day of Atonement would begin on the tenth day (Lev 23:23-32). Five days later ("the full moon"), the Feast of Tabernacles began (Lev 23:33-43). This eight-day festival was an opportunity to commemorate the Exodus, when God had delivered his people from Egypt and had watched over them as they journeyed through the wilderness. For three weeks, the people exuberantly celebrated with singing, playing instruments, and undoubtedly, feasting. Throughout the centuries and through this corporate worship, the people expressed praise to God for his faithfulness. When we come together to worship God on Sundays, we worship him for his great salvation through Jesus Christ and for the ways he reveals his presence with us. When we consider the duration of the Hebrew festivities, it challenges us to give far more attention to worshipping the Lord during the week.

Prayer. Lord, you are calling me to joyful, uplifting worship, praising you for your salvation through Christ. Forgive me for limiting my worship to one day a week. I know you want me to live with gratitude. I want to begin cultivating daily worship by thanking you for the countless blessings you shower upon me and your people throughout the week. Amen.

July 16 — Psalm 81:6–10

6 "I relieved his shoulder of the burden, his hands were freed from the basket. 7 You called in trouble and I rescued you; I answered you in the hiding place of thunder; I put you to the test at the waters of Meribah. Selah 8 Hear, My people, and I will admonish you; Israel, if you would listen to Me! 9 There shall be no strange god among you; nor shall you worship a foreign god. 10 I, the Lord, am your God, who brought you up from the land of Egypt; *open your mouth wide and I will fill it.*" (NASB)

Reasons for worship. After the call to worship, God invites his people to remember the ways he delivered them from Egypt. He freed them as slaves from hard labor and led them across the Red Sea, accompanied by thunder (vv. 6–7b; 77:18–20). In the wilderness God tested them (v. 7b) and yes, they failed. From these painful times, he wanted them to learn to listen to him, to obey him and forsake other gods (vv. 8–9). If they remember who God is and all that he had done for them, then he would abundantly bless his people (v. 10). Thomas Case paraphrases God's words about filling our mouths, "You cannot over expect God . . . widen and dilate the desires and expectations of your souls, and God is able to fill every chink to the vastest capacity. This honours God, when we greaten our expectations upon him, it is a sanctifying of God in our hearts." With a similar thought, Benjamin Beddome* suggests that God is asking us to have an "enlarged hope and expectation." Beddome exhorts us, "We cannot be too confident in our expectations from him . . . Open your mouth wide then, O Christian; stretch out your desires to the uttermost, grasp heaven and earth in your boundless wishes, and believe there is enough in God to afford the full satisfaction . . . Those who expect most from God are likely to receive the most. The desire of the righteous, let it be ever so extensive, shall be granted."

Prayer. Lord, although I cannot demand from you, would you increase my expectation of what you want to do for me in the future so that I might praise you? Amen.

July 17 — Psalm 81:11–16

11 "But my people did not listen to My voice, and Israel did not obey Me. 12 So I gave them over to the stubbornness of their heart, to walk by their own plans. 13 Oh that My people would listen to Me, that Israel would walk in My ways! 14 I would quickly subdue their enemies and turn My hand against their adversaries. 15 Those who hate the LORD would pretend to obey Him, and their time of punishment would be forever. 16 *But I would feed you with the finest of the wheat, and with honey from the rock I would satisfy you.*" (NASB)

Wholehearted worship. Just as remembering God's salvation should prompt us to praise him, so genuine worship should motivate us to change. For example, the Lord expects us to come into his presence by listening to his voice (vv. 11, 13) through Scripture. As we grow in our knowledge of the Bible, we are in a better position to obey him by walking in his ways (v. 13). Then we can wholeheartedly worship because we are focusing our hearts and minds on God. When we worship him this way, he is pleased, and he responds by blessing us (v. 16). Joseph Caryl elaborates on the blessings of verse 16, "I [God] would not have fed you with wheat only, that's good; but with the finest wheat, that's the best . . . They should not have had the bran, but the flour, and the finest of the flour; they should have had not only honey, but honey out of the rock, which, as naturalists observe, is the best and purest honey. Surely God cannot think anything of this world too good for his people, who has not thought the next world too good for them; certainly, God cannot think any of these outward enjoyments too good for his people, who has not thought his Son too good for his people." Caryl points us to the apostle Paul's words, "He who did not spare his own Son, but gave him up for us all—how will he not also, along with him, graciously give us all things?" (Rom 8:32).

Prayer. Lord, by dabbling in thoughts and activities which displease you, my worship is no more than half-hearted. By your grace, I want to change so that I might fully devote myself to you and experience your blessings. Amen.

July 18   Psalm 82

1 God has taken his place in the divine council; in the midst of the gods he holds judgment: 2 "How long will you judge unjustly and show partiality to the wicked? *Selah* 3 Give justice to the weak and the fatherless; maintain the right of the afflicted and the destitute. 4 Rescue the weak and the needy; deliver them from the hand of the wicked." 5 They have neither knowledge nor understanding, they walk about in darkness; all the foundations of the earth are shaken. 6 I said, "You are gods, sons of the Most High, all of you; 7 *nevertheless, like men you shall die, and fall like any prince.*" 8 Arise, O God, judge the earth; for you shall inherit all the nations! (ESV)

God's impartial justice. Unlike corrupt judges, God settles issues impartially with everyone including the "gods" (vv. 1, 6). Thomas Adams viewed these "gods" as human adjudicators. In his words, God "considered their pomp and dignity" and then declared that they judged unjustly like others. Adams expands on these human judges, "In power, wealth, train, titles, friends, they differ from others; in death they differ not from others. They are cold when winter comes, withered with age, weak with sickness, and melt away with death, as the meanest: all to ashes." Adams highlights 1 Peter 1:24 to remind us that humanity passes away like "the grass" and "the flower." Then he adds, "No great difference, the flower shows fairer, the grass stands longer, one scythe cuts down both. Beasts, fat and lean, fed in one pasture, killed in one slaughter. The prince in his lofty palace, the beggar in his lowly cottage, have double difference, local and ceremonial height and lowness; yet meet at the grave, and are mingled in ashes. We walk in this world as a man in a field of snow; all the way appears smooth, yet cannot we be sure of any step. All are like actors on a stage, some have one part and some another, death is still busy amongst us; here drops one of the players, we bury him with sorrow, and to our scene again: then falls another, yes all, one after another, till death be left upon the stage."

Prayer. Lord, when I hear of all those who act unjustly I am thankful that you will one day judge all people fairly. Stir my heart to pray for those who are treated unjustly. Help me to act fairly toward those I meet so that I may mirror you. Amen.

July 19   Psalm 83:1-8

1 God, do not remain quiet; do not be silent and, God, do not be still. 2 For behold, Your enemies make an uproar, and those who hate You have exalted themselves. 3 They make shrewd plans against Your people, and conspire together against Your treasured ones. 4 They have said, "Come, and let's wipe them out as a nation, so that the name of Israel will no longer be remembered." 5 *For they have conspired together with one mind;* they make a covenant against You: 6 the tents of Edom and the Ishmaelites, Moab and the Hagrites; 7 Gebal, Ammon, and Amalek, Philistia with the inhabitants of Tyre; 8 Assyria also has joined them; they have become a help to the children of Lot. *Selah* (NASB)

Ungodly power. Asaph describes the nations' hatred toward God's people (vv. 6-8) and their plan to destroy them (v. 4). To accomplish their goal, they develop strategies and form military alliances (vv. 3, 5). Thomas Watson highlights the unique nature of this alliance, "Though there may fall out a private grudge betwixt such as are wicked, yet they will all agree and unite against the saints: if two greyhounds are snarling at a bone, yet put up a hare between them, and they will leave the bone, and follow after the hare; so, if wicked men have private differences amongst themselves, yet if the godly be near them, they will leave snarling at one another, and will pursue after the godly." Reflecting on the power of united alliance, Matthew Henry first addresses the power of united evil. He asks, "Do the enemies of the church act with one consent to destroy it? Are the kings of the earth of one mind to give their power and honour to the beast?" Yes, evil is united against Christ. Around the globe, believers are persecuted for their faith. Second, he challenges believers to be united, "And shall not the church's friends be unanimous in serving her interests? If Herod and Pilate are made friends that they may join in crucifying Christ, sure Paul and Barnabas, Paul and Peter, will soon be made friends that they may join in preaching Christ."

Prayer. Lord, help your people to remain strong in the face of intense persecution. May we, your people, stand united with one another for your honor. Amen.

July 20   Psalm 83:9-15

9 Deal with them as with Midian, as with Sisera and Jabin at the river of Kishon, 10 who were destroyed at En-dor, who became like dung for the ground. 11 Make their nobles like Oreb and Zeeb, and all their leaders like Zebah and Zalmunna, 12 who said, "Let's possess for ourselves the pastures of God." 13 *My God, make them like the whirling dust, like chaff before the wind.* 14 Like fire that burns the forest, and like a flame that sets the mountains on fire, 15 so pursue them with Your heavy gale, and terrify them with Your storm. (NASB)

Godly power. The alliance of ruthless nations wants to kill God's people (v. 4) and possess the land which Yahweh gave them (v. 12). Asaph recalls Israel's past history and the ways God used seemingly weak people, such as Gideon and Jael, to defeat their enemies (vv. 9-11; Judg 4, 7). Knowing God's power, Asaph asks the Lord to destroy the current enemies and make them like "whirling dust" (vv. 13-15). Heinrich Möller* [Mollerus] unpacks this imagery for us, "Cause them to fall into such great calamities that they can find no counsel or remedy for their misfortunes, and that they may run hither and thither like a wheel or a ball, and yet see not where they ought to stop, or whither they ought to escape." Then he concludes, "Such are the minds of wicked men in calamities, wherever they turn they find no harbour wherein to rest, no certain consolation can they discover. They are tossed with perpetual disquietude; by running hither and thither and seeking various remedies they but weary themselves the more and plunge themselves the more deeply in their woes. This must necessarily happen to those who seek to cure evil with evil." Möller reminds us of Isaiah's words, "The wicked are like the tossing sea which cannot rest whose waves cast up mire and mud" (Isa 57:20). "There is no peace for the wicked," says the Lord (v. 21).

Prayer. Father, you know countless numbers persecute those who follow Jesus. Although they threaten and kill your people around the globe, I know that you can humble them. May they realize that they need a Savior who loves them and can deliver them from their own hate. Amen.

July 21   Psalm 83:16–18

16 Fill their faces with shame, that they may seek Your name, O Lord. 17 Let them be confounded and dismayed forever; yes, let them be put to shame and perish, 18 *That they may know that You, whose name alone is the* Lord, *are the Most High over all the earth.* (NKJV)

Responding to God's power. Knowing God's power, Asaph turns to him, asking that he would defeat the nations, not to be vindictive but in order that they might "seek" and "know" God (vv. 16, 18). The psalmist asks that those who have been put to shame (vv. 16–17) might come to know God's "name," the Lord, Most High (vv. 16, 18). The name "Lord" is an alternate name for Jehovah. Thomas Brooks states that "Jehovah is one of the incommunicable names of God, which signifies his eternal essence." While some of his attributes (such as love) find a partial similarity in humans, the name Jehovah "is never attributed to any but God." Thomas Goodwin points out that "Jehovah is the name of his essence, "I AM." Moses encountered Jehovah, the one who is "I AM" (Exod 3:6, 14–15). Jehovah is also the "Most High" (v. 18). About the name "Most High," Goodwin comments, "His being the High and lofty One, notes forth the transcendency and super excellency of his divine being in himself, and that it is utterly of another kind from creatures, and indeed that it only is truly being." When the psalmist calls God Jehovah, Most High, the psalmist "thereby argues his height from his name, that his name is alone Jehovah, and therefore he is most high, and in that very respect . . . he is MOST HIGH in respect of such a glorious being as is proper alone unto him." It is this God whom Asaph wants the enemies to know and seek, once they are defeated. At the least, Asaph wants them to acknowledge God's great power in victory (v. 18). At the most, Asaph prays that they will worship the true, living God.

Prayer. Father, for those who oppose you, I ask that they would see your victorious power through Jesus' resurrection and in people's lives. May they acknowledge who you are and willingly submit their lives to you. Amen.

July 22 — Psalm 84:1–4

1 How lovely is your dwelling place, Lord Almighty! 2 My soul yearns, even faints, for the courts of the Lord; my heart and my flesh cry out for the living God. 3 Even the sparrow has found a home, and the swallow a nest for herself, where she may have her young—a place near your altar, Lord Almighty, my King and my God. 4 Blessed are those who dwell in your house; they are ever praising you. (NIV)

Longing for God's presence. The psalmist is on a journey to Jerusalem to worship God at the temple. He calls it "lovely" because it is God's "dwelling place" (v. 1), where he makes his presence known to his people. As for the psalmist, he "yearns," "faints," and cries out to express his passionate longing to encounter the "living God" (v. 2). The birds who have made their nests and raised their young in the temple (v. 3) adds to the psalmist's yearning to "dwell" in God's house (v. 4). Both God and the psalmist will dwell together in the temple (v. 1). How can we and the psalmist do this? To dwell there, Richard Baker explains that we cannot "look in sometimes as we pass by, or to stay in it a time as we do at an inn." Rather, we must "be constant abiders in it day and night as to which we have devoted ourselves and vowed our service." In other words, abiding in God's presence involves possessing the right heart attitude before him. For example, John Howe tells us that the psalmist's heart is "so naturalized to [God's] presence as to effect an abode in it, and that he might lead his life with God, and dwell with him all his days; he could not be content with giving a visit now and then." Howe challenges us to have the right attitude or "disposition of spirit toward God" and "pursue" abiding in God's presence. With such a heart posture, we receive God's blessing (v. 4). Abiding with Christ allows us to enjoy the presence of an intimate relationship with him (John 15).

Prayer. Lord, I have failed to long for your presence in my life. But now I want to cultivate greater hunger for you and allow your presence to radiate through my life. I want you to be my true home which will fill my heart with praise and will bless my life. Amen.

July 23 — Psalm 84:5-8

5 Blessed are those whose strength is in you, whose hearts are set on pilgrimage. 6 *As they pass through the Valley of Baka, they make it a place of springs;* the autumn rains also cover it with pools. 7 They go from strength to strength, till each appears before God in Zion. 8 Hear my prayer, Lord God Almighty; listen to me, God of Jacob. (NIV)

Need for God's presence. Since our spiritual journey with Jesus is often arduous, we need his presence to meet life's demands (v. 5). One of the pilgrims' challenges involved going through Baka or the "Valley of Weeping," an arid place. With God's grace, they "make it a place of springs" (v. 6). Richard Baker describes how the pilgrims trusted God to turn "an impediment . . . to a furtherance; at least, no misery can be so great, no estate so barren, but a godly heart can make it a well, out of which to draw forth water of comfort; either water to cleanse, and make it a way to repentance; or water to cool, and make it a way to patience; or water to moisten, and make it a way of growing in grace." God's presence supplies what we need for our spiritual pilgrimage, and he uses us to transform barren situations into life-giving experiences so that others can continue on their spiritual journeys. Baker adds, "If natural forces be not sufficient, there shall be supernatural graces added to assist them, that though troubles of the world seem rubs in the way to blessedness, yet in truth they are none, they hinder not arriving at the mark we aim at, they hinder us not from being made members of Sion, they hinder us not from approaching the presence of God." His presence enables us to go "from to strength" (v. 7). In other words, Baker states, we go "from strength of patience to strength of hope; from strength of hope to strength of faith, to strength of vision." God supplies us with all that we need to live for him and others.

Prayer. Lord, I have gone through many painful times. I need your presence for my spiritual journey so that I can grow spiritually stronger amid life's challenges. I want your presence so that I can be a transformative person for others. Amen.

July 24 — Psalm 84:9–12

9 O God, look with favor upon the king, our shield! Show favor to the one you have anointed. 10 A single day in your courts is better than a thousand anywhere else! I would rather be a gatekeeper in the house of my God than live the good life in the homes of the wicked. 11 For the LORD God is our sun and our shield. He gives us grace and glory. *The* LORD *will withhold no good thing from those who do what is right.* 12 O LORD of Heaven's Armies, what joy for those who trust in you. (NLT)

Enjoying God's presence. After days on the road, the journey culminates with their arrival at Jerusalem's temple. To enjoy spending time with the Lord is far better than pursuing the "good life," the psalmist exclaims (v. 10). Why should seeking God's presence be our chief priority? God gives us all we need for daily living (v. 11). Richard Baker reflects on the psalmist's testimony that God withholds "no good thing" from the righteous, "But how is this true, when God oftentimes withholds riches and honours, and health of body from men, though they walk never so uprightly; we may therefore know that honours and riches and bodily strength, are none of God's good things; they are of the number of things indifferent which God bestows promiscuously upon the just and unjust, as the rain to fall and the sun to shine." God's common grace disperses riches, honors, health, rain and sun as he wills among all people. To those who have a personal relationship with God, he gives empowering grace. Baker continues, "The good things of God are chiefly peace of conscience and the joy in the Holy Ghost in this life; fruition of God's presence, and vision of his blessed face in the next, and these good things God never bestows upon the wicked [and] never withholds from the godly." Jesus tells us that he is the vine, and we are the branches (John 15:5). When we allow his presence, the Holy Spirit, to live through us, we will "bear much fruit" as Jesus' disciples (v. 8).

Prayer. Lord, I found the "good life" to be unsatisfying. There is nothing better than to be with you. I am content to experience your transforming and empowering presence for daily living. Use me for your glory. Amen.

July 25 — Psalm 85:1-7

1 Lord, You showed favor to Your land; You restored the fortunes of Jacob. 2 You forgave the guilt of Your people; You covered all their sin. *Selah* 3 You withdrew all Your fury; You turned away from Your burning anger. 4 Restore us, God of our salvation, and cause Your indignation toward us to cease. 5 Will You be angry with us forever? Will You prolong Your anger to all generations? 6 Will You not revive us again, so that Your people may rejoice in You? 7 *Show us Your mercy, Lord, and grant us Your salvation.* (NASB)

Spiritual revival. Adversities have a way of wearing us down and often create the desperate need for personal renewal. The Israelites had experienced painful times because of their disobedience. Now, they ask God to "restore" and "revive" them (vv. 4, 6). In light of their past behavior, should they expect that God would do this for them? No, he would not have to respond, but he did for one reason—his mercy (v. 7). Barton Bouchier* helps us to grasp the essence of divine mercy. "It is not merely of the Lord's mercies that we are not consumed, but all is mercy, from first to last—mercy that met us by the way— mercy that looked upon us in our misery—mercy that washed us from our sins in his own blood—mercy that covered our nakedness and clad us in his own robe of righteousness—mercy that led and guided us by the way— and mercy that will never leave nor forsake us till mercy has wrought its perfect work in the eternal salvation of our souls through Jesus Christ." This is God's mercy which redeems us and continues to bring spiritual revival to our downtrodden souls. The Hebrews could ask for God's mercy again because he had shown them mercy in the past by restoring "their fortunes" (vv. 1-4). Yes, God's mercies are new every morning (Lam 3:23), offering us the opportunity for a renewed relationship with Christ.

Prayer. Loving Father, every breath I take, every day I live, is an expression of your mercy. As you have shown mercy in the past by forgiving my sin and bringing me into a relationship with you, I need your mercy to overcome my discouraged heart by renewing my walk with you today. Amen.

July 26   Psalm 85:8–13

8 I will hear what God the Lord *will say; for He will speak peace to His people,* to His godly ones; and may they not turn back to foolishness. 9 Certainly His salvation is near to those who fear Him, that glory may dwell in our land. 10 Graciousness and truth have met together; righteousness and peace have kissed each other. 11 Truth sprouts from the earth, and righteousness looks down from heaven. 12 Indeed, the Lord will give what is good, and our land will yield its produce. 13 Righteousness will go before Him and will make His footsteps into a way. (NASB)

Evidence of revival. God hears and responds with mercy to broken people who cry out to him. He speaks peace or *shalom* to those who pursue godliness (v. 8a). While *shalom* may be a greeting, the word also denotes the wholeness or well-being which we experience in two realms, according to Edward Marbury. First, *shalom* describes a wholesome relationship with the Lord. When God's peace is given to his people, "The voice of the Lord is comfortable, and his words are sweet to those that fear him." The righteous do "not fear the voice of God." However, if his people return to "foolishness" (v. 8b), Marbury states, "It is a plain sign that all is not well with us, when the voice of God does cast us into fear, when we are afraid to hear the word preached, when just reproofs of our sins are unwelcome to us, and anger us, and make us think the less of our minister that chides and threatens us." Our attitude toward God's voice reveals whether or not we experience *shalom*. The second realm of *shalom* is our relationships within the community of faith. When God's peace exists within us, his love flows through us; we speak graciously and truthfully, and treat others rightly (vv. 10–11, 13). Wholesome relationships are evidence of people who have experienced spiritual revival with God.

Prayer. Lord, you are the true source of *shalom* and makes it possible for me to experience well-being. From my broken heart, I long for a wholesome relationship with you and others. Thank you for reviving me with your peace so that I may speak graciously and truthfully with others and treat them rightly. Amen.

July 27   Psalm 86:1–7

1 Incline your ear, LORD, and answer me; for I am afflicted and needy. 2 Protect my soul, for I am godly; You are my God, save Your servant who trusts in You. 3 Be gracious to me, Lord, for I call upon you all day long. 4 Make the soul of your servant joyful, for to you, Lord, I lift up my soul. 5 *For you, Lord, are good, and ready to forgive,* and abundant in mercy to all who call upon you. 6 Listen, LORD, to my prayer; and give Your attention to the sound of my pleading! 7 On the day of my trouble I will call upon You, for You will answer me. (NASB)

God forgives. When David is afflicted by trials, he asks God to listen and answer his prayer for protection and a joyful spirit (vv. 1–4, 6–7). In part, he bases his appeal on his own character. He is a godly person who trusts God and calls upon him throughout the day (vv. 2–3, 6). David sees God as his God and sees himself as God's "servant"; he knows the Lord will answer him (v. 2). Based on this personal relationship, he knows God to be gracious (vs. 3), "ready to forgive and abundant in mercy" (v. 5). Joseph Caryl elaborates on these qualities of God, "The mercy of God is a ready mercy, and his pardons are ready for his people; his pardons and mercies are not to seek, he has them at hand, he is 'good and ready to forgive.' Whereas most men, though they will forgive, yet they are not ready to forgive, they are hardly brought to it, though they do it at last. But God is 'ready to forgive'; he has, as it were, pardons ready drawn (as a man who would be ready to do a business, he will have such writings as concern the passing of it ready); there is nothing to do but to put in the date and the name; yes indeed, the date and the name are put in from all eternity."

Prayer. Father, I am thankful for your forgiveness of my sins through Jesus' death on the cross. It is humbling to know that you are ready to forgive me when I confess my sins to you. Your mercy is greater than my sin! Amen.

July 28   Psalm 86:8–13

8 There is no one like You among the gods, Lord, nor are there any works like Yours. 9 All nations whom You have made will come and worship before You, Lord, and they will glorify Your name. 10 For You are great, and You do wondrous deeds; You alone are God. 11 Teach me Your way, LORD; I will walk in Your truth; *unite my heart to fear Your name.* 12 I will give thanks to You, Lord my God, with all my heart, and I will glorify Your name forever. 13 For Your graciousness toward me is great, and You have saved my soul from the depths of Sheol. (NASB)

An undivided heart. Knowing God's "wondrous deeds" (vv. 8, 10), David testifies that no other god compares to God. Nations who acknowledge God's great works will worship him (v. 9). In recognition of who God is, David wants to obey him (v. 11a). John Flavel states, "Sincerity drives but one design, and that is to please and enjoy God; and what can more establish and fix the soul in the hour of temptation than this [desire to please]?" If we want to obey the Lord, we cannot have a divided heart. Flavel warns us, "The reason why the hypocrite is unstable in all his ways, is given us by the apostle: he is 'a double minded man' [Jas 1:8], a man of two souls in one body; as a profane wretch once boasted, that he had one soul for God, and another for anything." Flavel reminds us that God's "designs of a gracious heart are united in one; and so the entire stream of [an individual's] affections runs strong." Our heart's longings must be like a river without tributaries to reduce the force of the river's flow. Thus, if "the heart be united for God, then we may say of such a Christian, as was said of a young Roman, 'What he does is done with all his might.' A man of only one design, puts out all his strength to carry it; nothing can stand before him. Sincerity brings a man's will into subjection to the will of God." With a united heart for God, we will be willing to obey and praise him with our whole being.

Prayer. Lord, I want an undivided heart so that I may willingly obey, love and worship you. Amen.

July 29 — Psalm 86:14-17

14 God, arrogant men have risen up against me, and a gang of violent men have sought my life, and they have not set You before them. 15 But you, Lord, are a compassionate and gracious God, slow to anger and abundant in mercy and truth. 16 *Turn to me and be gracious to me; grant Your strength to Your servant and save the son of Your maidservant.* 17 Show me a sign of good, that those who hate me may see it and be ashamed, because You, Lord, have helped me and comforted me. (NASB)

God is faithful. We can feel overwhelmed by life's challenges. David faced a major battle against men who were proud, violent, and opposed to God (v. 14). He responds by turning to the Lord whose character he knows (v. 15) and asks him for divine strength to face the opposition (v. 16). Thomas Adams notes, "There is no stronger argument of God's infallible readiness to grant our requests, than the experience of his former concessions [answers]." Because God had delivered him from his enemies in the past (v. 13), David now confidently asks God to do the same again (v. 16). Adams explains David's reasoning, "The Lord that delivered me out of the paw of the lion, and out of the paw of the bear, he will deliver me out of the hand of this Philistine' (1 Sam 17:37)." The psalmist's confidence in the Lord comes from what he knows to be true about God, as God has taught him. David's prayer reflects "the voice of a strong faith that persuades the conscience God will be gracious to him, because he has been gracious." In the New Testament, Paul "grounded his assurance" in God who had "delivered him out of the lion's mouth" (2 Tim 4:17 KJV), and as a result, could declare that "the Lord shall deliver me still, from every evil work, and preserve me unto his heavenly kingdom" (v. 18 KJV). During challenges, our confidence in the Lord rests in how faithfully he has answered us in the past.

Prayer. Father, ground me in the knowledge of your unchanging character. Because I often panic in demanding situations, help me to grow in my confidence of who you are by reflecting on past experiences of your faithfulness to me. Amen.

July 30 — Psalm 87

1 On the holy mount stands the city he founded; 2 *the* Lord *loves the gates of Zion more than all the dwelling places of Jacob.* 3 Glorious things of you are spoken, O city of God. *Selah* 4 Among those who know me I mention Rahab and Babylon; behold, Philistia and Tyre, with Cush—"This one was born there," they say. 5 And of Zion it shall be said, "This one and that one were born in her"; for the Most High himself will establish her. 6 The Lord records as he registers the peoples, "This one was born there." *Selah* 7 Singers and dancers alike say, "All my springs are in you." (ESV)

Public worship. In this psalm the congregation joyfully worships God in his temple (vv. 1, 7). Reflecting on these verses causes David Clarkson to challenge believers to join in public Sunday worship. He observes, "Some absent themselves from public worship, under pretense that they can serve the Lord at home as well in private. How many are apt to say, they see not but their time may be as well spent at home, in praying, reading some good book, or discoursing on some profitable subject, as in the use of ordinances in public assemblies! They see not but private prayer may be as good to them as public, or private reading and opening the Scripture as profitable as public preaching . . . They see not the great blessings God has annexed to public worship more than to private." Since God has indicated his place for congregational worship (v. 2), Clarkson asks, "How do men of this conceit run counter to the Lord" by preferring their private family dwellings to worship God? The writer to the Hebrew believers instructs them (and us) to continue to worship together for mutual encouragement (Heb 10:25). In church, we witness God bringing people who once opposed him to "know" him personally (v. 4). While online Sunday services have value, the benefits of regularly worshipping with God's people are of far greater worth.

Prayer. Lord, it is easy to stay in the comfort of my home and worship you. You have challenged and encouraged me to see the importance of weekly worshipping and fellowshipping with your people for my spiritual growth. Amen.

July 31   Psalm 88:1-9

1 LORD, you are the God who saves me; day and night I cry out to you. 2 May my prayer come before you; turn your ear to my cry. 3 *I am overwhelmed with troubles and my life draws near to death.* 4 I am counted among those who go down to the pit; I am like one without strength. 5 I am set apart with the dead, like the slain who lie in the grave, whom you remember no more, who are cut off from your care. 6 You have put me in the lowest pit, in the darkest depths. 7 Your wrath lies heavily on me; you have overwhelmed me with all your waves. 8 You have taken from me my closest friends and have made me repulsive to them. I am confined and cannot escape; 9 my eyes are dim with grief. I call to you, LORD, every day; I spread out my hands to you. (NIV)

The reality of dark days. Heman, the writer of this psalm, experiences a painful time with no end in sight. "Assuredly, if ever there was a song of sorrow and a Psalm of sadness, this is one," remarks Charles Spurgeon. This gloomy account of a man's life may be discouraging but it paints a realistic picture. While some may portray the abundant Christian life as rosy, this psalm smashes any illusions of a trouble-free existence on earth. The psalmist tells us that he cries throughout the day because he is "overwhelmed with troubles" and he may soon die, with no hope of escaping (vv. 1-6, 8). He feels God's anger (v. 7), has lost his closest friends (v. 8) and yet, he still calls out to God (v. 9). Robert Bolton tells the story of a woman and two men who went through dark days. These "worthy servants of God" went through a "depth of spiritual distress" and were "plunged and pressed down" with their afflictions. The woman described herself as "horribly hemmed in with the sorrows of death." The two men described their conditions as "woeful and miserable" and "sorrowful torments." Some people suffer greatly, like Heman, yet continue to trust God. We are not alone with our pain because Jesus knows and empathizes with us.

Prayer. Lord, at times life seems so hopeless. I find comfort knowing that others have also experienced dark days. Knowing this alleviates my self-pity and unnecessary guilt. Thank you for understanding and your presence in the darkest days. Amen.

August 1   Psalm 88:10-18

10 Do you show your wonders to the dead? Do their spirits rise up and praise you? 11 Is your love declared in the grave, your faithfulness in Destruction? 12 Are your wonders known in the place of darkness, or your righteous deeds in the land of oblivion? 13 *But I cry to you for help*, Lord; in the morning my prayer comes before you. 14 Why, Lord, do you reject me and hide your face from me? 15 From my youth I have suffered and been close to death; I have borne your terrors and am in despair. 16 Your wrath has swept over me; your terrors have destroyed me. 17 All day long they surround me like a flood; they have completely engulfed me. 18 You have taken from me friend and neighbor—darkness is my closest friend. (NIV)

Grappling with dark days. Considering his miserable condition, Heman asks God several questions (vv. 10-12, 14). Rather than avoiding asking the hard questions and turning inwardly to himself, Heman expresses his concerns to the Lord. William Gurnall believes that we benefit spiritually when adopt this practice. He states, "There is something concomitant with the Christian's present darkness of spirit that distinguishes it from the hypocrite's horror; and that is the lively working of grace, which then commonly is very visible, when his peace and former comfort are most questioned by him." Gurnall provides examples of God's grace given to Heman (and us) when we keep seeking him in prayer. He comments, "The less joy he has from any present sense of the love of God, the more abounding you shall find him in sorrow for his sin that clouded his joy; the further Christ is gone out of his sight, the more he clings in his love to Christ, and vehemently cries after him in prayer, as we see in Heman here. O the fervent prayers that then are shot from his troubled spirit to heaven, the pangs of affection which are springing after God, and his face and favour!" As we wrestle with God during our afflictions, his grace supplies us with joy and a greater longing for him.

Prayer. Lord, amid the challenging questions I ask you in my darkest hours, I long for more of your presence, peace, and joy. Thank you that you are more than willing to generously provide all that I need during this dark time. Amen.

August 2   Psalm 89:1-4

1 *I will sing of the graciousness of the* LORD *forever;* to all generations I will make Your faithfulness known with my mouth. 2 For I have said, "Graciousness will be built up forever; in the heavens You will establish Your faithfulness." 3 "I have made a covenant with My chosen; I have sworn to My servant David, 4 I will establish your descendants forever and build up your throne to all generations." *Selah* (NASB)

Praise for God's faithfulness. The writer opens this psalm with a note of praise. He specifically thanks God for his faithfulness which he has graciously shown and will continue to demonstrate to his people (vv. 1-2). His faithfulness is rooted in the covenant relationship established between himself and David, and David's descendants (v. 3; 2 Sam 7:12-16). The promise of a long-term royal dynasty was certainly worthy of praise for God's goodness! However, later in this psalm the writer laments God's withdrawing his favor which causes pain and serious questioning (vv. 38-51). We may ask ourselves: How should I respond when I face the unexpected hard trials? Matthew Henry provides us with biblical counsel, "The Psalmist has a very sad complaint to make of the deplorable condition of the family of David at this time, and yet he begins the Psalm with songs of praise; for we must in everything, in every state, give thanks. We think when we are in trouble, we get ease by complaining: but we do more, we get joy, by praising. Let our complaints therefore be turned into thanksgiving; and in these verses we find that which will be in matter of praise and thanksgiving for us in the worst of times, whether upon a personal or public account." People within the early church also praised God in difficulties. When the religious leaders jailed and beat the apostles, these new followers of Jesus left rejoicing (Acts 5:41). Later, the Apostle Paul followed his own admonition to "rejoice in the Lord always" (Phil 4:4) after he and Silas were flogged and jailed (Acts 16:22-25). Giving thanks to God during tough times is possible by God's grace.

Prayer. Lord, I admit that I grumble and complain far too often when life unexpectedly becomes challenging. I ask for your forgiveness and empowering grace to join the innumerable past saints by praising you during hardships. Amen.

August 3 — Psalm 89:5–14

5 The heavens will praise Your wonders, Lord; Your faithfulness also in the assembly of the holy ones. 6 For who in the skies is comparable to the Lord? Who among the sons of the mighty is like the Lord, 7 a God greatly feared in the council of the holy ones, and awesome above all those who are around Him? 8 Lord God of armies, who is like You, mighty Lord? *Your faithfulness also surrounds You.* 9 You rule the surging of the sea; when its waves rise, You calm them. 10 You yourself crushed Rahab like one who is slain; You scattered Your enemies with Your mighty arm. 11 The heavens are Yours, the earth also is Yours; the world and all it contains, You have established them. 12 The north and the south, You have created them; Tabor and Hermon shout for joy at Your name. 13 You have a strong arm; Your hand is mighty, Your right hand is exalted. 14 Righteousness and justice are the foundation of Your throne; mercy and truth go before You. (NASB)

The scope of God's faithfulness. When trials tempt us to doubt God's trustworthiness, the breadth of his loyalty should encourage us. The psalmist testifies that the angelic "holy ones" praise God for faithfulness which "surrounds" him (v. 8). Thomas Goodwin describes this attribute of God, "Whatever he does, he is mindful of his faithfulness and covenant, before and behind, and on each side; he can look no way, but that is in his eye. And though he employs angels, and send them down into the world, and they stand round about him; yet he has better harbingers than these—mercy, and truth, and faithfulness, that wait round about him." We are surrounded by God's faithfulness revealed in his sovereignty (vv. 9–14), righteousness, justice, mercy, and truth (v. 14). Since God's actions are consistent with his moral nature, we can be assured of his allegiance to us.

Prayer. Lord, you know how often I doubt your faithfulness to me when hardships come my way. Open my eyes to the ways you express your faithfulness so that you may strengthen my faith. Amen.

August 4 — Psalm 89:15–18

15 *Blessed are the people who know the joyful sound!* LORD, *they walk in the light of Your face.* 16 *In Your name they rejoice all the day, and by Your righteousness they are exalted.* 17 *For You are the glory of their strength, and by Your favor our horn is exalted.* 18 *For our shield belongs to the* LORD, *and our king to the Holy One of Israel.* (NASB)

The blessing of God's faithfulness. God's nature is the bedrock for his activities in our world and his people. In addition to previously mentioned qualities (v. 14), God who is king provides a shield of protection for them (vv. 17–18). He also blesses his people who praise him with a "joyful sound" and walk in his presence (v. 15). Jonathan Edwards contrasts the joyful worship associated with Mount Zion (Ps 9:11) to a "dreadful sound" the Israelites heard on Mount Sinai (Exod 19:16). In addition to the thunder, the people were "far from beholding the glory of God's face . . . the people were kept at a distance, and the light of God's glory that they saw was so terrible to them, that they could not abide it [Exod 33:21–23]." With verse 15 in mind, Edwards states, "[The people] shall be admitted near, nearer than Moses, so as to see the glory of God's face or brightness of his countenance, and that not only transiently, as Moses saw God's back parts, but continually. The light of God's glory shall not be terrible to them, but easy and sweet, so that they may dwell in it and walk in it; and it shall be to them instead of the light of the sun; for the sun shall no more be their light by day, nor the moon by night, but God shall be their everlasting light." In God's glorious presence, we are gradually transformed into God's likeness "with ever-increasing glory" and become more like Jesus (2 Cor 3:18) who remains faithful to us.

Prayer. Lord, I need not dread your presence; instead, I want an intimate relationship with you. Create in my heart an even greater hunger for this relationship so that I can become more like Jesus, radiating his life to others. I praise you for your power to change my life and to sustain me day by day. Amen.

August 5   Psalm 89:19–29

19 Once You spoke in a vision to Your godly ones, and said, "I have given help to one who is mighty; I have exalted one chosen from the people. 20 I have found My servant David; with My holy oil I have anointed him, 21 with whom My hand will be established; My arm also will strengthen him. 22 The enemy will not deceive him, nor will the son of wickedness afflict him. 23 But I will crush his adversaries before him, and strike those who hate him. 24 My faithfulness and My favor will be with him, and in My name his horn will be exalted. 25 I will also place his hand on the sea, and his right hand on the rivers. 26 *He will call to Me, 'you are my Father, my God, and the rock of my salvation.'* 27 I will also make him My firstborn, the highest of the kings of the earth. 28 I will maintain My favor for him forever, and My covenant shall be confirmed to him. 29 So I will establish his descendants forever, and his throne as the days of heaven." (NASB)

Covenant faithfulness. The psalmist records God's choosing David to establish a covenant with him (vv. 3, 20; 1 Sam 16). As Israel's king, his success, including military conquests (v. 23) rested on God exalting him by showing faithfulness and favor to him (v. 24). Based on this covenant, David's reign would continue through his descendants, eventually culminating with Jesus Christ, the son of David (Matt 1:1, 17). Seeing a parallel between David and Christ, Stephen Charnock suggests that Jesus called out to his heavenly Father regarding salvation to be achieved through the cross (v. 26). Charnock states, "As he has authority to cry to God, so he has an assurance of the prevalence of his cry, in regard of the stability of the covenant of mediation, which shall stand fast with him." Jesus' earthly ministry concludes his exaltation "and a throne prepared for him at the right hand of God to that end" (v. 24). Though forsaken on the cross, Jesus is exalted through his resurrection, and by faith in Christ, we enter a "new covenant" relationship with him (v. 29).

Prayer. Lord, thank you for your faithfulness to me as a child of your covenant. I want to live faithfully for you by your grace. Amen.

August 6 — Psalm 89:30–37

30 "If his sons abandon My Law and do not walk in My judgments, 31 if they violate My statutes and do not keep My commandments, 32 then I will punish their wrongdoing with the rod, and their guilt with afflictions. 33 *But I will not withhold My favor from him, nor deal falsely in My faithfulness.* 34 I will not violate My covenant, nor will I alter the utterance of My lips. 35 Once I have sworn by My holiness; I will not lie to David. 36 His descendants shall endure forever, and his throne as the sun before Me. 37 It shall be established forever like the moon, and a witness in the sky is faithful." *Selah* (NASB)

Understanding God's faithfulness. During difficulties we may doubt God's faithfulness when he does not respond to our prayers. If David's descendants who rule on the throne do not obey God they must expect divine discipline (vv. 30–32). In those times, they will call out to him, but he will not answer by delivering them from their enemies. His blessings upon them are conditional upon their obedience to him. However, the Lord will not break his covenant with David, nor his descendants. His dynasty will not end (vv. 36–37) but will culminate in the birth of Jesus Christ. On God's faithfulness, William Greenhill elaborates, "Man's faith may fail him sometimes, but God's faithfulness never fails him: God will not suffer his faithfulness to fail. God's operations may have an aspect that way; the devil's temptations, and our unbelieving hearts, may not only make us think so, but persuade us it is so, whereas it cannot be so, for the Lord will not suffer it, he will not make a lie in his truth or faithfulness; so the Hebrew is: he is a God that cannot lie, he is Truth, speaks truth, and not one of his promises can or shall fail; which may afford strong consolation unto all that are under any promise of God." Even when we fail the Lord, he will be faithful to us (2 Tim 2:13).

Prayer. Lord, I am very thankful for the reassurance of your faithfulness to me during my trials. Neither do I want to take advantage of your faithfulness. By your grace, help me to be more faithful to you. Amen.

August 7   Psalm 89:38–45

38 But You have rejected and refused, You have been full of wrath against Your anointed. 39 You have repudiated the covenant of Your servant; You have profaned his crown in the dust. 40 You have broken down all his walls; You have brought his strongholds to ruin. 41 All who pass along the way plunder him; he has become a disgrace to his neighbors. 42 You have exalted the right hand of his adversaries; You have made all his enemies rejoice. 43 *You also turn back the edge of his sword and have not made him stand in battle.* 44 You have put an end to his splendour and cast his throne to the ground. 45 You have shortened the days of his youth; You have covered him with shame. *Selah* (NASB)

Questioning God's faithfulness. Absent now are the psalmist's expressions of confidence in God's faithfulness. With the royal crown laid in the "dust" (v. 39), God appears to repudiate his covenant promise to David. His enemies have destroyed the cities, and they gloat over his people, leaving them humiliated and disgraced (vv. 40–42). It is even more troubling that God has weakened his own people (v. 43). Matthew Henry states that the nation outwardly "cannot do execution as it has done" by the sword, and inwardly God has "taken off his [Israel's] courage" so that they cannot stand up to their foes in the heat of battle (v. 43). If we believe that we have the fortitude to fight spiritual battles, Henry cautions us, "The spirit of men is what the Father and Former of spirits makes them; nor can we stand with any strength or resolution, farther than God is pleased to uphold us. If men's hearts fail them, it is God that dispirits them; but it is sad with the church when those cannot stand that should stand up for it." As a result of these calamities, shame covers the Israelites (v. 45) who now conclude God has rejected them as his people (v. 38). Since circumstances can wrongly shape our perspective of God's relationship with us, we need Scripture to keep the truth before us (Rom. 8:38–39).

Prayer. Jesus, when afflictions come my way, I doubt your love for me. When I question your faithfulness to me, assure me of your steadfast love by your death on the cross and your word. Amen.

August 8   Psalm 89:46-52

46 How long, Lord? Will You hide Yourself forever? Will Your wrath burn like fire? *47 Remember what my lifespan is; for what futility You have created all the sons of mankind!* 48 What man can live and not see death? Can he save his soul from the power of Sheol? *Selah* 49 Where are Your former acts of favor, Lord, which You swore to David in Your faithfulness? 50 Remember, Lord, the taunt against Your servants; how I carry in my heart the taunts of all the many peoples, 51 with which Your enemies have taunted, Lord, with which they have taunted the footsteps of Your anointed. 52 Blessed be the Lord forever! Amen and Amen. (NASB)

Expecting God's faithfulness. The writer concludes his psalm by asking when God will once again reveal his faithfulness to his people (v. 46). The question, "How long, Lord?" prompts further queries (vv. 47–48). Waiting for God to act prompts questions about afflictions and the brevity of life (v. 47). Matthew Henry addresses this reality, "If we think that God has made man 'in vain,' because so many have short lives, and long afflictions in this world, it is true that God has made them so." However, psalmist's reference to "futility" must be qualified, according to Henry, who believes that our lives are not "made in vain." Henry explains, "For those whose days are few and full of trouble, yet may glorify God, and do some good, may keep their communion with God, and go to heaven, and then they are not made in vain." However, as for others, Henry states, "If we think that God has made men in vain, because the most of men neither serve him nor enjoy him, it is true, that as to themselves, they were made in vain, better for them they had not been born, than not be 'born again.'" They can blame only themselves, not God, for their plight. From his perspective, they are not created in vain because he has "made all things for himself" and "those whom he is not glorified by he will be glorified upon."

Prayer. Lord, I find myself impatiently questioning you during my troubles. Like the psalmist, I am your servant, and I wait for you to reveal your love. Meanwhile, use my difficulties to glorify you. Amen.

August 9 — Psalm 90:1–6

1 *Lord, you have been our dwelling place in all generations.* 2 Before the mountains were brought forth, or ever you had formed the earth and the world, from everlasting to everlasting you are God. 3 You return man to dust and say, "Return, O children of man!" 4 For a thousand years in your sight are but as yesterday when it is past, or as a watch in the night. 5 You sweep them away as with a flood; they are like a dream, like grass that is renewed in the morning: 6 in the morning it flourishes and is renewed; in the evening it fades and withers. (ESV)

Mortality and dependence on God. This psalm touches on our mortality. In his meditation, William Bradshaw expounds on verse 1 and its importance for us. He states that God "in all ages has had a special care of his saints and servants, to provide for them all things necessary for this life including a 'dwelling place,' or 'mansion house' . . . both for maintenance and protection." Bradshaw directs our attention to Abraham, Isaac, and Jacob and others who were pilgrims wandering in the wilderness "without house and home." They could only "abide in tents, booths, and cabins, having little hope to live a settled and comfortable life in any place." Moses, the author of this psalm, knew that his people "wandered up and down in a desolate wilderness, removing from place to place, and wandering, as it were in a maze. So that of all the people of the earth, God's own people had hitherto lived as pilgrims and banished persons, without house or home." Nevertheless, Bradshaw points out, the psalmist "professes that God himself more immediately by his extraordinary providence, for many ages together had protected them, and been as it were a mansion house unto them; that is, the more they were deprived of these ordinary comforts of this life, the more was God present with them, supplying by his extraordinary and immediate providence what they wanted in regard of ordinary means." He suggests that we can find "great joy and comfort" by depending on God while facing our mortality.

Prayer. Lord, with the brevity of life, you provide the security that I need during my spiritual journey. I am thankful for your constant care of me. Amen.

August 10   Psalm 90:7–17

7 For we have been consumed by Your anger, and we have been terrified by Your wrath. 8 You have placed our guilty deeds before You, our hidden sins in the light of Your presence. 9 For all our days have dwindled away in Your fury; we have finished our years like a sigh. 10 As for the days of our life, they contain seventy years, or if due to strength, eighty years, yet their pride is only trouble and tragedy; for it quickly passes, and we disappear. 11 Who understands the power of Your anger and Your fury, according to the fear that is due You? 12 *So teach us to number our days that we may present to You a heart of wisdom.* 13 Do return, Lord; how long will it be? And be sorry for Your servants. 14 Satisfy us in the morning with Your graciousness that we may sing for joy and rejoice all our days. 15 Make us glad according to the days You have afflicted us, and the years we have seen evil. 16 Let Your work appear to Your servants and Your majesty to their children. 17 May the kindness of the Lord our God be upon us; and confirm for us the work of our hands; yes, confirm the work of our hands. (NASB)

Mortality and living responsibly. Henry Smith exposes life's brevity (v. 12), and tells us "First, that death is the haven of every man; whether he sit on the throne, or keep in a cottage, at last he must knock at death's door . . . Secondly, that man's time is set, and his bounds appointed, which he cannot pass . . . Thirdly, that our days are few . . . and therefore Moses, speaking of our life, speaks of days, not of years, nor of months, nor of weeks . . . it is an easy thing even for a man to number his days, they be so few. Fourthly, the aptness of man to forget death rather than anything else; and therefore, Moses prayed [to] the Lord to teach him to number his days . . . Lastly, that to remember how short a time we have to live, will make us apply our hearts to that which is good."

Prayer. Lord, I often forget that life is so short. Help me to live responsibly and pleasingly before you. Amen.

August 11   Psalm 91:1–4

1 Those who live in the shelter of the Most High will find rest in the shadow of the Almighty. 2 *This I declare about the* LORD: *he alone is my refuge, my place of safety; he is my God, and I trust him.* 3 For he will rescue you from every trap and protect you from deadly disease. 4 He will cover you with his feathers. He will shelter you with his wings. His faithful promises are your armor and protection. (NLT)

God's security. When we feel threatened by overwhelming challenges, this psalm encourages us to find security in the Lord. In verses 1–2, the writer states that God is his "shelter," "shadow," "refuge," and "place of safety." His confidence rests in his God who is the "Most High," "Almighty," and "Lord." The psalmist testifies of God's protection of each of us (vv. 3–4). David Dickson explains the security God offers us, "If the severity and justice of God terrify, the Lord offers himself as a bird with stretched out wings to receive the supplicant (v. 4). If enemies who are too strong do pursue, the Lord opens his bosom as a refuge (v. 2). If the child be assaulted, he becomes a fortress (v. 2). If he be hotly pursued and enquired after, the Lord becomes a secret place to hide his child; if persecution be hot, God gives himself for a shadow; if potentates and mighty rulers turn enemies, the Lord interposes as the Most High and Almighty Saviour (v. 1). If his adversaries be crafty like fowlers or hunters, the Lord promises to prevent and break the snares (v. 3). Whether evils do come upon the believer night or day, secretly or openly, to destroy him, the Lord preserves his child from destruction; and if stumbling blocks be laid in his child's way, he has his instruments, his servants, his angels prepared to keep the believer that he stumble not" because the angels will watch guard over the saints (v. 11). Whatever our spiritual battles may be, we can be secure in God who offers us his caring and protective presence.

Prayer. Lord, I often feel insecure by my own inadequacies. Thank you for reminding me that my security rests in my relationship with you. You offer me your presence, power, and promises. Thank you! Amen.

August 12   Psalm 91:5-13

5 Do not be afraid of the terrors of the night, nor the arrow that flies in the day. 6 Do not dread the disease that stalks in darkness, nor the disaster that strikes at midday. 7 Though a thousand fall at your side, though ten thousand are dying around you, these evils will not touch you. 8 Just open your eyes, and see how the wicked are punished. 9 *If you make the* LORD *your refuge, if you make the Most High your shelter,* 10 *no evil will conquer you; no plague will come near your home.* 11 For he will order his angels to protect you wherever you go. 12 They will hold you up with their hands so you won't even hurt your foot on a stone. 13 You will trample upon lions and cobras; you will crush fierce lions and serpents under your feet! (NLT)

God's protection. John Arrowsmith reflects on the psalmist's affirmation of God's protection against all harm (v. 10), "There is a threefold preservation which the church and the members of it may look for from divine providence. One from, another in, and a third by, dangers." He explains these three modes of protection. First, based on the promise in verses 9–10, we have protection "from dangers." He points to God who thwarts evil plans against his people. Second, we have a safeguard "in dangers." For example, "The providence of God was with Daniel in the lions' den, shutting up the mouths of those furious beasts: and with the men in the fiery furnace, giving a prohibition to the fire that it should not burn, when they were in the jaws of danger, yes of death." Finally, God protects "by danger." Arrowsmith explains, "There is a preservation from greater evils by less. No poison but Providence knows how to make an antidote; so Jonah was swallowed by a whale, and by that danger kept alive. Joseph thrown into a pit, and afterwards sold into Egypt, and by these hazards brought to be a nursing father to the church." He notes, "Faith is endangered by security, but secure in the midst of danger . . . Our heavenly Father preserves us as those whom he resolves to keep forever, in and by dangers themselves."

Prayer. Lord, thank you for the ways you offer me your protection against all forms of evil. Amen.

August 13   Psalm 91:14-16

14 The LORD says, "I will rescue those who love me. I will protect those who trust in my name. 15 When they call on me, I will answer; *I will be with them in trouble.* I will rescue and honor them. 16 I will reward them with a long life and give them my salvation." (NLT)

God's promise. The psalmist's testimony (vv. 1-2), followed by his challenge to the congregation (vv. 3-13), would be meaningless without God's promise to help his people (vv. 14-16). They have a personal relationship with the Lord which is expressed by loving, trusting, and calling on him (vv. 14-15). Thomas Watson exclaims, "God has made promises of his special presence with his saints in suffering. If we have such a friend to visit us in prison, we shall do well enough; though we change our place, we shall not change our keeper." He continues, "God will hold our head and heart when we are fainting! What if we have more afflictions than others, if we have more of God's company? God's honour is dear to him; it would not be for his honour to bring his children into sufferings and leave them there; he will be with them to animate and support them; yes, when new troubles arise." Watson concludes by quoting Eliphaz who tells Job, "From six calamities he will rescue you; in seven no harm will befall you" (Job 5:19). The apostle Paul declares that nothing, including "trouble or hardship or persecution or famine or nakedness or danger or sword" will separate us from God's love in Christ (Rom 8:35, 38-39). Whatever happens to us, we are still secure in Jesus whose power is greater than the evil forces of this world.

Prayer. Lord, I am thankful for your numerous promises to help me throughout my life. I am also encouraged by many martyrs' testimonies which witness to your empowering grace through their ordeals. How reassuring to know for your promise to be with me always. Amen.

August 14   Psalm 92:1–4

1 It is good to give thanks to the LORD, and to sing praises to Your name, O Most High; 2 *To declare Your lovingkindness in the morning, and Your faithfulness every night,* 3 On an instrument of ten strings, on the lute, and on the harp, with harmonious sound. 4 For You, LORD, have made me glad through Your work; I will triumph in the works of Your hands. (NKJV)

Continual praise. This psalm begins by extolling the importance of worshipping God. The psalm's heading suggests that the congregation sang these words on the Sabbath, a day of rest and corporate worship. Verses 1–4 indicate that they worship God with exuberant singing accompanied with musical instruments. Later in this song of praise, the writer declares that God has defeated their (and his) enemies. Thanksgiving for his works is due to him (v. 4), regardless of the day or the circumstances. It is "good" to praise him for his daily "lovingkindness" and "faithfulness" (v. 2). Regarding this verse, William Gurnall reflects on the benefit of praising God daily and the drawback when we do not. "God is Alpha and Omega. It is fit we should begin and end the day with his praise, who begins and ends it for us with mercy. Well, you see your duty plainly laid before you. As you would have God prosper your labour in the day, and sweeten your rest in the night, clasp them both together with your morning and evening devotions. He that takes no care to set forth God's portion of time in the morning, does not only rob God of his due, but is a thief to himself all the day after, by losing the blessing which a faithful prayer might bring from heaven on his undertakings. And he that closes his eyes at night without prayer, lies down before his bed is made." Not only does the Lord deserve our praise, but he blesses us for doing so.

Prayer. Father, some days it is challenging to praise you. Help me to turn my mind and heart away from my difficulties and turn to who you are. Help me to see the ways you have expressed your love and faithfulness to me over the years. I will cling to your commitment to love me when difficulties come in the days to come. Amen.

August 15 — Psalm 92:5-8

5 O LORD, what great works you do! *And how deep are your thoughts.* 6 Only a simpleton would not know, and only a fool would not understand this: 7 though the wicked sprout like weeds and evildoers flourish, they will be destroyed forever. 8 But you, O LORD, will be exalted forever. (NLT)

Contemplative praise. God's expressions of love and his deep thoughts stir us to praise to him (vv. 2–5). Augustine* elaborates on the depth of God's thoughts, "Verily, my brethren, there is no sea so deep as these thoughts of God, who makes the wicked flourish, and the good suffer: nothing so profound, nothing so deep; therein every unbelieving soul is wrecked, in that depth, in that profundity." Since we are finite creatures, we will never plumb all thoughts of our eternal God although he has revealed much to us through his word. Nevertheless, we benefit when we pause to contemplate on God's greatness. After God poses several questions to Job, the latter is awed by the depth of God's thoughts and ways (Job 38-42:3). In Romans 11, after discussing the Gospel's coming to the Gentiles and eventually to the Jews through the Jews' initial rejection of Christ, Paul exclaims, "Oh, the depth of the riches of the wisdom and knowledge of God! How unsearchable are his judgments, and his paths beyond tracing out! Who has known the mind of the Lord? Or who has been his counselor?" (vv. 33–34) Among his many purposes, God has shown us how we pass from eternal death to eternal life. Augustine asks, "Do you wish to cross this depth? Remove not from the wood of Christ's cross; and you shall not sink: hold yourself fast to Christ." When the Holy Spirit illuminates our minds, we grasp more of his ways for our lives (1 Cor 2:16). Our increasing knowledge of Jesus Christ stirs us to contemplate on his greatness and to worship him.

Prayer. Father, marveling at the depth of your wisdom prompts me to. Rather than praise stirred only by emotions, it is good to reflect on your nature and actions which reveal your infinite wisdom. Amen.

August 16   Psalm 92:9-15

9 For surely your enemies, Lord, surely your enemies will perish; all evildoers will be scattered. 10 You have exalted my horn like that of a wild ox; fine oils have been poured on me. 11 My eyes have seen the defeat of my adversaries; my ears have heard the rout of my wicked foes. 12 The righteous will flourish like a palm tree, they will grow like a cedar of Lebanon; 13 planted in the house of the Lord, they will flourish in the courts of our God. 14 *They will still bear fruit in old age, they will stay fresh and green,* 15 proclaiming, "The Lord is upright; he is my Rock, and there is no wickedness in him." (NIV)

Cultivating praise. Pondering the psalm's metaphor of a palm tree, John Owen makes observations on the spiritual vitality of the elderly (v. 14). Although some older people may still appear "naturally vigorous, healthy, and strong," they may be "overtaken with spiritual decays" such as bitterness. As the body ages, one's relationship with Jesus offers the "principle of spiritual life and grace," providing older saints "strength and rigour in the exercise of grace." Therefore, the elderly who are godly "will produce a flourishing profession [testimony}" and "they still bring forth fruit in all duties of holy obedience." Vitality in old age is possible because God provides his grace so that the elderly can be "vigorous in the power of internal grace and flourishing in the expression of it in all duties of obedience." Praising God in one's latter years (v. 15) testifies to God's grace, "Consider the oppositions that lie against the flourishing of believers in old age, the difficulties of it, the temptations that must be conquered, the acting of the mind above its natural abilities which are decayed, the weariness that is apt to befall us in a long spiritual conflict, the cries of the flesh to be spared, and we shall see it to be an evidence of the faithfulness, power, and righteousness of God in covenant; nothing else could produce this mighty effect."

Prayer. Lord, as my body gets older, I need to increasingly rely on your grace so that I may flourish spiritually and praise you until my last breath. Amen.

August 17   Psalm 93

1 The LORD reigns; he is robed in majesty; the Lord is robed; he has put on strength as his belt. Yes, the world is established; it shall never be moved. 2 Your throne is established from of old; you are from everlasting. 3 The floods have lifted up, O LORD, the floods have lifted up their voice; the floods lift up their roaring. 4 Mightier than the thunders of many waters, mightier than the waves of the sea, the LORD on high is mighty! 5 *Your decrees are very trustworthy*; holiness befits your house, O LORD, forevermore. (ESV)

The King's decrees. This psalm is the first of seven songs focusing on God who reigns with majesty, strength, and eternality (vv. 1–2). Therefore, he is mightier than all the world's powerful forces (vv. 3–4). Not only is the King strong, but his "decrees are very trustworthy" (v. 5). Commenting on this verse, Matthew Poole states, "Having spoken of God's kingdom, he [the psalmist] now shows that the laws of that kingdom are just, and true, and holy." For all who accept God's reign in their lives, his decrees are good. These decrees are like promises because the King's words are trustworthy. These promises are "declarations of his mind and will to mankind. And he seems here to speak of those great and precious promises concerning the erection and establishment of his kingdom in the world." Thus, God's statutes are "infallibly true and shall certainly be accomplished in [his] time." We fully trust God's decrees because of his integrity and eternal nature. We gladly submit and obey our majestic King.

Prayer. Lord, I am prone to question your commandments by choosing the ones I like while discounting others which challenge my life. Thank you for reminding me that your decrees have come from you and so I can trust what you have to say to me. By your grace, help me to submit and obey what you ask me to do. You are my King! Amen.

August 18   Psalm 94:1–11

1 Lord, God of vengeance, God of vengeance, shine forth! 2 Rise up, Judge of the earth, pay back retribution to the proud. 3 How long, Lord, shall the wicked—how long shall the wicked triumph? 4 They pour out words, they speak arrogantly; all who do injustice boast. 5 They crush your people, Lord, and afflict your inheritance. 6 They kill the widow and the stranger and murder the orphans. 7 They have said, "The Lord does not see, nor does the God of Jacob perceive." 8 *Pay attention, you stupid ones among the people; and when will you understand, foolish ones? 9 He who planted the ear, does He not hear? Or He who formed the eye, does He not see? 10 He who disciplines the nations, will He not rebuke, He who teaches mankind knowledge? 11 The Lord knows human thoughts, that they are mere breath.* (NASB)

Spiritual blindness. When the psalmist speaks of the "stupid ones" (v. 8), Jonathan Edwards highlights their characteristics. They have a "certain spiritual disease" marked by "darkness and blindness of mind." They are ignorant and foolish. He notes the "great degree of this disease" by which their moral stupidity renders them to act like "beasts" toward others. Furthermore, the uncertainty of when they will understand points to the "obstinacy of this disease." Edwards states, "Their blindness and folly were not only very great, but deeply rooted and established, resisting all manner of cure." He points out "what nature this blindness is. It is especially in things pertaining to God. They were strangely ignorant of his perfections, like beasts: and had foolish notions of him, as though he did not see, nor know: and as though he would not execute justice, by chastising and punishing wicked men." We see the "unreasonableness and sottishness [senselessness] of the notion they had of God, that he did not hear, did not observe their reproaches of him and his people, is shown by observing that he planted the ear" (v. 9). They do not have the moral senses to understand or see God's intentions. Their unreasonableness is revealed by their expectation "to escape God's just chastisement and judgments for sin" (v. 10). Without God's help, humanity will suffer and die from its "dreadful disease."

Prayer. Lord, open my spiritual eyes that I may personally know you and your ways more clearly. Amen.

August 19   Psalm 94:12–15

12 *Blessed is the man whom You discipline,* Lord, *and whom You teach from Your Law,* 13 *so that You may grant him relief from the days of adversity, until a pit is dug for the wicked.* 14 *For the* Lord *will not abandon His people, nor will He abandon His inheritance.* 15 *For judgment will again be righteous, and all the upright in heart will follow it.* (NASB)

Spiritual discipline. Those whom God disciplines are blessed (v. 12), the psalmist tells us. Daniel Dyke illustrates the two schoolmasters of this discipline, the "sour schoolmaster of affliction," and God, the "chief and principal head schoolmaster." He elaborates, "The first schoolmaster is affliction . . . God does not willingly afflict us, but being necessarily thereunto enforced, by that strength of corruption in us, which otherwise will not be subdued. So physicians and surgeons are constrained to come to cutting, lancing, and burning, when milder remedies will not prevail. Let us therefore hereby take notice of the hardness of our hearts, the fallow ground whereof cannot be broken up but by this sharp plough of affliction. See what dullards and blockheads we are, how slow to understand spiritual things, not able to conceive of them by the instruction of words, unless they be even beaten and driven into our brains by blows. So thick and brawny is that foreskin which is drawn over our uncircumcised ears and hearts that no doctrine can enter, unless it be pegged, and hammered, and knocked into us by the fists of this sour and crabbed schoolmaster." Dyke continues, "The second schoolmaster is God himself. Afflictions of themselves, though severe schoolmasters, yet can do us no good, unless God come by his Spirit, and teach our hearts inwardly. Let us therefore pray that as in the ministry of God's word, so also of his works and judgments, we may be all taught of God. For it is his Spirit that quickens and animates the outward means, which otherwise are a dead letter. And this is the reason that many men have rather grown worse by their afflictions, than anything better; because God's Spirit has not gone with the affliction, to put life and spirit into it" (Deut 29:24).

Prayer. Lord, I admit that I do not always love your discipline, but it is an indication of your love for me! Enable me to be a teachable student willing to learn from trials and your word. Amen.

August 20 — Psalm 94:16–23

16 Who will stand up for me against evildoers? Who will take his stand for me against those who do injustice? 17 If the LORD had not been my help, my soul would soon have dwelt in the land of silence. 18 If I should say, "my foot has slipped," your faithfulness, LORD, will support me. 19 *When my anxious thoughts multiply within me, Your comfort delights my soul.* 20 Can a throne of destruction be allied with You, one which devises mischief by decree? 21 They band themselves together against the life of the righteous and condemn the innocent to death. 22 But the LORD has been my refuge, and my God the rock of my refuge. 23 He has brought back their injustice upon them, and He will destroy them in their evil; the LORD our God will destroy them. (NASB)

Spiritual comfort. When we go through trials (v. 12), we can experience God's comfort (v. 19) because he supports us during those times (vv. 16, 18). God specifically consoles us when "anxious thoughts multiply" within us (v. 19). Thomas Horton explains God's consolations, "In a word, they are the comforts which do flow from our communion with him. The comforts of his attributes, and the comforts of his promises, and the comforts of his gracious presence drawing near unto our souls, when it pleases him to shine upon us." God's comfort cures the "malady" of anxiety and sorrow within the soul. "Bodily pleasure will not satisfy for mind distraction: nothing will ease the soul but such comforts as are agreeable to itself, and such are these present comforts of God, they delight the soul." This spiritual comfort does not only "pacify the mind but they joy it; they do not only satisfy it, but ravish it; they not only quiet, but delight it." Horton concludes by saying that God does not only remove the anxiety and grief, but he replaces it with the "most unspeakable comfort and consolation; as the 'sun' does not only dispel darkness but likewise brings in a glorious light in the stead of it."

Prayer. Lord, you know my anxious thoughts which preoccupy me. I ask you to comfort me with your promises and presence so that I may delight in you. Amen.

August 21   Psalm 95:1–5

1 Oh come, let us sing to the LORD! Let us shout joyfully to the Rock of our salvation. 2 Let us come before His presence with thanksgiving; let us shout joyfully to Him with psalms. 3 For the LORD is the great God, and the great King above all gods. 4 *In His hand are the deep places of the earth*; the heights of the hills are His also. 5 The sea is His, for He made it; and His hands formed the dry land. (NKJV)

Praise for God's dominion. With the daily rising and setting of the sun, the waxing and waning of the moon, and the rotating seasons of the year, we can take these rhythms for granted. However, God "formed" or created our planet (v. 5) and now sustains it (v. 4). Concerning God's active involvement in this world, Stephen Charnock elaborates, "While his hand holds, his hand has a dominion over them. He that holds a stone in the air exercises a dominion over its natural inclination in hindering it from falling. The creature depends wholly upon God in its preservation; as soon as that divine hand which sustains everything were withdrawn, a languishment and swooning would be the next turn in the creature. He is called Lord, *Adonai,* in regard of his sustentation [preservation] of all things by his continual influx [of power]." Charnock continues, "The Hebrew root for *Adonai* signifies a basis or pillar that supports a building. God is the Lord of all, as he is the sustainer of all by his power, as well as the Creator of all by his word." Centuries later, the apostle Paul writes of God's active role of sustaining this world and states that Jesus Christ holds the universe together (Col 1:17). God's sustaining power has three implications for us. The first implication is that God is supreme over all other "gods" (v. 3). The second is that we have a "Rock" in whom to trust in the world (v. 1b). And the third is that we have manifold reasons to praise God (v. 1a).

Prayer. Father, although I often think that I do not need you, I must daily depend on you to sustain my life, whether in good or poor health. Help me to trust and worship you! Amen.

August 22   Psalm 95:6–7

6 Oh come, let us worship and bow down; let us kneel before the Lord *our Maker. 7 For He is our God, and we are the people of His pasture, and the sheep of His hand.* (NKJV)

Reverence before God. What do we learn about worship from the writer's words in this psalm? Reflecting on verse 6, John Boys shares his thoughts on worship. First, the psalmist extends an invitation to others to join him in worshipping God. Boys encourages us to imitate his example and invite others to come along, thereby avoiding "parents without their children, and children without their parents: husbands without their wives, and wives without their husband." Second, bowing down and kneeling before God is fitting because "our God, unto whom we must sing, in whom we must rejoice, before whom we must worship, is a great 'King above all gods.'" We humble ourselves before God alone, not before any other religious objects. As God's "sheep," we live in humble dependence on Jesus our Shepherd and "with all that is within us, with all that is without us" we worship him.

Prayer. Lord, I am thankful for the relationship I have with you. You are my Shepherd who has watched over me and cared for me. In recognition of my dependence on you, I bow in humble reverence to worship you. The opportunity of joyfully worshipping you with others is a testimony of your faithfulness to your people. Amen.

August 23　　　　　　　Psalm 95:8–11

8 *"Do not harden your hearts*, as in the rebellion, as in the day of trial in the wilderness, 9 When your fathers tested Me; They tried Me, though they saw My work. 10 For forty years I was grieved with that generation, and said, It *is a people who go astray in their hearts, and they do not know My ways.'* 11 So I swore in My wrath, 'They shall not enter My rest.' (NKJV)

The human heart. Worshipping God with humility requires us not to harden our hearts (v. 8). William Gouge states that the "heart" refers "to signify sometimes the whole soul, and sometimes the several faculties appertaining to the soul." He enumerates the specific ways Scriptures refer to the "heart." In one definition, the heart is "frequently put for the whole soul, and that for the most part when it is set alone; as where it is said, 'Serve the Lord with all your heart' (1 Sam 7:20)." A second definition refers to the "principal part of the soul which is called the mind or understanding (Eccl 1:17). In this respect darkness and blindness are attributed to the heart (Eph 6:18, Rom 1:21)." The third way the heart can be understood is as "the will: as when heart and soul are joined together, the two essential faculties of the soul are meant, namely, the mind and will: *soul* put for the mind, heart for the will (Deut 6:13)." In a fourth definition, the heart refers to the memory, "that faculty wherein matters are laid up and hid" (Ps 119:11). The heart can also be equated with our conscience as when David was "conscience-stricken" (1 Sam 24:5 NIV). Finally, the heart refers to the "affections" when Jesus says, "'You shall love the Lord your God with all your heart and with all your soul and with all your mind.'" (Matt 22:37 NKJV). Gouge explains, "By the mind is meant the understanding faculty; by the soul, the will; by the heart, the affections." When the Lord tells us not to harden our hearts (Ps 95:8), Gouge concludes, "The heart is put for the whole soul, even for mind, will, and affections."

Prayer. Lord, my heart is prone to wander from you. I want to guard it in order that I may love and obey you supremely. Search and purify my heart with your truth and Spirit. Amen.

August 24   Psalm 96:1–9

1 Sing to the Lord a new song; sing to the Lord, all the earth. 2 Sing to the Lord, praise his name; proclaim his salvation day after day. 3 *Declare his glory among the nations, his marvelous deeds among all peoples.* 4 For great is the Lord and most worthy of praise; he is to be feared above all gods. 5 For all the gods of the nations are idols, but the Lord made the heavens. 6 Splendor and majesty are before him; strength and glory are in his sanctuary. 7 Ascribe to the Lord, all you families of nations, ascribe to the Lord glory and strength. 8 Ascribe to the Lord the glory due his name; bring an offering and come into his courts. 9 Worship the Lord in the splendor of his holiness; tremble before him, all the earth. (NIV)

God the glorious deliverer. In these verses, the psalmist mentions the word "glory" four times (vv. 3, 6, 7, 8). Verse 3, with its two parallel statements, links God's "marvelous deeds" with "his glory." We declare God's glory whenever we tell others the wonderful things that he has done for us. The greatest act the Lord did for us was forgiving our sins through Jesus Christ and saving us. What we have personally experienced in our lives, we must tell others. David Dickson states, "It is a part of the commission given to the ministers of the gospel, not only to teach their congregations concerning Christ, but also to have a care that they who never did hear of him, may know what he is, what he has done and suffered, and what good may be had by his mediation. Nothing so glorious to God, nothing so wonderful in itself, as is the salvation of man by Christ; to behold God saving his enemies by the incarnation, sufferings, and obedience of Christ the eternal Son of God." We declare God's glory not only in in sharing his 'marvelous deeds,' but in our worship when we exalt the Lord who is above all other gods (v. 4).

Prayer. Lord, help me to declare your glory by telling others of your salvation and by worshipping you. I also want to reflect your glory by becoming more like Jesus. Amen.

August 25   Psalm 96:10–13

10 *Tell all the nations, "The* Lord *reigns!" The world stands firm and cannot be shaken.* He will judge all peoples fairly. 11 Let the heavens be glad, and the earth rejoice! Let the sea and everything in it shout his praise! 12 Let the fields and their crops burst out with joy! Let the trees of the forest sing for joy 13 before the Lord, for he is coming! He is coming to judge the earth. He will judge the world with justice, and the nations with his truth. (NLT)

God the reigning judge. The psalmist asserts that the "world stands firm and cannot be shaken" (v. 10). Yet, the psalms inform us that the natural world with earthquakes and stormy seas (46:2–3; 93:3–4) and the geopolitical world with wicked leaders (2:1–3; 46:6) is a tumultuous place. At the same time, the world is not shaken because God reigns and judges everyone (v. 10). The fear of what we see around us should be replaced by the certainty of God's reign over us. Matthew Henry provides us with a biblical perspective, "The natural world shall be established; the standing of the world, and its stability, is owing to the mediation of Christ. Sin had given it a shock, and still threatens it; but Christ, as redeemer, upholds all things, and preserves the course of nature. The world of mankind shall be established, shall be preserved, till all that belong to the election of grace are called in, though a guilty, provoking world. The Christian religion, as far as it is embraced, shall establish states and kingdoms, and preserve good order among men. The church in the world shall be established, that it cannot be moved, for it is built upon a rock, and the gates of hell shall never prevail against it; it is a 'kingdom that cannot be shaken.'" Yes, one day, the Lord will come to judge the nations with justice and truth (v. 13). This future act of God now stirs all of creation to praise to God for his reign over this world (vv. 11–12).

Prayer. Lord, I become fearful when I am barraged with news of global conflicts and natural disasters. Help me to apply the truth of your reign over this world to my daily life and trust you as my King. Amen.

August 26   Psalm 97:1–5

1 *The* LORD *reigns, let the earth be glad; let the distant shores rejoice.* 2 Clouds and thick darkness surround him; righteousness and justice are the foundation of his throne. 3 Fire goes before him and consumes his foes on every side. 4 His lightning lights up the world; the earth sees and trembles. 5 The mountains melt like wax before the LORD, before the Lord of all the earth. (NIV)

God the holy judge. The psalmist describes God's reign drawing from a time during Israel's years in the wilderness (v. 2; Exod 19:16, 18). William Sedgwick* suggests God is saying, "I am upon my throne. I am great; none is great but myself. I am King; I have the sceptre in my hand. I am powerful; none is powerful but I." He states the clear implications, "All the power of men is broken. All the thrones of men are shattered into dust. All the wisdom of men is turned into folly. All the strength of men is melted into weakness and water. The melting and mouldering [crumbling] away of the powers and dignities of the world, speak it aloud, 'The Lord reigns.'" Sedgwick continues, "All the pride and ambition, all the oppression and tyranny, and miscarriages that have been in the government of men, shall be wholly taken away. Pure righteousness and judgment and equity shall be infallibly dispensed; and infinite power, strength, holiness, goodness, and authority shall shine forth nakedly in the face of God; and that shall be the judge of all men. We shall no longer be abused and oppressed by the will of men, by the lusts of men. The poor people shall no longer groan under the burden of men's lusts, nor sweat for the pleasure and contents of men; nor their faces any longer be ground by the hardness of the spirit of men; but they shall be under the protection of God." With "reverence and awe" (Heb 12:28–29), we worship our mighty and holy God. Depicted by fire (v. 3), God's holiness is a call to examine ourselves so that we may walk rightly before him.

Prayer. Lord, when I see rampant evil in the world, I am thankful that you will judge this evil which has devastated so many lives. At the same time, help me to live reverently because I am conscious of your holiness. Amen.

August 27   Psalm 97:6-9

6 The heavens proclaim his righteousness, and all peoples see his glory. 7 All who worship images are put to shame, those who boast in idols—*worship him, all you gods!* 8 Zion hears and rejoices and the villages of Judah are glad because of your judgments, Lord. 9 For you, Lord, are the Most High over all the earth; you are exalted far above all gods. (NIV)

God the supreme Lord. The psalmist highlights the glory of God (v. 6) who is the "Most High" over everything, including people's gods (v. 9). In response, the people, the "heavens." and the "gods" or *Elohim* praise God (vv. 6–8). Suggesting "angels" as an alternative meaning of "gods" (1 Cor 8:5). John Owen notes, "They [the angels] have the name of God attributed unto them, and these are they whom the psalmist speaks unto. Having called on the whole creation to rejoice in the bringing forth of the kingdom of God, and pressed his exhortation upon things on the earth, he turns unto the ministering angels and calls on them to the discharge of their duty unto the King of that kingdom." Owen defines this kingdom, "A kingdom is described wherein God would reign, which should destroy idolatry and false worship; a kingdom wherein the isles of the Gentiles should rejoice, being called to an interest therein; a kingdom that was to be preached, proclaimed, declared, unto the increase of light and holiness in the world, with the manifestation of the glory of God unto the ends of all the earth: every part whereof declares the kingdom of Christ to be intended in the psalm, and consequently that it is a prophecy of the bringing in of the first begotten into the world." As citizens of God's kingdom, we affirm God's reign in our lives by worshipping Jesus Christ who supreme over all creation (Col 1:15).

Prayer. Lord, you are supreme over your creation and as one of your creatures I want you to reign in my life so that others may see you through me. Amen.

August 28   Psalm 97:10–12

10 *Let those who love the* LORD *hate evil,* for he guards the lives of his faithful ones and delivers them from the hand of the wicked. 11 Light shines on the righteous and joy on the upright in heart. 12 Rejoice in the LORD, you who are righteous, and praise his holy name. (NIV)

Our responses to the Lord. One way by which we express our love for God is to hate evil (v. 10). Richard Sibbes elaborates, "It is evident that our conversion is sound when we loathe and hate sin from the heart: a man may know his hatred of evil to be true, first, if it be universal: he that hates sin truly, hates all sin. Secondly, true hatred is fixed; there is no appeasing it but by abolishing the thing hated. Thirdly, hatred is a more rooted affection than anger: anger may be appeased, but hatred remains and sets itself against the whole kind. Fourthly, if our hatred be true, we hate all evil, in ourselves first, and then in others; he that hates a toad, would hate it most in his own bosom. Many, like Judah, are severe in censuring others (Gen 38:24), but partial to themselves. Fifthly, he that hates sin truly, hates the greatest sin in the greatest measure; he hates all evil in a just proportion. Sixthly, our hatred is right if we can endure admonition and reproof for sin, and not be enraged; therefore, those that swell against reproof do not appear to hate sin." If we hate evil, we also must look within ourselves. Sibbes explains, "God is a Spirit, and he looks to our very spirits; and what we are in our spirits, in our hearts and affections, that we are to him. Therefore, what ill we shun, let us do it from the heart, by hating it first. A man may avoid an evil action from fear, or out of other respects, but that is not sincerity. Therefore, look to your heart, see that you hate evil, and let it come from sincere looking to God . . . not only avoid it, but hate it; and not only hate it, but hate it out of love to God."

Prayer. Lord, out of my love for you, I want to confront evil in my own heart. Search me so that I may honor you. Amen.

August 29   Psalm 98:1–3

1 *Sing to the* L̲ord *a new song, for he has done marvelous things;* his right hand and his holy arm have worked salvation for him. 2 The L̲ord has made his salvation known and revealed his righteousness to the nations. 3 He has remembered his love and his faithfulness to Israel; all the ends of the earth have seen the salvation of our God. (NIV)

New songs. Along with other psalms, this one instructs us to praise God with "new" songs (v. 1; 33:3; 96:1). John Boys suggests possible meanings of these songs. First, the "new song" could be related to being a follower of Jesus Christ. Using the apostle Paul's terms of "old man" and "new man" (Eph 4:22, 24), Boys comments that "the old man sings old songs: only the new man sings a new song; he speaks with a new tongue, and walks in new ways, and therefore does new things, and sings new songs." Second, the new song could be a "fresh song" which is "new for a new benefit." For example, the psalmist mentions God's "salvation" (vv. 1–2) or victorious deliverance from his people's enemies. Daily experiencing his new mercies (Lam 3:23) prompts one to voice a new song for each of those blessings. Boys mentions Paul's words, "Give thanks always for all things" (Eph 5:20) and then he asks, "Have you been sick and now made whole? Praise God with the leper (Luke 17:11–19): sing a new song for this new salve. Do you hunger and thirst after righteousness, whereas heretofore you could not endure the words of exhortation and doctrine? Sing a new song for this new grace." Whatever way one experiences God's goodness, then we ought to "sing, sing, sing, a new song for this new mercy." Third, in light of the psalmist's words "he has done marvelous things" (v. 1b), a "new song" might not refer to a "common or ordinary song" but to a song that is "exceeding marvelous and extraordinary" because it is about a wonder God has performed. Throughout the psalms, the writers describe God's great miraculous events as "marvelous" (72:18; 119:23).

Prayer. Lord, I thank you for making me a new person through faith in your Son, Jesus. You are continuing to do new and wondrous things around me. For these many blessings, I give you thanks with a song in my heart! Amen.

August 30 — Psalm 98:4-9

4 Shout for joy to the LORD, all the earth, burst into jubilant song with music; 5 make music to the LORD with the harp, with the harp and the sound of singing, 6 with trumpets and the blast of the ram's horn—shout for joy before the LORD, the King. 7 *Let the sea resound, and everything in it, the world, and all who live in it. 8 Let the rivers clap their hands, let the mountains sing together for joy;* 9 let them sing before the LORD, for he comes to judge the earth. He will judge the world in righteousness and the peoples with equity. (NIV)

Expansive songs. The call to praise God now extends beyond his people. For those who have witnessed the victorious King's deliverance from oppression (v. 3), the psalmist now invites them to express their joy (vv. 4-6). Expressing words of praise is an acknowledgment of the joy experienced as a result of God freeing people from the ravages of evil. The skilled musicians also provide a majestic symphony of praise to the King. Then the focus shifts to God's future role as the Judge who will act fairly (v. 9), by punishing those who opposed him. The psalmist invites all creation to praise God for his equitable judgments (vv. 7-8) which bring freedom to everything which is subject to sin. In alignment with the psalmist, the apostle Paul mentions creation's bondage to sin which will be broken allowing creation to be liberated from sin (Rom 8:20-21). With this total liberation in mind, David Dickson expands on the responsive global praise, "The setting forth the praise of Christ for the redemption of sinners, may not only furnish work to all reasonable creatures; but also if every drop of water in the sea, and in every river and flood, every fish in the sea, every fowl of the air, every living creature on the earth, and whatsoever else is in the world: if they all had reason and ability to express themselves; yes, and if all the hills were able by motion and gesticulation to communicate their joy one to another; there is work for them all to set out the praise of Christ."

Prayer. Lord, because all creation rejoices in your works, I offer you my exuberant praise. You are worthy of all honor. Amen.

August 31   Psalm 99:1–5

1 The LORD is king! Let the nations tremble! He sits on his throne between the cherubim. Let the whole earth quake! 2 The LORD sits in majesty in Jerusalem, exalted above all the nations. 3 Let them praise your great and awesome name. *Your name is holy!* 4 Mighty King, lover of justice, you have established fairness. You have acted with justice and righteousness throughout Israel. 5 Exalt the LORD our God! Bow low before his feet, for he is holy! (NLT)

A holy King. Our King's just and right actions (v. 4) are rooted in his holy character (vv. 3, 5). Stephen Charnock expounds on God's holiness, "No attribute is sounded out so loftily, with such solemnity, and so frequently by angels that stand before his throne, as this [holiness]. Where do you find any other attribute trebled in the praises of it as this?" For example, the angels sing, "Holy, holy, holy, is the LORD of hosts" (Isa 6:3). Charnock observes, "His power of sovereignty as Lord of hosts is but once mentioned, but with a ternal [three-fold] repetition of his holiness. Do you hear in any evangelical song any other perfection of the divine nature thrice repeated? Where do we read of the crying out, Eternal, eternal, eternal; or Faithful, faithful, faithful, Lord God of hosts! Whatsoever other attribute is left out, this God would have to fill the mouths of angels and blessed spirits forever in heaven." Charnock believes God's holiness is his supreme attribute, "As it seems to challenge an excellence above all his other perfections, so it is the glory of all the rest; as it is the glory of the Godhead, so it is the glory of every perfection in the Godhead; as his power is the strength of them, so his holiness is the beauty of them; as all would be weak without almightiness to back them, so all would be uncomely without holiness to adorn them: should this be sullied all the rest would lose their honour and their comfortable efficacy; as at the same instant that the sun should lose its light, it would lose its heat, its strength, its generative and quickening virtue."

Prayer. Lord, I often overlook your holiness. Help me to focus more on your holiness so that I may live with reverence before you and loving obedience to you. Amen.

September 1   Psalm 99:6-9

6 Moses and Aaron were among His priests, and Samuel was among those who called upon His name; they called upon the LORD, and He answered them. 7 He spoke to them in the cloudy pillar; they kept His testimonies and the ordinance He gave them. 8 You answered them, O LORD our God; *You were to them God-Who-Forgives, though You took vengeance on their deeds.* 9 Exalt the LORD our God, and worship at His holy hill; For the LORD our God is holy. (NKJV)

A forgiving king. Due to his holiness, it is not surprising that God who is King acts with justice and righteousness (v. 4). However, it may be puzzling that a holy God forgives people (v. 8). Yet, he did exactly this with spiritual giants such as Moses, Aaron, and Samuel. Each man communicated with God (v. 6) and obeyed the Law which he had given to him (v. 7). When they sinned, God forgave them while punishing their actions (v. 8). Thomas Goodwin provides us with insight, "Because he loves the person, and hates only the sin; therefore, he preserves the one [and] destroys only the other. This is all the fruit, to take away his sin. The covenant that is made with us in Christ is not a covenant made with works, but with persons; and therefore, though the works be often hateful, yet he goes on to love the persons; and that he may continue to love them, destroys out of them what he hates, but cuts not them off." Goodwin draws a parallel between God's handling of our sin and our handling of our own diseases, "A member that is leprous or ulcerous, a man loves it as it is 'his own flesh' (Eph 5:29), though he loathes the corruption and putrefaction that is in it; and therefore, he does not presently cut it off but purges it daily." Rather than denying our sin, we do well to acknowledge our sin, knowing that Jesus Christ, who bore the punishment of death for our sin, has forgiven us.

Prayer. Holy Father, I am profoundly aware of my sinfulness in thought and deed. Since I do not take my sin lightly, I am thankful that you do forgive my sin through Jesus' death. I want to honor your holiness by obeying and loving you. Amen.

September 2   Psalm 100

1 Make a joyful noise to the Lord, all the earth! 2 Serve the Lord with gladness! Come into his presence with singing! 3 *Know that the* Lord, *he is God! It is he who made us, and we are his; we are his people, and the sheep of his pasture.* 4 Enter his gates with thanksgiving, and his courts with praise! Give thanks to him; bless his name! 5 *For the* Lord *is good; his steadfast love endures forever, and his faithfulness to all generations.* (ESV)

Knowing God. Matthew Henry believed that our knowledge about God (v. 3) must be applied to our lives. He states, "Know what God is in himself, and what he is to you. Knowledge is the mother of devotion, and of all obedience; blind sacrifices will never please a seeing God." When a person knows God, "[he/she] will be more close and constant, more inward and serious, in the worship of him." He focuses on seven truths that we must "know" (v. 3) about God to strengthen our worship. One, we must know that "the Lord he is God, the only living and true God; that he is a being infinitely perfect, self-existent, and self-sufficient, and the fountain of all being." The second is that God is our Creator. "We do not, we could not make ourselves; it is God's prerogative to be his own cause; our being is derived and depending." The third truth is God is our "rightful owner." That is, we belong to him because we are not our own. The fourth is that God is our "sovereign Ruler. We are 'his people,' or subjects, and he is our prince, our rector or governor . . . and will call us to an account for what we do." The fifth truth to know is that God is our "bountiful Benefactor; we are not only his sheep whom he is entitled to, but 'the sheep of his pasture,' whom he takes care of." The sixth is that the Lord is "a God of infinite mercy and good (v. 5a) . . . and therefore does good." The final truth is that God is "inviolable truth and faithfulness (v. 5b) . . . no word of his shall fall to the ground as antiquated or revoked."

Prayer. Lord, I want to know more about you to magnify you more in my worship. Amen.

September 3 — Psalm 101

1 I will sing of your love and justice, LORD. I will praise you with songs. 2 I will be careful to live a blameless life—when will you come to help me? *I will lead a life of integrity in my own home.* 3 I will refuse to look at anything vile and vulgar. I hate all who deal crookedly; I will have nothing to do with them. 4 I will reject perverse ideas and stay away from every evil. 5 I will not tolerate people who slander their neighbors. I will not endure conceit and pride. 6 I will search for faithful people to be my companions. Only those who are above reproach will be allowed to serve me. 7 I will not allow deceivers to serve in my house, and liars will not stay in my presence. 8 My daily task will be to ferret out the wicked and free the city of the LORD from their grip. (NLT)

Commitment to integrity. Regarding David's statement on integrity in verse 2, William Gurnall notes that domestic life "lies to the very heart of godliness." He states, "It is in vain to talk of holiness" if no one witnesses our "holy walking" in our relationships. "Oh, it is sad when they that have reason to know us best, by their daily converse with us, do speak least for our godliness!" For example, Gurnall challenges married men, "He is a bad husband that has money to spend among company abroad, but none to lay in provisions to keep his family at home." If he is self-indulgent but does not provide for his family, he is not living with integrity. Then there are the religious activities. "Can he be a good Christian that spends all his religion abroad, and leaves none for his nearest relations at home? That is, a great zealot among strangers, and little or nothing of God comes from him in his family?" Gurnall instructs Christian husbands not to boast of their faith but to practice being "loving and kind in their way to their wives." Is not this approach better than those who boast of their faith in Christ but "who are dogged and currish to the wife of their bosom?" Integrity requires consistency between the home and the community.

Prayer. Lord, help me to walk with greater integrity by your Spirit. Then I will be able to live courageously and consistently according to my moral convictions based on Scripture. Amen.

September 4   Psalm 102:1–11

1 Hear my prayer, O Lord, and let my cry come to You. 2 Do not hide Your face from me in the day of my trouble; incline Your ear to me; in the day that I call, answer me speedily. 3 For my days are consumed like smoke, and my bones are burned like a hearth. 4 My heart is stricken and withered like grass, so that I forget to eat my bread. 5 Because of the sound of my groaning my bones cling to my skin. 6 I am like a pelican of the wilderness; I am like an owl of the desert. 7 *I lie awake and am like a sparrow alone on the housetop.* 8 My enemies reproach me all day long; those who deride me swear an oath against me. 9 For I have eaten ashes like bread, and mingled my drink with weeping, 10 because of Your indignation and Your wrath; for You have lifted me up and cast me away. 11 My days are like a shadow that lengthens, and I wither away like grass. (NKJV)

Painful isolation. Due to opposition and God's silence, the psalmist expresses grief and isolation (v. 7). Timothy Rogers observes that "people in trouble love solitariness. They are full of sorrow . . . Grief is a thing that is very silent and private." After raising the question as to why "melancholy people delight to be so much alone" he offers three reasons. The first reason is that physical illness negatively affects a melancholic's disposition. He notes, "The Disease of Melancholy is so obstinate, and so unknown to all but those who have it, that nothing but the power of God can totally overthrow it." Two, The second reason melancholics choose to be alone is because others "deride them" in their physical and emotional condition. Rogers states, "The principal [and third] reason why people in trouble and sadness choose to be alone is, because they generally apprehend themselves singled out to be the marks of God's peculiar displeasure," like the psalmist who felt God's "indignation" (v. 10). "It even breaks their hearts to see how low they are fallen, how oppressed, that were once as easy, as pleasant, as full of hope as others are."

Prayer. Lord, I need a community of God's people who love me especially when I feel "down." I am thankful for your love expressed through them. Amen.

September 5   Psalm 102:12-17

12 But you, O Lord, will sit on your throne forever. Your fame will endure to every generation. 13 You will arise and have mercy on Jerusalem—and now is the time to pity her, now is the time you promised to help. 14 For your people love every stone in her walls and cherish even the dust in her streets. 15 Then the nations will tremble before the Lord. The kings of the earth will tremble before his glory. 16 For the Lord will rebuild Jerusalem. He will appear in his glory. 17 *He will listen to the prayers of the destitute.* He will not reject their pleas. (NLT)

Not alone. After voicing the pain of his isolation (vv. 1-11), the psalmist expresses hope that the Lord will not forget him or his people. God listens to the prayers of the "destitute," this afflicted writer and others (v. 17). According to Stephen Marshall, the destitute are those who are "forsaken," "despised," "stripped of all that is comfortable to them" and "utterly forlorn, like the barren heath [wasteland] in a desolate howling wilderness." Even though the Lord is full of glory (v. 15), remarkably he still pays attention to them by listening to their prayers. Marshall offers hope, "This is also a lesson of singular comfort to every afflicted soul to assure them their prayers and supplications are tenderly regarded before God. I have often observed such poor forsaken ones, who in their own eyes are brought very low, that of all other people they are most desirous to beg and obtain the prayers of their friends, when they see any that has gifts, and peace, and cheerfulness of spirit, and liberty, and abilities to perform duties, O how glad they are to get such a man's prayers!" However, such friends "would rather desire the poor, and the desolate, to be mediators for them; for, certainly, whomsoever God neglects, he will listen to the cry of those that are forsaken and destitute." If you feel rejected by the Lord, Marshall encourages you to "continue to pour out your soul to him; you have a faithful promise from him to be rewarded: he will regard the prayer of the destitute."

Prayer. Lord, although I have felt rejected, I am thankful I am not alone in my pain. You hear me! Amen.

September 6   Psalm 102:18–22

18 Let this be recorded for future generations, *so that a people not yet born will praise the* Lord. 19 Tell them the Lord looked down from his heavenly sanctuary. He looked down to earth from heaven 20 to hear the groans of the prisoners, to release those condemned to die. 21 And so the Lord's fame will be celebrated in Zion, his praises in Jerusalem, 22 when multitudes gather together and kingdoms come to worship the Lord. (NLT)

Praising God. While we know that God expects us to praise him, we may need to be reminded of the reasons. Reflecting on verse 18, Stephen Marshall offers a three-fold rationale for praising the Lord. The first reason is that God retains the right to receive all the praise and glory. In Marshall's words, "The Lord has reserved nothing to himself but only his glory . . . his glory and his praise is his own, and that which he has wholly reserved; of that he is jealous, lest it should either be denied, eclipsed, diminished, or any the least violation offered to it in any kind. All God's people know this of him, and therefore they cannot but endeavour to preserve it for him." We must be sure that God receives the praise he rightfully deserves. The second is that God chose or elected individuals so that "they might give him all the glory and praise of his mercy ('I have, said God, created him, formed, and made him for my glory' Isa 43:7)." Marshall reminds us that this is "the law of his new creation, which is as powerful in them as the law of nature, or the first creation . . . therefore with a holy and spiritual naturalness (if I may so call it), the hearts of all the saints are carried to give God the glory . . . this is fixed in their hearts, the work of grace has moulded them to it, that they can do no other but endeavour to exalt God, it being the very end why their spiritual life and all their other privileges are conferred upon them." The third reason for praising God is the blessings we enjoy; they are an opportunity to praise God, the source of all the benefits that we experience.

Prayer. Lord, as one of your children, I want to praise you because you are worthy of all glory, and I thank you for all your blessings. Amen.

September 7   Psalm 102:23–28

23 He broke my strength in midlife, cutting short my days. 24 But I cried to him, "O my God, who lives forever, don't take my life while I am so young! 25 Long ago you laid the foundation of the earth and made the heavens with your hands. 26 They will perish, but you remain forever; they will wear out like old clothing. You will change them like a garment and discard them. 27 *But you are always the same*; you will live forever. 28 The children of your people will live in security. Their children's children will thrive in your presence." (NLT)

Our unchanging God. When we feel alone (v. 7) and feel our frailty (v. 23), the psalmist directs us to God's eternality and immutability (vv. 24, 27). Commenting on these attributes, Stephen Charnock states, "The essence of God, with all the perfections of his nature, are pronounced the same, without any variation from eternity to eternity. So that the text does not only assert the eternal duration of God, but [also] his immutability in that duration." These two attributes are inter-related, "To endure, argues indeed this immutability as well as eternity; for what endures is not changed, and what is changed does not endure . . . He could not be the same if he could be changed into any other thing than what he is." Therefore, Charnock observes that the psalmist does not describe God's existence in the past ("have been") or future ("will be") tenses but in the present tense ("you are"). He is "the same God, the same in essence and nature, the same in will and purpose." While God can change anything he wants, he is "immutable in every respect and receives no shadow of change." God is the unchanging "I AM," a title which excludes "everything else from partaking in that perfection." The psalmist suggests that God's unchanging nature has practical value for our lives. The unfailing Lord will sustain for us and provide for the needs of future generations (vv. 24, 28). Like God his father, Jesus is unchanging and supreme (Heb 1:10–12) and gives us confidence for daily life (Heb 13:8).

Prayer. Lord, I am thankful that I can rely on your unchanging promises, strength, and eternal life with you. Amen.

September 8   Psalm 103:1–5

1 *Bless the* LORD, *my soul, and all that is within me, bless his holy name.* 2 Bless the LORD, my soul, and do not forget any of his benefits; 3 who pardons all your guilt, who heals all your diseases; 4 who redeems your life from the pit, who crowns you with favor and compassion; 5 who satisfies your years with good things, so that your youth is renewed like the eagle. (NASB)

Our blessing to God. David, the songwriter, overflows with thanksgiving for the many "benefits" (v. 2) which God gives to his children. He pardons our guilt, heals us, redeems our lives, crowns us with his compassion, satisfies and renews our lives (vv. 3–5). Filled with a superabundance of God's blessings to us, we generously respond by blessing or praising the Lord (vv. 1–2). We express our gratitude with our "soul" or whole being ("all that is within me" v. 1). John Stevenson* elaborates on the rich meaning of the soul, "Let your conscience 'bless the Lord' by unvarying fidelity. Let your judgment bless Him, by decisions in accordance with his word. Let your imagination bless him, by pure and holy musings. Let your affections praise him, by loving whatsoever he loves. Let your desires bless him, by seeking only his glory. Let your memory bless him, by not forgetting any of his benefits. Let your thoughts bless him, by meditating on his excellencies. Let your hope praise him, by longing and looking for the glory that is to be revealed. Let your every sense bless him by its fealty, your every word by its truth, and your every act by its integrity." As we bless God, he stirs every area of our lives to respond with thanksgiving, prompting us to deeply love and willingly obey him.

Prayer. Lord, you have blessed my life in so many ways. Out of sheer gratitude for all your blessings, I praise you for your goodness to me which is so undeserved. But more than this, I want your blessings to seep into every crevice of my being so that my relationship with you will be stronger and transformed by your Spirit. Amen.

September 9   Psalm 103:6–10

6 The LORD performs righteous deeds and judgments for all who are oppressed. 7 He made known His ways to Moses, His deeds to the sons of Israel. 8 *The LORD is compassionate and gracious, slow to anger and abounding in mercy.* 9 He will not always contend with us, nor will He keep His anger forever. 10 He has not dealt with us according to our sins, nor rewarded us according to our guilty deeds. (NASB)

God's blessings to us. Although Moses and the Israelites have been oppressed (vv. 6–7), they experience God's love when he frees them from their Egyptian captors (Exod 14) and being supplied with food (Exod 15 and 16). In addition, God does not destroy them when they build a golden calf idol (Exod 32:9). Soon afterwards, Moses tells the people that God is "compassionate and gracious, slow to anger, abounding in love and faithfulness" (Exod 34:6). Regarding God's attributes, Richard Baker elaborates, "O my soul, here are four properties spoken of to be in God, and are all so necessary, that we could not miss one of them. If he were not 'merciful' we could hope for no pardon; and if he were no more but merciful we could hope for no more but pardon; but when besides his being merciful he is also 'gracious,' this gives us a further hope, a hope of a donative [special gift]; and then it will not be what we are worthy to receive, but what it is fit for him to give. If he were not 'slow to anger' we could expect no patience; but when besides his slowness to anger he is also 'full of compassion' this makes us expect he will be the good Samaritan, and not only bind up our wounds, but take care also for our further curing. What though he chide and be angry for a time; it is but our being patient a while with him, as he a long time hath been patient with us."

Prayer. Lord, thank you for the innumerable blessings which are expressions of your love. Thank you for the physical comforts which I enjoy. Thank you for the joyful blessing of relationships which allow me to be loved and to love. Thank you for the many memorable experiences which I have enjoyed. Above all else, I am thankful for the blessing of knowing you! Amen.

September 10   Psalm 103:11–18

11 For as the heavens are high above the earth, so great is His mercy toward those who fear Him; 12 As far as the east is from the west, so far has He removed our transgressions from us. 13 *As a father pities his children, so the* LORD *pities those who fear Him.* 14 For He knows our frame; He remembers that we are dust. 15 As for man, his days are like grass; as a flower of the field, so he flourishes. 16 For the wind passes over it, and it is gone, and its place remembers it no more. 17 But the mercy of the LORD is from everlasting to everlasting on those who fear Him, and His righteousness to children's children, 18 to such as keep His covenant, and to those who remember His commandments to do them. (NKJV)

God's pity. In the previous verses, David has been ruminating on God's great love. By his immense mercy he removes our sins far away from us akin to the great distances between heaven and earth, and between the east and the west (vv. 11–12). David next compares God's mercy to a father's mercy toward a child (v. 13). Matthew Henry notes, "The father pities his children that are weak in knowledge, and instructs them; pities them when they are forward [disobedient], and bears with them; pities them when they are sick, and comforts them; when they are fallen, and helps them up again; when they have offended, and upon their submission, forgives them; when they are wronged, and rights them." God's pity for us is based on his knowledge of us (v. 14). Since he knows us better than we know ourselves, he is full of compassion for his spiritual children. Although we are frail human beings, God showers his love upon us who know and follow him (vv. 15–18). Years later, Paul writes that no height or depth, or anything in God's creation will separate us from God's love (Rom 8: 39).

Prayer. Lord, I am grateful for the times you have shown me your mercy. When I was down and struggled to find my way in life, you came and delivered me. Your encouragement kept me going. Amen.

September 11   Psalm 103:19-22

19 *The LORD has established his throne in heaven, and his kingdom rules over all.* 20 Praise the LORD, you his angels, you mighty ones who do his bidding, who obey his word. 21 Praise the LORD, all his heavenly hosts, you his servants who do his will. 22 Praise the LORD, all his works everywhere in his dominion. Praise the LORD, my soul. (NIV)

Praise the compassionate King. In this psalm, David eloquently describes God's unfathomable love. He is confident about this love because God is the King who rules over all (v. 19). Or, as Thomas Adams states, "His Lordship is universal;" then explains three ways God reigns. First, God rules over time because he is the "I AM" (Exod 3:14) who is eternal (Ps 90:2; 102:27). Adam notes, "Eternity is properly the duration of an uncreated Ens [entity]." God has created everything eternal such as angels, human souls, eternal life and eternal fire. God also rules "over all places, heaven, earth, hell (Ps 135:6)." He continues, "Kings are limited, and cannot do many things they desire: they cannot command the sun to stand still, nor the wind to blow which way they would: in the lofty air, in the depths of the sea no king reigns." The third way God reigns is "over all creatures." God stopped the lions from devouring Daniel and his companions (Dan 6:22), he directed a raven to provide food for Elijah (I Kgs 17:4), and he sent a large fish to swallow Jonah and prevent him from drowning (Jonah 1:17; 2:10). God rules over lightning and hail (Ps 148:8), and "he makes iron to swim, stones to cleave asunder." The Lord rules over and delivers us from "the devils" who "must obey him though unwillingly . . . Therefore, at all times, in all places, and against all creatures, let us trust in him for deliverance." God, our King who rules over everything, deserves the praise of his creation (vv. 20-22).

Prayer. Lord, I know this calendar date is painful for many people, and I must admit that I panic when I see the turmoil in this world. I am thankful that you are in control, and I joyfully praise you as my King. Amen.

September 12   Psalm 104:1–6

1 Bless the LORD, my soul! LORD my God, You are very great; You are clothed with splendor and majesty, 2 covering Yourself with light as with a cloak, stretching out heaven like a tent curtain. 3 He lays the beams of His upper chambers in the waters; He makes the clouds His chariot; He walks on the wings of the wind; 4 He makes the winds His messengers, flaming fire His ministers. 5 *He established the earth upon its foundations, so that it will not totter forever and ever.* 6 You covered it with the deep sea as with a garment; the waters were standing above the mountains. (NASB)

God's creation. This entire hymn praises God for his creation. Before the psalmist provides a detailed account of the creation of the world, these opening verses serve as a prelude which lays down foundational truths. The psalmist wants us to know that God is actively involved in the creation events. His creative action indicates that he is supreme and distinct from the creation, not a part of it. Also, God's creation is majestic and worthy of praise (v. 1). Finally, God established a foundation which will not "totter" (v. 5). Joseph Caryl addresses the nature of this foundation, "The stability of the earth is of God, as much as the being and existence of it. There have been many earthquakes or movings of the earth in several parts of it, but the whole body of the earth was never removed so much as one hair's breadth out of its place, since the foundations thereof were laid." In response to one who thought he could move the earth, Caryl states, "It was a great brag; but the Lord has laid it too fast for man's removing. Himself can make it quake and shake, he can move it when he pleases; but he never has nor will remove it. He has laid the foundations of the earth that it shall not be removed, nor can it be at all moved, but at his pleasure."

Prayer. Father, help me to respect your creation by caring for it, and by worshipping you as its creator. I am also glad that I can trust you who sustains this troubled world by your power. Amen.

September 13 Psalm 104:7-18

7 They fled from Your rebuke, at the sound of Your thunder they hurried away. 8 The mountains rose; the valleys sank down to the place which You established for them. 9 You set a boundary so that they will not pass over, so that they will not return to cover the earth. 10 He sends forth springs in the valleys; they flow between the mountains; 11 they give drink to every animal of the field; the wild donkeys quench their thirst. 12 The birds of the sky dwell beside them; they lift up their voices from among the branches. 13 He waters the mountains from his upper chambers; the earth is satisfied with the fruit of His works. 14 *He causes the grass to grow for the cattle, and vegetation for the labor of mankind, so that they may produce food from the earth,* 15 *and wine, which makes a human heart cheerful, so that he makes his face gleam with oil, and food, which sustains a human heart.* 16 The trees of the LORD drink their fill, the cedars of Lebanon which He planted, 17 where the birds build their nests, and the stork, whose home is the juniper trees. 18 The high mountains are for the wild goats; the cliffs are a refuge for the rock hyrax. (NASB)

God's provisions in creation. The psalmist marvels at how God provides food and drink for all living creatures. Matthew Henry gives three reasons why we should be thankful for these provisions. First, we should give thanks because "God not only provides for us, but for our servants; the cattle that are of use to man, are particularly taken care of; grass is made to grow in great abundance for them." The second reason for giving thanks is that we have food which is "ready to us: having our habitation on the earth, there we have our storehouse." Finally, we thank God that the produce from the earth is "not only for necessity, but for ornament and delight, so good a master do we serve." In fact, God's provision of wine "refreshes" and "exhilarates" the human spirit "when it is soberly and moderately used; that we may not only go through our business but go through it cheerfully." In response, we should be grateful for what we have (v. 15). We have no cause to "complain of want" with God's abundant provision.

Prayer. Lord, thank you for your gifts to sustain your creatures and for the opportunity to enjoy your creation. With a deeper appreciation for the wise design of your creation to provide for all creatures, I worship you! Amen.

September 14   Psalm 104:19–23

19 He made the moon to mark the seasons, and the sun knows when to go down. 20 You bring darkness, it becomes night, and all the beasts of the forest prowl. 21 *The lions roar for their prey and seek their food from God.* 22 The sun rises, and they steal away; they return and lie down in their dens. 23 Then people go out to their work, to their labor until evening. (NASB)

God's rhythms in creation. The psalmist revels in God's established rhythms within creation for the animal kingdom. The annual seasons and the daily sunlight and darkness certainly provide a pattern for the animals' rising and resting (v. 23). Joseph Caryl shows God's goodness through these rhythms, "God feeds not only sheep and lambs, but wolves and lions. It is a strange expression that young lions when they roar after their prey, should be said to seek their meat of God; implying that neither their own strength nor craft could feed them without help from God. The strongest creatures left to themselves cannot help themselves. As they who fear God are fed by a special providence of God, so all creatures are fed and nourished by a general providence. The lion, though he be strong and subtle, yet cannot get his own prey; we think a lion might shift for himself; no, it is the Lord that provides for him; the young lions seek their meat of God." Since the Lord's providential care includes the animals, this theological truth has a practical implication for us. Caryl states, "Surely, then, the mightiest of men cannot live upon themselves; as it is of God that we receive life and breath, so all things needful for the maintenance of this life." Since God cares for the birds and the flowers, Jesus encourages us to be pre-occupied not with worry but with God's kingdom (Matt 6:25–34). Along with Jesus' comments, the psalmist's words challenge those who mistakenly assume that they are self-sufficient, in the hope that they will recognize their dependence on God. All living creatures, including humanity, rely on the Creator who demonstrates his grace by providing daily needed sustenance.

Prayer. Lord, since you so powerfully provide for your creatures, work in my heart to trust and submit to your ways. Amen.

September 15   Psalm 104:24–30

24 LORD, how many are Your works! In wisdom You have made them all; the earth is full of Your possessions. 25 There is the sea, great and broad, in which are swarms without number, animals both small and great. 26 The ships move along there, and Leviathan, which You have formed to have fun in it. 27 They all wait for You to give them their food in due season. 28 You give to them, they gather it up; You open Your hand, they are satisfied with good. 29 You hide Your face, they are terrified; You take away their breath, they perish and return to their dust. 30 *You send forth Your Spirit, they are created; and You renew the face of the ground.* (NASB)

God's providence in creation. God's creation reveals his wisdom (v. 24) and life-giving power (v. 30). Joseph Caryl states, "The Spirit of God creates every day: what is it that continues things in their created being, but providence? That is a true axiom in divinity, Providence is creation continued." With reference to the words, "You send forth your Spirit, they are created" (vs. 30a), he remarks, "The work of creation was finished in the first six days of the world, but the work of creation is renewed every day, and so continued to the end of the world. Successive providential creation as well as original creation is ascribed to the Spirit." God not only continues to create but he renews. Referring to the psalmist's sentence "you renew the face of the ground" (v. 30b), Caryl comments, "You [God] make a new world; and thus, God makes a new world every year, sending forth his Spirit, or quickening power, in the rain and sun to renew the face of the earth. And as the Lord sends forth his power in providential mercies, so in providential judgments." Thus, Caryl explains the psalmist's perspective, whereby through God's Spirit, God is continually involved with creation (v. 30; Col 1:16–17).

Prayer. Father, I am thankful for my physical and spiritual birth which you made possible. Knowing that each breath I take is a gift from you, I want to live with gratitude, consciously aware of my dependence on you. Renew my life for your purposes. Amen.

September 16   Psalm 104:31–35

31 May the glory of the Lord endure forever; may the Lord rejoice in His works. 32 He looks on the earth, and it trembles; He touches the hills, and they smoke. 33 I will sing to the Lord as long as I live; I will sing praise to my God while I have my being. *34 May my meditation be sweet to Him; I will be glad in the Lord.* 35 May sinners be consumed from the earth, and the wicked be no more. Bless the Lord, O my soul! Praise the Lord! (NKJV)

Praise for God's creation. This hymn's theme on creation climaxes with praise. God rejoices over his creation which mirrors the attributes of his glory (v. 31), such as his power and wisdom (vv. 24, 30). Also, those who have meditated on God's works respond with praise (v. 34). Regarding meditation, Thomas Horton expounds, "First. Take this as an assertion. The meditation on God is sweet. And the sweetness of it should stir us up to the putting of it in practice. Secondly. Take it as a resolution—that he would make it for his own practice; that is, that he would comfort himself in such performances as these are; whilst others took pleasure in other things, he would please himself in communion with God, this should be his solace and delight upon all occasions. David promises himself a great deal of contentment in this exercise of divine meditation which he undertook with much delight: and so likewise do others of God's servants of the same nature and disposition with him in the like undertakings. Thirdly. Take it as a prayer and petition." With the words, "I will be glad," Horton suggests that the psalmist is saying, "Let my meditation, or prayer, or converse, be sweet unto him." Since God's creation delights the psalmist so much, he wants his verbal response to be pleasing to the Lord. Anyone opposed to God's glory must and will be consumed by him (v. 35). The ending of evil prompts the psalmist to conclude the psalm as he began it with the refrain "Bless the Lord, O my soul!" Hallelujah!

Prayer. Lord, meditating on your creation motivates me to praise you for your revealed glory. Help me to trust you for your provisions made possible through your creation. Amen.

September 17 — Psalm 105:1–7

1 Give thanks to the LORD, call upon His name; make His deeds known among the peoples. 2 Sing to Him, sing praises to Him; tell of all His wonders. 3 Boast in His holy name; may the heart of those who seek the LORD be joyful. 4 Seek the LORD and His strength; *seek His face continually.* 5 Remember His wonders which He has done, His marvels and the judgments spoken by His mouth, 6 you descendants of Abraham, His servant, you sons of Jacob, His chosen ones! 7 He is the LORD our God; his judgments are in all the earth. (NASB)

Pursuing the Lord. This psalm celebrates the ways God expresses love to his people throughout the generations. An appropriate response to God involves multi-faceted praise. With our mouths, we verbalize our thanks in speech and songs (vv. 1–2). When we remember God's great deeds (v. 5), our hearts become joyful. Our praise also includes pursuing God. The psalmist urges us to seek the Lord three times (vv. 3–4). Only those who know God can seek him. Apart from God's grace working in one's life, the Psalter is clear about sinful human nature which has no interest in seeking God (14:1–3; 53:1–3). Those who have a relationship with God praise him by acknowledging he is the one who provides strength (v. 4). When the psalmist invites us to seek God's face, Matthew Henry explains that we are invited to "seek to have his favour to eternity and therefore continue seeking it to the end of the time of [our] probation." This seeking does not earn God's favor but instead, it is a response of gratitude to him. He adds, "Seek it while you live in this world, and you shall have it while you live in the other world, and even there, shall be forever seeking it, in an infinite progression, and yet be forever satisfied in it." When we see Jesus' face to face one day this will be our ultimate blessing (Rev 22:4).

Prayer. Lord, as I reflect on your profound love, it is my heart's desire to continually seek you in gratitude for all you have done for me. I long for a deeper relationship with you. Amen.

September 18   Psalm 105:8–15

8 He has remembered His covenant forever, the word which He commanded to a thousand generations, 9 the covenant which He made with Abraham, and His oath to Isaac. 10 Then He confirmed it to Jacob as a statute, to Israel as an everlasting covenant, 11 saying, "To you I will give the land of Canaan as the portion of your inheritance," 12 when they were only a few people in number, very few, and strangers in it. 13 And they wandered from nation to nation, from one kingdom to another people, 14 *He allowed no one to oppress them, and He rebuked kings for their sakes*, saying, 15 "Do not touch My anointed ones, and do not harm My prophets." (NASB)

God provides security. The psalmist recounts God's covenant promise of land (vv. 8–11) for his people. He protected them from enemies who wanted to destroy them (vv. 14–15). Thomas Goodwin shares three reflections on these verses. First, he says, "Here is the nearness and the dearness of the saints unto God. They are dearer to him than kings and states, simply considered; that is, otherwise than as they in their persons are also saints; for you see that for their sakes he reproved kings, and so shows that he prefers them to kings." Second, he describes God's warning to their enemies, "Let me see if you dare so much as touch them . . . upon your peril if you do so." God kept his word because he did not allow anyone to "oppress" his people. However, Goodwin astutely notes, this does not mean that God prevented "all wrong and injuries, for they received many as they went through those lands; but at no time did he let it go unpunished. In that sense he suffered them not." God destroyed the Egyptian pursuers, for example. Third, Goodwin shifts from God's punitive action to his "care and protection" of his people. Though they were few in number, he gave them "power and strength" so that their enemies would not "do them any wrong . . . without recompense and satisfaction." While we are not immune to harm, we are always secure in the Father's hands (John 10:29).

Prayer. Lord, in the most painful times when I am prone to fear, may my trust in you grow as I look to you for my ultimate security. Amen.

September 19   Psalm 105:16–23

16 And He called for a famine upon the land; He broke the whole staff of bread. 17 He sent a man before them, Joseph, who was sold as a slave. 18 They forced his feet into shackles, he was put in irons; 19 until the time that his word came to pass, the word of the LORD refined him. 20 The king sent and released him, the ruler of peoples, and set him free. 21 *He made him lord of his house, and ruler over all his possessions,* 22 *to imprison his high officials at will, that he might teach his elders wisdom.* 23 Israel also came into Egypt; so Jacob lived in the land of Ham. (NASB)

God overrules circumstances. Difficulties can cause us to question God's purposes. After his brothers sold Joseph, he ended up in Egypt (Gen 37:25–36) and he could have wondered what God was doing with him. Christopher Ness describes how Joseph would later see God's hand on his life (vv. 21–22), "He [Joseph] was received into the Royal Society of the right honourable the king's privy councillors, and was constituted as Chairman of the council table, which, though Moses does not express, yet David intimates [vv. 21–22]. All the privy councillors, as well as the private people were bound (possibly by oath) to obey him in all things, and, as out of the chair, he magisterially taught these senators wisdom." He continues, "He bound the princes to his soul (or according to his will) and made wise his elders; teaching them not only civil and moral, but also divine wisdom, for which cause God sent Joseph . . . into Egypt, that some sound of the redemption of fallen mankind might be heard in that kingdom, at that time the most flourishing in the world." Ness notes that Joseph was a "master of wisdom, or father to Pharaoh (Gen 45:8)." For all that he offered to the Egyptians, they amply supplied food for Joseph's reunited family. God took Joseph's brothers' mean-spirited plans and used them for his divine purposes (Gen 50:20).

Prayer. Lord, sometimes I wonder why I find myself in tough situations. However, as I reflect on these experiences I recognize your sovereign hand on my life. Thank you for guiding me even when I did not know it! Amen.

September 20   Psalm 105:24–38

24 And He made his people very fruitful and made them stronger than their enemies. 25 *He turned their heart to hate His people, to deal cunningly with His servants.* 26 He sent his servant Moses, and Aaron, whom He had chosen. 27 They performed His wondrous acts among them, and miracles in the land of Ham. 28 He sent darkness and made it dark; and they did not rebel against His words. 29 He turned their waters into blood and caused their fish to die. 30 Their land swarmed with frogs even in the chambers of their kings. 31 He spoke, and a swarm of flies and gnats invaded all their territory. 32 He gave them hail for rain, and flaming fire in their land. 33 He also struck their vines and their fig trees and smashed the trees of their territory. 34 He spoke, and locusts came, and creeping locusts, beyond number, 35 and they ate all the vegetation in their land, and ate the fruit of their ground. 36 He also fatally struck all the firstborn in their land, the first fruits of all their vigor. 37 Then He brought the Israelites out with silver and gold, and among His tribes there was not one who stumbled. 38 Egypt was glad when they departed, for the dread of them had fallen upon the Egyptians. (NASB)

God delivers. God both blessed his people in Egypt and aroused their captors' hatred (vv. 24–25). He turned their oppressors' hearts, Matthew Poole suggests, "not by putting this wicked hatred into them, which is not consistent either with the holiness of God's nature, or with the truth of his word, and which was altogether unnecessary, because they had that and all other wickedness in them by nature; but partly by withdrawing the common gifts and operations of his Spirit, and all the restraints and hindrances to it, and wholly leaving them to their own mistakes, and passions, and corrupt affections, which of their own accord were ready to take that course; and partly, by directing and governing that hatred, which was wholly in and from themselves, so as it should fall upon the Israelites rather than upon other people." God used hatred, an unlikely means, to bring about the Israelites' "glad" departure.

Prayer. Lord, help me to see that you even use adversities to accomplish your plans in my life. Although your love is so mysterious at times, I will trust in your sovereign purposes. Amen.

September 21 Psalm 105:39-45

39 He spread out a cloud as a covering, and fire to illumine by night. 40 They asked, and He brought quail, and satisfied them with the bread of heaven. 41 He opened the rock and water flowed out; it ran in the dry places like a river. 42 For He remembered His holy word with His servant Abraham; 43 and He led out His people with joy, His chosen ones with a joyful shout. 44 He also gave them the lands of the nations, so that they might take possession of the fruit of the peoples' labor, 45 *and that they might keep His statutes and comply with His laws; praise the* LORD! (NASB)

God cares. After the Israelites left Egypt and traversed the desert, God provided his people with the necessities for survival. He sustained them with a cloud to protect them from the sun and fire to keep them warm during the cold desert nights (v. 39). He also generously supplied them with meat, bread, and water (vv. 40-41). He also addressed a spiritual matter. In keeping with his covenant with Abraham (Gen 15:4-16), he provided the land promised to Abraham and his descendants (vv. 42-44). He kept his promise because he chose and loved them (Deut 7:7-8). As the children of Israel experienced God's undeserved goodness (grace), the Lord expected one important response. They were to obey him (v. 45) as an expression of gratitude for all God had done for them (Deut 6:1-5). Charles Spurgeon* reflects on their obedience, "This was the practical design of it all. The chosen nation was to be the conservator of truth, the exemplar of morality, the pattern of devotion: everything was so ordered as to place them in advantageous circumstances for fulfilling this trust. Theirs was a high calling and a glorious election. It involved great responsibilities, but it was in itself a distinguished blessing, and one for which the nation was bound to give thanks. Most justly then did the music close with the jubilant but solemn shout of HALLELUJAH. Praise the Lord. If this history did not make Israel praise God, what would?"

Prayer. Lord, you have been so good to me in countless ways. I know this is only by your grace, and in gratitude to your undeserved love, I want to respond by loving and obeying you. Amen.

September 22   Psalm 106:1-5

1 Praise the Lord! Oh give thanks to the Lord, for He is good; for His mercy is everlasting. 2 *Who can speak of the mighty deeds of the Lord, or can proclaim all His praise?* 3 How blessed are those who maintain justice, who practice righteousness at all times! 4 Remember me, Lord, in Your favor toward Your people. Visit me with Your salvation, 5 so that I may see the prosperity of Your chosen ones that I may rejoice in the joy of Your nation that I may boast with Your inheritance. (NASB)

Praise for mercy. While this psalm's opening has a link to the previous psalm with the same exclamation "Praise the Lord" or Hallelujah (v. 1; 105:45), this psalm is different. Although the prior psalm emphasizes God's faithfulness throughout the generations, this psalm dwells on the Israelites' ongoing disobedience. Thus, the invitation to praise the Lord may appear surprising (v. 1) in this context. The psalmist rhetorically asks who can declare God's mighty deeds so that he receives "all" the praise (v. 2). Henry Jeanes explains that such rhetorical questions express a person's difficult situation (Ps 42:1, 3, 9, 11). Therefore, in response to the psalmist's question, Jeanes comments that "few can do it [praise] in an acceptable manner, and none can do it in a perfect manner." The context suggests that those who have sinned may experience God's mercy, and they will praise him (vv. 44–47). However, God's mercies are so numerous that "without a full confession of mercies it is not possible to make either a due valuation of them, or a just requital [return] of them." In comparison to God's ongoing mercy to us, we cannot fully return the praise that is due to Him. To illustrate, Jeanes quotes David's words, "Many, O Lord, my God, are the wonders you have done. The things you planned for us, no one can recount to you; were I to speak and tell of them, they would be too many to declare" (Ps 40:5). In other words, "how impossible a thing it is fully to recount [God's] mercies." Since God is so faithful to us, we should be loyal in our obedience to him (v. 3).

Prayer. Lord, although I do not praise you enough, your mercy fills my being with gratitude. I am thankful that you receive my worship. Amen.

September 23 Psalm 106:6–12

6 We have sinned like our fathers, we have gone astray, we have behaved wickedly. 7 Our fathers in Egypt did not understand Your wonders; they did not remember Your abundant kindnesses, but rebelled by the sea, at the Red Sea. 8 Nevertheless He saved them for the sake of His name, so that He might make His power known. 9 So He rebuked the Red Sea and it dried up, and He led them through the mighty waters, as through the wilderness. 10 So He saved them from the hand of one who hated them, and redeemed them from the hand of the enemy. 11 The waters covered their adversaries; not one of them was left. 12 Then they believed His words; they sang His praise. (NASB)

Spiritual amnesia. The psalmist shifts from praising God to the people's sinfulness (vv. 6–8). Sin infects each person and every generation so that all humanity rebels against God's moral law by behaving "wickedly" (v. 6). Sin also impairs our minds, including our spiritual memory. William Bridge states that the Israelites saw God's wonders "with their eyes, but they did not understand them with their heart." They did not grasp the "design and scope and end of God in those wonders" and so they did not "remember" God's mercies (v. 7). Some postulate that God's mercies "were very few" and therefore they forgot. But Bridge points out that God's mercies were "abundant" (v. 7). Others might propose that the people had a type of "infirmity or weakness." However, rather than being victims of sin, they actively "rebelled" against God (v. 7). Neither could they foolishly blame their spiritual amnesia on their harsh circumstances while "they were in Egypt, or among the Egyptians." Bridge responds, "but when they were come out of Egypt, and only had to deal with God, and saw his glorious power at the Red Sea, then they rebelled against him." Crossing the Red Sea was an unforgettable event, to be retold to the following generations. Like disobedient children, they deliberately chose to set aside this past event to do what they wanted.

Prayer. Lord, I confess that I deliberately forget your will in order to get my own way. I cannot blame my circumstances, nor you who has loved me. I can only take responsibility for my willful disobedience and ask for your forgiveness. Amen.

September 24 Psalm 106:13–18

13 They quickly forgot His works; they did not wait for His plan, 14 but became lustfully greedy in the wilderness, and put God to the test in the desert. 15 So He gave them their request, but sent a wasting disease among them. 16 When they became envious of Moses in the camp, and of Aaron, the holy one of the Lord, 17 the earth opened and swallowed up Dathan, and engulfed the company of Abiram. 18 And a fire blazed up in their company; the flame consumed the wicked. (NASB)

Unholy impatience. The people deliberately ignored God's great acts of past deliverance because they were impatient and did not wait "for his plan" (v. 13). Joseph Caryl believes that this phrase has two interpretations. He suggests that they did not wait for God's "open or declared counsel, to direct them what to do, but without asking his advice would needs venture and run on upon their own heads, to do what seemed good in their own eyes." Or alternatively, they did not wait for his plan to be fulfilled. In Caryl's words, "They would not tarry God's time for the bringing forth and bringing about his counsels." Whatever view one accepts, Caryl comments, "Not to wait upon God either way is very sinful. Not to wait for his counsel to direct us what to do, and not to wait for his doing or fulfilling his own counsel, argues at once a proud and an impatient spirit; in the one, men so even slight the wisdom of God, and in the other vainly presume and attempt to prevent his providence." Their impatience stemmed from their discontent with God's provision (manna) and their greed for meat (v. 14; Num 11). Their attitude toward God provoked his anger (v. 15). At another time, Saul, in impatience, disobeyed God and performed a forbidden burnt offering (1 Sam 13:8–12). As a result, his family dynasty ended (13:13). Because of our proclivity to rush ahead of God, we need patience, a fruit of the Spirit (Gal 5:22), to walk in step with God's purposes.

Prayer. Lord, too often I rush ahead and am impatient to wait, even when I know what you want me to do. When I do this, I only get myself in more trouble. Create in me a patient heart, willing to obey you. Amen.

September 25   Psalm 106:19-23

19 They made a calf in Horeb and worshiped a cast metal image. 20 So they exchanged their glory for the image of an ox that eats grass. 21 They forgot God their Savior, who had done great things in Egypt, 22 wonders in the land of Ham, and awesome things by the Red Sea. 23 Therefore He said that He would destroy them, *if Moses, his chosen one, had not stood in the gap before Him*, to turn away His wrath from destroying them. (NASB)

Idolatry. Once again, the people forgot, or more accurately, ignored God (v. 21) and chose to deliberately build and worship an idol (v. 19; Exod 32). God was angry enough to destroy them, if Moses "had not stood in the gap before him" (v. 23). To explain "the gap," William Greenhill states that "the hedge of religion and worship was broken down by a golden calf" but Moses "diverted the wrath of God." Greenhill applies this incident to our lives, "We, through infinite mercy, have had some like Moses and Aaron, to make up our hedges, raise up our foundations, and stop some gaps; but all our gaps are not yet stopped." He asks us to consider any gaps we might have which would impede our relationships with God and friends: "Are there not gaps in the hedge of doctrine? If it were not so, how came in such erroneous, blasphemous, and wild opinions amongst us? . . . Are there not gaps in the worship of God? Do not too many tread down all churches, all ordinances, yea, the very Scriptures? . . . Are there not gaps in the hedge of love; is not that bond of perfection broken? Are there not bitter envyings and strife amongst us; do we not bite and devour one another? Are there not gaps in the hedge of conscience? Is not the peace broken between God and your souls? Does not Satan come in oft at the gap, and disturb you? Are there not gaps also in your several relations, whereby he gets advantage? Surely, if our eyes be in our heads, we may see gaps enough."

Prayer. Lord, seeking idolatries by loving and prioritizing things other than you has injured my relationship with you. May your Spirit change me so that I may wholeheartedly and sacrificially love you and others. Amen.

September 26   Psalm 106:24–31

24 Then they rejected the pleasant land; they did not believe His word, 25 but grumbled in their tents; they did not listen to the voice of the Lord. 26 Therefore He swore to them that He would have them fall in the wilderness, 27 and that He would bring down their descendants among the nations and scatter them in the lands. 28 They also followed Baal-peor, and ate sacrifices offered to the dead. 29 So they provoked Him to anger with their deeds, and a plague broke out among them. 30 Then Phinehas stood up and intervened, and so the plague was brought to a halt. 31 And it was credited to him as righteousness, to all generations forever. (NASB)

Grumbling. The litany of the Israelites' sins, mentioned in the previous verses, continues to grow and now includes grumbling (v. 25). While their complaining does not seem as serious as idolatry (v. 19), John Willison* reminds us that "murmuring has in it much unbelief and distrust of God" (v. 24). His comments point to the time the ten spies, other than Caleb and Joshua, "rejected the pleasant land" of Canaan (v. 24; Num 13:31–33). Then all the people "grumbled" against Moses (v. 25; Num 14:2–4) because, as Willison explains, "They could not believe that the wilderness was the way to Canaan, that God would provide and furnish a table for them there and relieve them in all their straits." He applies the Israelites' response to our lives. He notes, "So it is with us in trouble. We quarrel with God's providence, because we do not believe his promises; we do not believe that this can be consistent with love or can work for good in the end." We must heed the sin of grumbling and quarreling with God, or else this sin will lead to our idolatry as it did with the Israelites (vv. 28–29; Num 25:1–2) is convincing. Paul wants us, his readers, to serve without grumbling because God's working in us provides what we need to minister to others (Phil 2:12–14).

Prayer. Lord, there are too many things that I grumble and complain too much. My attitude tells me that I am doubting your purposes in my life and the need for change. I need to ponder your faithfulness and goodness over the years so that my doubts will lessen. Amen.

September 27   Psalm 106:32–39

32 They also provoked Him to wrath at the waters of Meribah, so that it went badly for Moses on their account. 33 Because they were rebellious against His Spirit, He spoke rashly with His lips. 34 *They did not destroy the peoples, as the* LORD *had commanded them,* 35 *but they got involved with the nations and learned their practices,* 36 *and served their idols, which became a snare to them.* 37 *They even sacrificed their sons and their daughters to the demons,* 38 *and shed innocent blood, the blood of their sons and their daughters whom they sacrificed to the idols of Canaan; and the land was defiled with the blood.* 39 So they became unclean in their practices and were unfaithful in their deeds. (NASB)

Spiritual decline. After settling in the land God had promised them, the Israelites continued to rebel. Commenting on their spiritual condition, Matthew Henry states that "they corrupted themselves and forsook God." He notes the progressive stages of their "apostasy." First, "They spared the nations which God had doomed to destruction (v. 34). When they had got the good land God had promised them, they had no zeal against the wicked inhabitants, whom the Lord commanded them to extirpate." Second, "When they spared them, they promised themselves, that for all this, they would not join in any dangerous affinity with them; but the way of sin is downhill; omissions make way for commissions; when they neglect to destroy the heathen, the next news we hear is, they were mingled among the heathen. . . so that they learned their works (v. 35). Third, "They thought they would never join with them in their worship; but by degrees they learned that too (v. 36). They served their idols in the same manner, and with the same rites that they served them." Fourth, "When they joined with them in some of their idolatrous services, which they thought had least harm in them, they little thought that ever they should be guilty of that barbarous and inhuman piece of idolatry, the sacrificing of their living children to their dead gods: but they came to that at last (vv. 37–38)."

Prayer. Lord, I cannot be complacent about my relationship with you! Sin is a snare. By your grace, keep me close to you so that my life my honor you. Amen.

September 28   Psalm 106:40–48

40 Therefore the anger of the LORD was kindled against His people, and He loathed His inheritance. 41 So He handed them over to the nations, and those who hated them ruled over them. 42 Their enemies also oppressed them, and they were subdued under their power. 43 Many times He would rescue them; they, however, were rebellious in their plan, and they sank down into their guilt. 44 Nevertheless He looked at their distress when He heard their cry; 45 *and He remembered His covenant for their sake and relented according to the greatness of His mercy.* 46 He also made them objects of compassion in the presence of all their captors. 47 Save us, LORD our God, and gather us from the nations, to give thanks to your holy name and glory in your praise. 48 Blessed be the LORD, the God of Israel, from everlasting to everlasting. And all the people shall say, "Amen." Praise the LORD! (NASB)

True love. The people's sin stirred God to anger (v. 40). Charles Spurgeon* states that God felt the "deepest indignation" toward those he deeply loved. They did not fully love God because as Spurgeon notes, "Sin never creates true love." Consequently, God allowed them to be "oppressed" (v. 42). With "a taste of the result of sin," the people cried out, and God with his "father's heart" heard his children's cries (v. 44). Their "sorrows touched his soul, the sound of their cries overcame his heart, and he looked upon them with compassion." In love, God responded to his people based on his covenant commitment to them (v. 45). Spurgeon states, "The covenant is the sure foundation of mercy, and when the whole fabric of outward grace manifested in the saints lies in ruins this is the fundamental basis of love which is never moved, and upon it the Lord proceeds to build again a new structure of grace. Covenant mercy is sure as the throne of God." When we sin, God grieves (Eph 4:30), but his fatherly discipline, motivated by love, seeks to renew our love for him in order that we may wholeheartedly praise him (vv. 47–48).

Prayer. Lord, I acknowledge that my sin grieves you. I am thankful that your love pursues me so that I may more deeply love and follow you. Amen.

September 29   Psalm 107:1–9

1 Give thanks to the Lord, for He is good, for His mercy is everlasting. 2 The redeemed of the Lord shall say so, those whom He has redeemed from the hand of the enemy 3 and gathered from the lands, from the east and from the west, from the north and from the south. 4 They wandered in the wilderness in a desert region; they did not find a way to an inhabited city. 5 They were hungry and thirsty; their souls felt weak within them. 6 Then they cried out to the Lord in their trouble; He saved them from their distresses. 7 He also had them walk on a straight way, to go to an inhabited city. 8 *They shall give thanks to the Lord for His mercy, and for His wonders to the sons of mankind!* 9 For He has satisfied the thirsty soul, and He has filled the hungry soul with what is good. (NASB)

God mercifully delivers. It is not unusual to praise God after a past painful experience. The psalmist reflects on a challenging time in Israel's history. He describes the exiles' return from Babylon to their homeland (vv. 2–3) as an arduous journey with physical deprivations (vv. 4–6; Isa 40:1–5). In despair, they finally did what God waited for them to do—they cried out to him (v. 6). While we might dismiss those who have rejected us, God responds differently. The psalmist twice speaks of God showing "mercy" to his distressed people (vv. 1, 8). He reaches down to show them the "straight way" to Jerusalem (v. 7; Isa 40:3). He satisfies their thirsty and hungry souls with "what is good" (v. 8). In response to God's extravagant mercy, the psalmist calls the people to give thanks to God (vv. 1, 8). Matthew Henry notes, "We must acknowledge God's goodness . . . to others as well as to ourselves." As for God, John Trapp comments that "he is content that we have the comfort of his blessings, so he may have the honour of them."

Prayer. Lord, I have often spurned your love and yet you did not give up on me. You waited until I cried out in desperation for you. Thank you for mercifully rescuing me out of my mess. I praise you for your continual mercy. Amen.

September 30   Psalm 107:10–16

10 There were those who lived in darkness and in the shadow of death, prisoners in misery and chains, 11 because they had rebelled against the words of God and rejected the plan of the Most High. 12 *Therefore He humbled their heart with labor; they stumbled and there was no one to help.* 13 Then they cried out to the Lord in their trouble; He saved them from their distresses. 14 He brought them out of darkness and the shadow of death and broke their bands apart. 15 They shall give thanks to the Lord for His mercy, and for His wonders to the sons of mankind! 16 For He has shattered gates of bronze and cut off bars of iron. (NASB)

God purposefully humbles. For seventy years the Israelites lived in Babylon because they continually refused to heed God's call to repentance. The psalmist describes their actions as a rebellious rejection of God (v. 11). Based on his covenant commitment to his people, he humbled them (v. 12a). John Willison* applies this humbling experience to us, "O believer, God may see you have many and strong lusts to be subdued, and that you need many and sore afflictions to bring them down. Your pride and obstinacy of heart may be strong, your distempers deeply rooted, and therefore the physic must be proportioned to them." As much as we would like God to rescue us immediately from affliction, he does not always do this (v. 12b). David Dickson observes, "Affliction is then come to the height and its complete measure, when the sinner is made sensible of his own weakness, and does see there is no help for him, save in God alone." By experience, we know the dark times (vv. 10, 14) when we feel that God has abandoned us. Fortunately, God does not reject his people. After the Israelites lived in a foreign country, God allowed the Israelites to return from Babylon to their homeland. Likewise, after circumstances humble us, God's grace allows us to walk in the light of his presence (v. 14; Jas 4:6). Rather than seeking self-aggrandizement, we find ourselves praising God for his mercy.

Prayer. Lord, you have humbled me throughout my life. Although the experiences have been painful, they have drawn me closer to you. Thank you for your mercy which gives me hope to continue my journey with you. Amen.

October 1   Psalm 107:17-22

17 Fools, because of their rebellious way, and because of their guilty deeds, were afflicted. 18 *Their souls loathed all kinds of food, and they came close to the gates of death.* 19 Then they cried out to the LORD in their trouble; He saved them from their distresses. 20 He sent His word and healed them and saved them from their destruction. 21 They shall give thanks to the LORD for His mercy, and for His wonders to the sons of mankind! 22 They shall also offer sacrifices of thanksgiving and tell of His works with joyful singing. (NASB)

God truly satisfies. "Fools," people who lose their moral sensibilities and act rebelliously seriously, hurt their own lives (vv. 17-18; Exod 11:33-34). Joseph Caryl elaborates on their fate, "The best of creature comforts are but vain comforts. What can dainty meat do a man good, when he is sick and ready to die? Then gold and silver, lands and houses, which are the dainty meat of a covetous man, are loathsome to him. When a man is sick to death, his very riches are sapless and tasteless to him; wife and children, friends and acquaintance, can yield but little comfort in that dark hour, yes, they often prove miserable comforters: when we have most need of comfort, these things administer least or no comfort at all to us." He advises, "Is it not our wisdom, then, to get a stock of such comforts, as will hold and abide fresh with us, when all worldly comforts either leave us, or become tasteless to us? Is it not good to get a store of that food, which how sick soever we are, our stomachs will never loathe?" Caryl instructs us to "feed" on Jesus (John 6:55). "Feed upon him by faith, in health and sickness, you will never loathe him . . . A hungry craving appetite after Christ, and sweet satisfaction in him, are inseparable, and still the stronger is our appetite, the greater is our satisfaction." He encourages us to have the "strongest appetite" for Jesus who is our "greater happiness."

Prayer. Father, I admit that my chasing after the good things in life has left me dissatisfied. I return to you with an increased hunger to draw my spiritual nourishment from you. Amen.

October 2   Psalm 107:23–32

23 Those who go down to the sea in ships, who do business on great waters; 24 they have seen the works of the LORD, and His wonders in the deep. 25 For He spoke and raised a stormy wind, which lifted the waves of the sea. 26 They rose up to the heavens, they went down to the depths; their soul melted away in their misery. 27 They reeled and staggered like a drunken person and were at their wits' end. 28 *Then they cried out to the* LORD *in their trouble*, and he brought them out of their distresses. 29 He caused the storm to be still, so that the waves of the sea were hushed. 30 Then they were glad because they were quiet, so he guided them to their desired harbor. 31 They shall give thanks to the LORD for His mercy, and for His wonders to the sons of mankind! 32 They shall also exalt Him in the congregation of the people and praise Him at the seat of the elders. (NASB)

God mercifully responds. Overwhelmed by life's storms (vv. 23–27), we attempt at first to survive by our own means, but then in desperation cry for God's help (v. 28). John Ryther* describes three of God's attributes which "are much honoured in calling upon him, especially in times of danger and distresses." First, we "honour his sovereignty. God says to these proud waves, 'So far and no farther!' So, 'the storm and hail,' they fulfil his will, and when he pleases he commands a calm." Second, Ryther states, "Prayer in time of danger honours God's wisdom, when we see no way open for mercies and deliverance to come in at, then to look up to him, believing, 'He knows how to deliver out of temptation.'" God is "never at a loss as to ways of bringing in mercy and deliverance." Third, Ryther suggests, "The faithfulness of God is much honoured in times of danger, when he is called upon. The faithfulness of a friend does most appear in a strait: now if you can rely upon his promise, God's faithfulness is the best line men sinking at sea can lay hold on."

Prayer. Lord, when I am in trouble, I want to call out to you, so that you may be honored by helping me. Thank you for your mercy! Amen.

October 3   Psalm 107:33-43

33 He turns rivers into a wilderness, and springs of water into a thirsty ground; 34 and a fruitful land into a salt waste, because of the wickedness of those who dwell in it. 35 He turns a wilderness into a pool of water, and a dry land into springs of water; 36 and He has the hungry live there, so that they may establish an inhabited city, 37 and sow fields and plant vineyards, and gather a fruitful harvest. 38 He also blesses them and they multiply greatly, and He does not let their cattle decrease. 39 When they become few and lowly because of oppression, misery, and sorrow, 40 He pours contempt upon noblemen and makes them wander in a pathless wasteland. 41 But He sets the needy securely on high, away from affliction, and makes his families like a flock. 42 The upright see it and are glad; but all injustice shuts its mouth. 43 *Who is wise? He is to pay attention to these things and consider the mercy of the* LORD. (NASB)

God providentially cares. After describing God's love for his people (vv. 33–41), the writer asks us to pay attention to divine providence (v. 43). John Collinges cautions, "There are many careless observers of providence, who indeed see events rather than providence; they see much that comes to pass in the world but consider nothing of God in them." They devote their attention to discovering the "immediate causes and reasons" behind God's providence. Collinges encourages us to focus on divine providence in order to "affect our heart." This heart change can occur when we seek to "understand his loving kindness and gain a spiritual wisdom." With this attitude, followers of Jesus can cultivate "a trembling, humble heart that they might learn by them more to acknowledge, love, fear, adore, and revere the great and mighty God whose works these are." He challenges us, "Let not yours be such an observation [of events in the world]; but let your eye, beholding God in his providential dispensations, affect your hearts with that adoration and veneration that love and fear of the great and mighty God, which such works of God do call to you for."

Prayer. Lord, I want to be attentive to your providential dealings with me and with the world, so that I may respond to you with love and awe. Amen.

October 4   Psalm 108:1–5

1 *O God, my heart is fixed*; I will sing and give praise, even with my glory. 2 Awake, psaltery and harp: I myself will awake early. 3 I will praise thee, O Lord, among the people: and I will sing praises unto thee among the nations. 4 For thy mercy is great above the heavens: and thy truth reacheth unto the clouds. 5 Be thou exalted, O God, above the heavens: and thy glory above all the earth; (KJV)

A steadfast heart. When troubles arise, we need God to steady our unsettled internal world. David declares that his "heart is fixed" (v. 1). Nathanael Ranew states that the heart must be sharpened like a tent peg, and then "drive it in and fix it" on God. He points out that prayer and meditation help to keep the heart fixed, "So ask seriously and often, that your heart may be ready, and may also be fixed, and this by a habit which brings readiness and fixedness, as in other holy duties, so in that of meditation." John Wells elaborates on this thought. He comments, "Meditation is a fixed duty. It is not a cursory work. Man's thoughts naturally labour with a great inconsistency; but meditation chains them and fastens them upon some spiritual object. The soul when it meditates lays a command on itself, that the thoughts which are otherwise flitting and feathery should fix upon its object; and so this duty is very advantageous." He illustrates, "As we know a garden which is watered with sudden showers is more uncertain in its fruit than when it is refreshed with a constant stream; so when our thoughts are sometimes on good things, and then run off; when they only take a glance of a holy object, and then flit away, there is not so much fruit brought into the soul. In meditation, then, there must be a fixing of the heart upon the object" as psalmist declares in verse 1. Wells summarizes with these thoughts, "Meditation is not only the busying [of] the thoughts, but the centering of them; not only the employing of them, but the staking them down upon some spiritual affair."

Prayer. Lord, too often I am inattentive to you, leaving me vulnerable to life's storms. Help me to fix my mind and heart on you so that I am anchored in those storms. Amen.

October 5   Psalm 108:6-13

6 That your beloved ones may be delivered, give salvation by your right hand and answer me! *7 God has promised in his holiness:* "With exultation I will divide up Shechem and portion out the Valley of Succoth. 8 Gilead is mine; Manasseh is mine; Ephraim is my helmet, Judah my scepter. 9 Moab is my washbasin; upon Edom I cast my shoe; over Philistia I shout in triumph." 10 Who will bring me to the fortified city? Who will lead me to Edom? 11 Have you not rejected us, O God? You do not go out, O God, with our armies. 12 *Oh grant us help against the foe,* for vain is the salvation of man! 13 With God we shall do valiantly; it is he who will tread down our foes. (ESV)

A steadfast confidence. By continuing to focus on God (v. 1), David and his people face their enemies with confidence (vv. 6-9). David Dickson points out three reasons for this confidence. First, they are "beloved" by God (v. 6). He writes that the church is the Lord's beloved and "more loved than anything else in the world . . . Because the church is God's beloved, the care of it should be most in our mind, and the love of the preservation of it should draw forth our prayer most in favour of it." With confidence, we can pray for God's protection over his global church which he loves. The second reason for confidence is God's divine promises of help (vv. 7-9). When we have faith in God's promises, this faith will "furnish joy to the believer before he enjoys the performance of it." We can praise the Lord even before he acts and fulfills his promises to us. Finally, we have confidence in God because he provides help (v. 12). Dickson challenges us, "He who would have God's help in any business, must quit confidence in man's help; and the seeing of the vanity of man's help must make the believer to trust the more unto, and expect the more confidently God's help, as here is done."

Prayer. Lord, I am thankful that I am your child because of your love. With this confidence in your strength, wisdom and your promises, I come to you with my challenges. I am thankful that you are able to help me. Amen.

October 6 — Psalm 109:1–5

1 God of my praise do not be silent! 2 For they have opened a wicked and deceitful mouth against me; they have spoken against me with a lying tongue. 3 They have also surrounded me with words of hatred and have fought against me without cause. 4 *In return for my love they act as my accusers; but I am in prayer.* 5 So they have repaid me evil for good, and hatred for my love. (NASB)

Responding to slander. In this psalm, David asks God to protect him against slander motivated by hatred and filled with lies and falsehoods (vv. 2–3). David shows love to his enemies but they, with their continuing accusations, reject him (vv. 4–5). In pain, David turns to God in prayer, his response to these mean-spirited men. Joseph Caryl asks the question, "But for whom did he pray? Doubtless he prayed and prayed much for himself; he prayed also for them." He suggests two ways that David prayed for his accusers. Reflecting the psalmist's prayer, Caryl states, "First I pray against their plots and evil dealings with me (prayer was David's best strength always against his enemies), yet that was not all. But, secondly . . . that the Lord would pardon their sin, and turn their hearts, when they are doing me mischief; or, though they have done me mischief, I am wishing them the best good." On other occasions when David is slandered, he prays to God, voicing condemnation on his enemies. However, in this instance, as evidence of a non-vindictive spirit, David turns to God and asks him to deal with the evil (v. 1). John Calvin* believed that David's response indicates that he, "free from all inordinate passion, breathed forth his prayers under the influence of the Holy Spirit." We do well to turn to the Lord regarding those who verbally attack us and thus guard our hearts against mean-spiritedness.

Prayer. Lord, rather than loving those who have criticized me, I have reacted and deeply hurt them. Help me to turn to you so you can change my heart. I need to pray for them, not against them, and thereby honor you. Amen.

October 7   Psalm 109:6-15

6 Appoint a wicked person over him, and may an accuser stand at his right hand. 7 When he is judged, may he come out guilty, *and may his prayer become sin.* 8 May his days be few; may another take his office. 9 May his children be fatherless, and his wife a widow. 10 May his children wander about and beg; and may they seek sustenance far from their ruined homes. 11 May the creditor seize everything that he has, and may strangers plunder the product of his labor. 12 May there be none to extend kindness to him, nor any to be gracious to his fatherless children. 13 May his descendants be eliminated; may their name be wiped out in a following generation. 14 May the guilt of his fathers be remembered before the LORD, and do not let the sin of his mother be wiped out. 15 May they be before the LORD continually, so that He may eliminate their memory from the earth. (NASB)

Two kinds of prayer. Rather than personally seeking revenge on his enemies, David asks God to judge the wicked and to declare them guilty (vv. 6-7a). Then, David requests that their prayers "become sin" (v. 7b). Matthew Henry interprets the wicked's prayers as "sin" to parallel "the clamours of a condemned malefactor, [which] not only find no acceptance, but are looked upon as an affront to the court. The prayers of the wicked now become sin, because soured with the leaven of hypocrisy and malice." Joseph Caryl contributes further insight into hypocritical prayers, "The prayer of the hypocrite is sin formally, and it is sin in the effect, that is, instead of getting any good by it, he gets hurt, and the Lord instead of helping him because he prays, punishes him because of the sinfulness of his prayers. Thus, his prayer becomes sin to him, because he receives no more respect from God when he prays than when he sins. And sin doe not only mingle with his prayer (as it does with the prayers of the holiest), but his prayer is nothing else but a mixture or mingle mangle (as we speak) of many sins."

Prayer. Lord, although I often wish the worst for evil doers, I am thankful that you are the judge and will deal equitably with them. Rather than seeking personal revenge against others, teach me to pray for your will to be done. Amen.

October 8 — Psalm 109:16–20

16 Because he did not remember to show mercy, but persecuted the afflicted and needy person, and the despondent in heart, to put them to death. 17 *He also loved cursing, so it came to him; and he did not delight in blessing, so it was far from him.* 18 *But he clothed himself with cursing as with his garment, and it entered his body like water, and like oil into his bones.* 19 *May it be to him as a garment with which he covers himself, and as a belt which he constantly wears around himself.* 20 May this be the reward of my accusers from the Lord, and of those who speak evil against my soul. (NASB)

Divine justice. We have noted that David's prayer does not express personal revenge, but trust in God to act justly based on his moral law (Deut 27:15–26; 28:15–68). A person's sinful choices will come back to haunt him or her in the future. If one slanders others, the individual can expect them to slander in return. When an individual withholds mercy with those who desperately need mercy, curses and death will come to that person (vv. 16–19). John Bunyan explains that these grave consequences are brought upon by God whose actions are a "retaliation" for the evil perpetrated upon the afflicted who needed mercy. The unmerciful will reap what they have sowed. God will also seek "revenge" because he "will right the wrongs that sinners have done him [and] will repay vengeance for the despite and reproach wherewith they have affronted him." God's revenge may seem cruel, but his actions are consistent with his holiness. John Bunyan elaborates on divine justice, "This curse lies in a deprivation of all good, and in a being swallowed up of all the most fearful miseries that a holy and just and eternal God can righteously inflict or lay upon the soul of a sinful man." While the subject of divine justice is distasteful to modern society, Bunyan reminds us that Scripture promises judgment will come one day (2 Thess 1:7–9). Those who have been brutally oppressed are thankful for God's justice which offers them hope.

Prayer. Father, I am thankful that one day you will deal justly with those who victimize the vulnerable. In the meantime, I pray that they may come to know and love Jesus. Amen.

October 9   Psalm 109:21–29

21 But You, God, the Lord, deal kindly with me for the sake of Your name; because Your mercy is good, rescue me; 22 for I am afflicted and needy, and my heart is wounded within me. 23 I am passing like a shadow when it lengthens; I am shaken off like the locust. 24 My knees are weak from fasting, and my flesh has grown lean, without fatness. 25 I also have become a disgrace to them; when they see me, they shake their head. 26 Help me, Lord my God; save me according to Your mercy. 27 And may they know that this is Your hand; you, Lord, have done it. 28 They will curse, but You bless; when they arise, they will be ashamed, but Your servant will be glad. 29 May my accusers be clothed with dishonor, and may they cover themselves with their own shame as with a robe. (NASB)

God's great mercy. God's nature is multi-faceted. He exercises justice to address evil and shows mercy to the afflicted (vv. 21–22). In the face of his enemies, David again cries to the Lord for help. Thomas Goodwin reflects on God's mercy, "Deliverance was good; yes, but the mercy of God apprehended therewith was infinitely more good to him, which was the greatest inducement to him to seek deliverance. And indeed God's mercy does eminently bear the style of goodness." He further explains, "Unto a truly broken, humbled sinner, the mercies that are in God, out of which he pardons, should have infinitely more of goodness and sweetness in them than the pardon itself, or all things else that are in the promises. This a soul that has tasted how good the Lord is will instantly acknowledge." Goodwin continues, "A promise of life to a condemned man is sweet, for life is sweet" but God's "steadfast love is better than life" (Ps 63:3 ESV). God's mercy is sweeter than life itself. When we ask God's mercy for our situations, we sometimes forget to pray that God will be glorified. David has a higher vision, asking mercy for himself and for the sake of God's character (v. 21).

Prayer. Lord, because I am a needy person, I thank you for your great mercy which you show to me daily. Reveal your goodness to those who doubt your care for people. Amen.

October 10 — Psalm 109:30-31

30 With my mouth I will give thanks abundantly to the LORD; and I will praise Him in the midst of many. 31 For He stands at the right hand of the needy, to save him from those who judge his soul. (NASB)

The needy rejoice. Until now, this song of lament has painfully reflected David's darkest days. Now this psalm ends on a high note of praise, with hope filling David's heart as he thanks the Lord who deals with his enemies. The dark clouds lift as he anticipates God's mercy and as he waits, David erupts, with praise to God (v. 30). He describes God standing at the right hand of the needy, not as an accuser but as a savior to exonerate them (v. 31). This is cause for praise! John Calvin* elaborates on this praise, "In the celebration of God's praises, there can be no question that these must issue from the heart ere they can be uttered by the lips; at the same time, it would be an indication of great coldness, and of want of fervour, did not the tongue unite with the heart in this exercise. The reason why David makes mention of the tongue only is, that he takes it for granted that, unless there be a pouring out of the heart before God, those praises which reach no farther than the ear are vain and frivolous; and, therefore, from the very bottom of his soul, he pours forth his heart felt gratitude in fervent strains of praise; and this he does from the same motives which ought to influence all the faithful—the desire of mutual edification; for to act otherwise would be to rob God of the honour which belongs to him." In addition to this wholehearted praise, David worships with others who are either witnesses or learners of God's mercy (v. 30b).

Prayer. Heavenly Father, you know that I have gone through dark days. When life seemed hopeless, you brought hope as my Advocate who defended me against the lies of the Accuser. Rather than allowing a vindictive spirit to control me, you helped me with your unending mercy in my time of need! Help me to be a witness to others of your mercy. Amen.

October 11   Psalm 110

1 The Lord says to my Lord: "Sit at my right hand, until I make your enemies your footstool." 2 The Lord sends forth from Zion your mighty scepter. Rule in the midst of your enemies! 3 Your people will offer themselves freely on the day of your power, in holy garments; from the womb of the morning, the dew of your youth will be yours. 4 The Lord has sworn and will not change his mind, "you are a priest forever after the order of Melchizedek." 5 The Lord is at your right hand; he will shatter kings on the day of his wrath. 6 He will execute judgment among the nations, filling them with corpses; he will shatter chiefs over the wide earth. 7 He will drink from the brook by the way; therefore he will lift up his head. (ESV)

The messianic king. This psalm is an oracle of God, "the Lord," speaking to the messianic King, "my Lord," Jesus (v. 1). Edward Reynolds states, "This psalm is one of the fullest and most compendious prophecies of the person and offices of Christ in the whole Old Testament." Within these seven verses, Reynolds sees the major Christian doctrines of our faith, the Trinity, the incarnation of Christ, the sufferings of Christ, his "completed work and conquest over all his enemies and sufferings," his resurrection, the universal church, the last judgment, the forgiveness of sins, and the resurrection of the body. Some verses of this psalm are quoted again in the New Testament. For example, verse 1 appears in Matthew 26:64, Mark 14:6, Luke 22:69, Acts 5:31, 7:55–56, Romans 8:34, Ephesians 1:20, and Colossians 3:1. Hebrews 7 elaborates on verse 4 to teach about Jesus's heavenly priesthood, his resurrection and ascension. The New Testament mentions this psalm at least fourteen times. Psalm 110 also has practical value for us. First, it helps us trust the Old Testament prophecies which have been fulfilled and will be again in the future. Second, it presents Jesus as the messianic King who is above all earthly royalty and who is worthy of our worship.

Prayer. Father, thank you for your son, Jesus, who is the anointed King above all other kings. May people see Jesus for who he truly is and then join the global worship due to him. Amen.

October 12 — Psalm 111

1 Praise the Lord! I will thank the Lord with all my heart as I meet with his godly people. 2 How amazing are the deeds of the Lord! All who delight in him should ponder them. 3 Everything he does reveals his glory and majesty. His righteousness never fails. 4 He causes us to remember his wonderful works. How gracious and merciful is our Lord! 5 He gives food to those who fear him; he always remembers his covenant. 6 He has shown his great power to his people by giving them the lands of other nations. 7 All he does is just and good, and all his commandments are trustworthy. 8 They are forever true, to be obeyed faithfully and with integrity. 9 He has paid a full ransom for his people. He has guaranteed his covenant with them forever. What a holy, awe-inspiring name he has! 10 *Fear of the Lord is the foundation of true wisdom. All who obey his commandments will grow in wisdom.* Praise him forever! (NLT)

Living wisely. We are called to live wisely because God is the "foundation of true wisdom" (v. 10). The writer arrives at this conclusion after considering all that God does in the world. Among his deeds, he provides for (vv. 5–6) and redeems his people (v. 9). In recognition of who God is and what he does, we are wise to pay serious attention to him. Unfortunately, many look to whatever society offers them for meaning, security and love while ignoring God. John Boys recommends that if one's goal in life is "to get an opulent fortune," to "live joyfully," or to "get honour," the individual should turn to God who offers "great gain" in godliness (1 Tim 6:6), joy with an upright heart (Ps 97:11), and his favor. To receive these divine blessings we must obey God's commands (v. 10). Henry Smith notes, "They which do the commandments have a good understanding; not they which speak of the commandments, nor they which write of the commandments, nor they which preach of the commandments, but they which do the commandments, have a good understanding." This is practical godliness.

Prayer. Lord, I want to live wisely by building my life on you. Help me to honor you by knowing and living according to your Word. Amen.

October 13   Psalm 112

1 Praise the Lord! Blessed is the man who fears the Lord, who greatly delights in his commandments! 2 His offspring will be mighty in the land; the generation of the upright will be blessed. 3 Wealth and riches are in his house, and his righteousness endures forever. 4 Light dawns in the darkness for the upright; he is gracious, merciful, and righteous. 5 It is well with the man who deals generously and lends; who conducts his affairs with justice. 6 For the righteous will never be moved; he will be remembered forever. 7 *He is not afraid of bad news; his heart is firm, trusting in the Lord.* 8 His heart is steady; he will not be afraid, until he looks in triumph on his adversaries. 9 He has distributed freely; he has given to the poor; his righteousness endures forever; his horn is exalted in honor. 10 The wicked man sees it and is angry; he gnashes his teeth and melts away; the desire of the wicked will perish! (ESV)

Facing bad news. Wise people revere God, delight in his revealed word, and deal generously and fairly with others (vv. 1, 5, 9). They also do not fear bad news because they trust the Lord (v. 7). Thomas Manton elaborates on trusting God, "A man that puts his confidence in God, if he hears bad news of mischief coming towards him, as suppose a bad debt, a loss at sea, accidents by fire, tempests, or earthquakes, as Job had his messengers of evil tidings, which came thick and threefold upon him, yet he is not afraid, for his heart is fixed on God: he has laid up his confidence in God, therefore his heart is kept in an equal poise." To illustrate this confidence in the face of unwelcome news, Manton quotes Job, "The Lord gave, and the Lord has taken away; may the name of the Lord be praised," (Job 1:21 NIV)." Even when difficulties come into our lives, we can thank God because we trust him (v. 7) and be blessed.

Prayer. Lord, I fear sad and disturbing news, and I need your grace to cultivate a firm and steady heart to trust you in turbulent times. Continue to deepen my trust in you! Amen.

October 14   Psalm 113

1 Praise the LORD! Yes, give praise, O servants of the LORD. Praise the name of the LORD! 2 Blessed be the name of the LORD now and forever. 3 Everywhere—from east to west—praise the name of the LORD. 4 *For the LORD is high above the nations; his glory is higher than the heavens. 5 Who can be compared with the LORD our God, who is enthroned on high?* 6 He stoops to look down on heaven and on earth. 7 He lifts the poor from the dust and the needy from the garbage dump. 8 He sets them among princes, even the princes of his own people! 9 He gives the childless woman a family, making her a happy mother. Praise the LORD! (NLT)

Our King's supremacy. Like the two previous psalms, this one opens with "Praise the LORD," the English equivalent of the Hebrew "hallelujah." This psalm also marks the commencement of the Egyptian Halle psalms (113–118). Sung at the beginning of the Passover meal, families commemorate the great acts of God who is "high above the nations" and is "enthroned on high" (vv. 4–5). In the seventeenth century, when Thomas Hodges preached on these verses to England's Members of Parliament, he first observed that God is so high that "all creatures bow before him and do homage to him according to their several aptitudes and abilities." For example, "angels and saints worship him, acknowledging his highness, by denying their own, but setting up his will as their supreme law . . . even inanimate creatures" subject themselves to God's greatness (Isa 48:13). Hodges' second point was that God is so high that he "surmounts all created capacity to comprehend him" (Job 11:7–9). God's greatness cannot be fathomed (Ps 145:3) either by the physical eye or by the "eye of understanding." His final point was that God is high above everything because he is perfect in his very being. While we reflect "some small drops" of God's character, such as his love, Hodges noted that "[God] is an infinite ocean of perfection, without either brink or bottom." Yes, God is the "LORD Most High" (7:17; 97:7).

Prayer. Lord Most High, I acknowledge your greatness and my inability to fathom you. I gladly and willingly submit and worship you. Amen.

October 15   Psalm 114

1 When Israel went out from Egypt, the house of Jacob from a people of strange language, 2 Judah became his sanctuary, Israel his dominion. 3 The sea looked and fled; Jordan turned back. 4 The mountains skipped like rams, the hills like lambs. 5 What ails you, O sea that you flee? O Jordan that you turn back? 6 O mountains that you skip like rams? O hills, like lambs? 7 Tremble, O earth, at the presence of the Lord, at the presence of the God of Jacob, 8 *who turns the rock into a pool of water, the flint into a spring of water.* (ESV)

God's transforming power. This second Hallel song celebrates God's victorious deliverance of his people from Egypt. The psalmist wants us to recognize that the "presence" of God (repeated twice) has power to do the unthinkable (vv. 7–8). If God can turn a rock into a pool of water, John Boys asks, "Shall not our hard and flinty hearts, in consideration of our own miseries, and God's unspeakable mercies in delivering us from evil, (if not gush forth into fountains of tears) express so much as a little standing water in our eyes?" Since empowering grace can transform our lives, Boys leads us in prayer, "O Lord, touch the mountains and they shall smoke, touch our lips with a coal from your altar, and our mouth shall show forth your praise. Smite, Lord, our flinty hearts as hard as the nether millstone, with the hammer of your word, and mollify them also with the drops of your mercies and dew of your Spirit; make them humble, fleshy, flexible, circumcised, soft, obedient, new, clean, broken, and then 'a broken and a contrite heart, O God, you will not despise.'" (Ps 51:17 NIV). He concludes his prayer, "O Lord my God, give me grace from the very bottom of my heart to desire you; in desiring, to seek you; in seeking, to find; in finding, to love you; in loving, utterly to loathe my former wickedness that . . . I may possess the heavenly Canaan and happy land of promise."

Prayer. Lord, in light of all you have done for me, I ask that you soften my hardened heart. Transform it so that I may be responsive to your love by loving and obeying you. Amen.

October 16   Psalm 115:1–8

1 *Not to us,* Lord, *not to us, but to Your name give glory,* because of Your mercy, because of Your truth. 2 Why should the nations say, "Where, then, is their God?" 3 But our God is in the heavens; He does whatever He pleases. 4 Their idols are silver and gold, the work of human hands. 5 They have mouths, but they cannot speak; they have eyes, but they cannot see; 6 they have ears, but they cannot hear; they have noses, but they cannot smell; 7 they have hands, but they cannot feel; they have feet, but they cannot walk; they cannot make a sound with their throat. 8 Those who make them will become like them, everyone who trusts in them. (NASB)

God's glory. Our life goal should be to glorify God. Stephen Charnock states that the psalmist's twice-repeated phrase "not to us" (v. 1) implies "our natural tendency to self-idolatry, and to magnifying of ourselves, and the difficulty of cleansing our hearts from these self-reflections. If it be angelical to refuse an undue glory stolen from God's throne (Rev 12:8–9), it is diabolical to accept and cherish it . . . So much as we sacrifice to our own credit, to the dexterity of our hands, or the sagacity of our wit, we detract from God." When we seek self-glory, we are robbing glory from God. Thomas Manton emphasizes glorifying God, "This [verse 1] is not a doxology, or form of thanksgiving, but a prayer. Not for our safety or welfare, so much as for your [God's] glory, be pleased to deliver us. Not to satisfy our revenge upon our adversaries; not for the establishment of our own interest; but for the glory of your grace and truth do we seek your aid, that you may be known to be a God keeping covenant; for mercy and truth are the two pillars of that covenant. It is a great dishonouring of God when anything is sought from him more than himself, or not for himself." As Manton observes, "Self and God are the two things that come in competition . . . God must have the preeminence."

Prayer. Lord, too often I seek glory for what I have done. This is so wrong, and I confess it with a greater resolve to see you receive all the glory you rightly deserve. Amen.

October 17   Psalm 115:9–18

9 Israel, trust in the Lord; He is their help and their shield. 10 House of Aaron, trust in the Lord; He is their help and their shield. 11 You who fear the Lord, trust in the Lord; He is their help and their shield. 12 The Lord has been mindful of us; He will bless us. He will bless the house of Israel; He will bless the house of Aaron. 13 *He will bless those who fear the Lord, the small together with the great.* 14 May the Lord increase you, you and your children. 15 May you be blessed of the Lord, Maker of heaven and earth. 16 The heavens are the heavens of the Lord, but the earth He has given to the sons of mankind. 17 The dead do not praise the Lord, nor do any who go down into silence; 18 but as for us, we will bless the Lord from this time and forever. Praise the Lord! (NASB)

God's mercy. Thomas Manton comments on verse 13, "Mercy, according to the covenant of grace, gives the same grounds of faith and hope to everyone within the church; so that whatever of favour is shown to one of God's people, it is of a general use and profit to others. This Scripture shews that as the duty of trusting in the Lord is common to all sorts of persons, so the blessing of trust is common, and does belong to all sorts of believers, small and great . . . Now these have all the same privileges. If God be the help and shield of the one, he will be the help and shield of the other; if he bless the one he will bless the other. Every one that fears God . . . may expect his blessing as well as public persons; the meanest peasant as well as the greatest prince, as they have leave to trust in God, so they may expect his blessing. The reason is that they have all an equal interest in the same God, who is a God of goodness and power, able and willing to relieve all those that trust in him."

Prayer. Lord, I am thankful for your generous mercy, but I question your mercy shown to those I consider to be unworthy. Forgive my pride and my lack of appreciation for your great mercy. Amen.

October 18   Psalm 116:1–6

1 I love the LORD, because He hears my voice and my pleas. 2 Because He has inclined His ear to me, therefore I will call upon Him as long as I live. 3 The snares of death encompassed me and the terrors of Sheol came upon me; I found distress and sorrow. 4 Then I called upon the name of the LORD: "Please, LORD, save my life!" 5 *Gracious is the LORD, and righteous; yes, our God is compassionate.* 6 The LORD watches over the simple; I was brought low, and He saved me. (NASB)

Our confidence in God. Amid life-threatening troubles (v. 3), the psalmist wisely calls on God to come to his aid (v. 4), and God does (v. 1). While we might attribute God's response to the intensity of his prayer or piety, God replies because of who he is (v. 5). True to Puritan tradition, Richard Baker relates the theology of these verses to practical life. He rhetorically asks, "He [God] is gracious in hearing, he is "righteous" in judging, he is "merciful" in pardoning, and how, then, can I doubt of his will to help me? He is righteous to reward according to deserts [what one deserves]; he is gracious to reward above deserts; yes, he is merciful to reward without deserts; and how, then, can I doubt of his will to help me? He is gracious, and this shows his bounty; he is righteous, and this shows his justice; yes, he is merciful, and this shows his love; and how, then, can I doubt of his will to help me? If he were not gracious I could not hope he would hear me; if he were not righteous, I could not depend upon his promise; if he were not merciful, I could not expect his pardon; but now that he is gracious and righteous and merciful too, how can I doubt of his will to help me?" During times of crisis, by meditating on God's unchanging attributes we best address our doubts and strengthen our trust in him.

Prayer. Father, sometimes I assume that my fervent prayers will prompt you to hear and answer my requests. Now I want to gain a great knowledge of your character better so that I might grow in confidence in my prayer life. Amen.

October 19 — Psalm 116:7–11

7 Return to your rest, my soul, for the LORD has dealt generously with you. 8 For you have rescued my soul from death, my eyes from tears, and my feet from stumbling. 9 *I shall walk before the* LORD *in the land of the living.* 10 I believed when I said, "I am greatly afflicted." 11 I said in my alarm, "All people are liars." (NASB)

Resting and doing. In response to God answering his prayer, the psalmist speaks of resting his soul and walking before the Lord (vv. 7, 9). While these two actions, resting and walking, may be seemingly contradictory for our spiritual lives, Nathanael Hardy offers some insights, "You must know that walking and rest here mentioned, being of a divine nature, do not oppose each other; spiritual rest makes no man idle, and therefore it is no enemy to walking; spiritual walking makes no man weary, and therefore it is no enemy to rest." Hardy continues discussing this relationship, "Indeed, they are so far from being opposite that they are subservient to each other, and it is hard to say whether that rest be the cause of this walking, or this walking a cause of that rest. Indeed, both are true, since he that rests in God cannot but walk before him, and by walking before, we come to rest in God. Returning to rest is an act of confidence, since there is no rest to be had but in God, nor in God but by believing affiance in, and reliance on him. Walking before God is an act of obedience; when we disobey we wander and go astray, only by obedience we walk." Hardy drives home his point, "Now these two are so far from being enemies that they are companions and ever go together; confidence being a means to quicken obedience, and obedience to strengthen confidence." Jesus tells us that we must abide in him if we want to walk obediently in his will (John 15:5, 10). Some church traditions place priority on contemplation, while others emphasize activism. These priorities are complementary in the Christian life.

Prayer. Lord, sometimes I place too much emphasis on doing and other times, I want to devote time to being in your presence. Give me wisdom to manage these two areas so I walk in your presence throughout the day. Amen.

October 20   Psalm 116:12–19

12 What shall I render to the Lord for all His benefits toward me? 13 I will take up the cup of salvation and call upon the name of the Lord. 14 I will pay my vows to the Lord now in the presence of all His people. 15 Precious in the sight of the Lord is the death of His saints. 16 O Lord, *truly I am Your servant; I am Your servant*, the son of Your maidservant; You have loosed my bonds. 17 I will offer to You the sacrifice of thanksgiving and will call upon the name of the Lord. 18 I will pay my vows to the Lord now in the presence of all His people, 19 in the courts of the Lord's house, in the midst of you, O Jerusalem. (NKJV)

God's servant. How do I express gratitude to God for answering my prayers? After asking himself this question (v. 12), the psalmist responds. He takes in his hands the "cup of salvation" which is God's gift extended to him (v. 13). In gratitude to this grace of salvation, he makes vows of obedience to the Lord (v. 14). Finally, he offers a "sacrifice of thanksgiving" praising God for his goodness shown to him (v. 17). He praises and obeys God because he sees himself as God's "servant" (v. 16). Thomas Adams elaborates on this role, "The saints have ever had a holy pride in being God's servants; there cannot be a greater honour than to serve such a Master as commands heaven, earth, and hell. Do not think you do honour God in serving him; but this is how God honours you, in vouchsafing [guaranteeing you] then to be his servant." The psalmist's role as a servant is spoken "not in the phrase of a human compliment, but in the humble confession of a believer." Adams compares the psalmist to the apostle Paul who in his letters writes "the title of servant before that of an apostle; first servant, then apostle. Great was his office in being an apostle, greater his blessing in being a servant of Jesus Christ; the one is an outward calling, the other an inward grace."

Prayer. Lord, having received your salvation by grace through Jesus Christ, in gratitude I offer myself as your servant with the desire to love and follow you the rest of my life. Amen.

October 21   Psalm 117

1 *Praise the* LORD, *all you Gentiles! Laud Him, all you peoples!*
2 *For His merciful kindness is great toward us, and the truth of the* LORD *endures forever. Praise the* LORD*!* (NKJV)

An international call. This fifth Hallel psalm celebrates God's kindness shown to people from among the Gentiles such as Ruth and Naaman who join Israel in praising God for his "merciful kindness" shown to them (v. 2). In the New Testament, the apostle Paul quotes verse 1 to confirm that the Gentiles in his day encountered God through Jesus Christ and experienced his salvation (Rom 15:8–9). For those who personally know God, praise for his salvation is fitting. Noting the phrase "Praise the Lord" at the beginning and the end of this song, Abraham Wright* suggests, "The praise of God is here made both the beginning and the end of the Psalm; to show, that in praising God the saints are never satisfied with their own efforts, and would infinitely magnify him, even as his perfections are infinite . . . When we have said our utmost for God's praise, we must not be content but begin anew." He notes that since the nations are included in this psalm, we must "consecrate our whole lives to the singing and setting forth of God's worthy praises." If verse 1 is a general call to worship God, verse 2 provides the specifics for our praise to God, namely his mercy and truth. In Wright's words, "Through ordinances and "providences," God "comes and communicates himself to his people not only mercy, though that is very sweet, but truth also. Their blessings come to them in the way of promise from God, as bound to them by the truth of his covenant." He continues, "Upon this account, God's mercy is ordinarily in the Psalms bounded by his truth; that none may either presume him more merciful than he hath declared himself in his word; nor despair of finding mercy *gratis*, according to the truth of his promise." Wright applies these truths, "Therefore though your sins be great, believe the text, and know that God's mercy is greater than the sins."

Prayer. Father, I am thankful for your eternal truth and unfailing mercy which makes it possible for people around the globe to experience your salvation through Jesus Christ. Amen.

October 22 — Psalm 118:1–9

1 Oh give thanks to the LORD, for he is good; for his steadfast love endures forever! 2 Let Israel say, "His steadfast love endures forever." 3 Let the house of Aaron say, "His steadfast love endures forever." 4 Let those who fear the LORD say, "His steadfast love endures forever." 5 Out of my distress I called on the LORD; the LORD answered me and set me free. 6 *The LORD is on my side; I will not fear.* What can man do to me? 7 The LORD is on my side as my helper; I shall look in triumph on those who hate me. 8 It is better to take refuge in the LORD than to trust in man. 9 It is better to take refuge in the LORD than to trust in princes. (ESV)

Confident in his love. This sixth and final Hallel psalm opens with a fourfold affirmation of God's "steadfast love" (vv. 1–4) and concludes with the same refrain (v. 29). Twice the psalmist declares that the Lord is on his side (vv. 6–7). Considering God's great love, the psalmist has no need to fear and can expect to triumph over his enemies (vv. 7–8). His bold claim does not come from personal arrogance but from his confidence in God's covenant which is a commitment to steadfastly love his people. William Greenhill paraphrases the psalmist's confidence in the face of his enemy, "Let him do his worst, frown, threat, plot, arm, strike; the Lord is on my side, he has a special care for me, he is a shield unto me, I will not fear, but hope." He applies the truth of God's committed love to our lives, "God's presence should put life into us. When inferior natures are backed with a superior, they are full of courage: when the master is by, the dog will venture upon creatures greater than himself and fear not; at another time he will not do it when his master is absent. When God is with us, who is the supreme, it should make us fearless." Because we have a covenant relationship with Jesus Christ, nothing will separate us from God's great love (Rom 8:39).

Prayer. Father, often circumstances or feelings of unworthiness cause me to doubt your love for me. May your promises increase my confidence in your committed and unreserved love for me. Amen.

October 23   Psalm 118:10-18

10 All nations surrounded me; in the name of the LORD I cut them off! 11 *They surrounded me, surrounded me on every side; in the name of the* LORD *I cut them off!* 12 They surrounded me like bees; they went out like a fire among thorns; in the name of the LORD I cut them off! 13 I was pushed hard, so that I was falling, but the LORD helped me. 14 The LORD is my strength and my song; he has become my salvation. 15 Glad songs of salvation are in the tents of the righteous: "The right hand of the LORD does valiantly, 16 the right hand of the LORD exalts, the right hand of the LORD does valiantly!" 17 I shall not die, but I shall live, and recount the deeds of the LORD. 18 The LORD has disciplined me severely, but he has not given me over to death. (ESV)

Confident in adversity. Although it is relatively easy to make bold claims which ooze with confidence in God's love (v. 6), life's harsh realities test our certainty of his love. Four times in two verses the psalmist testifies that his enemies surrounded him (vv. 10–12). In difficult situations, we may wonder how much God loves us. Thomas Adams comments on such persecution, "Whether Tertullus persecute the church with his tongue [Acts 24:1–9], or Elymas [Acts 13:9] with his hand, God has the command of both. Indeed, the wicked are the mediate causes of our troubles: the righteous are as the centre, the other the circumference; which way soever they turn, they find themselves environed; yet still the centre is fixed and immovable, being founded upon Christ." Our confidence rests in Jesus Christ and his love commitment to us. Adams suggests that we should see value in adversity. He notes, "It is good for some men to have adversaries . . . They speak evil of us: if true, let us amend it; if false, contemn it; whether false or true, observe it. Thus, we shall learn good out of their evil; make them our tutors and give them our pupillage. In all things, let us match them, in nothing fear them."

Prayer. Father, I tremble when I experience hostility. Thank you for your promises which remind me that you are with me and can bring good out of adversity. Amen.

October 24　　Psalm 118:19-29

19 Open to me the gates of righteousness that I may enter through them and give thanks to the Lord. 20 This is the gate of the Lord; the righteous shall enter through it. 21 I thank you that you have answered me and have become my salvation. 22 *The stone that the builders rejected has become the cornerstone.* 23 This is the Lord's doing; it is marvelous in our eyes. 24 This is the day that the Lord has made; let us rejoice and be glad in it. 25 Save us, we pray, O Lord! O Lord, we pray, give us success! 26 Blessed is he who comes in the name of the Lord! We bless you from the house of the Lord. 27 The Lord is God, and he has made his light to shine upon us. Bind the festal sacrifice with cords, up to the horns of the altar! 28 You are my God, and I will give thanks to you; you are my God; I will extol you. 29 Oh give thanks to the Lord, for he is good; for his steadfast love endures forever! (ESV)

Confident in Jesus Christ. Returning from battle (vv. 10-12), the victorious warrior who enters Jerusalem's gates with thanksgiving (vv. 19-21) becomes the "cornerstone," or the most important stone in a building (v. 22). On this victorious day, the congregation express thanksgiving to God who saved them (vv. 24-25). This passage foreshadows Jesus' triumphal entry into Jerusalem (Matt 21:1-11) with the crowds shouting to him "Hosanna," a cry for him to save his people (21:9). Jesus' salvation would not be a military conquest, but a spiritual one which would begin by people rejecting Jesus (v. 22). Robert Leighton* elaborates, "They cast him away by their reproaches, and by giving him up to be crucified and then cast into the grave, causing a stone to be rolled upon this stone which they had so rejected, that it might appear no more, and so thought themselves sure. But even from thence did he arise" and became the cornerstone of our faith (Eph 2:19). Leighton reminds us, "It is the spirit of humility and obedience, and saving faith that teach men to esteem Christ, and build upon him."

Prayer. Lord, I am thankful for salvation in you in whom I place my full confidence. You are worthy of my praise! Amen.

October 25   Psalm 119:1-8

1 Blessed are those whose ways are blameless, who walk according to the law of the Lord. *2 Blessed are those who keep his statutes and seek him with all their heart—3 they do no wrong but follow his ways. 4 You have laid down precepts that are to be fully obeyed. 5 Oh, that my ways were steadfast in obeying your decrees! 6 Then I would not be put to shame when I consider all your commands. 7 I will praise you with an upright heart as I learn your righteous laws. 8 I will obey your decrees; do not utterly forsake me.* (NIV)

The blessed life. The longest psalm opens with God's blessing on those who wholeheartedly obey him (vv. 1–2). Paul Baynes comments on the two meanings of blessing through two scenarios, "If I speak of a sick man, and say he is happy, for he has met with a good physician; here I pronounce him blessed because he has found one who will restore him to health. If I say of the same man, he is a happy man, he can now digest very well what he eats, he can sleep, and walk abroad; I speak of him now as actually blessed with health of body." The first scenario reminds us that blessedness is "attributed to faith in Christ, to forgiveness of sin, and to justification of life which we obtain in Christ." The second scenario illustrates the results of a blessed life. Those who are blessed reflect the fruit of the Spirit by "walking in God's way." Referring to the habit of living according to God's will, Bayne observes, "If we have not the habit of doing anything, we do it with difficulty, we are ready to cease from doing it." For people who do not habitually walk with God, there is "no greater misery than to see themselves doing good duties uncheerfully, no sooner entering them than out again, and desisting from them." They will be "miserable till they form the habit which makes them with facility and constancy walk with God . . . they count it of all things most blessed to have attained some degree of permanent habit in godliness."

Prayer. Lord, seeking your blessing is essential for my life. I want to cultivate the habit of walking with you to experience your favor. Amen.

October 26   Psalm 119:9–16

9 How can a young man cleanse his way? By taking heed according to Your word. 10 With my whole heart I have sought You; Oh, let me not wander from Your commandments! 11 Your word I have hidden in my heart that I might not sin against You. 12 Blessed are You, O LORD! Teach me Your statutes. 13 With my lips I have declared all the judgments of Your mouth. 14 I have rejoiced in the way of Your testimonies, as much as in all riches. 15 *I will meditate on Your precepts and contemplate Your ways.* 16 I will delight myself in Your statutes; I will not forget Your word. (NKJV)

Meditating on God's truth. The psalmist is committed to meditating on Scripture (v. 15). This practice is worthwhile because, as Nathanael Ranew notes, "It makes the mind wise, the affections warm, the soul fat and flourishing, and the conversation greatly fruitful." To experience these blessings, we must exercise personal discipline. Ranew observes, "In meditation it is hard (sometimes at least) to take off our thoughts from the pre-engagements of other subjects and apply them to the duty." We need to discipline our minds because they wander easily as he notes, "It is harder to become duly serious in acting in it [meditation}, harder yet to dive and ponder; and hardest of all to continue in an abode of thoughts, and dwell long enough" especially when we are reading a passage which seems familiar and "old" and the "freshness and newness" is no longer there. In these cases, he admits that our devotional time can go "flat" unless we rouse ourselves with a "warm affection" for Scripture and make a "strong and quick repeated resolution" with the Lord's strength. He encourages us to imitate David who said, "I will meditate (v. 15)." David needed this resolve to begin his meditation on Scripture but also "for continuance in it, to keep up his heart from flagging, till he well-ended his work." Meditation reaps great rewards according to Ranew, "It is not the digging into the golden mine, but the digging long, that finds and fetches up the treasure. It is not the diving into the sea, but staying longer, that gets the greater quantity of pearls."

Prayer. Lord, cultivate in me a hunger to meditate on the Bible so that I may grow in my relationship with you. Amen.

October 27   Psalm 119:17–24

17 Be good to your servant while I live, that I may obey your word. 18 *Open my eyes that I may see wonderful things in your law.* 19 I am a stranger on earth; do not hide your commands from me. 20 My soul is consumed with longing for your laws at all times. 21 You rebuke the arrogant, who are accursed, those who stray from your commands. 22 Remove from me their scorn and contempt, for I keep your statutes. 23 Though rulers sit together and slander me, your servant will meditate on your decrees. 24 Your statutes are my delight; they are my counselors. (NIV)

Spiritual illumination. Since Scripture is God's written revelation to us (2 Tim 3:16), we, like the psalmist, need God's enabling grace to open our eyes to "see" or understand what it says to us (v. 18). However, Moses informs the Israelites that "the Lord has not given you a mind that understands or eyes that see or ears that hear" (Deut 29:4). Joseph Caryl mentions that the Israelites saw with their own eyes the many signs and miracles God performed to free them from Egyptian captivity. He explains, "They had sensitive eyes and ears, yes, they had a rational heart or mind; but they wanted a spiritual ear to hear, a spiritual heart or mind to apprehend and improve those wonderful works of God; and these they had not, because God had not given them such eyes, ears, and hearts." For those who do not personally know Jesus Christ, the Holy Spirit must remove the spiritual blindness so that they can see the light of God's truth (1 Cor 2:14; 2 Cor 4:3-4, 6). Caryl concludes, "Wonders without grace cannot open the eyes fully; but grace without wonders can. And as man has not an eye to see the wonderful works of God spiritually, until it is given; so, much less has he an eye to see the wonders of the word of God till it be given him from above." The Holy Spirit enables us to see those wonders in Scripture so that we may apply biblical truth to our lives.

Prayer. Lord, open my eyes to the richness of Scripture so that I may grasp what you are saying and allow it to speak into my life so that I may be transformed. Amen.

October 28   Psalm 119:25–32

25 My soul clings to the dust; revive me according to Your word. 26 I have declared my ways, and You answered me; teach me Your statutes. 27 Make me understand the way of Your precepts; so shall I meditate on Your wonderful works. 28 My soul melts from heaviness; strengthen me according to Your word. 29 Remove from me the way of lying and grant me Your law graciously. 30 I have chosen the way of truth; Your judgments I have laid before me. 31 I cling to Your testimonies; O Lord, do not put me to shame! 32 I will run the course of Your commandments, for You shall enlarge my heart. (NKJV)

Spiritual revival. At various points in our lives, we may feel that our spiritual vitality has diminished, and we can empathize with the psalmist's frequent petition to God to "revive" him (vv. 25, 37, 50, 91, 107, 154). He expresses a common need within us. While the Hebrew word for "revive" can refer to physical life, Matthew Henry captures the word's other meaning, "By your providence put life into my affairs, by your grace put life into my affections; cure me of my spiritual deadness and make me lively in my devotion." Paul Baynes describes our need for spiritual invigoration, "To whom shall the godly fly when life fails but to that Wellspring of all life?" Of course, to no one but the Lord! Baynes continues, "Even as to remove cold the next way is to draw near the fire, so to dispel any death the next way is to look to him who is our root, by whom we live this natural life. All preservatives and restoratives are nothing, all colleges of physicians are vanity, if compared with him." For the psalmist, it is Scripture which offers spiritual revival through its promises and its assurances of God's love and presence with us. With confidence we can ask God to reignite our souls, knowing that "God deal[s] with this flame of life which he has kindled." Spiritual revival is possible through God's working in our lives.

Prayer. Lord, when I felt so spiritually dry, I kept foolishly pressing on even though I was physically and spiritually exhausted. Breathe your life into me to revive the fire in my heart so that I may fervently love and serve you and others. Amen.

October 29 Psalm 119:33–40

33 Teach me, Lord, the way of your decrees, that I may follow it to the end. 34 *Give me understanding, so that I may keep your law and obey it with all my heart.* 35 Direct me in the path of your commands, for there I find delight. 36 Turn my heart toward your statutes and not toward selfish gain. 37 Turn my eyes away from worthless things; preserve my life according to your word. 38 Fulfill your promise to your servant, so that you may be feared. 39 Take away the disgrace I dread, for your laws are good. 40 How I long for your precepts! In your righteousness preserve my life. (NIV)

Wholehearted obedience. In this section of Psalm 119, the writer wants to obey the Lord wholeheartedly (v. 34). Thomas Manton explains why such obedience should be our desire, "The whole man is God's by every kind of right and title; and therefore, when he requires the whole heart he does but require that which is his own. God gave us the whole by creation, preserves the whole, redeems the whole, and promises to glorify the whole." God did not create us to keep a part of ourselves from him; nor does he divide up our whole being at death, or "take a part to heaven." God is involved in sanctifying "the whole in a gospel sense, that is every part" of our being (I Thess 5:23). "not only [the] conscience, but will and affections, appetite and body." God has, is, and will always be involved with our whole being! Our response is to glorify God with our bodies and spirit (1 Cor. 6:20 KJV), to give "all to him for his use . . . not a part, but the whole." God's word (v. 34) helps us, "gives strength, that excites the sluggish will, and breaks the force of corrupt inclinations; it removes sluggish will and the darkness which corruption and sin have brought upon the mind, and makes us pliable and ready to obey."

Prayer. Lord, too often my heart has divided allegiances, robbing you of the love you deserve. Loving you more and loving other things less is a lifelong process which requires your Spirit's enabling grace. Work in my heart so that I may wholeheartedly love and obey you. Amen.

October 30   Psalm 119:41–48

41 May your unfailing love come to me, Lord, your salvation, according to your promise; 42 then I can answer anyone who taunts me, for I trust in your word. 43 Never take your word of truth from my mouth, for I have put my hope in your laws. 44 I will always obey your law, for ever and ever. 45 *I will walk about in freedom, for I have sought out your precepts.* 46 *I will speak of your statutes before kings and will not be put to shame,* 47 *for I delight in your commands because I love them.* 48 *I reach out for your commands, which I love, that I may meditate on your decrees.* (NIV)

Esteem for God's word. The psalmist serves as a good example of one who spoke God's word in the face of those who taunted him (v. 42). Matthew Henry mentions "five things [the psalmist] promises himself here in the strength of God's grace," following each promise with a paraphrase of his thoughts. First, "he should be free and easy in his duty: I will walk at liberty: freed from that which is evil, not hampered with the fetters of my own corruptions, and free to that which is good" (v. 45). God's word does not restrict believers but gives freedom from the power of sin. Second, "he should be bold and courageous in his duty: I will speak of thy testimonies before kings" (v. 46). He would speak boldly like Daniel and Paul who faced kings. Third, "he should be cheerful and pleasant in his duty: I will delight myself in your commandments, in conversing with them, in forming to them" (v. 47). His love for God's word shaped his life. Fourth, "he should be diligent and vigorous in his duty: I will lift up my hands unto your commandments; which notes not only a vehement desire towards them, but a close application of mind to the observance of them" (v. 48). He wants God's revelation to be practical for his life. Fifth, "he should be thoughtful and considerate in his duty: I will meditate in thy statutes." Meditation on biblical truth will shape his and our speech and actions.

Prayer. Lord, I need not be ashamed of your word when I consider how it has transformed so many lives, including my own. Amen.

October 31 Psalm 119:49-56

49 Remember the word to Your servant, upon which You have caused me to hope. 50 *This is my comfort in my affliction, for Your word has given me life.* 51 The proud have me in great derision, yet I do not turn aside from Your law. 52 I remembered Your judgments of old, O Lord, and have comforted myself. 53 Indignation has taken hold of me because of the wicked, who forsake Your law. 54 Your statutes have been my songs in the house of my pilgrimage. 55 I remember Your name in the night, O Lord, and I keep Your law. 56 This has become mine because I kept Your precepts. (NKJV)

God's word comforts. Although the writer is indignant toward those who forsake God's word (v. 53) and ridicule him (v. 51), yet, he experiences comfort in his affliction through God's word (vv. 50, 52). Richard Sibbes explains this comfort that Scripture reassures us, "God has given us his Scriptures, his word; and the comforts that are fetched from thence are strong ones, because they are his comforts, since they come from his word. The word of a prince comforts, though he be not there to speak it. Though it be by a letter, or by a messenger, yet he whose word it is, is one that is able to make his word good. He is Lord and Master of his word. The word of God is comfortable [able to comfort], and all the reasons that are in it, and that are deduced from it, upon good ground and consequence, are comfortable, because it is God's word." Even though we may experience comfort from others, the Bible comforts us because its words come from the Lord. Sibbes continues, "Those comforts in God's word, and reasons from thence, are wonderful in variety. There is comfort from the liberty of a Christian, that he has free access to the throne of grace; comfort from the prerogatives of a Christian, that he is the child of God, that he is justified, that he is the heir of heaven, and such like; comforts from the promises of grace, of the presence of God, of assistance by his presence."

Prayer. Lord, thank you for your promises and personal presence which reassure and sustain me during my doubts and trials! Amen.

November 1   Psalm 119:57–64

57 You are my portion, O Lord; I have said that I would keep Your words. 58 *I entreated Your favor with my whole heart; be merciful to me according to Your word.* 59 I thought about my ways and turned my feet to Your testimonies. 60 I made haste, and did not delay to keep Your commandments. 61 The cords of the wicked have bound me, but I have not forgotten Your law. 62 At midnight I will rise to give thanks to You, because of Your righteous judgments. 63 I am a companion of all who fear You, and of those who keep Your precepts. 64 The earth, O Lord, is full of Your mercy; teach me Your statutes. (NKJV)

God's word shapes prayer. Like the psalmist, we may find ourselves pleading with our whole being for God to answer our requests (v. 58). When we come before God, we should desire for him to respond according to his will which is revealed in Scripture. Richard Greenham agrees that Scripture "must be the rule of our prayers, and then we shall receive." He notes that David "prayed not for what he lusted after, but for that which the Lord promised." Edmund Calamy states that Scripture's promises are "the food of faith, and the soul of faith." He explains, "As faith is the life of a Christian, so the promises are the life of faith: faith is a dead faith if it has no promise to quicken it. As the promises are of no use without faith to apply them, so faith is of no use without a promise to lay hold on." Thomas Manton adds, "God's word is the rule of our confidence" for our prayer requests. Praying according to God's promises ultimately depends on God's mercy (v. 58). Manton notes, "If we would have favour and mercy from God, it must be upon his own terms . . . Many would have mercy but will not observe God's direction. We must ask according to God's will, not without a promise, nor against a command."

Prayer. Lord, I confess that often my prayers are according to my selfish desires and interests. In response to your word, I want Scripture to shape my prayers so that they are according to your good purposes in order to nourish me to face today's opportunities and challenges. Amen.

November 2   Psalm 119:65-72

65 Do good to your servant according to your word, LORD. 66 Teach me knowledge and good judgment, for I trust your commands. 67 *Before I was afflicted I went astray, but now I obey your word.* 68 You are good, and what you do is good; teach me your decrees. 69 Though the arrogant have smeared me with lies, I keep your precepts with all my heart. 70 Their hearts are callous and unfeeling, but I delight in your law. 71 It was good for me to be afflicted so that I might learn your decrees. 72 The law from your mouth is more precious to me than thousands of pieces of silver and gold. (NIV)

God's word and afflictions. The psalmist confesses that he strayed away from the Lord and his word before God used afflictions to draw him back into an obedient relationship (vv. 67, 71). Ezekiel Hopkins addresses affliction in our lives. He states, "God in wisdom deals with us as some great person would do with a disobedient son that forsakes his house, and riots among his tenants. His father gives orders that they should treat him ill, affront, and chase him from them, and all, that he might bring him back. The same does God: man is his wild and debauched son; he flies from the commands of his father, and cannot endure to live under his strict and severe government. He resorts to the pleasures of the world, and revels and riots among the creatures. But God resolves to recover him, and therefore commands every creature to handle him roughly." Like the "beggared prodigal" the individual returns to his father's loving embrace. Not surprisingly, the psalmist admits that the affliction was "good" because he learned God's word (v. 71) and now he values its truth. This greater appreciation for God's revealed word motivates him to obey it even when others slander him (vv. 67, 69). When we face animosity from others, the commitment to obey God's truth enables us to respond with "good judgment" (v. 66).

Prayer. Lord, when life goes well, I can unconsciously adopt a lackadaisical attitude toward you. As a result, I stray from your word and deliberately disobey you. I want to submit to afflictions so that I may have renewed passion to obey your truth. Amen.

November 3   Psalm 119:73–80

73 Your hands made me and formed me; *give me understanding to learn your commands.* 74 May those who fear you rejoice when they see me, for I have put my hope in your word. 75 I know, Lord, that your laws are righteous, and that in faithfulness you have afflicted me. 76 May your unfailing love be my comfort, according to your promise to your servant. 77 Let your compassion come to me that I may live, for your law is my delight. 78 May the arrogant be put to shame for wronging me without cause; but I will meditate on your precepts. 79 May those who fear you turn to me, those who understand your statutes. 80 May I wholeheartedly follow your decrees, that I may not be put to shame. (NIV)

God's word enlightens. We have God's commands to understand how to live (v. 73). To influence our thoughts and actions, God speaks his truth into our consciences. William Fenner explains the role of prayer in helping us act rightly, "Let us pray unto God that he would open our understandings, that as he has given us consciences to guide us, so also he would give eyes to these guides that they may be able to direct us aright. The truth is, it is God only that can soundly enlighten our consciences; and therefore, let us pray unto him to do it." He continues, "All our studying, and hearing, and reading, and conferring will never be able to do it; it is only in the power of him who made us to do it. He who made our consciences, he only can give them this heavenly light of true knowledge and right understanding; and therefore, let us seek earnestly to him for it." He also sheds light on those areas within us which need healing. The psalmist's afflictions wounded him and required comfort from God's Word (vv. 75–76). Richard Stock likens the Bible to a pharmacy, "In the Scriptures, there are cures for any infirmities; there is comfort against any sorrows, and by conferring chapter with chapter, we shall understand them. The Scriptures are not wanting [lacking] to us, but we to ourselves; let us be conversant in them, and we shall understand them."

Prayer. Lord, I want your inspired word to shape my conscience and bring healing to my deep wounds. Amen.

November 4 — Psalm 119:81–88

81 My soul faints with longing for your salvation, *but I have put my hope in your word.* 82 My eyes fail, looking for your promise; I say, "When will you comfort me?" 83 Though I am like a wineskin in the smoke, I do not forget your decrees. 84 How long must your servant wait? When will you punish my persecutors? 85 The arrogant dig pits to trap me, contrary to your law. 86 All your commands are trustworthy; help me, for I am being persecuted without cause. 87 They almost wiped me from the earth, but I have not forsaken your precepts. 88 In your unfailing love preserve my life, that I may obey the statutes of your mouth. (NIV)

God's word provides hope. Facing persecution (vv. 85–86), the psalmist waits for God to punish his antagonists (v. 84). Physically and emotionally exhausted (vv. 81–83a), the writer wonders when God will act. God sustains and gives him hope according to his "trustworthy" word (vv. 81, 86) but David's persecutors still threaten him. Samuel Rutherford writes of the need for faith at such times, "Believe under a cloud, and wait for him when there is no moonlight nor starlight. Let faith live and breathe, and lay hold of the sure salvation of God, when clouds and darkness are about you, and appearance of rotting in the prison before you." He adds, "Who dreams that a promise of God can fail, fall a swoon, or die? Who can make God sick, or his promises weak? When we are pleased to seek a plea with Christ, let us plead that we hope in him . . . Faith's eyes that can see through a millstone, can see through a gloom of God, and under it read God's thoughts of love and peace. Hold fast Christ in the dark; surely you shall see the salvation of God." David Dickson also encourages us, "It is good in all times of persecution or affliction to have an eye both on the promises and on the precepts; for the looking to the promise does encourage [us] to hope, and the eyeing of the precepts does prove the hope to be sound." This hope enables us to obey God (v. 88).

Prayer. Lord, thank you for your trustworthy word which gives me genuine hope during my troubles. Amen.

November 5   Psalm 119:89–96

89 Your word, LORD, is eternal; it stands firm in the heavens. 90 Your faithfulness continues through all generations; you established the earth, and it endures. 91 Your laws endure to this day, for all things serve you. 92 If your law had not been my delight, I would have perished in my affliction. 93 I will never forget your precepts, for by them you have preserved my life. 94 *Save me, for I am yours*; I have sought out your precepts. 95 The wicked are waiting to destroy me, but I will ponder your statutes. 96 To all perfection I see a limit, but your commands are boundless. (NIV)

A love relationship. The writer declares that he belongs to God his relationship with God (v. 94), a declaration from which Joseph Symonds shares some insights. First, if a father is good to his child, or a husband to his wife, then God does this "more perfectly, fully, and gloriously" because "there is no father like him, no friend, [and] no husband like him." Also, this love relationship between the psalmist and God is based on the covenant which "God has made with us, wherein he is become our father and friend (Isa 63:16)." Since God is our Father, we can call on him to help us. If a person can say, "'I am yours,' God much more will say to the creature, 'I am yours.' If we have so much love to offer ourselves to God, to become his; much more will the love of God make him to become ours; for God loves first, and most, and surest. If my heart rises toward God, much more is the heart of God toward me; because there love is in the fountain." From a "love of thankfulness," the psalmist responds to God's love, "Lord, I am yours." Symonds notes, "The gracious man will willingly acknowledge himself to be the Lord's." In Psalm 116:16, when the psalmist twice affirms, "I am your servant," Symonds explains, "To say it once was not enough; he said it again, to show the sincerity of his spirit, and to witness that his heart was fully pleased with this, that he was not his own, but the Lord's."

Prayer. Father, I am grateful that you have adopted me into your family, which gives me the assurance you will always love me. I am yours! Amen.

November 6   Psalm 119:97-104

97 Oh, how I love Your law! It is my meditation all the day. 98 You, through Your commandments, make me wiser than my enemies; for they are ever with me. 99 I have more understanding than all my teachers, for Your testimonies are my meditation. 100 *I understand more than the ancients because I keep Your precepts.* 101 I have restrained my feet from every evil way that I may keep Your word. 102 I have not departed from Your judgments for You Yourself have taught me. 103 How sweet are Your words to my taste, sweeter than honey to my mouth! 104 Through Your precepts I get understanding; therefore I hate every false way. (NKJV)

God's word provides wisdom. The psalmist declares that Scripture has made him "wiser" than others (vv. 99-100). Thomas Manton explains his understanding, "Malice sharpens the wit of enemies, and teaches them the arts of opposition; teachers are furnished with learning because of their office; and ancients grow wise by experience; yet David, by the study of the word, excelled all these." The psalmist is wiser than his enemies because he walks under God's protection, is "guided by the Spirit of God," and walks "with God step by step." In regard to the wisdom of the "ancients" (v. 100), Manton shares three reasons why gaining wisdom through God's word is better than learning from experience. First, understanding informed by Scripture is "more exact," because it covers all areas which pertain to a blessed life. Second, biblical understanding is a "more sure way of learning wisdom, whereas experience is more uncertain." Manton refers to the Israelites who were rescued from Egypt, but they failed to "gather wisdom" from the Exodus (Deut 29:2-4). Third, learning from Scripture is a "safer and cheaper way of learning," in contrast to experience, a "too expensive" way to learn because of the "many thousand miseries" we create for ourselves. Fourth, gaining understanding through Scripture is "shorter" in contrast to the "long way" a person often chooses which results in "miseries and troubles."

Prayer. Father, too often I have learned the hard way which has only brought heartache and pain to me and others. Now, I want to grow in wisdom through your word so that my life will honor you and others. Amen.

November 7   Psalm 119:105–12

105 Your word is a lamp for my feet, a light on my path. 106 I have taken an oath and confirmed it, that I will follow your righteous laws. 107 I have suffered much; preserve my life, LORD, according to your word. 108 Accept, Lord, the willing praise of my mouth, and teach me your laws. 109 Though I constantly take my life in my hands, I will not forget your law. 110 The wicked have set a snare for me, but I have not strayed from your precepts. 111 Your statutes are my heritage forever; they are the joy of my heart. 112 *My heart is set on keeping your decrees to the very end.* (NIV)

God's word provides joy. Scripture provides a path for us to follow to avoid sin ensnaring us (vv. 105, 110). When we stay on God's pathway, we experience "the joy" of his word (v. 111). The "heart" (vv. 111–12) must be rightly related to God for persistent obedience and joy to occur. Examining our heart attitude is important because various heart conditions can rob us of true joy, according to Nathanael Ranew. We may have a "sinful heart" which loves "upon earthly things, upon evil things, or upon impertinent and unseasonable things," rather than paying attention to God's ways. A person may have a "carnal heart" which is pulled like a magnet toward sin whereas a heart for God "must be of another property, and act in a higher way." Even a moralist's "good heart" is a barrier to experiencing God's joy because this heart "thinks too much earthward" with a focus on doing good things. Ranew mentions that the psalmist knew that his heart could be distant from God's precepts, and to unite his heart to Him, he "inclined his heart to God's commandments both to keep them and to meditate on them." As we allow God's grace to work within us by meditating on Scripture, we experience genuine joy "to the very end" (v. 112), the joy of an unfailing reward. God's word and joy are true rewards!

Prayer. Lord, even though I seek to obey you, I often lack joy because my heart has been drawn to idols which rob me of joy. Create within me a pure heart so that I may obey you and rediscover the true joy found in you. Amen.

November 8   Psalm 119:113–20

113 I hate double-minded people, *but I love your law.* 114 You are my refuge and my shield; I have put my hope in your word. 115 Away from me, you evildoers, that I may keep the commands of my God! 116 Sustain me, my God, according to your promise, and I will live; do not let my hopes be dashed. 117 Uphold me, and I will be delivered; I will always have regard for your decrees. 118 You reject all who stray from your decrees, for their delusions come to nothing. 119 All the wicked of the earth you discard like dross; therefore I love your statutes. 120 My flesh trembles in fear of you; I stand in awe of your laws. (NIV)

God's word cultivates love. The psalmist wholeheartedly loves God's word, and therefore he despises a double-minded approach to life (v. 113). A hunger for biblical truth exposes duplicity and cultivates a singular devotion to God. Stephen Charnock underscores the importance of a love relationship with the Lord. He exhorts, "Ballast your heart with a love to God." Then he explains, "Love will, by a pleasing violence bind down our thoughts: if it [love] does not establish our minds, they will be like a cork, which, with a light breath, and a short curl of water, shall be tossed up and down from its station." His words echo James' description of double-minded people who are "blown and tossed by the wind" (Jas 1:6). In contrast, one who loves Christ "will have frequent glances and flights toward him." Even while one is working during the day, the individual can go to Jesus "several times in a day to give him a visit." While ardent love for God's truth counters double mindedness, love also "increases our delight in God." In our "very act of loving" him, God is pleased and blesses us. Experiencing his pleasure "will prevent the heart's giving entertainment" to a double-minded attitude toward God. With a love for Scripture, the psalmist places his hope in it (v. 114), trusts God's promises to sustain him (v. 116), and obeys the commands during opposition (v. 115).

Prayer. Lord, use your word to expose my double-minded thoughts and enable me to wholeheartedly love you and your word. I want my trust in you to deepen and my obedience flow out of my love for you Amen.

November 9   Psalm 119:121–28

121 I have done what is righteous and just; do not leave me to my oppressors. 122 Ensure your servant's well-being; do not let the arrogant oppress me. 123 My eyes fail, looking for your salvation, looking for your righteous promise. 124 Deal with your servant according to your love and teach me your decrees. 125 I am your servant; give me discernment that I may understand your statutes. 126 It is time for you to act, LORD; *your law is being broken.* 127 Because I love your commands more than gold, more than pure gold, 128 and because I consider all your precepts right, I hate every wrong path. (NIV)

God's word provides boundaries. Today's verses rightly challenges those who claim that there are no absolutes. The psalmist sees only two options from which to choose: God's precepts are right and many paths are wrong (v. 128). These two alternatives reflect more than the psalmist's opinion. For example, he mentions that the "law" comes from the Lord (v. 126). The decrees, statutes, commandments, law, and precepts are his (vv. 124–28). A righteous God is the author of moral laws by which we are to conduct our lives. However, people willfully and deliberately break God's laws (v. 126) and choose their own paths in which they oppress and hurt others (v. 122). Joseph Caryl comments, "They would not only sin against the Law, but sin away the Law, not only withdraw themselves from the obedience of it, but drive it out of the world; they would make void and repeal the holy acts of God, that their own wicked acts might not be questioned; and lest the Law should have a power to punish them, they will deny it a power to rule them." Instead of denying God's law, the psalmist loves God's commands (v. 127) which motivate him to learn, understand and obey his moral laws (vv. 121, 124–25).

Prayer. Lord, despite social pressure to deny moral absolutes, I want to hold firm to your unchanging truth. However, I confess that I intentionally violate your word and disobey you. Forgive me and increase my love for Scripture so that I may increasingly live in accordance with it. Amen.

November 10   Psalm 119:129-36

129 *Your statutes are wonderful; therefore I obey them.* 130 The unfolding of your words gives light; it gives understanding to the simple. 131 I open my mouth and pant, longing for your commands. 132 Turn to me and have mercy on me, as you always do to those who love your name. 133 Direct my footsteps according to your word; let no sin rule over me. 134 Redeem me from human oppression, that I may obey your precepts. 135 Make your face shine on your servant and teach me your decrees. 136 Streams of tears flow from my eyes, for your law is not obeyed. (NIV)

God's word is wonderful. Thomas Manton mentions ways God's "statutes are "wonderful" (v. 129). First, they are wonderful "in their majesty and composure, which strikes reverence into the hearts of those that consider; the Scripture speaks to us at a God like rate." Second, they are wonderful "for the matter and depth of mystery . . . concerning God, and Christ, the creation of the world, the souls of men, and their immortal and everlasting condition, the fall of man" and much more. Third, they are wonderful "for purity and perfection." The statutes "reaches to the very soul, and all the motions of the heart," in order that we may fulfill our "whole duty" before God. Fourth, they are wonderful "for the harmony and consent of all the parts." There is a unified focus to promote obedience or the "subjection of the creature to God." Finally, they are wonderful "for the power . . . There is a mighty power which goes along with the word of God and astonishes the hearts of those that consider it and feel it."

Prayer. Lord, in the words of Thomas a Kempis* "Blessed is the man whom eternal Truth teacheth, not by obscure figures and transient sounds, but by direct and full communication . . . Thy ministers can pronounce the words but cannot impart the spirit; they may entertain the fancy with the charms of eloquence, but if thou art silent they do not inflame the heart. They administer the letter, but thou openest the sense; they utter the mystery, but thou reveal its meaning; they point out the way of life, but you bestow strength to walk in it; they water, but thou givest the increase." Amen.

November 11   Psalm 119:137-44

137 You are righteous, LORD, and your laws are right. 138 The statutes you have laid down are righteous; they are fully trustworthy. 139 My zeal wears me out, for my enemies ignore your words. 140 Your promises have been thoroughly tested, and your servant loves them. 141 Though I am lowly and despised, I do not forget your precepts. 142 Your righteousness is everlasting and *your law is true.* 143 Trouble and distress have come upon me, but your commands give me delight. 144 Your statutes are always righteous; give me understanding that I may live. (NIV)

God's word is true. Scripture's truthfulness is related to God who is righteous (vv. 137, 142) and consequently, his laws and statutes are right or righteous and true (vv. 137–38, 142, 144). Thomas Manton explains the ways that God's word is true. First, Scripture is the "chief" or the primary truth one needs to know. He states, "There is some truth in the laws of men and the writings of men, even of heathens; but they are but sorry fragments and scraps of truth, that have escaped since the fall." Second, Scripture is "the only truth; that is, the only revelation of the mind of God that you can build upon. It is the rule of truth." There are no other divine revelations from God or any other self-ascribed gods. Third, his written revelation is "the pure truth. In it there is nothing but the truth, without the mixture of falsehood; every part is true as truth itself. It is true in the promises, threatenings, doctrines, histories, precepts, prohibitions." Finally, the Bible contains "the whole truth. It contains all things necessary for the salvation of those that yield up themselves to be instructed by it." The psalmist dares not to forget God's precepts because they are "fully trustworthy" (vv. 138, 141). He wants the truth to permeate his mind so that he can grow in understanding (v. 144). With a love and delight for God's laws, he obeys them (vv. 140, 143). Scripture's truthfulness should influence the way we live. Having trust, understanding, and a delight in God's word strengthens us in the face of life's adversities (v. 139).

Prayer. Lord, I am thankful for the truthfulness of your word which sustains me through each day's ups and downs. Incline my heart to faithfully delight in the truth of Scripture so that I may obey you. Amen.

November 12   Psalm 119:145-52

145 I call with all my heart; answer me, Lord, and I will obey your decrees. 146 I call out to you; save me and I will keep your statutes. 147 *I rise before dawn and cry for help*; I have put my hope in your word. 148 My eyes stay open through the watches of the night that I may meditate on your promises. 149 Hear my voice in accordance with your love; preserve my life, Lord, according to your laws. 150 Those who devise wicked schemes are near, but they are far from your law. 151 Yet you are near, Lord, and all your commands are true. 152 Long ago I learned from your statutes that you established them to last forever. (NIV)

God's word is practical. Although he faces nearby adversaries, the psalmist knows that God is also near (vv. 150–51), giving him confidence to call out to him (vv. 145–47). The writer also has an unwavering confidence in God's truthful word (vv. 147, 151) which motivates him to devote time with the Lord. Matthew Henry makes a few observations. First, "David was an early riser, which perhaps contributed to his eminency. He was none of those that say, 'Yet a little sleep.'" Second, "He began the day with God; the first thing he did in the morning, before he admitted any business, was to pray, when his mind was most fresh and in the best frame. If our first thoughts in the morning be of God, it will help to keep us in his fear all the day long. Third, "His mind was so full of God and the cares and delights of his religion, that a little sleep served his turn, even in 'the night watches' when he awaked from his first sleep, he would rather meditate and pray, than turn him and go to sleep again." Fourth, "He would redeem time for religious exercises; he was full of business all day, but that will excuse no man from secret devotion; it is better to take time from sleep, as David did, than not find time for prayer."

Prayer. Father, busyness often crowds out my time with you, but this is a poor excuse. Help me to spend more uninterrupted time talking and listening to you in the quietness of the early morning or late in the evening. Amen.

November 13   Psalm 119:153–60

153 Consider mine affliction and deliver me: for I do not forget thy law. 154 Plead my cause and deliver me: quicken me according to thy word. 155 Salvation is far from the wicked: for they seek not thy statutes. 156 Great are thy tender mercies, O Lord: quicken me according to thy judgments. 157 Many are my persecutors and mine enemies; yet do I not decline from thy testimonies. 158 I beheld the transgressors, and was grieved; because they kept not thy word. 159 Consider how I love thy precepts: quicken me, O Lord, according to thy lovingkindness. 160 Thy word is true from the beginning: *and every one of thy righteous judgments endureth for ever.* (KJV)

God's word is eternal. Adversities, such as serious illnesses, threaten our existence. The psalmist suffered relentlessly, persecuted by his enemies (vv. 153, 157). Three times he asked God to "quicken" (vv. 154, 156, 159). The Hebrew word for "quicken" includes the ideas of renewal or revival. When the Lord touches an individual's physical being, he also uplifts one's spirit or emotions. The psalmist's confident pleas for God to renew his life are rooted in God's promise (v. 154), laws (v. 156), his love (v. 159), and the laws' eternal truthfulness (v. 160). On this truthfulness of Scripture, Anthony Tuckney refers to verse 160 which mentions that God's word is "true from the beginning." He asserts, "It's well, it begins well. But will it last as well?" He responds with a "yes" based on the enduring nature of God's truth (v. 160). He discusses the practical implications of the eternal nature of God's precepts. He states, "God's commandment and promise is exceeding broad, reaching to all times . . . A good promise is a good nurse, both to the young babe and to the decrepit old man . . . Has a promise cheered you, say, twenty, thirty, forty years ago? Taste it but now afresh, and you shall find it as fresh, and as full of refreshment as ever. If it has been your greatest joy in your joyful youth, I tell you, it has as much joy in it for thy sad old age."

Prayer. Father, with society's changing values, I am thankful for your eternal truth. When I am exhausted by the cultural shifts, breathe your lifegiving truth into my heart and renew me. Amen.

November 14   Psalm 119:161–68

161 Rulers persecute me without cause, but my heart trembles at your word. 162 I rejoice in your promise like one who finds great spoil. 163 I hate and detest falsehood but I love your law. 164 Seven times a day I praise you for your righteous laws. 165 *Great peace have those who love your law, and nothing can make them stumble.* 166 I wait for your salvation, Lord, and I follow your commands. 167 I obey your statutes, for I love them greatly. 168 I obey your precepts and your statutes, for all my ways are known to you. (NIV)

God's word sustains. God's truth sustains the psalmist in the face of adversity. Rather than trembling at his persecutors, he trembles before God's word (v. 161). Thomas Manton states that there is an "awe of the word" which makes us "tender of violating it or doing anything contrary to it. This is not the fruit of slavish fear, but of holy love; it is not afraid of the word but delights in it." The psalmist also praises God amid adversity (vv. 162, 164). John Cotton states that the psalmist rejoices like a soldier who gets "a booty [great gain] out of every commandment, promise, or threatening he hears" (v. 162). While the psalmist hates falsehoods, he loves God's laws (vv. 163, 165). Thomas Manton points out that "where the enmity is not great against the sin," in other words, where sin is tolerated, it will greatly diminish our appetite for God's truth. He adds. "Slight hatred of a sinful course is not sufficient to guard us against it [falsehood]." Rather than loving sin, love for God's truth furnishes us with peace (v. 165). Finally, steadfast obedience to God's word (vv. 167–68) sustains the psalmist because he believes in the promise of deliverance (vv. 162, 166) amid adversity. To do otherwise is foolish as Nathanael Vincent notes, "He that casts the commands behind his back is very presumptuous in applying the promises to himself." Thomas Shephard asks if the psalmist should put the priority on loving the commandments in order to obey them. He responds that the psalmist used a "holy and most heavenly circle" by which he "kept them and loved them and loved them and kept them."

Prayer. Lord, may your word sustain me when life is both challenging and comfortable. Amen.

November 15 Psalm 119:169–76

169 May my cry come before you, Lord; give me understanding according to your word. 170 May my supplication come before you; deliver me according to your promise. 171 May my lips overflow with praise, for you teach me your decrees. 172 May my tongue sing of your word, for all your commands are righteous. 173 May your hand be ready to help me, for I have chosen your precepts. 174 I long for your salvation, Lord, and your law gives me delight. 175 Let me live that I may praise you, and may your laws sustain me. 176 *I have strayed like a lost sheep. Seek your servant, for I have not forgotten your commands.* (NIV)

God's word is for us. Although we may not measure up to the writer's devotion to God in this psalm, his admission of straying is a reminder that we all are sinners who constantly need the Lord (v. 176). In regard to the psalmist's straying, Joseph Caryl points out that Satan can deceive us until God convicts us through Scripture and draws us back to him. Barton Bouchier* comments, "I do not think that there could possibly be a more appropriate conclusion of such a Psalm as this, so full of the varied experience and the ever changing frames and feelings even of a child of God, in the sunshine and the cloud, in the calm and in the storm, than this ever clinging sense of his propensity to wander, and the expression of his utter inability to find his way back without the Lord's guiding hand to restore him; and at the same time with it all, his fixed and abiding determination never to forget the Lord's commandments. What an insight into our poor wayward hearts does this verse give us—not merely liable to wander, but ever wandering, ever losing our way, ever stumbling on the dark mountains, even while cleaving to God's commandments! But at the same time what a prayer does it put into our mouths, 'Seek your servant'—'I am yours, save me.' Yes, blessed be God!"

Prayer. Lord, I love your word, but I stray by disobeying it. My heart is prone to wander from you! Woo me back to a deeper intimacy with you so that I will have a stronger resolve to obey you. Amen.

November 16   Psalm 120

1 I took my troubles to the LORD; I cried out to him, and he answered my prayer. 2 Rescue me, O LORD, from liars and from all deceitful people. 3 O deceptive tongue, what will God do to you? How will he increase your punishment? 4 *You will be pierced with sharp arrows and burned with glowing coals.* 5 How I suffer in far-off Meshech. It pains me to live in distant Kedar. 6 I am tired of living among people who hate peace. 7 I search for peace; but when I speak of peace, they want war! (NLT)

Motivation for the journey. Living far from home, the psalmist is a stranger (v. 5) among people who lie to him, hate him and hate peace (vv. 2, 6–7). In response, he asks a question (v. 3) and then answers with the punishment God will bring to them (v. 4). Joseph Caryl explains God's retribution, "As such speakers shoot arrows, like the arrows of the mighty, and as they scatter coals, like the coals of juniper, so they usually get an arrow in their own sides, and not only burn their fingers, but heap coals of fire upon their own heads. Ungodly men will do mischief to other men purely for mischief's sake: yet when once mischief is done it proves most mischievous to the doers of it." Thus, distance and an antagonistic culture birth the longing to return home which shapes the first of fifteen pilgrim songs or songs of ascent to the elevated city of Jerusalem. Robert Nisbet* mentions that this first song offers us a "painful but useful lesson." He states that "all who manifest a resolution to obey the commands and seek the favour of God, may expect to encounter opposition and reproach in such a course . . . But their refuge is in him they worship; and, firmly convinced that he never can forsake his servants, they look up through the cloud of obloquy [slander] to his throne and implore the succour [help] which they know that his children shall ever find there." We too are strangers and pilgrims in an antagonistic world (1 Pet 5:11–12).

Prayer. Lord, help me to resist the evil in this culture and to pursue you in my spiritual journey. I need your word to teach me and your Holy Spirit to change me so that I may become more like you, rather than a product of this culture. Amen.

November 17 — Psalm 121

1 I will lift up my eyes to the hills—from whence comes my help? 2 My help comes from the LORD, who made heaven and earth. 3 He will not allow your foot to be moved; He who keeps you will not slumber. 4 Behold, He who keeps Israel shall neither slumber nor sleep. 5 *The LORD is your keeper; the LORD is your shade at your right hand.* 6 The sun shall not strike you by day, nor the moon by night. 7 The LORD shall preserve you from all evil; He shall preserve your soul. 8 The LORD shall preserve your going out and your coming in from this time forth, and even forevermore. (NKJV)

Not alone on the journey. Our spiritual journey is fraught with risks and dangers ranging from discouragement to Satan's attacks. Drawing from the Israelites' early days of wandering through the wilderness under God's caring protection, the psalmist encourages the travelers as they commence their pilgrimage to Jerusalem. For example, God is the "keeper" who will protect them (v. 5). Joseph Caryl reflects on verses 5–8, and the ways God cares for his people, then and now, "How large a writ or patent of protection is granted here! No time shall be hurtful, neither 'day nor night' which includes all times. Nothing shall hurt, neither sun nor moon, nor heat nor cold. These should include all annoyances. Nothing shall be hurt." When the psalmist refers to the "soul" and various activities (vv. 7–8), Caryl states, "These include the whole person of man, and him in all his just affairs and actions. Nothing of man is safe without a guard, and nothing of man can be unsafe which is thus guarded. They should be kept who can say, 'The Lord is our keeper'; and they cannot be kept, no, not by legions of angels, who have not the Lord for their keeper. None can keep us but he, and he has promised to keep us forevermore." As Jesus ascended to heaven, he told his disciples that he would always be with them through their life journey (Matt 28:20). His promise is also for us.

Prayer. Lord, you have been with me through my spiritual journey with all its high moments and crises. I thank you for being my faithful companion through it all. Amen.

November 18   Psalm 122

1 I was glad when they said to me, "Let us go to the house of the Lord." 2 And now here we are, standing inside your gates, O Jerusalem. 3 Jerusalem is a well-built city; its seamless walls cannot be breached. 4 *All the tribes of Israel—the Lord's people—make their pilgrimage here.* They come to give thanks to the name of the Lord, as the law requires of Israel. 5 Here stand the thrones where judgment is given, the thrones of the dynasty of David. 6 Pray for peace in Jerusalem. May all who love this city prosper. 7 Jerusalem, may there be peace within your walls and prosperity in your palaces. 8 For the sake of my family and friends, I will say, "May you have peace." 9 For the sake of the house of the Lord our God, I will seek what is best for you, O Jerusalem. (NLT)

A communal journey. After a lengthy trek, the people finally arrive in Jerusalem. They see its walls and gates (vv. 2–3) but not through the eyes of tourists. They are singularly focused on the house of the Lord where they want to worship as a community of God's people (vv. 1, 2, 4). David Dickson observes that the city exists "for a community" of those who seek the Lord. He applies this community life to the church, characterized by "the union, concord, community of laws, mutual commodities, and conjunction of strength which should be among God's people." Also, comparable to Jerusalem's temple, the localized church is "a place for his people to meet together for his worship." However, like the twelve tribes, the church is "scattered in several places of the earth, yet as they are the Lord's people, they should entertain a communion and conjunction among themselves as members of one universal church." Therefore, as Dickson reminds us, "As the tribes, so all particular churches, how far soever scattered, have one Lord, one covenant, one law and Scripture." We must be in community with a local church while we also remember that we have a mystical connection with the global church.

Prayer. Lord, even though our culture emphasizes individualism, you call us to take this spiritual journey with others. I need others who will encourage, instruct, laugh with, and challenge me while we walk together with Jesus through this life. Amen.

November 19 — Psalm 123

1 I lift my eyes to you, O God, enthroned in heaven. 2 *We keep looking to the* LORD *our God for his mercy*, just as servants keep their eyes on their master, as a slave girl watches her mistress for the slightest signal. 3 Have mercy on us, LORD, have mercy, for we have had our fill of contempt. 4 We have had more than our fill of the scoffing of the proud and the contempt of the arrogant. (NLT)

The arduous journey. The psalmist twice mentions that he and his people have had enough of others' contempt (vv. 3–4). Thomas Manton discusses what motivates people to scornfully mistreat others, "When men go on prosperously, they are apt wrongfully to trouble others, and then to shout at them in their misery, and to despise the person and cause of God's people. This is the sure effect of great arrogancy and pride. They think they may do what they please; they have no changes [adversities], therefore they fear not God, but put forth their hands against such as be at peace with them (Ps 4:19, 20); whilst they go on prosperously and undisturbed, they cannot abstain from violence and oppression. This is certainly pride, for it is a lifting up of the heart above God and against God and without God . . . When men sit fast, and are well at ease, they are apt to be insolent and scornful. Riches and worldly greatness make men insolent and despisers of others, and not to care what burdens they impose upon them; they are entrenched within a mass of wealth and power and greatness, and so think none can call them to an account." With a demanding spiritual journey, the psalmist directs us to focus on the Lord (vv. 1–2). John Trapp states that we need the Lord's "direction, defence, maintenance, mercy in time of correction, help when the service is over hard." When we cannot verbalize our prayers due to afflictions, we can follow the example of the psalmist who, in Trapp's words, essentially feels "mine afflictions having swollen my heart too big for my mouth," turns his eyes to the Lord for help (v. 1).

Prayer. Lord, I need to be prepared for this tough spiritual journey by leaning on all your resources so that I can persevere in adversity. Amen.

November 20 — Psalm 124

1 *What if the* LORD *had not been on our side?* Let all Israel repeat: 2 What if the LORD had not been on our side when people attacked us? 3 They would have swallowed us alive in their burning anger. 4 The waters would have engulfed us; a torrent would have overwhelmed us. 5 Yes, the raging waters of their fury would have overwhelmed our very lives. 6 Praise the LORD, who did not let their teeth tear us apart! 7 We escaped like a bird from a hunter's trap. The trap is broken, and we are free! 8 Our help is from the LORD, who made heaven and earth. (NLT)

Divine aid for the journey. The writer describes the enemies' vicious attacks on the Israelites (vv. 3–7), using imagery of a predator, a devastating flood, and an animal's trap. Matthew Henry comments concerning these enemies, "[They] are very subtle and spiteful, they lay snares for God's people, to bring them into sin and trouble, and to hold them there. Sometimes they seem to have prevailed so far as to gain their point, the children of God are taken in the snare, and are as unable to help themselves out as any weak and silly bird is." However, God is on the Israelites' side which the congregation affirms (vv. 1–2). Henry paraphrases the psalmist's sentiment, "God was on our side; he took our part, espoused our cause, and appeared for us. He was our helper, and a very present help, a help on our side, nigh at hand. He was with us; not only for us, but among us, and commander-in-chief of our forces." He mentions that God's attributes made it possible for Israel's deliverance, "That God was Jehovah; there the emphasis lies. If it had not been Jehovah himself, a God of infinite power and perfection that had undertaken our deliverance, our enemies would have overpowered us. Happy the people therefore whose God is Jehovah, a God all sufficient. Let Israel say this to his honour and resolve never to forsake him." Our God who is greater than the forces of the Evil One will supply what we need for our spiritual journey (Rom 8:37–39; 1 John 4:4).

Prayer. Lord, my faith walk could not survive without you accompanying and supplying me your empowering grace. Thank you! Amen.

November 21 — Psalm 125

1 Those who trust in the LORD are as secure as Mount Zion; they will not be defeated but will endure forever. 2 *Just as the mountains surround Jerusalem, so the* LORD *surrounds his people, both now and forever.* 3 The wicked will not rule the land of the godly, for then the godly might be tempted to do wrong. 4 O LORD, do good to those who are good, whose hearts are in tune with you. 5 But banish those who turn to crooked ways, O LORD. Take them away with those who do evil. May Israel have peace! (NLT)

Trusting God for the journey. The psalmist calls on us to trust in the Lord (v. 1a) who encircles his people forever (v. 2). Consequently, they will "endure forever" (v. 1b). John Owen mentions that what this psalm "promised the saints is a perpetual preservation of them in that condition wherein they are . . . As mount Zion abides in its condition, so shall they; and as the mountains about Jerusalem continue, so does the Lord continue his presence unto them." He adds, "The Lord is round about them, not to save them from this or that incursion, but from all; not from one or two evils, but from everyone whereby they are or may be assaulted. He is with them, and round about them on every side that no evil shall come nigh them. It is a most full expression of universal preservation, or of God's keeping his saints in his love and favour, upon all accounts whatsoever." However, we dare not presume upon God's constant care by choosing to live contrary to his will (v. 3). Rather, we hate evil because we align our hearts with God's ways (vv. 4–5). Jude calls upon his readers to practice godliness knowing that God "is able to keep you from falling and to present you before his glorious presence without fault and with great joy' (Jude 24). The Lord offers us incomparable security!

Prayer. Lord, I realize that I place too much of my security with my finances, possessions, and relationships. However, they displace you who should be my ultimate security. Help me to trust you, the Eternal God, above all that is temporal in this world. Amen.

November 22   Psalm 126

1 When the Lord brought back his exiles to Jerusalem, it was like a dream! 2 We were filled with laughter, and we sang for joy. And the other nations said, "What amazing things the Lord has done for them." 3 *Yes, the Lord has done amazing things for us!* What joy! 4 Restore our fortunes, Lord, as streams renew the desert. 5 Those who plant in tears will harvest with shouts of joy. 6 They weep as they go to plant their seed, but they sing as they return with the harvest. (NLT)

Rhythms in our journey. This psalm captures a range of experiences that we go through during our spiritual pilgrimage. The Christian life is neither an ongoing celebratory party; nor is it a dreary, somber life. Instead, the rhythm of both joy and sadness fills our journey; both witnessing God's "amazing" activity and toiling in the humdrum of daily work. The pilgrims' joy stemmed from what God had done for them (v. 3). Thomas Taylor states, "This verse is the marrow of the whole psalm . . . Their deliverance was so great and incredible that when God brought it to pass they were as men in a dream, thinking it rather a dream, and a vain imagination, than a real truth." God's works were so "amazing" (v. 3), Taylor points out, first, because God delivered them from a "great and lasting a bondage" in Babylon; second, because the deliverance was "sudden and unexpected;" third, because, in a desperate situation, "nothing more unlikely or impossible" could occur; and finally, because the "manner was so admirable (without the counsel, help, or strength of man: no, it was beyond and against all human means)." Verses 4 through 6 address the reality of adversities in life after a joyful return to Jerusalem. Alexander Henderson remarks that "the afflictions of God's people are as sowing in tears." There are both the "great pains" and "great hazard" with "many dangers" in the Christian life. For the one who perseveres and sees the harvest, personal joy erupts (vv. 5–6).

Prayer. Lord, forgive me for believing the lie that never-ending happiness should fill my life. Keep me spiritually balanced with the rhythms of joy and sadness. I need to remember and depend on you during both times. Amen.

November 23 — Psalm 127

1 Unless the LORD builds the house, the builders labor in vain. Unless the LORD watches over the city, the guards stand watch in vain. 2 *In vain you rise early and stay up late, toiling for food to eat*—for he grants sleep to those he loves. 3 Children are a heritage from the LORD, offspring a reward from him. 4 Like arrows in the hands of a warrior are children born in one's youth. 5 Blessed is the man whose quiver is full of them. They will not be put to shame when they contend with their opponents in court. (NIV)

The priority for our journey. Solomon, the psalmist, warns us that if we attempt to establish our lives apart from God, we should not be surprised if our efforts fall short or fail (vv. 1–2). Thomas Manton explains further that those with a worldly perspective "beat their brains, tire their spirits, rack their consciences, yet many times all is for nothing . . . labour without God cannot prosper; against God and against his will in his word, will surely miscarry." He continues to describe their situation as "living a life of misery and labours, fretting at their own disappointments, eaten up with envy at the advancement of others, afflicted overmuch with losses and wrongs. There is no end of all their labours. Some have died of it, others been distracted and put out of their wits; so that you are never like to see good days as long as you cherish the love of the world but will still lie under self-tormenting care and trouble of mind, by which a man grates on his own flesh." Rather than this dead-end path, Solomon encourages us to put God first throughout our spiritual journey. The benefits which come from trusting the Lord, Manton tells us, are contentment, sleep, rest, "silence submitting to the will of God, and quietness waiting for the blessing of God." He issues a challenge, "Acknowledge the providence that you may come under the blessing of it." A priority in our spiritual journey requires relying on God in our domestic responsibilities which may include the blessing of family life (vv. 3–5).

Prayer. Lord, I am tired of seeking the "good life" on my terms. Help me to live wisely by making you a priority in every sphere of my daily existence. Amen.

November 24   Psalm 128

1 *Blessed is everyone who fears the* LORD, *who walks in his ways!* 2 *you shall eat the fruit of the labor of your hands; you shall be blessed, and it shall be well with you.* 3 *Your wife will be like a fruitful vine within your house; your children will be like olive shoots around your table.* 4 *Behold, thus shall the man be blessed who fears the* LORD. 5 *The* LORD *bless you from Zion! May you see the prosperity of Jerusalem all the days of your life!* 6 *May you see your children's children! Peace be upon Israel!* (ESV)

The blessed journey. The psalmist tells us that we can be "blessed" by God (vv. 1–2, 4–5) when we fear him (v. 1). Robert Leighton* admits that "fear sounds rather contrary to blessedness; has an air of misery." This fear of God is equivalent to revering him. Thus, Leighton states, "He that so fears [God], fears not: he shall not be afraid; all petty fears are swallowed up in this great fear; and this great fear is as sweet and pleasing as little fears are anxious and vexing." Our human fears are lost in reverence for God who we gladly obey (v. 1) in many areas of life (vv. 2–3, 5–6). The evidence of God's blessing in these relationships is peace (v. 6). To define what peace is not, Alexander Henderson writes, "The great blessing of peace, which the Lord bas promised to his people even in this life . . . does not consist in this, that the people of God shall have no enemies; no, for there is an immortal and endless enmity against them. Neither does their peace consist in this, that their enemies shall not assault them; neither does it consist in this, that their enemies shall not molest or afflict them. We do but deceive ourselves if so be that we imagine, so long as we are in this our pilgrimage, and in our warfare here, if we promise to ourselves a peace of this kind; for while we live in this world, we shall still have enemies, and these enemies shall assault us, and persecute and afflict us."

Prayer. Lord, I want your blessing on my life, not for my sake but for your honor. Help me to revere you with glad obedience. Amen.

November 25   Psalm 129

1 *"Greatly have they afflicted me from my youth"*—let Israel now say—2 "Greatly have they afflicted me from my youth, yet they have not prevailed against me. 3 The plowers plowed upon my back; they made long their furrows." 4 The Lord is righteous; he has cut the cords of the wicked. 5 May all who hate Zion be put to shame and turned backward! 6 Let them be like the grass on the housetops, which withers before it grows up, 7 with which the reaper does not fill his hand nor the binder of sheaves his arms, 8 nor do those who pass by say, "The blessing of the Lord be upon you! We bless you in the name of the Lord!" (ESV)

Spiritual conflict along the journey. The psalmist and the Israelites frequently experience others' hatred and wounding (vv. 1–3, 5). Viewing the "wicked" in this psalm as "enemies of the church," David Dickson describes them as "one adverse army," constantly waging war. However, there is hope amid the cruel oppression because God has "cut the cords of the wicked" (v. 4). Although the wicked "do no more regard her [the church] than they do the earth under their feet and do seek to make their own advantage of her," God delivers "his church from oppression of the enemy," like he cuts "the cords of the wicked" (v. 4). In addition, God uses enemies to "break up the fallow ground of his people's proud and stiff hearts with the plough of persecution, and to draw deep and long furrows on them." God allows the enemies to bring suffering to his people "for maturing the church, which is his field, albeit they intend no good to God's church, yet they serve in God's wisdom to prepare the Lord's people for receiving the seed of God's word." Finally, when "the wicked have performed so much of God's husbandry as he thinks good to suffer them, then he stops their design, and loosens their plough."

Prayer. Lord, sometimes when life is going well, I forget that I am in an ongoing spiritual battle with Satan. While this conflict could be frightening, I am thankful for the spiritual resources you have given me so that I can experience victory. Through it all, you are accomplishing your purposes, and transforming my life. Amen!

November 26   Psalm 130

1 Out of the depths I have cried to You, O Lord; 2 Lord, hear my voice! Let Your ears be attentive to the voice of my supplications. 3 If You, Lord, should mark iniquities, O Lord, who could stand? *4 But there is forgiveness with You, that You may be feared.* 5 I wait for the Lord, my soul waits, and in His word I do hope. *6 My soul waits for the Lord more than those who watch for the morning—yes, more than those who watch for the morning.* 7 O Israel, hope in the Lord; for with the Lord there is mercy, and with Him is abundant redemption. 8 And He shall redeem Israel from all his iniquities. (NKJV)

Hope for the journey. Amid despair, hope is available to the psalmist and God's people (vv. 1, 5, 7) because of God's forgiveness of sin (vv. 3–4a). Writing as if speaking to God, William Gurnall says, "There is forgiveness in your nature, you carry a pardoning heart in your bosom; yes, there is forgiveness in your promise; your merciful heart does not only incline you to thoughts of forgiving; but your faithful promise binds you to draw forth the same unto all that humbly and seasonably lay claim thereunto." God forgives us so that we may serve him with fear (v. 4b), loving and revering God. The pilgrim also waits for God himself (v. 6). Richard Baker turns his meditation on waiting into a prayer, "To wait upon him, to do him service, to wait for him, to be enabled to do him better service; to wait upon him, as being Lord of all; and to wait for him, as being the rewarder of all; to wait upon him whose service is better than any other command, and to wait for him whose expectation is better than any other possession. Let others, therefore, wait upon the world, wait for the world; I, O God, will wait upon you, for you, seeing I find more true contentment in this waiting than all the world can give me in enjoying; for how can I doubt of receiving reward by my waiting for you when my waiting for you is itself the reward of my waiting upon you?"

Prayer. Lord, I find hope in you through your forgiveness and wait for you to act on my behalf. Amen.

November 27   Psalm 131

1 LORD, my heart is not haughty, nor my eyes lofty. Neither do I concern myself with great matters, nor with things too profound for me. 2 *Surely I have calmed and quieted my soul, like a weaned child with his mother; like a weaned child is my soul within me.* 3 O Israel, hope in the LORD from this time forth and forever. (NKJV)

Content on the journey. Verse 1 may hearken back to the time when David could have but was unwilling to seize the kingship from Samuel. Rather than pride controlling his actions, David chose to wait on God's timing (1 Sam 24, 26) because he had a calm heart (v. 2a). Oliver Heywood, speaking as David, captures his meditation, "It is none of these earthly things that my heart is set upon; my soul is set on things above, my treasure is in heaven, and I would have my heart there also." Since he loves God more than anything else, he is satisfied not to be the king. His contentment to accept his present status is much like a weaned infant (v. 2b). Thomas Manton discusses this growth in our lives, "Though the weaned child has not what it would have, or what it naturally most desires, the milk of the breast—yet it is contented with what the mother gives—it rests upon her love and provision. So are we to be content with what providence allows us" (Heb 13:5). When the child is weaned, he notes that the child must still depend on the mother for food and therefore, "for everything whatsoever should we depend upon God, refer ourselves to God, and expect all things from him (Ps 62:5). With such a simplicity of submission we rest and depend upon God. Let us take heed of being over wise and provident for ourselves but let us trust our Father which is in heaven, and refer ourselves to his wise and holy government." Manton succinctly states, "Whatever pleases our heavenly Father should please us." This is the pathway to learning true contentment, regardless of the circumstances (Phil 4:11).

Prayer. Lord, I want to stop demanding from you and learn to wait on your timing, and willingly submit to you so that I may learn to be truly content with your will. Amen.

November 28   Psalm 132:1–10

1 Remember, O LORD, in David's favor, all the hardships he endured, 2 how he swore to the LORD and vowed to the Mighty One of Jacob, 3 *"I will not enter my house or get into my bed, 4 I will not give sleep to my eyes or slumber to my eyelids, 5 until I find a place for the LORD, a dwelling place for the Mighty One of Jacob."* 6 Behold, we heard of it in Ephrathah; we found it in the fields of Jaar. 7 "Let us go to his dwelling place; let us worship at his footstool!" 8 Arise, O LORD, and go to your resting place, you and the ark of your might. 9 Let your priests be clothed with righteousness, and let your saints shout for joy. 10 For the sake of your servant David, do not turn away the face of your anointed one. (ESV)

God's presence for the journey. This passage recollects David's promise to build a permanent home for the ark of the covenant (vv. 1–5) and its journey to Jerusalem (vv. 6–10). He wants to honor God's "dwelling place" (v. 5) or presence. Commenting on David not sleeping (vv. 3–4) until the ark returned to Jerusalem, Arthur Jackson notes, "I rather take these to be hyperbolical expressions of the continual, exceeding great care wherewith he was perplexed about providing a settled place for the ark to rest." He would not be content until he completed the task. After David locates the ark and orchestrates its transfer, he invites others to join him to worship at God's "footstool" (v. 7), another description for the ark of the covenant (1 Chron 28:2). Reflecting on the Lord's presence, Charles Spurgeon* exclaims, "What matters where we meet with him so long as we do behold him . . . If Christ be in a wood he will yet be found of those who seek for him. He is as near in the rustic home, embowered among the trees, as in the open streets of the city; yes, he will answer prayer offered from the heart of the black forest where the lone traveller seems out of all hope of hearing . . . Where Jehovah is, there shall he be worshipped."

Prayer. Lord, wherever I am during the day, I want to be conscious of your presence and worship you. Amen.

November 29   Psalm 132:11–18

11 The LORD swore to David a sure oath from which he will not turn back: "One of the sons of your body I will set on your throne. 12 If your sons keep my covenant and my testimonies that I shall teach them, their sons also forever shall sit on your throne." 13 For the LORD has chosen Zion; he has desired it for his dwelling place: 14 "This is my resting place forever; here I will dwell, for I have desired it. 15 *I will abundantly bless her provisions; I will satisfy her poor with bread.* 16 Her priests I will clothe with salvation, and her saints will shout for joy. 17 There I will make a horn to sprout for David; I have prepared a lamp for my anointed. 18 His enemies I will clothe with shame, but on him his crown will shine." (ESV)

Enjoying God's presence on the journey. After its arrival in Jerusalem, the ark, representing God's presence, resided in the Holy of Holies within the temple's sanctuary. God chose and desired to dwell among his people forever (vv. 13–14). As David Dickson states, "The Lord's pitching upon any place to dwell there comes not of the worthiness of the place, or persons, but from God's good pleasure alone." The people enjoy God's presence among them in numerous ways. Noting God's abundant blessing of provisions for believers (v. 15), then and later, John Janeway comments, "The Lord gives [the believer] all the experiences of his power and goodness to his Church" like enjoying God's providence, answered prayers, and the Lord's Supper. Janeway continues, "Beside all this, [the believer] has the sweet and refreshing incomes of the Spirit, filling him with such true pleasure, that he can easily spare the most sumptuous banquet, the noblest feast, and highest worldly delights, as infinitely short of one hour's treatment in his Friend's chamber." Being in God's presence, allows us to experience his strength, referred to as a "horn," and his guidance, referred to as a "lamp" for daily living (v. 17). This lamp, as Ebenezer Erskine notes, refers to the "word of God" which gives "light to people in the darkness of the night."

Prayer. Lord, I am thankful for your indwelling presence, so that I can experience you and enjoy your blessings in my spiritual journey. Amen.

November 30   Psalm 133

1 *Behold, how good and how pleasant it is for brethren to dwell together in unity!* 2 *It is like the precious oil upon the head, running down on the beard, the beard of Aaron, running down on the edge of his garments.* 3 *It is like the dew of Hermon, descending upon the mountains of Zion; for there the* LORD *commanded the blessing—life forevermore.* (NKJV)

Enjoying the journey together. Joseph Caryl defines what it means to live in unity with one another (v. 1). First, he says, unity exists "When [people] join or are one in opinion and judgment, when they all think the same thing, and are of one mind in the truth." Unity is also present among people "when they join together and are one in affection, when they are all of one heart, though possibly they are not all of one mind; or, when they meet in affection, though not in opinion." When unity exists, people do good. "It is a blessed thing to see them joining together in duty," and "turning from evil." Thomas Horton gives reasons why unity is good. Because God is the "author and owner" of unity and peace, unity is "good, as any grace is good. It is good morally. Love is a fruit of the Spirit." The goodness of unity is seen in its "effects and consequences and concomitants of it: it has much good . . . A great deal of advantage comes by brethren's dwelling together in unity, especially spiritual advantage, and for the doing and receiving of good." Commenting on the psalmist's description of unity as "pleasant," Horton first says, "It is pleasant to God, it is such as is very acceptable to him; it is that which he much delights in, wheresoever he observes it; being himself a God of peace, he does therefore so much the more delight in peaceable Christians, and such as do relate to himself." In addition, he points out that "This brotherly unity is also pleasant to ourselves, who accordingly shall have so much the greater pleasure in it and from it." And finally, unity is "pleasing to others" in the community who are observing our lives (Rom 14:18).

Prayer. Lord, rather than being a divisive person, may I seek unity with others so that my life is pleasing to them and you. Amen.

December 1   Psalm 134

1*Behold*, bless the LORD, all you servants of the LORD, who by night stand in the house of the LORD! 2 Lift up your hands in the sanctuary and bless the LORD. 3 The LORD who made heaven and earth bless you from Zion! (NKJV)

Service and worship. The pilgrims sang the Songs of Ascent from the beginning of their journey in a foreign country (Ps 120). Now they finally arrive in Jerusalem and upon entering the temple, they sing the last of the Songs, Psalm 134. With their greeting "Behold," the pilgrims bless the "servants" (vv. 1–2), who are the priests and Levites. This greeting is significant according to John Calvin* who states that the temple ministers have a "duty before their eyes, for they were to be stimulated to devotion by looking constantly to the Temple. We are to notice the Psalmist's design in urging the duty of praise so earnestly upon them. Many of the Levites, through the tendency which there is in all men to abuse ceremonies, considered that nothing more was necessary than standing idly in the Temple and thus overlooked the principal part of their duty. The Psalmist would show that merely to keep nightly watch over the Temple, kindle the lamps, and superintend the sacrifices, was of no importance, unless they served God spiritually, and referred all outward ceremonies to that which must be considered the main sacrifice—the celebration of God's praises. You may think it a very laborious service, as if he had said, to stand at watch in the Temple, while others sleep in their own houses; but the worship which God requires is something more excellent than this and demands of you to sing his praises before all the people." In the New Testament, the apostle Paul emphasizes this interrelated theme of service and worship with his challenge to surrender one's life to God as an expression of "reasonable service." (Rom 12:1–2 NKJV). The Greek word for "service" is *leitourgia*, from which we get the word "liturgy," prescribed words and acts associated with public worship. Parallel to the priests' ministry, our daily service to others expresses our worship to God.

Prayer. Lord, I confess that my activities can be dutifully done devoid of worship. Cultivate in my heart a willingness to gladly serve others as an expression of worship to you. Amen.

December 2   Psalm 135:1–7

1 Praise the LORD! *Praise the name of the* LORD; Praise Him, O you servants of the LORD! 2 You who stand in the house of the LORD, in the courts of the house of our God, 3 *Praise the* LORD, *for the* LORD *is good; Sing praises to His name, for it is pleasant.* 4 For the LORD has chosen Jacob for Himself, Israel for His special treasure. 5 For I know that the LORD is great, and our LORD is above all gods. 6 Whatever the LORD pleases He does, in heaven and in earth, in the seas and in all deep places. 7 He causes the vapors to ascend from the ends of the earth; He makes lightning for the rain; He brings the wind out of His treasuries. (NKJV)

God's goodness and greatness. Three times in these verses, the psalmist calls on the people to praise the LORD (vv. 1, 3). The second call to praise mentions the "name of the LORD." Stephen Charnock relates "LORD" to God's self-ascription as "I AM," the name which God used for himself when he spoke to Moses (Exod 3:14). This name "signifies the Divine eternity, as well as immutability" of his nature. Charnock continues, "It was not a temporary name, but a name for ever, his 'memorial to all generations' (v. 15)" including today's believers who have a covenant relationship with Jesus Christ. The psalmist also mentions that the LORD is "good" (v. 3). That means, according to John Trapp, God is "good and does good (Ps 119:68) and is therefore to be praised with mind, mouth, and practice." David Dickson comments, "When we praise God most we get much benefit by so doing: it is so comely in itself, so pleasant unto God, and profitable to the person that offers praises, so fit to cheer up his spirit, and strengthen his faith in God." God is also "great" because he is "above all gods" (v. 5). Yes, it is "pleasant" to praise him (v. 3) because there are ample reasons for congregations to worship God.

Prayer. Lord, my praise is often motivated by what you have done for me. I want to focus more on praising you for your nature, including your faithfulness, goodness, and greatness. Amen.

December 3   Psalm 135:8–14

8 He destroyed the firstborn in each Egyptian home, both people and animals. 9 He performed miraculous signs and wonders in Egypt against Pharaoh and all his people. 10 He struck down great nations and slaughtered mighty kings—11 Sihon king of the Amorites, Og king of Bashan, and all the kings of Canaan. 12 He gave their land as an inheritance, a special possession to his people Israel. 13 *Your name, O* Lord, *endures forever; your fame, O* Lord, *is known to every generation.* 14 For the Lord will give justice to his people and have compassion on his servants. (NLT)

God's changelessness. Since God is supreme over the universe and all gods (vv. 5–7), he exercises authority over the nations. For example, he gave the Israelites the land he had promised them (v. 12). However, could they expect God to continue to exert the same authority in the future? The response is a resounding "yes" based on the eternal name of God (v. 13) whose nature never changes. Stephen Charnock provides insights into God's changelessness. He states, "Immutability is a glory belonging to all the attributes of God. It is not a single perfection of the Divine nature, nor is it limited to particular objects thus and thus disposed . . . The wisdom of God is not his power, nor his power his holiness; but immutability is the centre wherein they all unite. There is not one perfection which may not be said to be, and truly is, immutable." In other words, all God's attributes are immutable or unchanging. Charnock imagines if it were otherwise. "How cloudy would his blessedness be, if it were changeable; how dim his wisdom, if it might be obscured; how feeble his power, if it were capable of becoming sickly and languishing; how would mercy lose much of its lustre, if it could change into wrath, and justice much of its dread, if it could be turned into mercy." God's unchanging nature offers hope because he will exercise his justice and love to the present and future generations (vv. 13–14) as he has done in the past.

Prayer. Lord of the universe, in an ever-changing world, I am thankful that you are unchanging. Your immutability gives me great assurance that I can rely on your justice and sovereign purposes. Amen.

December 4   Psalm 135:15-21

15 The idols of the nations are silver and gold, the work of men's hands. 16 They have mouths, but they do not speak; eyes they have, but they do not see; 17 they have ears, but they do not hear; nor is there any breath in their mouths. 18 Those who make them are like them; so is everyone who trusts in them. 19 *Bless the* LORD, *O house of Israel! Bless the* LORD, *O house of Aaron!* 20 Bless the LORD, O house of Levi! You who fear the LORD, bless the LORD! 21 Blessed be the LORD out of Zion who dwells in Jerusalem! Praise the LORD! (NKJV)

God's supremacy. People's idols are extremely limited (vv. 15-17) and worshipping these finite gods is illogical. The idol-makers foolishly worship their own created objects! Matthew Poole argues that the idols "should rather, if it were possible, worship man, as their creator and lord, than be worshipped by him." Regarding the idols' resemblance to the human body, David Dickson remarks, "So many members as the images have, serving to represent perfections ascribed to them, so many are the lies." It is no wonder that he remarks, "Idolatry is a benumbing sin, which bereaves the idolater of the right use of his senses." In stark contrast to the created idols, God is supreme above all "gods" (v. 3) because he is the creator who exhibits his power over the nations (vv. 6-12). Since he is supreme, the psalmist tells us four times to "bless" the Lord (vv. 19-20). Since God blesses us, blessing God may seem unusual. Thomas Goodwin explains, "[The] blessing of God is to wish well to, and speak well of God, out of goodwill to God himself, and a sense of his goodness to ourselves." Addressing us as individuals, Goodwin continues, "God loves your good word, that is, to be spoken of well by you; he rejoices in your well wishes, and to hear from you expressions of rejoicings in his own independent blessedness." We bless God by praising him throughout the week.

Prayer. Lord, since you are supreme over all creation, forgive me for creating idols in my life which rob me from loving you. I want to bless you for your many acts of undeserved goodness shown to me over the years. I am humbled and thankful. Amen.

December 5   Psalm 136:1–9

1 Oh, give thanks to the LORD, for He is good! *For His mercy endures forever.* 2 Oh, give thanks to the God of gods! For His mercy endures forever. 3 Oh, give thanks to the LORD of lords! For His mercy endures forever: 4 To Him who alone does great wonders, For His mercy endures forever; 5 To Him who by wisdom made the heavens, For His mercy endures forever; 6 To Him who laid out the earth above the waters, For His mercy endures forever; 7 To Him who made great lights, For His mercy endures forever—8 The sun to rule by day, for His mercy endures forever; 9 The moon and stars to rule by night, for His mercy endures forever. (NKJV)

God's love through creation. This psalm, the Great Hallel, is filled with praise to God. After the call to praise him (vv. 1–3), the congregation responds twenty-six times with the refrain "his mercy endures forever." The word "mercy" or "loving-kindness" (NIV) refers to God's covenant relationship with his people. Robert Harris comments on two aspects of this covenant love. First, he relates this love or mercy to God's nature. "His essential mercy is eternity itself; for it is himself, and God has not, but is, things. He is beginning, end, being; and that which is of himself and even himself is eternity itself." God's merciful love is "endless" and "incapable of end." Harris also links our needs to God's mercy which is "everlasting, too, in a sense; for the creatures, ever since they had being in him, or existence in their natural causes, ever did and ever will need mercy, either preserving or conserving." We constantly need God's faithful love for as long as we live. This psalm affirms that "God's mercy (chiefly to his church) is an endless mercy; it knows no end, receives no interruption." Because God is good, "Mercy pleases him. It is no trouble for him to exercise mercy. It is his delight: we are never weary of receiving, therefore he cannot be of giving." As an expression of his mercy, God sustains us through his creation (vv. 4–9) which is good reason to praise our Creator.

Prayer. Lord, reflecting on your creation and its capability to sustain me, I am thankful for this expression of your enduring love. Amen.

December 6   Psalm 136:10–16

10 To Him who struck Egypt in their firstborn, for His mercy endures forever; 11 and brought out Israel from among them, for His mercy endures forever; 12 with a strong hand, and with an outstretched arm, for His mercy endures forever; 13 to Him who divided the Red Sea in two, for His mercy endures forever; 14 *and made Israel pass through the midst of it, for His mercy endures forever;* 15 but overthrew Pharaoh and his army in the Red Sea, for His mercy endures forever; 16 *to Him who led His people through the wilderness,* for His mercy endures forever; (NKJV)

God's love through deliverance. Drawing from the Israelites' exodus from Egypt, the psalmist uses details of God's deliverance to indicate his love to his people. Addressing the crossing of the Red Sea (v. 14), David Dickson remarks, "It is a work of no less mercy and power to give his people grace to make use of an offered means of delivery, than to prepare the deliverance for them; but the constancy of God's mercy does not only provide the means, but also gives his people grace to make use thereof in all ages." God offers his grace to deliver us from the power of sin. After the Israelites cross the Red Sea, God continues to lead and deliver them from the dangers of living in the wilderness. Leading his people through the wilderness is far different than leading his people to water and green pastures (Ps 23:2). Yet, although "The barren wilderness has no green pastures, the parched and arid desert has no still waters," Barton Bouchier* reminds us that God promises to provide water in the desert for his people (Isa 35:6–7). Thus, "It is one of the Lord's sweet truths that so perplex those that are without, but which are so full of consolation to his own children, that the wilderness and mercy are linked together of God in indissoluble union here." This mercy, Bouchier points out, also found in Hosea 2:14 where God promises to speak tenderly to his people in the desert.

Prayer. Lord, I am thankful not only for the times you have rescued me from harm, but also for your provision for me during my wilderness experiences. These are expressions of your mercy. Amen.

December 7   Psalm 136:17–26

17 [T]o him who struck down great kings, for his steadfast love endures forever; 18 and killed mighty kings, for his steadfast love endures forever; 19 Sihon, king of the Amorites, for his steadfast love endures forever; 20 and Og, king of Bashan, for his steadfast love endures forever; 21 and gave their land as a heritage, for his steadfast love endures forever; 22 a heritage to Israel his servant, for his steadfast love endures forever. 23 *It is he who remembered us in our low estate, for his steadfast love endures forever;* 24 and rescued us from our foes, for his steadfast love endures forever; 25 he who gives food to all flesh, for his steadfast love endures forever. 26 Give thanks to the God of heaven, for his steadfast love endures forever. (ESV)

God's love through remembrance. The psalmist continues to indicate the ways God showed mercy to his people. Ralph Venning suggests that God reveals several "degrees" of his mercy or enduring love to them (v. 23). First, God does not forget but thinks about us. Second, he does not neglect us but takes notice of us. Third, by his mercy, God shows compassion to us (Jer 31:20). Fourth, he accepts us and is "well pleased" with us (Ps 20:3). Fifth, in his mercy, God hears and grants our requests (1Sam 1:19–20, 27). Sixth, God delivers us "from that which we were appointed to, from the low estate" (Gal 2:10). In the context of this psalm, God remembered to deliver his people from their enemies (v. 24). Venning makes two applications. We should thank the "Author of the mercy, God; a God that was offended by us, a God that needed us not, and a God that gains nothing by us; and yet this God remembered us in our low estate; that should engage us." Also, we need to consider that we are not only "undeserving but an ill-deserving" people of God's mercy. Therefore, we ought to consider our "obligations" before him, such as giving thanks to God because, as Venning notes, "His mercy endures forever. There is no reason to be given for grace but grace; there is no reason to be given for mercy but mercy."

Prayer. Lord, thank you for the generous and unfathomable mercy you have extended to me, even before I knew you. Amen.

December 8   Psalm 137

1 Beside the rivers of Babylon, we sat and wept as we thought of Jerusalem. 2 We put away our harps, hanging them on the branches of poplar trees. 3 *For our captors demanded a song from us.* Our tormentors insisted on a joyful hymn: "Sing us one of those songs of Jerusalem!" 4 But how can we sing the songs of the Lord while in a pagan land? 5 If I forget you, O Jerusalem, let my right hand forget how to play the harp. 6 May my tongue stick to the roof of my mouth if I fail to remember you, if I don't make Jerusalem my greatest joy. 7 O Lord, remember what the Edomites did on the day the armies of Babylon captured Jerusalem. "Destroy it!" they yelled. "Level it to the ground!" 8 O Babylon, you will be destroyed. Happy is the one who pays you back for what you have done to us. 9 Happy is the one who takes your babies and smashes them against the rocks! (NLT)

Life as an exile. Exiled to Babylon, the Jews find themselves sitting by the local rivers (vv. 1–2), lamenting Jerusalem's destruction (v. 7). To add to their grief, the captors insist that the Jews sing joyful songs of their beloved but plundered city (vv. 3–6). Thomas Manton describes their captors' mockery "No jest relishes with a profane spirit so well as when Scripture is abused and made to lackey [serve] to their sportive jollity." Thomas Chalmers* accurately summarizes this scenario, "The Babylonians asked them in derision for one of the songs of Zion. They loaded with ridicule their pure and venerable religion and aggravated the sufferings of the weary and oppressed exiles by their mirth and their indecency." In their pain, they turn to God asking him to deal work vengeance on each of their captors (vv. 8–9). "He that sows evil shall reap evil," Thomas Adams observes; "he that sows the evil of sin, shall reap the evil of punishment." Like the Jews in Babylon, we are "aliens and strangers in the world" (1 Pet 2:11 NIV) who need God's wisdom to respond to social antipathy.

Prayer. Lord, many in society mock you and those who follow you. Considering their derision, I need wisdom to know how to respond so that you are honored. Amen.

December 9 — Psalm 138

1 I give you thanks, O Lord, with my whole heart; before the gods I sing your praise; 2 I bow down toward your holy temple and give thanks to your name for your steadfast love and your faithfulness, for you have exalted above all things your name and your word. 3 On the day I called, you answered me; my strength of soul you increased. 4 All the kings of the earth shall give you thanks, O Lord, for they have heard the words of your mouth, 5 and they shall sing of the ways of the Lord, for great is the glory of the Lord. 6 *For though the* Lord *is high, he regards the lowly,* but the haughty he knows from afar. 7 Though I walk in the midst of trouble, you preserve my life; you stretch out your hand against the wrath of my enemies, and your right hand delivers me. 8 The Lord will fulfill his purpose for me; your steadfast love, O Lord, endures forever. Do not forsake the work of your hands. (ESV)

God exalts the humble. In this first of a small collection of eight psalms written by David, he praises God for numerous reasons, including the exaltation of the "lowly" (v. 6; Luke 1:52; 1 Pet 5:12). Ebenezer Erskine offers three reasons why God lifts the humble. First, this act "best serves God's great design of lifting up and glorifying his free grace." God wants to "display the riches of his free and sovereign grace." The second reason for exalting the lowly is that "God has such respect unto the humble soul because it is a fruit of the Spirit inhabiting the soul, and an evidence of the soul's union with the Lord Jesus Christ, in whom alone we are accepted." The third reason is that, by exalting the humble, God "makes the soul like Christ; and the more alike that a person is to Christ, God loves him all the better." Erskine reminds us that Jesus was humble (Matt 11:29), coming to earth as a servant (Phil 2:7), and "though he was rich, yet he was content to become poor, that we through his poverty might be rich."

Prayer. Father, I want to live in humble dependence on your Spirit, so that people see your grace and see Jesus in my life which will exalt you. Amen.

December 10   Psalm 139:1-6

1 You have searched me, LORD, and you know me. 2 *You know when I sit and when I rise; you perceive my thoughts from afar.* 3 You discern my going out and my lying down; you are familiar with all my ways. 4 Before a word is on my tongue you, LORD, know it completely. 5 You hem me in behind and before, and you lay your hand upon me. 6 Such knowledge is too wonderful for me, too lofty for me to attain. (NIV)

God who knows all. In this psalm, David elaborates on three of God's attributes which collectively address the personal prayer at the psalm's conclusion (vv. 19-24). Today's meditation focuses on the omniscience of God who knows David's actions and thoughts "from afar" (v. 2). About this phrase, William Greenhill comments, "Not that God is at a distance from our thoughts; but he understands them while they are far off from us." Before we are conscious of our own ponderings, God knows them. Regarding our thoughts, Matthew Henry remarks that God "understands the chain of [our thoughts] and can make out their connection, when so many of them slip [our] notice." Stephen Charnock similarly states, "If the Lord knows them before their existence, before they can be properly called ours, much more does he know them when they actually spring up in us." In contrast to our limited understanding, God's knowledge is unfathomable (v. 6). Henry Duncan* states, "Compared with our stinted knowledge, how amazing is the knowledge of God! As he made all things, he must be intimately acquainted, not only with their properties, but with their very essence. His eye, at the same instant, surveys all the works of his immeasurable creation. He observes, not only the complicated system of the universe, but the slightest motion of the most microscopic insect; not only the most sublime conception of angels, but the meanest propensity of the most worthless of his creatures." For application, Greenhill suggests, "Look well to your hearts, thoughts, risings, whatever comes into your mind; let no secret sins, or corruptions, lodge there; think not to conceal anything from the eye of God."

Prayer. Father, although your knowing my thoughts is intimidating, I am glad that you know me so well. Draw to my attention to those thoughts which you need to purify. Amen.

December 11   Psalm 139:7-12

7 Where can I go from your Spirit? Where can I flee from your presence? 8 If I go up to the heavens, you are there; if I make my bed in the depths, you are there. 9 If I rise on the wings of the dawn, if I settle on the far side of the sea, 10 even there your hand will guide me, your right hand will hold me fast. 11 If I say, "Surely the darkness will hide me and the light become night around me," 12 even the darkness will not be dark to you; the night will shine like the day, for darkness is as light to you. (NIV)

God who is everywhere. In these verses, David knows it is impossible escape from God's presence. Henry Smith states, "When we think that we fly from God, in running out of one place into another, we do but run from one hand to the other; for there is no place where God is not." To avoid misunderstanding God's presence, William Jones* clarifies, "The Psalm was not written by a Pantheist. The Psalmist speaks of God as a Person everywhere present in creation, yet distinct from creation . . . God is everywhere, but he is not everything." John Mason* further explains God's omnipresence, "The presence of God's glory is in heaven; the presence of his power on earth; the presence of his justice in hell; and the presence of his grace with his people. If he deny us his powerful presence, we fall into nothing; if he deny us his gracious presence, we fall into sin; if he deny us his merciful presence, we fall into hell." Thomas Adams observes that it would be "strange" if we could be separated from God's presence because "his gracious presence is ever with us; that no sea is so broad as to divide us from his favour; that wheresoever we feed, he is our host; wheresoever we rest, the wings of his blessed providence are stretched over us." When the world betrays us, God's caring presence everywhere encourages us. Even during his darkest days (vv. 11–12), David writes that God's omnipresence guides and holds on to him (v. 10).

Prayer. Lord, I am thankful for your encompassing presence, especially when I feel so alone. You are with me! Amen.

December 12   Psalm 139:13–18

13 For you created my inmost being; you knit me together in my mother's womb. 14 *I praise you because I am fearfully and wonderfully made; your works are wonderful, I know that full well.* 15 My frame was not hidden from you when I was made in the secret place, when I was woven together in the depths of the earth. 16 Your eyes saw my unformed body; all the days ordained for me were written in your book before one of them came to be. 17 How precious to me are your thoughts, God! How vast is the sum of them! 18 Were I to count them, they would outnumber the grains of sand—when I awake, I am still with you. (NIV)

God who is extensively creative. The psalmist describes God knitting or weaving together his body in the womb (vv. 13, 15). Thomas Manton describes this body as "a garment of needlework, of divers colours, richly embroidered with nerves and veins." He expresses his wonder over God's handiwork, "What shall I speak of the eye, wherein there is such curious workmanship, that many upon the first sight of it have been driven to acknowledge God? Of the hand, made to open and shut, and to serve the labours and ministries of nature without wasting and decay for many years? If they should be of marble or iron, with such constant use they would soon wear out; and yet now they are of flesh they last so long as life lasts. Of the head? Fitly placed to be the seat of the senses, to command and direct the rest of the members. Of the lungs? A frail piece of flesh, yet, though in continual action, of a long use . . . In short, therefore, every part is so placed and framed, as if God had employed his whole wisdom about it." God also created the soul and Manton marvels at the soul which is "quick, nimble, various, and indefatigable in its motions! How comprehensive in its capacities! How it animates the body, and is like God himself, all in every part! Who can trace the flights of reason? What a value has God set upon the soul!"

Prayer. Father, your creation of the human body reveals your handiwork and indicates the sacredness of human life. I must treat it with respect for your purposes. Amen.

December 13   Psalm 139:19–24

19 If only you, God, would slay the wicked! Away from me, you who are bloodthirsty! 20 They speak of you with evil intent; your adversaries misuse your name. 21 Do I not hate those who hate you, Lord, and abhor those who are in rebellion against you? 22 I have nothing but hatred for them; I count them my enemies. *23 Search me, God, and know my heart; test me and know my anxious thoughts. 24 See if there is any offensive way in me, and lead me in the way everlasting.* (NIV)

God who searches all. With his encounter with mean-spirited people and his attitude toward them (vv. 19–22), David asks God to search him thoroughly for any wrongdoing (vv. 23–24). Since David had already stated that God had searched him (v. 1), Joseph Caryl asks, "Why did he beg God to do that which he had done already?" He gives a reason, "David was a diligent self-searcher, and therefore he was so willing to be searched, yes, he delighted to be searched by God . . . he knew God could do it better. He knew by his own search that he did not live in any way of wickedness against his knowledge, and yet he knew there might be some way of wickedness in him that he knew not of." Caryl describes David's thoughts, "Lord, I have searched myself, and can see no wicked way in me; but, Lord, your sight is infinitely clearer than mine, and if you will but search me you may see some wicked way in me which I could not see, and I would fain see and know the worst of myself, that I might amend and grow better; therefore, Lord, if there be any such way in me, cause me to know it also." David not only wants to know his sin but asks God to "lead me in the way everlasting (v. 24), expressing his desire to be purified from future sin. Caryl remarks that David "feared there might be some dross in him that he had not found; and now he would be retried that he might come forth purest gold."

Prayer. Lord, I have not enjoyed the thought of you exploring the depths of my heart. Now that I see how much that you love me, I want you to search my inner life to reveal anything that is displeasing to you so that I may live for your glory. Amen.

December 14   Psalm 140:1–5

1 Deliver me, O Lord, from evil men; preserve me from violent men, 2 who plan evil things in their heart and stir up wars continually. 3 *They make their tongue sharp as a serpent's and under their lips is the venom of asps.* Selah 4 Guard me, O Lord, from the hands of the wicked; preserve me from violent men, who have planned to trip up my feet. 5 The arrogant have hidden a trap for me, and with cords they have spread a net; beside the way they have set snares for me. *Selah* (ESV)

The poisoned life. Poison in our hearts creates harmful actions and words (vv. 2–3). William Crashaw comments on the poisoned soul, namely, one's inner life, "The bane or poison of the soul is much more hideous, horrible and hateful than that of the body." From sinful lives "what can come but poisonous words and actions from them whose very inward nature is all poison within!" Crashaw elaborates on the poisonous nature of sin, "Poison, wherever it enters, stays not there, but diffuses itself all over the body, and never ceases till it has infected all. Such is the nature of sin; enter where it will it creeps from one member of the body to another, and from the body to the soul, till it has infected the whole man." He reiterates, "Poison, having entered anywhere, as it seeks to creep presently over all, so desires it especially to seize upon the heart; such a malice and pride lies in the malignant nature of it, that it aspires to the heart; and such a craft and cunning lurks in it, that having once entered, it creeps closely and unfelt till it gets to the heart; but having possessed itself of that sovereign part of man, then like a tyrant, it reigns and rages, and infecting first the vital blood and noble parts, it diffuses itself over all and every part. And such is the nature of sin, the spiritual poison of the soul; enter where it will, it is the heart it aims at, and it will never stay till it comes there."

Prayer. Lord, sin has poisoned every area of my life! By ignoring this poison, I have hurt others by my actions and words. Purify my heart through your word and Spirit. Amen.

December 15   Psalm 140:6–13

6 I say to the Lord, you are my God; give ear to the voice of my pleas for mercy, O Lord! 7 O Lord, my Lord, the strength of my salvation, you have covered my head in the day of battle. 8 Grant not, O Lord, the desires of the wicked; do not further their evil plot, or they will be exalted! *Selah* 9 As for the head of those who surround me, let the mischief of their lips overwhelm them! 10 Let burning coals fall upon them! Let them be cast into fire, into miry pits, no more to rise! 11 Let not the slanderer be established in the land; let evil hunt down the violent man speedily! 12 I know that the Lord will maintain the cause of the afflicted, and will execute justice for the needy. 13 *Surely the righteous shall give thanks to your name; the upright shall dwell in your presence.* (ESV)

Responding to others' poison. In response to those who attack David, he prays with a seemingly malicious request (v. 10). Thomas Fenton* explains David's prayer, "In these imprecations he considered his enemies as the enemies of God, rather than as his own; and he thus cursed them, as knowing, in the quality of a prophet, that God himself had cursed them: and therefore, these sorts of imprecations do not authorize other persons to curse their enemies." While we are to pray that people surrender their lives to Jesus Christ, we are also to ask God to uphold his moral laws by dealing justly with those who oppose him. With a heart and mind aligned with the Lord's will, David further exemplifies how we should respond to mean-spirited attacks (v. 13). Based on his response, Thomas Wilcox suggests two principles. We should be "continually thankful" because God is "continually merciful" to us. Also, we must consider our future "excellent estate and condition" which shall "break forth with fulness of glory." Expressing our thanks to God is an appropriate response because in his "presence" (v. 13), we can talk to him about our crises and allow him to search for any wrongful attitudes in our hearts. Then we are in a better position to rightly respond to others' hurtful attacks.

Prayer. Lord, cleanse my heart and enable me to respond to others' spite in ways which will be pleasing to you. Amen.

December 16   Psalm 141

1 O Lord, I am calling to you. Please hurry! Listen when I cry to you for help! 2 Accept my prayer as incense offered to you, and my upraised hands as an evening offering. 3 *Take control of what I say, O Lord, and guard my lips.* 4 *Don't let me drift toward evil or take part in acts of wickedness. Don't let me share in the delicacies of those who do wrong.* 5 Let the godly strike me! It will be a kindness! If they correct me, it is soothing medicine. Don't let me refuse it. But I pray constantly against the wicked and their deeds. 6 When their leaders are thrown down from a cliff, the wicked will listen to my words and find them true. 7 Like rocks brought up by a plow, the bones of the wicked will lie scattered without burial. 8 I look to you for help, O Sovereign Lord. You are my refuge; don't let them kill me. 9 Keep me from the traps they have set for me, from the snares of those who do wrong. 10 Let the wicked fall into their own nets but let me escape. (NLT)

Godliness. In verses 3 and 4, David makes two requests to avoid sinning against God. First, by praying for the right words to say before his enemies (v. 3), John Owen explains that David does not want to express a "distempered passion in any of his words or sayings." Second, David asks for God's help regarding his conduct (v. 4). With the "power of God's grace influencing his mind and soul," David does not want his heart to be drawn into "any communion" with "his wicked adversaries." He wants to avoid the "delicacies" (v. 4) which include "the lust of the eyes, the lust of the flesh, or the pride of life." He wants to be "preserved from a liking of, or a longing after those things, which are the baits and allurements" of sin. David also asks God that he will be humble enough to accept the correction of the godly (v. 5). Owen notes that corrective words from the godly are better than the sweet enticements of sin offered by those who have little regard for us.

Prayer. Lord, by your Spirit's enabling and people's godly counsel, may my life please you in an antagonistic world. Guard my heart against the appeal of sin and strengthen my resolve to obey you. Amen.

December 17 — Psalm 142

1 I cry aloud to the LORD; I lift up my voice to the LORD for mercy. 2 I pour out before him my complaint; before him I tell my trouble. 3 *When my spirit grows faint within me, it is you who watch over my way.* In the path where I walk people have hidden a snare for me. 4 Look and see, there is no one at my right hand; no one is concerned for me. I have no refuge; no one cares for my life. 5 I cry to you, LORD; I say, "You are my refuge, my portion in the land of the living." 6 Listen to my cry, for I am in desperate need; rescue me from those who pursue me, for they are too strong for me. 7 Set me free from my prison that I may praise your name. Then the righteous will gather about me because of your goodness to me. (NIV)

Hope in confinement. Like the heading to Psalm 37, this psalm's heading tells us that the writer is cornered in a cave; he hopes that God will set him free from his prison-like situation (v. 7). Even though he is trapped, he knows God is watching over him (v. 3). When we are in inescapable situations, John Newton* encourages the downhearted, "The Lord is not withdrawn to a great distance, but his eye is upon you. He sees you not with the indifference of a mere spectator; but he observes with attention, he knows, he considers your path: yes, he appoints it, and every circumstance about it is under his direction. Your trouble began at the hour he saw best, it could not come before; and he has marked the degree of it to a hair's breadth, and its duration to a minute. He knows likewise how your spirit is affected; and such supplies of grace and strength, and in such seasons as he sees needful, he will afford in due season. So that when things appear darkest, you shall still be able to say, 'Though chastened, not killed. Therefore, hope in God, for you shall yet praise him.'"

Prayer. Lord, I have been feeling trapped for some time and feel that you have abandoned me. I need the assurance of your love. Your presence will bring great peace and assurance to my troubled soul. Amen.

December 18   Psalm 143:1-6

1 Hear my prayer, O LORD; give ear to my pleas for mercy! *In your faithfulness answer me, in your righteousness!* 2 Enter not into judgment with your servant, for no one living is righteous before you. 3 For the enemy has pursued my soul; he has crushed my life to the ground; he has made me sit in darkness like those long dead. 4 Therefore my spirit faints within me; my heart within me is appalled. 5 I remember the days of old; I meditate on all that you have done; I ponder the work of your hands. 6 I stretch out my hands to you; my soul thirsts for you like a parched land. *Selah* (ESV)

God is merciful, faithful and righteous. Pursued by his enemies (v. 3), David asks God to spare his life by appealing to God's faithfulness and righteousness (v. 1b). Richard Baker captures the sentiment of David's prayer, "It was your righteousness that you did make the promise, but it is your faithfulness that you will keep your promise: and seeing I am certain of you making it, how can I be doubtful of you keeping it? If you should not answer me in your righteousness, yet you should be righteous still; but if you should not answer me in your faithfulness, you should not be faithful still." Since God cannot act contrary to his nature, David can rightly make such an appeal. However, considering God's character, David recognizes that he, like everyone else, is not righteous (v. 2b). Aware both of his own faults and the prospect of divine judgment (v. 2a), he could only ask God to spare him. Many years later, Paul underscored our unrighteousness before God (Rom 3:10-12). This approaching Christmas season reminds us that Jesus came to this world to become our righteousness (3:21-26). Through him, we receive a right standing (righteousness) before God. With a new relationship with him, we have the assurance that he will not reject us but will graciously and lovingly care for us (Rom 8:31-39).

Prayer. Father, I know that I am unworthy to stand before you, apart from your mercy, and placing my trust in the righteousness of the sinless Jesus Christ. I am thankful for my secure standing before you, and the assurance of your unconditional love which you repeatedly express to me. Amen.

December 19   Psalm 143:7–12

7 Answer me quickly, O LORD! My spirit fails! Hide not your face from me, lest I be like those who go down to the pit. 8 Let me hear in the morning of your steadfast love, for in you I trust. Make me know the way I should go, for to you I lift up my soul. 9 Deliver me from my enemies, O LORD! *I have fled to you for refuge.* 10 *Teach me to do your will, for you are my God! Let your good Spirit lead me on level ground!* 11 For your name's sake, O LORD, preserve my life! In your righteousness bring my soul out of trouble! 12 And in your steadfast love you will cut off my enemies, and you will destroy all the adversaries of my soul, for I am your servant. (ESV)

Our response to God's righteousness. David trusts his righteous God to be his "refuge" (vv. 9, 11). Through Christ's righteousness, we obtain a perfect standing with God. Therefore, Ralph Robinson implores individuals to "fly to Christ" and "hide themselves with Christ." Robinson explains, "Faith is the key that opens the door of this hiding-place and locks it again." With a new relationship with Jesus, we express our gratitude to him by obeying his will (v. 10). Vincent Alsop remarks, "We are to pray that God would teach us to know, and then teach us to do, his will. Knowledge without obedience is lame, obedience without knowledge is blind." Thomas Shephard notes, "Seeing he [Christ] has purchased our lives in redemption . . . we should now live unto him, in all thankful and fruitful obedience, according to his will revealed in the moral law." However, without God's Spirit (v. 10), we cannot obey God's word. "The Spirit is indeed the efficient cause of our obedience, and hence we are said to be "led by the Spirit" (Rom 8:14) . . . the Spirit is the wind that drives us in our obedience; the law is our compass, according to which it steers our course for us: the Spirit and the law, the wind and the compass, can stand well together."

Prayer. Lord, for all you have done for me, by your Spirit I want to obey your word and follow you. Amen.

December 20   Psalm 144:1–8

1 Blessed be the LORD, my rock, who trains my hands for war, and my fingers for battle; 2 he is my steadfast love and my fortress, my stronghold and my deliverer, my shield and he in whom I take refuge, who subdues peoples under me. 3 O LORD, what is man that you regard him, or the son of man that you think of him? 4 Man is like a breath; his days are like a passing shadow. *5 Bow your heavens, O LORD, and come down! Touch the mountains so that they smoke!* 6 Flash forth the lightning and scatter them; send out your arrows and rout them! 7 Stretch out your hand from on high; rescue me and deliver me from the many waters, from the hand of foreigners, 8 whose mouths speak lies and whose right hand is a right hand of falsehood. (ESV)

The incarnation. Facing another battle, David looks to God who fights for him (vv. 1–2). Amazed that God should be concerned about mortal humans (vv. 3–4), David asks him to "come down" from the heavens and fight his enemies (v. 5). Jonathan Edwards comments on God's coming to earth, "This was never so remarkably fulfilled as in the incarnation of Jesus Christ, when heaven and earth were, as it were, brought together. Heaven itself was, as it were, made to bow that it might be united to the earth. God did, as it were, come down and bring heaven with him. He not only came down to the earth, but he brought heaven down with him to men and for men. It was a most strange and wonderful thing." During the Christmas season, we commemorate the birth of Jesus who would eventually disarm the evil powers and authorities through his death on the cross (Col 2:15). This event was not the end of the story as Edwards notes, "This [bringing heaven down] will be more remarkably fulfilled still by Christ's second coming, when he will indeed bring all heaven down with him . . . Heaven shall be left empty of its inhabitants to come down to the earth; and then the mountains shall smoke, and shall indeed flow down at his presence."

Prayer. Thank you, Father, for sending to this world Jesus to fight and win the battle against Satan and his evil forces. Amen.

December 21 — Psalm 144:9-15

9 I will sing a new song to you, O God; upon a ten-stringed harp I will play to you, 10 who gives victory to kings, who rescues David his servant from the cruel sword. 11 Rescue me and deliver me from the hand of foreigners, whose mouths speak lies and whose right hand is a right hand of falsehood. 12 May our sons in their youth be like plants full grown, our daughters like corner pillars cut for the structure of a palace; 13 may our granaries be full, providing all kinds of produce; may our sheep bring forth thousands and ten thousands in our fields; 14 may our cattle be heavy with young, suffering no mishap or failure in bearing; may there be no cry of distress in our streets! 15 *Blessed are the people to whom such blessings fall! Blessed are the people whose God is the* Lord! (ESV)

Heaven's victory and blessings. Anticipating God's coming to defeat his enemies (v. 10), David exuberantly praises the Lord (v. 9) and asks for his blessing on the families and their productivity (vv. 12–15). God blesses because he is the "Lord" (v. 15), a name equivalent to Jehovah who keeps a covenant relationship with his people. Nathanael Homes states that "to have God to be our Jehovah is the insurance of happiness to us." In other words, "this name is our security of God's performance" including his blessings on us. Regarding the essence of God's blessings, Thomas Brooks observes, "God is the author of all true happiness; he is the donor of all true happiness; he is the maintainer of all true happiness, and he is the centre of all true happiness; and, therefore, he that has him for his God, and for his portion, is the only happy man in the world." In the New Testament, God continued to bless his people with true happiness. Through Elizabeth's words inspired by the Holy Spirit (Luke 1:41), Mary receives two blessings. God blesses her as the mother of Jesus, the Son of God, and blesses her faith to believe this is so (Luke 1:42, 45). Then Mary praises God with a song (2:46–55) known as the *Magnificat*, meaning "my soul magnifies the Lord."

Prayer. Lord, I praise you for the many blessings I have received through your goodness. You are the source of true happiness! Amen.

December 22   Psalm 145:1–7

1 I will exalt you, my God and King, and praise your name forever and ever. 2 I will praise you every day; yes, I will praise you forever. 3 Great is the Lord! *He is most worthy of praise! No one can measure his greatness. 4 Let each generation tell its children of your mighty acts; let them proclaim your power. 5 I will meditate on your majestic, glorious splendour and your wonderful miracles. 6 Your awe-inspiring deeds will be on every tongue; I will proclaim your greatness. 7 Everyone will share the story of your wonderful goodness; they will sing with joy about your righteousness.* (NLT)

Praise for God's great acts. The psalm's title "A psalm of praise" indicates David as its author. Thomas Goodwin believes David's name is mentioned "because this [psalm] wholly consists of praise; he was elevated therein to a frame of spirit made up of the pure praise of God, without any touch of what was particular to himself. It was not thanks, but altogether praise, and wholly praise." Matthew Henry identifies two characteristics of praise (vv. 1–2). David's words first express a quality of praise. This quality consists of "the fervency of his affection to this work, the fixedness of his purpose to abound in it, and the frequency of his performances therein." David's praise is not necessarily loud but wholehearted, coming from the depths of his soul. The second characteristic of David's praise is its persistence. David "resolved to continue in this work to the end of his life, throughout his "forever" (vv. 1–2). Therefore, "the psalms he penned should be made use of in praising God by the church to the end of time (2 Chron 29:30)." David "hoped to be praising God to all eternity in the other world: they that make it their constant work on earth, shall have it their everlasting bliss in heaven." Dwelling on God's great acts in history (vv. 4–6) inspires David's praise. The Christmas season reminds us of God's mighty act of sending his Son, Jesus, to be born of human flesh. This is the reason for wholehearted, ongoing praise to the Lord!

Prayer. Lord, I praise you for sending Jesus to our world to become a human being and our Savior to show your great love for humanity. Amen.

December 23   Psalm 145:8–13

8 The Lord is gracious and full of compassion, slow to anger and great in mercy. 9 *The Lord is good to all, and His tender mercies are over all His works.* 10 All Your works shall praise You, O Lord, and Your saints shall bless You. 11 They shall speak of the glory of Your kingdom, and talk of Your power, 12 To make known to the sons of men His mighty acts, and the glorious majesty of His kingdom. 13 Your kingdom is an everlasting kingdom, and Your dominion endures throughout all generations. (NKJV)

God's mercy and the Incarnation. God's great acts in history are expressions of his mercy to his creation (vv. 8–9). David Clarkson comments, "When the sensible sinner is seeking faith of God, he may plead the *largeness* of mercy. God's mercy is like the firmament spread over all this lower world; and every infirm creature partakes more or less of its influence." He adds that "there is 'mercy over all,' even over such vile and loathsome creatures as these" and by God's saving grace, they cry out, "Oh, let that mercy, whose glory it is to stretch itself over all, reach my soul also! Oh, that the blessed and powerful influence thereof would beget faith in my heart!" God's merciful acts are also expressed by his "kingdom" or reign over all his creation (vv. 11–13). Upon the announcement of the upcoming birth of Jesus, Mary praises God for his mercy and alludes to Christ's coming kingdom which will overthrow human rulers and care for the needy (Luke 1:51–53). At the outset of his ministry, Jesus exercised his kingdom rulership over sickness and demonic spirits by mercifully healing those so afflicted (Matt 4:23–24). Considering God's mercy and reign revealed through the coming of Jesus, Matthew Henry emphasizes, "Of all God's works, his saints, the workmanship of his grace, the first fruits of his creatures, have most reason to bless him."

Prayer. Father, thank you for extending your great mercy to me through salvation in your Son, Jesus. During this season, I want to sing carols as expressions of my praise to you. I submit to you so that you may reign in me! Amen.

December 24   Psalm 145:14–21

14 The LORD helps the fallen and lifts those bent beneath their loads. 15 The eyes of all look to you in hope; you give them their food as they need it. 16 When you open your hand, you satisfy the hunger and thirst of every living thing. 17 The LORD is righteous in everything he does; he is filled with kindness. 18 *The LORD is close to all who call on him, yes, to all who call on him in truth.* 19 He grants the desires of those who fear him; he hears their cries for help and rescues them. 20 The LORD protects all those who love him, but he destroys the wicked. 21 I will praise the LORD and may everyone on earth bless his holy name forever and ever. (NLT)

Jesus is near. Comparing a friend's nearness to God's closeness to us (v. 18), Thomas Brooks writes, "The nearness or remoteness of a friend is very material and considerable in our troubles, distresses, wants, dangers etc. I have such a friend and he would help me, but he lives so far off; and I have another friend that has a great love for me, that is able to counsel me, and to speak a word in season to me, and that in my distress would stand close to me, but he is so remote. I have a special friend, that did he know how things stand with me would make my burdens his, and my wants his, and my sorrows his; but he is in a far country, he is at the Indies, and I may be undone before I can hear from him. But it is not thus with you, O Christians! who have a God so nigh unto you, who have the signal presence of God in the midst of you, yes, who have a God always standing by you, 'The Lord stood by me' (2 Tim 4:17)." Jesus' name, Immanuel, meaning "God with us" (Matt 1:23), reminds us of his former dwelling on earth and his present indwelling in those whom Jesus calls his friends (John 15:3, 15). Jesus is a friend who is near to us!

Prayer. Jesus, you are the best friend I could ever have. Your nearness through the indwelling Spirit is a timeless gift to me! Amen.

December 25   Psalm 146

1 Praise the Lord. Praise the Lord, my soul. 2 I will praise the Lord all my life; I will sing praise to my God as long as I live. 3 *Do not put your trust in princes, in human beings, who cannot save.* 4 When their spirit departs, they return to the ground; on that very day their plans come to nothing. 5 Blessed are those whose help is the God of Jacob, whose hope is in the Lord their God. 6 He is the Maker of heaven and earth, the sea, and everything in them—he remains faithful forever. 7 He upholds the cause of the oppressed and gives food to the hungry. The Lord sets prisoners free, 8 the Lord gives sight to the blind, the Lord lifts up those who are bowed down, the Lord loves the righteous. 9 The Lord watches over the foreigner and sustains the fatherless and the widow, but he frustrates the ways of the wicked. 10 The Lord reigns forever, your God, O Zion, for all generations. Praise the Lord. (NIV)

The God who saves. This is the first of five psalms which begin with "Praise the Lord." God is worthy of praise because he saves us in ways that no one else can (v. 3). Joseph Caryl elaborates, "True, may some say, it were a folly to trust in weak princes, to trust in them for help who have no power to help; but we will apply to mighty princes; we hope there is help in them. No; those words 'in whom there is no help' [KJV], are not a distinction of weak princes, from strong, but a conclusion that there is no help in the strongest. That's strange. What? No help in strong princes! If he had said, no help in mean men, carnal reason would have consented; but when he says, 'Trust not in princes, nor in any son of man' [KJV], one or other, who can believe this? Yet this is divine truth; we may write insufficiency, insufficiency, and a third time, insufficiency, upon them all.'" Instead, our help comes from God who provides for the needy (vv. 5–9). Jesus came to this world, announcing that he would do the same for us (Luke 4:18–19).

Prayer. Jesus, I praise you, the true Prince who came into the world to save sinners such as me. Amen.

December 26   Psalm 147:1–11

1 Praise the Lord! For it is good to sing praises to our God; for it is pleasant, and a song of praise is fitting. 2 The Lord builds up Jerusalem; he gathers the outcasts of Israel. 3 *He heals the brokenhearted and binds up their wounds.* 4 He determines the number of the stars; he gives to all of them their names. 5 Great is our Lord, and abundant in power; his understanding is beyond measure. 6 The Lord lifts up the humble; he casts the wicked to the ground. 7 Sing to the Lord with thanksgiving; make melody to our God on the lyre! 8 He covers the heavens with clouds; he prepares rain for the earth; he makes grass grow on the hills. 9 He gives to the beasts their food, and to the young ravens that cry. 10 His delight is not in the strength of the horse, nor his pleasure in the legs of a man, 11 but the Lord takes pleasure in those who fear him, in those who hope in his steadfast love. (ESV)

The God who heals. The Christmas season is difficult for many people. Like the exiles who return to Jerusalem to face their city's devastation (v. 2), today there are individuals who, after returning from the festivities, face their own anguish all by themselves. However, God mercifully offers healing to those who are hurting (v. 3). William Fenner explains why Jesus offers healing. First, God gives him the grace to heal others (Luke 4:18). Fenner notes, "If he be created master of this art, even for this purpose, to heal the broken in heart, he will verily heal them, and none but them." Second, Fenner states, "When a skillful Physician has undertaken a cure, he will surely do it . . . if Christ undertake it, you may be sure of it." Third, this healing is "Christ's charge, and he will look to his own calling: 'The Lord hath sent me to bind up the broken hearted" (Isa 61:1 KJV). Fourth, Jesus delights to respond to the brokenhearted because "this is a physician's desire, that his patient would cast himself upon him; if he will not, the physician has no desire to meddle with him."

Prayer. Jesus, you know those who are hurting at this time of year. Come and bring healing to wounded hearts. Amen.

December 27   Psalm 147:12–20

12 Praise the LORD, O Jerusalem! Praise your God, O Zion! 13 For he strengthens the bars of your gates; he blesses your children within you. 14 He makes peace in your borders; he fills you with the finest of the wheat. 15 He sends out his command to the earth; his word runs swiftly. 16 He gives snow like wool; he scatters frost like ashes. 17 He hurls down his crystals of ice like crumbs; who can stand before his cold? 18 He sends out his word and melts them; he makes his wind blow and the waters flow. 19 He declares his word to Jacob, his statutes and rules to Israel. 20 *He has not dealt thus with any other nation; they do not know his rules.* Praise the LORD! (ESV)

God's good gifts. Joseph Alleine notes that in this psalm, the writer sets "forth the mercy of God, both towards all creatures in general in his common providence, and towards his church in particular." Following the previous verses 1–11, the psalmist continues to show the ways God generously supplies the needed provisions to sustain all his creatures, including us. First, God shows his common grace to all creatures by supplying food and water (vv. 14, 17–18). By doing so, John Trapp says, God is "teaching us what to do for God's poor." Second, Alleine mentions that God mercifully gave his revealed law to the Israelites (v. 19) so that his people can obey the truth. In other words, God dealt uniquely with them in comparison to the other nations (v. 20). Alleine makes his point, "God deals in a singular way of mercy with his people above all other people." Therefore, since God shows mercy to those with whom he has a personal relationship, he "expects singular praises from his people." On this note, Alleine summarizes this psalm by observing that the "sweet psalmist of Israel, a man skillful in praises, does begin and end this psalm with Hallelujah [Praise the Lord]."

Prayer. Father, I worship you because you have mercifully and generously given me physical and spiritual provisions for my life. Amen.

December 28   Psalm 148:1–6

1 Praise the LORD! Praise the LORD from the heavens; praise him in the heights! 2 *Praise him, all his angels; praise him, all his hosts!* 3 Praise him, sun and moon, praise him, all you shining stars! 4 Praise him, you highest heavens, and you waters above the heavens! 5 Let them praise the name of the LORD! For he commanded and they were created. 6 And he established them forever and ever; he gave a decree, and it shall not pass away. (ESV)

Cosmic praise. This song celebrates the cosmos praising God. John Trapp points out, "As God in framing the world begun above, and wrought [created] downward, so does the Psalmist proceed in this his exhortation to all creatures to praise the Lord." On this theme, Barton Bouchier* ponders, "Is this universal praise never to be realized? Is it only the longing, intense desire of the Psalmist's heart, which will never be heard on earth, and can only be perfected in heaven? Is there to be no jubilee in which the mountains and the hills shall break forth into singing, and all the trees of the field shall clap their hands? If there is to be no such day, then is the word of God of none effect; if no such universal anthem is to swell the chorus of heaven and to be reechoed by all that is on earth, then is God's promise void. It is true, in this Psalm our translation presents it to us as a call or summons for everything that has or has not breath to praise the Lord—or as a petition that they may praise; but it is in reality a prediction that they shall praise. This Psalm is neither more nor less than a glorious prophecy of that coming day, when not only shall the knowledge of the Lord be spread over the whole earth, as the waters cover the sea, but from every created object in heaven and in earth, animate and inanimate, from the highest archangel through every grade and phase of being, down to the tiniest atom—young men and maidens, old men and children, and all kings and princes, and judges of the earth shall unite in this millennial, anthem to the Redeemer's praise."

Prayer. Lord, if the universe praises you, I must do likewise because you are worthy of all my praise. Amen.

December 29   Psalm 148:7–14

7 Praise the Lord *from the earth, you great sea creatures and all deeps, 8 fire and hail, snow and mist, stormy wind fulfilling his word! 9 Mountains and all hills, fruit trees and all cedars! 10 Beasts and all livestock, creeping things and flying birds! 11 Kings of the earth and all peoples, princes and all rulers of the earth! 12 Young men and maidens together, old men and children! 13 Let them praise the name of the Lord, for his name alone is exalted; his majesty is above earth and heaven. 14 He has raised up a horn for his people, praise for all his saints, for the people of Israel who are near to him. Praise the* Lord*!* (ESV)

Global praise. The psalmist invites the earth's animals, natural landscape, and elements (vv. 7–10) to praise God. Stephen Charnock believes that these do "bear a part in this work of praise. Not that they are able to do it actively, but to show that man is to call in the whole creation to assist him passively and should have so much charity to all creatures as to receive what they offer, and so much affection to God as to present to him what he receives from him." When we do not take nature for granted, but appreciate the sheer beauty, delicious food and rapturous sounds of creation, we turn to God and express our love to him for all that he has provided for our enjoyment. Thus, through our praise and enjoyment of creation, creation indirectly praises the Lord. Likewise, elements such as the hail and snow (v. 8) "cannot bless and praise God, but man ought to bless God for those things, wherein there is a mixture of trouble and inconvenience, something to molest our sense, as well as something that improves the earth for fruit." While a snowstorm and hail may be unpleasant, Charnock invites us to look beyond ourselves to see how the environment benefits. Commenting on the "creeping things" (v. 10) praising God, Thomas Goodwin states, "In public worship all should join. The little strings go to make up a concert, as well as the great." If nature praises God, it is appropriate for all people to praise him (vv. 11–14).

Prayer. Father, as our planet with its gifts praises you through my thankfulness, I praise you for your creation! Amen.

December 30   Psalm 149

1 Praise the LORD! Sing to the LORD a new song, his praise in the assembly of the godly! 2 Let Israel be glad in his Maker; let the children of Zion rejoice in their King! 3 Let them praise his name with dancing, making melody to him with tambourine and lyre! 4 For the LORD takes pleasure in his people; he adorns the humble with salvation. 5 Let the godly exult in glory; let them sing for joy on their beds. 6 *Let the high praises of God be in their throats and two-edged swords in their hands,* 7 to execute vengeance on the nations and punishments on the peoples, 8 to bind their kings with chains and their nobles with fetters of iron, 9 to execute on them the judgment written! This is honor for all his godly ones. Praise the LORD! (ESV)

Believers' praise. Since God has carried out his judgment on all those who opposed him (vv. 7–9), the congregation praises God with their mouths and by carrying their weapons (vv. 1–6). Commenting on the "high praises" (v. 6), Samuel Fairclough suggests that this phrase includes both "the high acts for which God is to be praised" and the "high praises to be given unto God for those high acts." The "excellency" of worship is "man's work in praising God, and not only of the work of God, for which he is to be praised." In addition, our praise is of a "high nature" because God has a "high estimation" of our praise and is "appreciative" of those who acknowledge what he has done for them. Fairclough concludes, "Now the Lord, who is of the most perfect understanding, and deepest skill and knowledge, declares himself to take infinite delight in his people's praises." Like the Israelites with their high praises and two-edged swords, today we, as God's people, praise him for his high acts and use the powerful weapon of his word, the sword of the Spirit. As God's people, we have his word which is a powerful weapon. Though we are engaged in spiritual warfare (Eph 6:12), Christ's church will experience victory now and until the end of history (Rev 12:11; 19:11–16) because God triumphs as the ultimate Victor.

Prayer. Lord, your past, present, and future triumphs over evil forces magnify your glory. You alone are the ultimate Victor. Amen.

December 31   Psalm 150

1 *Praise the* Lord! *Praise God in his sanctuary; praise him in his mighty heavens!* 2 Praise him for his mighty deeds; praise him according to his excellent greatness! 3 Praise him with trumpet sound; praise him with lute and harp! 4 Praise him with tambourine and dance; praise him with strings and pipe! 5 Praise him with sounding cymbals; praise him with loud clashing cymbals! 6 Let everything that has breath praise the Lord! Praise the Lord! (ESV)

Praise upon praise. This psalm, the last of the hallelujah (or "praise the Lord") songs, reaches a climactic crescendo with voices, and instruments used for joyous celebrations. Matthew Henry describes how we should praise God (vv. 3–5). He notes, "Praise God with a strong faith; praise him with holy love and delight; praise him with an entire confidence in Christ; praise him with a believing triumph over the powers of darkness; praise him with an earnest desire towards him, and a full satisfaction in him; praise him by a universal respect to all his commands; praise him by a cheerful submission to all his disposals; praise him by rejoicing in his love, and solacing yourselves in his great goodness; praise him by promoting the interests of the kingdom of his grace; praise him by a lively hope and expectation of the kingdom of his glory." According to David Dickson, the use of the instruments indicates, "the greatness of his [the believer's] joy to be found in God, and to teach what stirring up should be of the affections and powers of our soul, and of one another, unto God's worship; what harmony should be among the worshippers of God, what melody each should make in himself, singing to God with grace in his heart, and to show the excellency of God's praise." As Dickson concludes his thoughts, he encourages us, "When we have said all we are able to say for God's praise, we are but to begin anew." Charles Spurgeon* asks us kindly, "Reader, will you not at this moment pause a while, and worship the Lord your God?"

Prayer. Lord, you have loved me through life's lows and highs, through times of accusations and praise, isolation and intimacy, fears and confidence, dryness and refreshment, defeats and victories, crying and singing. I pause now to worship you, for you are worthy of all praise! Hallelujah! Amen!

Appendix

Adams, Thomas (1583–1652). Jan 2, 10; Feb 7; Apr 15; May 23; Jun 5; Jul 18, 29; Sept 11; Oct 20, 23; Dec 8, 11
Alleine, Richard (1611–1681). Feb 27
Alleine, Joseph (1634–1668). Jun 19; Dec 27
Alsop, Vincent (1630–1703). Dec 19
Ambrose, Isaac (1604–1664). Feb 4
Annesley, Samuel (1620–1696). Jun 4
Arrowsmith, John (1602–1659). Aug 12; Dec 11
Augustine* (353–429). Aug 15
Baker, Richard (c. 1568–1645). Mar 4, 19; Apr 18, 19, 20; Jul 22, 23, 24; Sept 9; Oct 18; Nov 26; Dec 18
Baxter, Richard (1615–1691). Jan 13
Baynes, Paul (c. 1573–1617). Oct 25, 28
Beddome, Benjamin* (1717–1795). Jul 16
Bellarmine, Robert* (1542–1621). Apr 9
Bolton, Robert (1572–1631). Jul 31
Bouchier, Barton* (1794–1865). Jul 25, Nov 15; Dec 6, 28
Boys, John (1571–1625). Feb 12; Apr 3, 8; May 26; Aug 22, 29; Oct 12, 15
Bradshaw, William (1570–1618). Aug 9
Bridge, William (1600–1671). Sept 23
Brooks, Thomas (1608–1680). Jan 14, Feb 23; Mar 7, 8; May 13; Jun 1; Jul 21; Dec 21, 24
Bunyan, John (1628–1688). Jan 18; Apr 27, 28; May 31; Oct 8; Nov 26
Burroughs, Jeremiah (c. 1600–1646). Jan 23; May 16, 21; Jun 3
Calamy, Edmund (1600–1666). Nov 1
Calvin, John* (1509–1564). May 5; June 14; July 3; October 6, 10; Dec 1
Carson, Alexander* (1776–1844). Jun 23
Caryl, Joseph (1602–1673). Jan 1, 4, 25, 31; Feb 9, 22; Mar 3, 18; Apr 2, 11; May 2, 3, 8, 12, 17, 28; Jun 10, 15, 29; Jul 4, 17, 27; Sept 12, 14, 15, 24; Oct 1, 6, 7, 27; Nov 9, 15, 16, 17, 30; Dec 13, 25
Case, Thomas (1598–1682). Jul 16
Chalmers, Thomas* (1780–1847). Dec 8
Charnock, Stephen (1628–1680). Jan 11; Apr 29; Aug 5, 21, 31; Sept 7; Oct 16; Nov 8; Dec 2, 3, 10

Christophers, Samuel Woolcock* (1810–1899). Apr 5
Clarkson, David (1622–1686). Jan 5; Mar 1, 25, 31; May 18; Jul 30; Dec 23
Collinges, John (1624–1691). Oct 3
Cotton, John (1584–1652). Jun 9; Nov 14
Crashaw, William (1572–1626. Dec 14
Dickson, David (c. 1583–1662). Feb 25; Apr 1, 24, 25, 26; Jun 11, 29; Jul 12, 14; Aug 11, 24, 30; Sept 30; Oct 5; Nov 4, 18, 25, 29; Dec 2, 4, 6, 31
Downame, George (c. 1563–1634). Jan 20
Duncan, Henry* (1774–1846). Dec 10
Dyke, Daniel (d. 1614). Aug 19
Edwards, Jonathan (1703–1758). Mar 10; Apr 7; Aug 4, 18; Dec 20
Erskine, Ebenezer (1680–1754). Jun 25; Nov 29; Dec 9
Erskine, Ralph (1685–1752). Apr 6
Fairclough, Samuel (1594–1677). Dec 30
Fenner, William (c. 1600–c. 1640). Nov 3; Dec 26
Fenton, Thomas* (c. 1688–1743). Dec 15
Flavel, John (1628–1691). Jan 26; Feb 6; Mar 24; Apr 4, 30; Jul 28
Frame, James E.* (n.d.). Jun 6
Frank, Mark* (1613–1664). Jun 2
Gill, John* (1697–1771). May 30; Jul 15
Gilpin, Richard (1625–1700). Feb 24; May 1
Goodwin, Thomas (1600–1680). Jan 27; Mar 23, 26; Apr 23; May 22; Jul 9; Aug 3; Sept 1, 18; Oct 9; Dec 4, 22
Gouge, William (1575–1653). Feb 8; Aug 23
Greenham, Richard (c. 1542–1594). Jan 21; Nov 1
Greenhill, William (1598–1671). May 3; Jul 11; Aug 6; Sept 3, 25; Oct 22; Dec 10
Gurnall, William (1616–1679). Jan 3, 9; Feb 10, 17; Mar 28; Apr 14, 22; May 10; Jun 28; July 1, 2; Aug 1, 14; Sept 3; Nov 26
Hardy, Nathanael (1619–1670). Feb 14; Mar 20; Apr 17; Oct 19
Harris, Robert (1581–1658). Dec 5
Henderson, Alexander (c. 1583–1646). Nov 22
Henry, Matthew (1662–1714). Feb 3, 5, 13, 21; Mar 27; May 4, 6, 15, 19, 20; Jul 10, 19; Aug 2, 7, 8, 25; Sept 2, 10, 13, 17, 27, 29; Oct 7, 28, 30; Nov 12, 20; Dec 10, 22, 23, 31
Hervey, James* (1714–1758). Mar 13
Heywood, Oliver (1630–1702). Jan 30; Jun 7; Nov 27
Hodges, Thomas (c. 1600–1672). Oct 13
Holmes (Homes), Nathanael (1599–1678). Dec 21
Hopkins, Ezekiel (1634–1690). Jan 16; Mar 9; Apr 13; Nov 2
Horton, Thomas (d. 1673). Aug 20; Sept 16; Nov 30

APPENDIX 369

Howe, John (1630–1705). Jan 24; Mar 12; May 25; July 22.
Jackson, Arthur (c. 1593–1666). Nov 28
Janeway, James (1636–1674). Jan 22; Mar 6, 15
Janeway, John (1633–1657). Nov 29
Jeanes, Henry (1611–1662) Sept 22
Jones, William* (1746–1794). Dec 11
 Kempis, Thomas à* (1380–1471). Nov 10
Lee, Samuel (1625–1691). May 11
Leighton, Robert* (1612–1684). Oct 24; Nov 24
Love, Christopher (1618–1651). Feb 28
Luther, Martin* (1483–1546). Apr 5
Manton, Thomas (1620–1677). Jan 8, 17; Feb 1, Mar 22; Jun 17; Oct 13, 16,
    17, 29; Nov 1, 6, 10, 11, 14, 19, 23, 27; Dec 8, 12
Marbury, Edward (d.1655). Jan 28; Jul 26
Marshall, Stephen (1595–1655). Sept 5, 6
Martin, Samuel* (1817–1878). May 29
Mason, John* (1706–1763). Dec 11
Möller [Mollerus], Heinrich* (1530–1589). Jul 20
Musculus, Wolfgang* (1497–1563). Jun 20
Nisbet, Robert* (1814–1874). Nov 16
Ness, Christopher (1621–1705). Jul 7, Sept 19
Newton, John* (1725–1807). Dec 17
Owen, John (1616–1683). Jan 19; May 9; Jun 24, 26; Aug 16, 27; Nov 21;
    Dec 16
Poole, Matthew (1624–1679). May 7; Aug 17; Sept 20; Dec 4
Preston, John (1587–1628). Jul 5
Pridham, Arthur* (1815–1879). Jul 6
Ranew, Nathanael (c. 1602–1677). Oct 4, 26; Nov 7
Reynolds, Edward (1599–1676). Feb 26; Oct 11
Robinson, Ralph (1614–1655). Dec 19
Rogers, Timothy (1658–1728). Jan 6, 7; May 24; Jun 27; Sept 4
Rutherford, Samuel (c. 1600–1661). Nov 4
Ryther, John* (c. 1634–1681). Oct 2
Sedgwick, Obadiah (c. 1600–1658). Feb 2
Sedgwick, William* (1609–1664). Mar 11; Aug 26
Shephard, Thomas (1605–1649). Nov 14, Dec 19
Sibbes, Richard (1577–1635). Feb 11, 15, 18, 19; Mar 2, 29, 30; Apr 12; Jun
    12, 18; Aug 28; Oct 31
Smith, Henry (1560–1591). Jan 12; Aug 10; Oct 12; Dec 11
Spurgeon, Charles* (1834–1857). May 21, Jul 8, 13, 31; Sept 21, 28; Nov
    28; Dec 31

Steele, Richard (1629–1692). Mar 16
Stevenson, John* (d. 1893). Sept 8
Stock, Richard (c. 1569–1626). Nov 3
Swinnock, George (c. 1627–1673). Feb 16; Mar 14; Apr 10; May 14; Jun 16, 30
Symonds, Joseph (d. 1652). Nov 5
Taylor, Francis (1589–1656). June 21
Taylor, Thomas (1576–1632). Feb 29, Nov 22
Trapp, John (1601–1669). Jan 29; Apr 21; May 27; Sept 29; Nov 19; Dec 2, 27, 28
Tuckney, Anthony (1599–1670). Nov13
Venning, Ralph (c. 1622–1674). Dec 7
Vincent, Nathanael (1638–1697). Nov 14
Watson, Thomas (c. 1620–1686). Jan 15; Feb 20; Mar 5, 17, 21; Apr 16; Jun 8, 13, 22; Aug 13; Dec 27.
Wells, John (1623–1676). Oct 4
Wilcox, Thomas (c. 1549–1608). Dec15
Willison, John* (1680–1750). Sept 26, 30
Wright, Abraham* (1611–1690). Oct 21

Bibliography

Calvin, John. "The Author's Preface." In *Commentary on the Book of Psalms*. Translated by James Anderson. Edinburgh: Calvin Translation Society, 1845.

op 't Hof, W. J. "Piety in the Wake of Trade: The North Sea as an Intermediary of Reformed Piety up to 1700." In *The North Sea and Culture (1550-1800): Proceedings of the International Conference Held at Leiden 21-22 April 1995*, edited by Juliette Roding and Les Heerma van Voss. Hilversum: Verloren, 1996.

Pederson, Randall J. *Unity in Diversity: English Puritans and the Puritan Reformation, 1603-1689*. Leiden: Brill, 2014.

Plumer, William S. *Psalms: A Critical and Expository Commentary with Doctrinal and Practical Remarks*. 1867. Reprint, Edinburgh: Banner of Truth, 1975.

Roding, Juliette and Lex Heerma van Voss, eds. *The North Sea and Culture (1550-1800): Proceedings of the International Conference Held at Leiden 21-22 April 1995*. Hilversum: Verloren, 1996.

Spurgeon, Charles Haddon. *Treasury of David: Containing an Original Exposition of the Book of Psalms; A Collection of Illustrative Extracts from the Whole Range of Literature; A Series of Homiletical Hints Upon Almost Every Verse; And Lists of Writers Upon Each Psalm*. 6 vols. London, Edinburgh, and New York: Marshall Brothers [London: Passmore and Alabaster, 1869-1885].

www.ingramcontent.com/pod-product-compliance
Lightning Source LLC
Chambersburg PA
CBHW071949220426
43662CB00009B/1068